THE WESTERN JOURNALS OF NEHEMIAH AND HENRY SANFORD, 1839–1846

The Western Journals of Nehemiah and Henry Sanford, 1839–1846

Edited by Kenneth E. Lewis

Michigan State University Press | *East Lansing*

♻ The paper used in this publication meets the minimum requirements
of ANSI/NISO Z39.48-1992 (R 1997) (Permanence of Paper).

Michigan State University Press
East Lansing, Michigan 48823-5245

Printed and bound in the United States of America.

28 27 26 25 24 23 22 21 20 19   1 2 3 4 5 6 7 8 9 10

LIBRARY OF CONGRESS CATALOGING-IN-PUBLICATION DATA
Names: Sanford, Nehemiah (Nehemiah Curtis), 1792–1841, author. | Sanford, H. S.,
1823–1891, author. | Lewis, Kenneth E., editor. | Container of (work): Sanford, Nehemiah
(Nehemiah Curtis), 1792–1841. Diaries. Selections. | Container of (work): Sanford, H. S.,
1823–1891. Diaries. Selections.
Title: The Western journals of Nehemiah and Henry Sanford, 1839–1846
/ edited by Kenneth E. Lewis.
Description: East Lansing : Michigan State University Press, [2019]
| Includes bibliographical references and index.
Identifiers: LCCN 2018020130 | ISBN 9781611863147 (cloth : alk. paper)
| ISBN 9781609175931 (pdf) | ISBN 9781628953596 (epub) | ISBN 9781628963601 (kindle)
Subjects: LCSH: Sanford, Nehemiah (Nehemiah Curtis), 1792–1841—Diaries.
| Sanford, H. S., 1823–1891—Diaries. | Sanford, Nehemiah (Nehemiah Curtis),
1792–1841—Travel—Middle West. | Sanford, H. S., 1823–1891—Travel—Middle West.
| Middle West—Description and travel. | LCGFT: Diaries.
Classification: LCC F353 .S265 2019 | DDC 917.704—dc23
LC record available at https://lccn.loc.gov/2018020130

Book design by Charlie Sharp, Sharp Designs, East Lansing, MI
Cover design by Shaun Allshouse, www.shaunallshouse.com
Cover art is a photograph of the *Great Western*, used with permission
of the Vessel Photograph Collection, Historical Collections of the Great Lakes,
Bowling Green State University.

Michigan State University Press is a member of the Green Press Initiative and is
committed to developing and encouraging ecologically responsible publishing
practices. For more information about the Green Press Initiative and the use of
recycled paper in book publishing, please visit *www.greenpressinitiative.org*.

Visit Michigan State University Press at *www.msupress.org*

*To the memory of my fourth great-grandparents,
Antoine Marson LaPierre and Mary Louise Misapis,
whose marriage was a product of the mixing of people
and cultures that fascinated young Henry Sanford
during his western travels.*

CONTENTS

MAPS AND FIGURES

PREFACE

The writings of Henry Sanford and his parents, Nehemiah and Nancy Sanford, are the personal accounts of members of an eastern family who traveled to the American West. By themselves, their journeys were not unusual in that they reflect the much larger movement of immigrants into the continent's interior during the antebellum period. Americans poured across the Appalachian Mountains to take up agricultural lands and exploit the resources made available by the young nation's territorial expansion and the expulsion of Native peoples. Those who came west did so for many reasons, the motives for which shaped the form of the accounts they left behind. The distinctive nature of the Sanfords' interests set them apart from many other travelers and makes their accounts stand out among other contemporary descriptions of western travel.

Perhaps the greatest impetus for immigration was agricultural expansion. By mid-nineteenth century the movement of farmers to the Great Lakes and other regions was in full swing, and narratives based on knowledge provided by explorers and other traveling reporters in newspapers, magazines, books, pamphlets, and other published forms entertained readers and informed newcomers of conditions and opportunities in the new country.[1] The western experience generated other accounts as well, consisting generally of diaries, letters, and unpublished narratives that were not aimed at a specific audience, or often any audience at all. These documents are perhaps the most personal and focus most closely on the interests of the writers. As such, they reveal details otherwise unavailable about the activities and motivations of individuals traveling west.

Evangelical zeal led religious organizations to send missionaries to evangelize aboriginal people as well as members of pioneer communities, and travelers roamed newly opened territories seeking adventure and knowledge. The reports and correspondence of missionaries provided details of their activities and help raise funds for future proselytizing efforts. Although many saw print, others remained in manuscript form, recording the day-to-day activities of their authors and their efforts to accomplish the goals of their endeavors.[2]

Westward expansion also created economic opportunities for eastern capitalist entrepreneurs. Among those who sought to expand business into

---

1. James Schramer and Donald Ross, *American Travel Writers, 1776–1864* (Detroit: Gale Research, 1997), xviii–xx. Contemporary published accounts of antebellum travels in the Great Lakes region include C. Colton, *Tour of the American Lakes, and among the Indians of the North-West Territory, in 1830*, 2 vols. (London: Frederick Wesley and A. H. Davis, 1833); Charles A. Lanman, *A Summer in the Wilderness: Embracing a Canoe Voyage up the Mississippi and around Lake Superior* (New York: D. Appleton, 1847); Henry R. Schoolcraft, *Narrative Journal of Travels from Detroit Northwest through the Great Chain of American Lakes to the Sources of the Mississippi River in 1820* (Ann Arbor: University Microfilms, 1966); Patrick Shirreff, *A Tour through North America* (Edinburgh: Oliver and Boyd, 1835).

2. Some missionary journals were published as contemporary accounts of travel in the Great Lakes region, including James L. Scott, *A Journal of a Missionary Tour through Pennsylvania, Ohio, Indiana, Illinois, Iowa, Wiskonsin, and Michigan* (Providence, RI: By the author, 1843). Other journals were compiled and published later, such as George P. Clark, ed., *Into the Old Northwest: Journals with Charles H. Titus, 1841–1846* (East Lansing: Michigan State University Press, 1994); and Maurice F. Cole, comp., *Voices from the Wilderness* (Ann Arbor: University of Michigan Press, 1961).

the newly opened lands were speculators in frontier lands. Nehemiah and Henry Sanford were members of the eastern elite who saw the purchase of western lands for resale at a profit as a viable investment of capital generated by their industrial endeavors at home in Connecticut. In the 1830s they began acquiring large quantities of land, but not for their own use. The Sanfords visited Michigan and surrounding states to examine and obtain properties and coordinate the activities of the agents who handled their management and sales in the owners' absence. Although the speculators' business was carried out for selfish motives, their efforts nevertheless had wider implications for the development of the regions they visited. The operations of the Sanfords and others did not occur in a vacuum, and their actions in selecting land and promoting its sale influenced the geographical form of frontier immigration and affected the location and success of new settlements. In Michigan, as elsewhere in the antebellum West, the machinations of land speculators helped shape the landscape of colonization, and their writings help reveal the manner in which they did so.[3]

The Sanfords' journeys took place amid substantial change in the development of the young nation. During the 1830s and 1840s the United States increased its territorial domain across the continent, gaining territory by conquest and negotiation and added six new states to the union. An expansion of the transportation network, propelled by technological innovation, accompanied this spatial growth and worked together with it to promote development in the West. Traveling through the new country, the Sanfords took advantage of such changes to conduct and expand their business on the frontier, but could not help but notice the transformations that they brought about in so short a time.

---

3. A classic example of the role of outside speculators' activities in shaping settlement in Michigan and adjacent areas is Levi Beardsley, *Reminiscences* (New York: Charles Vinten, 1852), 252–261. Joshua D. Rothman addressed the role of speculators in shaping settlement in the Old Southwest in *Flush Times and Fever Dreams: A Story of Capitalism and Slavery in the Age of Jackson* (Athens: University of Georgia Press, 2012).

The Sanford journals comprise a small portion of the voluminous records of Henry Shelton Sanford, a man whose life took him to many places beyond the West of the 1840s. His subsequent exploits as a diplomat, foreign agent, spymaster, politician, and agricultural developer have far overshadowed his role as land speculator and traveler in the antebellum West. Nevertheless, Henry's accounts of two extensive western journeys and his parents' record of their travels in the Great Lakes region provide an enlightening firsthand chronicle of business and travel in a landscape in transition, and one that would cease to exist within the lifetime of its inhabitants.

The Sanford journals rest in the Sanford Museum of the City of Sanford, Florida, the site of Henry Sanford's final venture. I could not be more appreciative of the museum's staff for their assistance in compiling the Sanford journals. In particular, curator Alicia Clarke facilitated access to the museum's collections and encouraged my pursuit of the Sanford journals. She cheerfully made materials available to me even at a distance and more than once called to my attention documents I might otherwise have overlooked. Her innumerable suggestions regarding their content made the task of developing context for the Sanfords' journeys considerably easier. I owe a debt of gratitude to museum assistant Brigitte A. Stephenson for her insights with regard to Henry Sanford's correspondence as well as her help in accessing documents in the collections. Her assistance facilitated the process of assembling the journal materials, and her efforts in securing the images of the Sanford family are deeply appreciated.

Over the course of the Sanford project Keith Widder provided constant encouragement and reviewed earlier drafts of the text. His keen interest in and extensive knowledge of Great Lakes history, together with his expertise as a writer, helped guide my research. Although I am responsible for the final results, they are better for his efforts. My work also benefited from the attention of Carolyn Baker Lewis and Woody Bowden, whose diligence helped overcome my shortcomings in logic and prose. I also wish to acknowledge the comments and suggestions of the two anonymous reviewers and the members of the editorial board of the Michigan State University Press.

In researching the historical and geographical context of the Sanfords' travels my task was made easier by those with knowledge of the region's past. In this regard I wish to thank William Lovis of Michigan State University and Sean Dunham of the US Forest Service for their assistance. For the use of contemporary images relating to the Sanfords' travels, I am indebted to Mark Spang of the Historical Collections of the Great Lakes at Bowling Green State University and Lisa R. Marine of the Wisconsin Historical Society. Several individuals provided additional information helpful in completing this study, and I wish to thank Anne Vawser and Karin Roberts of the National Park Service.

Last but certainly not least, the staff of the Michigan State University Press has as always been helpful and attentive in converting my manuscript into a finished product. It has been my pleasure to work with assistant director and editor in chief Julie Loehr and digital production specialist Annette Tanner. No study of travel is complete without maps, and those accompanying the text are the work of Ellen White of MSU.

INTRODUCTION

n early October 1846 Henry Shelton Sanford returned to Derby, Connecticut, having spent the previous four months on a trip to the trans-Mississippi West. This was not his first venture beyond the family's New England home to explore the wider world, nor was it Henry's first journey to the young nation's frontier. In his twenty-three years he had already completed several Atlantic crossings to visit Gibraltar and Portugal in the fall of 1841 and to conduct an extended seven-month excursion the following year to Turkey, Greece, and Malta, with a side trip to the Alps. He toured England in the spring of 1845 on his third voyage. In addition to these foreign journeys, Henry Sanford also made three western expeditions in 1844, 1845, and 1846, which was his last. These took him through the Ohio Valley as well as the Great Lakes and the lands beyond during a time of accelerated expansion and change in antebellum America. Well educated and intellectually curious, his financial security ensured by his family's manufacturing fortune, Sanford mixed pleasure with family business on journeys that became adventures in which he sought to describe as well

COURTESY OF THE SANFORD MUSEUM, CITY OF SANFORD, FLORIDA.

Henry Shelton Sanford, at the time of his first visit to Europe in 1841. He was already a seasoned traveler when he set out for his first western journey three years later.

as understand the new world he encountered. The youthful Sanford's narrative of his travels, recorded in his journals and letters, provide a fascinating description of the regions and their inhabitants.[1]

Henry Sanford's interest in the West represented more than his own curiosity and appetite for adventure. It also grew from his family's entrepreneurial inclinations and quest for profitable investments. Living in a time of American economic growth and dramatic geographical expansion that gave rise to the notion of Manifest Destiny, the Sanfords joined their countrymen in seeking fortune in the West.[2] Earlier, his father, Nehemiah Curtis Sanford, had taken an interest in the new country on the Middle Border, a land his correspondents described as "delightful" and a place

---

1. Joseph A. Fry, *Henry S. Sanford: Diplomacy and Business in Nineteenth-Century America* (Reno: University of Nevada Press, 1982), 5; Harriet Chappell Owsley, *Register: Henry Shelton Sanford Papers* (Nashville: Tennessee State Library and Archives, 1960), 6.
2. See David S. Reynolds, *Waking Giant: America in the Age of Jackson* (New York: HarperCollins, 2008), 1–4.

Nehemiah Curtis Sanford was a successful merchant and co-owner of the Shelton Tack Factory in Birmingham, Connecticut. An investor in western lands, he journeyed to the Great Lakes in 1835, and four years later he and his wife Nancy conducted an extensive tour of properties in Michigan.

Nancy Shelton Sanford, who accompanied her husband on his business trip to Michigan and Chicago in 1839.

where newcomers might live "in the midst of eastern people in a healthy and pleasant village."[3] The promise of profit in the sale of western lands attracted the attention of the elder Sanford as a member of the rising eastern business elite. Nehemiah Curtis Sanford and Nancy Shelton Sanford both came from old New England families whose economic interests were closely intertwined. Like the Sheltons, the Sanfords were an old and

---

3. William D. Abernathy to Nehemiah C. Sanford, Dec. 3, 1832, Henry Shelton Sanford Papers (HSSP), Box 69, Folder 1. Abernathy was a resident of Jacksonville, Illinois.

Edward Shelton, Henry Sanford's maternal uncle. Together with Nehemiah Sanford, Shelton toured the Great Lakes in 1835 and joined his brother-in-law as an investor in western lands. Upon Nehemiah's death in 1841, he assumed control of the family land business as well as the tack factory in Connecticut. He served as a mentor to his nephew until Henry reached his majority and became his business partner.

COURTESY OF THE SANFORD MUSEUM, CITY OF SANFORD, FLORIDA.

respected family with deep roots in Connecticut. Born in 1792, Nehemiah married Nancy Bateman Shelton in 1822, a year before the birth of their only child, Henry. The elder Sanford had made his fortune as a merchant in Woodbury, Connecticut, and in 1836 pooled his resources with those of his brother-in-law Edward N. Shelton to open the Shelton Tack Factory in Birmingham on the Housatonic River in the same state. The Sanford family then moved to the nearby village of Derby, where Nehemiah became a highly regarded member of the business community.[4]

Edward Shelton was one of Derby's leading businessmen and a continuing influence on Henry Sanford throughout his life. In addition to his partnership in the tack factory, he was involved with other enterprises, including two banks and the Shelton box company. As president of the Ousatonic Water Company he was a driving force behind the construction of the dam that provided water power for manufacturing. Politically active, Edward Shelton served in the Connecticut senate and maintained close

---

4. Richard J. Amundson, "The American Life of Henry Shelton Sanford" (PhD dissertation, Florida State University, 1963), 4–5; Fry, *Henry S. Sanford*, 2–5.

ties with the New York mercantile community. Following the early death of his father in 1841, young Henry's uncle Edward became his mentor in business, advising him as well as acting as his attorney in the acquisition and management of land and stock investments. Even after Henry left the tack factory and other commercial activities in Derby, his uncle continued to communicate with him regarding his businesses ventures.[5]

In 1835 Nehemiah's interest prompted him and his brother-in-law Edward Shelton to commence a voyage of exploration on the steamboat *Thomas Jefferson* on the Great Lakes, visiting Cleveland and Chicago.[6] During their voyage they undoubtedly became aware of the booming land market in Michigan and the potential for reaping profits from the resale of land to immigrants. By the fourth decade of the nineteenth century the southern portion of Michigan's Lower Peninsula was beginning to fill with immigrant farmers and was fast becoming a viable agricultural region whose new settlements had begun to grow into emerging centers of population and industry. This development was part of the larger spatial growth of the United States and its expanding antebellum economy, a process propelled by enlarged markets, technical innovations in production and transportation, the systematization of land distribution, and changing perceptions of western environments.[7] Eastern investors like Sanford and

---

5. Amundson, "American Life of Henry Shelton Sanford," 51–54; Fry, *Henry S. Sanford*, 7, 29, 78, 89. Edward Shelton represented the Fifth District in 1869. "Edward N. Sheldon," http://electronicvalley.org/derby//HallofFame/Shelton.Ed.htm; "Connecticut: State Senate, 1860s," The Political Graveyard, politicalgraveyard.com.
6. The *Thomas Jefferson* was built at Erie and finished at Buffalo in 1834. It was a low-pressure steamboat of 428 tons. It was part of a larger fleet of steamboats operated on the Great Lakes by Charles Manning Reed in the 1830s and 1840s. J. B. Mansfield, *Great Lakes Maritime History*, vol. 1, *1831–1840* (Chicago: J. H. Beers & Co., 1899), chapter 35; Joel Stone, *Floating Palaces of the Great Lakes: A History of Passenger Steamships on the Inland Seas* (Ann Arbor: University of Michigan Press, 2015), 71–72; Nehemiah Sanford Journal, June 5, 23, 1837, HSSP, Box 2, Folder 7.
7. The remarkable growth of the antebellum American economy and the increasingly central role of the Northeast were directly tied to the western expansion of production and the spread of settlement. See Susan Previant Lee and Peter Passell,

Shelton played an important role in guiding western development. Unlike migrants who sought new homes or places for business, they traveled as consumers who sought to exploit the economic opportunities presented by distant western resources. From their secure homes in the East they sought to manipulate markets in lands, agriculture, and labor and through their efforts wielded an "invisible hand" that played a major role in directing the economic development of frontier regions.[8]

Shelton's and Sanford's choices to invest their surplus capital in land reflected a broader strategy to profit from difficulties inherent in current land policy. Since the early years of the Republic, a series of federal land acts had regulated the size of tracts as well as their cost.[9] Initially the

---

A New Economic View of American History (New York: Norton, 1979), 52–62; Douglass C. North, *The Economic Growth of the United States, 1790–1860* (New York: Norton, 1966), 189–190; Charles Sellers, *The Market Revolution: Jacksonian America, 1815–1846* (New York: Oxford University Press, 1991), 16–21; D. W. Meinig, *The Shaping of America: A Geographical Perspective on 500 Years of History*, vol. 2, *Continental America, 1800–1867* (New Haven: Yale University Press, 1993), 197, 264–273. Economic expansion and the organization of the colonial economy in antebellum Michigan shaped the composition, distribution, and function of its settlements. Kenneth E. Lewis, *West to Far Michigan: Settling the Lower Peninsula, 1815–1860* (East Lansing: Michigan State University Press, 2002), 208–215, 301–310.

8. The role of eastern investors in the development of western regions has been explored elsewhere by Joshua D. Rothman, *Flush Times and Fever Dreams: A Story of Capitalism and Slavery in the Age of Jackson* (Athens: University of Georgia Press, 2012); and Edward E. Baptist, *Creating an Old South: Middle Florida's Plantation Frontier before the Civil War* (Chapel Hill: University of North Carolina Press, 2002), 91–96.

9. The alienation of federal lands to settlers was a separate procedure that involved additional steps. In order to distribute land in an orderly manner, the government relied on the systematic survey of the public domain into regular units consisting of six-mile-square townships divided into thirty-six sections. The townships were fixed in space within a larger grid system, the axes of which were formed by an east-west-oriented baseline and a north-south meridian. Additional baselines and medians permitted the incorporation of new territories into a consolidated network of survey lines that shaped the form of the new country. While the survey system provided a means to subdivide land, it required a concomitant infrastructure and rules to implement its transfer. The General Land Office provided the administrative

government allowed the purchase of land on credit, but subsequent speculation in western lands led to an inflation of prices and their collapse in the Panic of 1819. In response, the Land Act of 1820 eliminated credit sales of federal lands, a change that ignored the important role credit played in financing many immigrants' purchases. This action encouraged the entry of land speculators who purchased large frontier tracts to resell for a higher price in smaller units. Speculators filled a need for cash-poor pioneers and played a significant role in the transfer of western lands before 1860.[10] As commercial middlemen, they possessed the potential to direct the spread of settlement to suit their private interests. Although viewed by many as exploiters who profited from others' misfortunes, the mortgages speculators offered were virtually the only source of credit

oversight for the marketing of federal lands. Under its auspices lands were offered for sale in contiguous blocks in order of the completion of their survey. These were organized into districts, each of which was administered by the staff of a land office that collected payments and recorded the locations of tracts sold. John Frazier Hart, *The Look of the Land* (Englewood Cliffs, NJ: Prentice-Hall, 1975), 51–55; Richard A. Bartlett, *The New Country: A Social History of the American Frontier, 1776–1890* (New York: Oxford University Press, 1974), 68–71. The survey of Michigan lands began in 1815, and within the next twenty years approximately one-third of the Lower Peninsula had been surveyed. Work progressed rapidly northward and by 1840 the principal meridian and baselines were completed and practically all of the Lower Peninsula and the eastern Upper Peninsula surveyed. Knox Jamison, "The Survey of Public Lands in Michigan," *Michigan History* 42 (1958): 201–205.

10. During the 1850s pressure arose from reformers to distribute public lands free to immigrant settlers. Though the law was opposed by speculators who believed it would depreciate land values, Congress passed homestead legislation as early as 1860. Although initially vetoed by President Buchanan, Abraham Lincoln signed the Homestead Act into law in 1862. Willard W. Cochrane, *The Development of American Agriculture: A Historical Analysis* (Minneapolis: University of Minnesota Press, 1979), 59, 80–81; Roy M. Robbins, *Our Landed Heritage: The Public Domain, 1776–1970* (Lincoln: University of Nebraska Press, 1976), 30–33; Malcolm J. Rohrbough, *Land Office Business: The Settlement and Administration of American Public Lands, 1789–1837* (New York: Oxford University Press, 1968), 138–141; Arthur H. Cole, "Cyclical and Sectional Variations in the Sale of Public Lands, 1816–1860," in *The Public Lands: Studies in the History of the Public Domain*, ed. Vernon Carstensen (Madison: University of Wisconsin Press, 1963), 246.

available to many frontier farmers and made speculators economically integral to settlement.[11]

To be successful, however, speculators had to carefully select the land they purchased to avoid undesirable tracts that would be unlikely to attract pioneer farmers. In addition, for their investment to be profitable, speculators could afford to hold land only for the short time in which anticipated profits remained greater than taxes. Because their success depended on the rapid turnover of lands, a symbiotic relationship between speculators and settlers arose that tempered personal greed with the necessity of creating a workable system for transferring land for credit at reasonable rates.[12] The loss of lands for taxes remained a threat to Shelton and Sanford and others who dealt in lands, and they took pains to make sure that payments were current. The specter of repossession that threatened frontier farmers unable to pay taxes on their lands also offered an opportunity for speculators who were poised to acquire title to them for bargain prices at sheriffs' sales.

Within two years of their lake voyage, the brothers-in-law had begun to purchase tracts in Michigan, and their interest in western lands had become known. In the spring of 1837 Elias B. Sherman, a resident of Cassopolis, Michigan, approached them, offering to sell lands that Sanford and Shelton had acquired in Cass County.[13] Sherman proposed to act as

---

11. Reginald Horsman, "Changing Images of the Public Domain: Historians and the Shaping of Midwest Frontiers," in *This Land Is Ours: The Acquisition and Disposition of the Public Domain* (Indianapolis: Indiana Historical Society, 1978), 66; Allen G. Bogue, "Land Credit for Northern Farmers, 1789–1940," *Agricultural History* 50 (1976): 68–100.

12. Paul W. Gates, "The Role of the Speculator in Western Land Development," in Carstensen, *The Public Lands*, 360–363.

13. A native of Oneida, New York, Elias B. Sherman came to Michigan in 1825 and was admitted to the bar in Ann Arbor four years later. Later that year he moved to Cass County as a resident land speculator. He served as district surveyor as well as prosecuting attorney and probate judge. Together with Alexander H. Redfield he developed the town of Cassopolis as the county seat in 1831 and later became a director of the First National Bank there. In 1833 he married Sarah Silver, the daughter of Jacob Silver, a merchant who maintained a large store in Cassopolis. He was a

their agent, disposing of their lands in Michigan in return for a commission and expenses.[14] Apparently in response to his offer, Nehemiah Sanford engaged Sherman to manage their affairs and provided a general power of attorney to allow him to make deeds, take mortgages on lands, pay taxes, and conduct other financial matters in Shelton's and Sanford's names. Sanford also agreed to participate jointly with him in the purchase of additional parcels.[15]

The late 1830s was an auspicious time for eastern speculators who possessed the capital to enter the western land market. Although the decade was witnessed marked economic growth in the United States, it closed with an economic downturn touched off by the Panic of 1837. This financial crisis triggered a nationwide recession that lasted until 1844 and precipitated the decline of commodity prices, the collapse of banks, the failure of businesses, and massive unemployment. Despite these conditions, the Shelton Tack Factory seems to have flourished and furnished its owners with the financial wherewithal not only to survive but to seek further gains through investment. The negative impact of the downturn on the financial fortunes of western farmers furthered opportunities for speculators by increasing the number of failures and the tracts auctioned for failure to pay taxes.[16]

---

member of a commission that laid out a road running from White Pigeon and Prairie Ronde to Kalamazoo and Grand Rapids and from Constantine and Cassopolis to the mouth of the St. Joseph River. Alfred Mathews, *History of Cass County, Michigan* (Chicago: Waterman, Watkins & Co., 1882), 70–71, 76–77, 87, 154–155, 167; *History of St. Joseph County, Michigan* (Philadelphia: L. H. Everts, 1877), 27, 30; Howard S. Rogers, *History of Cass County, Michigan from 1825 to 1875* (Dowagiac, MI: Captain Samuel Felt Chapter, the Daughters of the American Revolution, 1942), 236–240, 385–386; Samuel W. Durant, *History of Kalamazoo County, Michigan* (Philadelphia: Everts & Abbott, 1880), 164; Crisfield Johnson, *History of Branch County, Michigan* (Philadelphia: Everts, 1879), 53–54; HSSP, Box 63, folder 14.

14. E. B. Sherman to N. C. Sanford, May 21, 1837, HSSP, Box 63, Folder 14.

15. E. B. Sherman to N. C. Sanford and E. N. Shelton, Oct. 24, 1837, HSSP, Box 63, Folder 14; E. B. Sherman to E. N Shelton, May 16, 1842, HSSP, Box 63, Folder 14.

16. Douglass C. North, *The Economic Growth of the United States, 1790–1860* (New York:

In the late spring of 1839 Nehemiah, together with his wife Nancy, set out from Derby to examine the lands he and Sheldon owned in Michigan and investigate the possibility of additional land purchases elsewhere. During this trip Nehemiah consulted with Sherman and explored portions of Cass and Berrien Counties in southwestern Michigan as well as northern Indiana. Farther north, in Kalamazoo County, he had earlier engaged the services of James Smith Jr. as a second agent. An ambitious merchant and early resident of Prairie Ronde, Smith had begun purchasing lands in the county, and Sanford visited him to settle accounts and direct him to acquire further tracts as they were sold for taxes. As Shelton and Sanford's second agent in Michigan, Smith represented their interests until his death in 1842.[17] Upon completing transactions in Michigan the Sanfords traveled westward to Chicago. Although Nehemiah could not resist the urge to investigate new prospects in western lands, the visit also permitted him to meets with old friends and marked the beginning of a leisurely homeward voyage via the Great Lakes. When the Sanfords returned to Detroit on their way home, Nehemiah once again contacted Sherman to coordinate the payment of taxes on his western properties and to inquire about acquiring additional tax lands. Nevertheless, the Sanfords' western trip involved more than business and revealed the family's interest in exploring new places.

■　　■　　■

Nehemiah Sanford's sudden death in early 1841 placed the operation of the Michigan land venture in his brother-in-law's hands. Nehemiah's son and heir Henry was ill and deeply shaken by his father's passing and not yet of

---

Norton, 1966), 128–203; Peter Temin, *The Jacksonian Economy* (New York: Norton, 1969), 136–155.

17. James Smith Jr. came to southwestern Michigan from Vermont in 1830 and the following year purchased land and established a store at Schoolcraft. He formed several partnerships during the following decade and greatly enlarged his business; however, the failure of various ventures led to his financial ruin, and he died in 1842. Durant, *History of Kalamazoo County*, 532–534.

legal age to assume control of his interests. On the advice of his physician he embarked that fall on the first of two voyages to Europe to recover his health. Only upon his return in 1843 did he begin to participate in his family's businesses.[18] In the intervening time Edward Shelton continued to carry out the family land business at a distance. His agent, Sherman, managed the heirs' estates in southwestern Michigan despite difficulties in paying taxes and collecting debts from those who absconded or were reluctant or unable to pay. Furthermore, a recent state bankruptcy law in Michigan favoring debtors complicated the situation and brought a downturn in the land market.[19] Even so, Sherman had reason to be optimistic about the future. He believed that the westward progress of the Michigan Southern Railroad would contribute to an increase in immigration and improve business for land speculators.[20] His own losses due to misfortune and less than satisfactory management of his client's funds, however, would strain their relationship and prompt Henry Sanford's first western trip in the summer of 1844.

Following his return home from Europe and the Mediterranean in the spring of 1843, Henry Sanford was now of age and assumed a major role in his late father's businesses. Having inherited a half interest in the ownership of the western lands as well as in the Sanford & Shelton Tack Company, he soon became active in both. Twenty-one-year-old Henry became a sales agent for the company in New York, but in spite of booming business he was soon enlisted by his uncle and partner to investigate the condition of their Michigan landholdings. Sometime after agent Smith's death, Shelton had hired William L. Booth, a former resident of Connecticut who now

18. Fry, *Henry S. Sanford*, 5; Amundson, "American Life of Henry Shelton Sanford," 6–7. Nehemiah Sanford died unexpectedly on June 23, 1841, at age forty-nine. His widow, Nancy Shelton Sanford, survived him by thirty-nine years, passing away on Dec. 21, 1880. "Connecticut Deaths and Burials, 1650–1934," Ancestry, https://www.ancestry.com.
19. E. B. Sherman to E. N. Shelton, June 10, 1843, HSSP, Box 63, Folder 14.
20. E. B. Sherman to E. N. Shelton, Jan. 25, 1844, HSSP, Box 63, Folder 14.

lived in Kalamazoo County, to represent the family's land interests there.[21] Directed by his uncle to meet with the new agent to view the lands he purchased and provide sufficient funds to pay taxes, Henry was also to visit agent Sherman to collect interest he owed them as well as payments due from land buyers. Shelton also instructed his nephew to examine and evaluate the lands Sherman had mortgaged.[22] Uncle Edward further directed Henry to proceed to Chicago to inquire about the soundness of L. W. Clark, a customer indebted to the company. In addition young Sanford was to investigate a competitor's business in that city.[23]

Henry left Derby for the "Great West" in late July. For the first part of his journey his mother and aunt Elizabeth "Lizzie" Shelton, accompanied the young adventurer to New York City and then up the Hudson River and overland to Saratoga Springs, the spa famous for its mineral waters. Believed to have curative powers, the springs attracted large numbers of visitors to the elegant hotels erected there. Although many visited the springs solely for their purported health benefits, others took advantage of the artificial social environment the spas provided, one that offered opportunity for members of both sexes to interact in various organized and impromptu activities and amusements not available elsewhere. Saratoga Springs also became a destination where the socially conscious could see and been seen, and many prominent people were seasonal residents.[24] A cultured and charming young man, Henry seemed to be in his element in

---

21. A native of Stratford, Connecticut, William L. Booth came to Michigan in 1842 and settled in Texas Township in Kalamazoo County. He later held several township offices and was a member of a partnership that operated a steam mill. Franklin Ellis, *History of Berrien and Van Buren Counties, Michigan* (Philadelphia: D. W. Ensign, 1880), 449, 535; Durant, *History of Kalamazoo County*, 541.
22. E. B. Sherman to E. N. Shelton, Aug. 6, 1844, HSSP, Box 73, Folder 1.
23. E. B. Sherman to E. N. Shelton, Aug. 15, 1844, HSSP, Box 73, Folder 1.
24. Thomas A. Chambers, "Seduction and Sensibility: The Refined Society of Ballston, New York, 1800," *New York History* 78 (July 1997): 253–257; Jeffrey W. Limerick, "The Grand Hotels of America," *Perspecta* 15 (1975): 88; "History of Saratoga," Saratoga Springs Heritage Area Visitor Center, saratogaspringsvisitorcenter.com.

Nancy Shelton Sanford in 1845, as she appeared at the time she accompanied Henry Sanford on his first trip to the West.

company with those who attended the social events during his short stay at Saratoga, and he quickly found introductions to many of the wealthy, middle-aged female guests. The ease with which he gained confidences would serve him well as a stranger on the frontier as well as in his later career as a diplomat.[25] Henry then escorted his mother and aunt to the residence of his father's brother John in Amsterdam, New York. After a short stay, his party traveled to Buffalo on Lake Erie, where Henry left his relatives to begin his journey to Michigan and points west.[26]

Henry's route took him across Lake Erie to Detroit by steamboat and overland across Michigan's Lower Peninsula to Chicago and Galena, Illinois,

---

25. Fry, *Henry S. Sanford*, 9–11.
26. John Sanford was a successful manufacturer who owned a carpet mill in Amsterdam, New York. Active in politics, he later served as a member of Congress. Samuel Orcott and Ambrose Beardsley, *The History of the Old Town of Derby, Connecticut, 1642–1880* (Bowie, MD: Heritage Books, 1998), 354; Owsley, *Register*; William Cothren, *History of Ancient Woodbury, Connecticut from the First Indian Deed in 1659 to 1854* (Waterbury, CT: Bronson Bros., 1854), 473.

and then by various means, to Dubuque, Iowa, and up the Mississippi River to the Falls of St. Anthony at present-day Minneapolis. Although this part of the journey is not recorded in his journal, he apparently returned home via Chicago and Cincinnati. His more southerly route contrasted with that of his outward journey and may have followed the path he described in detail in his journal of a trip made two years later.

The 1844 trip became more than a business venture to investigate the family's land dealings in Michigan, and Henry's journal introduces the reader to the broader interests that were a mark of his character and that helped influence his actions for the remainder of his life. Always fascinated by technology and innovation, as well as the new and unusual, he was intrigued by the varied activities of immigrant entrepreneurs on the frontier. Forever attracted to the possibility of new investment opportunities, he carefully examined and recorded their activities in hopes of potential future profit as well as out of curiosity about the unfamiliar. After viewing properties in Michigan and conducting business in Chicago, he extended his western tour to visit the lead-mining region in northern Illinois, southern Wisconsin, and Iowa. The lead ore deposits there had been mined successfully since the late eighteenth century, and production there expanded rapidly in the 1820s, particularly following the acquisition of Indian lands at the close of the Blackhawk War in 1832.[27] Reserved by the federal government and leased to individual miners, these valuable mineral lands were centered in the market town of Galena, Illinois. Lead was mined and smelted here and shipped down the Mississippi to St. Louis and New Orleans or from Green Bay and Milwaukee to New York via the lakes.[28]

---

27. Lucy Eldersveld Murphy, *A Gathering of Rivers: Indians, Métis and Mining in the Western Great Lakes, 1737–1832* (Lincoln: University of Nebraska Press, 2000), 105–110.
28. Walter Renton Ingalls, *Lead and Zinc in the United States: Comprising an Economic History of the Mining and Smelting of the Metals and the Conditions Which Have Affected the Development of the Industries* (New York: Hill Publishing Co., 1908), 120–131; Gary Henry, "Galena, Illinois during the Lead Mine Era" (MA thesis, Eastern

As immigrants poured into the mining district in the 1830s, mining camps sprang up across the region that soon extended into adjacent portions of Wisconsin and Iowa. By the time of Sanford's visit, the mining boom was well underway, and the region along the Fever River in Illinois and the vicinity of Dubuque presented an irresistible attraction to the young explorer. Always looking for investment opportunities, Henry visited sites of industrial development on the frontier in 1844. But his travels also took him to places of historical and cultural interest and reveal a curiosity and sense of adventure that would carry him even farther west as well as to other more remote destinations in later years. Although his journal closed at Dubuque in early September, Henry continued his travels on the Mississippi River, visiting the nascent settlement of St. Paul, Minnesota, as well as the Mormon colony at Nauvoo, Illinois, and returning via the Ohio River.[29]

■   ■   ■

Henry Sanford's experiences in 1844 led him to make two subsequent western trips. Unlike the first excursion, however, these appear to have been undertaken largely for the purpose of pleasure, much like his European tours. Financially secure and with limited business responsibilities, he had time to satisfy his intellectual curiosity and engage in the pastimes he most enjoyed. Traveling on the lakes and overland, Henry visited and carefully studied the inhabitants of the communities he encountered, but as an avid sportsman, he also sought to take advantage of the abundant fish and game in the West, engaging in the promiscuous practice of hunting and fishing at a time when the abundance of American wildlife seemed limitless and was only there for the taking.

The first excursion took place in the summer of 1845, shortly after he

Illinois University, 1976), 52–58; *The History of Jo Daviess County, Illinois* (Chicago: H. F. Kett & Co., 1878), 245–246.

29. E. B. Sherman to E. N. Shelton, Sept. 12, 1844, HSSP, Box 73, Folder 1.

returned home from a trip to England in May of that year.[30] Unlike his early foray into the West, this one produced no firsthand account of the journey, and little is known about it aside from information contained in two letters he received from his uncle Edward Shelton and his friend Gilead Smith.[31] Both were written on July 28, 1845, following his return to Buffalo four days earlier on the steamboat *Cleveland*.[32] Smith's letter reveals that Henry had been gone for at least three weeks, apparently spending some of the time in Chicago. The purpose of the trip is unstated, for neither correspondent mentioned business transactions in Michigan or the West. His uncle's acknowledgment of his visit to St. Joseph, Michigan, and his sending of a draft to William L. Booth, their land agent in Kalamazoo, however, imply that Henry was again looking after the family's land investments there. His westward travels followed much the same route as his outward journey of the previous year, taking him from Buffalo across the lake to Michigan to Chicago. But there he departed radically from his earlier itinerary.

At Chicago, Henry's trip seems to have been cut short by illness, possibly asthma or the eye affliction that arose during his sophomore year in college and troubled him sporadically for the remainder of his life.[33]

---

30. Henry S. Sanford, "Two Weeks' Tour of Great Britain, April 1845," HSSP, Box 3, Folder 3; Owsley, *Register*.
31. Gilead A. Smith was a close friend of Henry Sanford's from his days at Washington (now Trinity) College. Born in Pennsylvania in 1821, he became a businessman residing in New York City. In 1852 he married Anne M. Parsons and in later years was a banker and merchant. "New York City, Marriages, 1600s-1800s," Ancestry, https://www.ancestry.com; "New York State Census, 1855," Ancestry, https://www.ancestry.com; "Passport Applications, 1795–1905," Ancestry, https://www.ancestry.com; "U. S. Civil War Draft Registration Records, 1863–1865," Ancestry, https://www.ancestry.com.
32. The steamboat *Cleveland* was launched at Huron, Ohio, on June 24, 1837. Its deck measured 180 feet in length and 28 in breadth. The cabin occupied nearly the entire length of the deck, with accommodations for 200 passengers. "Another New Steamboat," *Cleveland (OH) Weekly Advertiser*, Oct. 6, 1836; "Steam Boat Launch," *Cleveland (OH) Daily Herald & Gazette*, June 22, 1837.
33. Fry, *Henry S. Sanford*, 4–5.

Upon his return he informed his Uncle Edward that he had become sick and had gone north to Mackinac Island, located at the straits between Lakes Huron and Michigan, to recover his health. Unlike his parents, who had made only a passing visit there six years previously, Henry lingered to enjoy the beneficial climate of the region and the boundless advantages it offered the sportsman. An avid hunter and fisherman, he found recreational opportunities there that he would continue to pursue in his subsequent western excursions. Apparently Henry's health improved during his extended stay on Mackinac Island. Actively pursuing his sporting interests, he traveled north across Michigan's Upper Peninsula to Sault Ste. Marie to fish for trout, engaging a guide named Le Comer. His experiences in this new country in the north so impressed him that he repeated the visit on his 1846 journey to the northern Plains.[34] Henry retraced his route homeward later that summer, passing through to Buffalo and stopping at Saratoga Springs in late July before returning to Derby.[35]

■   ■   ■

The new year brought a notable change in the life of the young bachelor, well known for his fondness for the society of young ladies. Among the eligible women in Henry's life was the daughter of a prominent Derby physician, Janey Howe, with whom he had been acquainted for several years. Their engagement in 1846 held the promise of bringing stability to Henry's life, much to the satisfaction of his mother. Nancy Shelton Sanford had long disapproved of her son's independence and pleasure-seeking ways and hoped marriage to a sensible young lady would bring a desired discipline and stability. Henry was deeply in love with Janey, and in his correspondence he not only conveyed his feelings for her, but also attempted to take her along on his journey through his descriptions of

34. Henry S. Sanford, July 21, "Journal: Buffalo Hunt, July–September, 1846," and undated letter Henry Sanford to Spirit, HSSP, Box 3, Folder 5.
35. Gilead Smith to Henry Sanford, July 28, 1845, HSSP, Box 73, Folder 3; E. N. Shelton to Henry S. Sanford, July 28, 1845, HSSP, Box 131, Folder 3.

people and places he encountered and the events he observed. His letters to his fiancée add a distinctive perspective to his last western trip.[36]

Henry Sanford's final western journey of 1846 was an epic trek that took him to the Great Plains in what is now South Dakota and culminated in a buffalo hunt on the Vermillion River. Recounted in his journal and letters, the trip took young Sanford on a new route to the West. Avoiding the lake passage westward from New York, he instead traveled by railroad down the Eastern Seaboard from New York, visiting Philadelphia and Baltimore before heading overland across the Alleghenies to Pittsburgh on the Ohio River and proceeding by steamboat to the great inland port of Cincinnati, currently a major embarkation point for American troops on their way to war in Mexico. From there he journeyed across Ohio to Sandusky and by Lake Erie to Detroit, from which he again traversed Michigan's Lower Peninsula to St. Joseph, by now familiar territory to him. After crossing Lake Michigan to Chicago, he continued by steamboat northward on the lake to Mackinac Island via several points along the lake. Proceeding north to Sault Ste. Marie, Henry stopped briefly before beginning his journey to the western frontier. He sailed the length of Lake Superior to Wisconsin and then trekked westward to St. Paul on the Mississippi River. Following a bout of asthma that nearly forced him to cut his trip short and return to the East, he continued onward over the prairie through Minnesota and into present South Dakota. In his travels Henry passed through regions largely beyond Euro-American settlement, although its resident aboriginal inhabitants had already begun to experience the trauma of white expansion, as mining, logging, and other industrial ventures spread into the trans-Mississippi West. The buffalo hunt on the Vermillion River was the raison d'être for his western sojourn and marked the climax of Henry's great adventure.

As the purpose of Henry's third western expedition differed markedly

36. Fry, *Henry S. Sanford*, 7; Amundson, "American Life of Henry Shelton Sanford," 15–16.

from that of his earlier trips, his attention shifted from business to the pleasures of exploration, travel, and sport. Although opportunities for investment in copper and timber ventures drew his attention, his principal interests were elsewhere. With the almost boundless natural resources of the lakes, rivers, and countryside before him, Sanford fished and hunted throughout his trip, noting in detail the animals taken in his travels. Indeed, he and his companions often depended upon wild game for their subsistence, living off the land as traversed ever more distant territory. Sanford reveled in the natural wonders of the landscape through which he passed and expressed great fascination with the people he encountered, especially the Native Americans and métis, who comprised a growing proportion of the inhabitants. For the first time he ventured well beyond the familiar settlements along the Mississippi River, moving farther into the world of Indians, traders, missionaries, soldiers, and others who inhabited a land outside the comfortable confines of antebellum America and over which its government exercised progressively less control. Its scope made it perhaps the greatest adventure yet for the young explorer, although it would certainly not be the last one in a life filled with future challenges.

Henry's return journey eastward followed a more leisurely course. He traveled by water from South Dakota along the Missouri River to St. Louis and via the Mississippi and Ohio Rivers to Louisville, Kentucky. In Kentucky he toured plantations and country estates, witnessing the institution of slavery and its effects firsthand. Like many in the eastern business and commercial establishment, Sanford was conscious of the value of economic ties with the southern states and the goods they produced, and remained less than sympathetic toward those trapped in bondage. After spending several days in Lexington, he continued eastward by stage to Virginia, again crossing the Appalachians to view the sights along a scenic route that led eventually to Richmond, from whence he traveled to New York by way of Washington, DC, Baltimore, and Philadelphia.[37]

---

37. Fry, *Henry S. Sanford*, 31, 83.

As they traveled in the West both Henry Sanford and his father observed varied and unfamiliar landscapes often quite distinct from those of the Eastern Seaboard they called home. These children of old New England stock appear to have been far from complacent members of an old order who were resistant to change or technological innovation. Like many contemporary entrepreneurs, they were not averse to exploring new investment opportunities in far places. Both Sanfords' travels seem to reflect an enthusiasm for examining the unfamiliar. Perhaps Nehemiah's early trips on the Great Lakes involved more than investigating the region's economic potential. Certainly Henry often found himself judging the countryside as much by its unspoiled allure as its capacity to produce crops. Their mixed perceptions mirrored those of other Americans, who by the 1830s had become familiar with the environments of Michigan and other western states and territories. On the one hand they were influenced by utilitarian concerns that reflected beliefs that grew out of the capitalist nature of the national economy. The need to supply the wants of production commodified nature, and many Americans viewed it as a storehouse of raw materials to be marketed for profit. On the other their images were also guided by romantic notions that saw the natural world of the wilderness as the perfection of divine beauty and grandeur that, when experienced by the senses, rejuvenated and purified the observer.[38] Clearly the Sanfords sought land desirable for farming and paid careful attention to those environmental characteristics that identified such tracts, but cultural ideals of beauty and splendor also affected the way they beheld the undeveloped regions they encountered influenced their perceptions of its value.

Perceptions of the environment rested upon immigrant farmers' knowledge of its agricultural potential, the understanding of which had begun to change with the settlement of western lands.[39] By the time American

38. John A. Jakle, *Images of the Ohio Valley: A Historical Geography of Travel, 1740–1860* (New York: Oxford University Press, 1977), 9–10.
39. Earlier beliefs that associated fertility with the humus created by forest growth led New England agriculturists to choose woodlands as the preferred location for

settlers had begun to colonize southwestern Michigan in the mid-1820s, they had abandoned the notion that wooded timberlands marked the location of the richest soils and come to accept that the open lands they encountered here were not only just as productive, but less laborious to clear, and they appealed to the eye as well. In southwestern Michigan the oak openings presented a parklike appearance that contrasted with the heavy eastern woodlands, and the treeless prairies often overwhelmed eastern observers with their vast expanse.[40]

In their travels, Nehemiah and Henry Sanford were aware of the degree to which perceptive factors affected the easterners' evaluation of land and thus its sales potential. As lands along Michigan's southern border opened to settlement in the 1820s and 1830s, surveyors as well as immigrants found an aesthetically pleasing landscape of fertile lands. The Sanfords purchased the bulk of their lands in the western portion of the Kalamazoo and St.

---

farms. Colonial farmers associated particular trees with soil quality and ranked land according to its vegetation. William Cronon, *Changes in the Land: Indians, Colonists, and the Ecology of New England* (New York: Hill and Wang, 1983), 114–115. This notion was challenged as emigrants crossed the Appalachians and successfully cultivated the thinly timbered oak woodlands of western New York. The relative ease by which such "openings" could be cleared and placed in production changed the perception of timbered lands as the most desirable for agricultural and encouraged expansion into open lands in the West. Bernard C. Peters, "Changing Ideas about the Use of Vegetation as an Indicator of Soil Quality: Example of New York and Michigan," *Journal of Geography* 72 (1973): 19–21; Brian Birch, "British Evaluations of the Forest Openings and Prairie Edges of the North Central States, 1800–1850," in *The Frontier: Comparative Studies*, vol. 2, ed. William W. Savage and Stephen I. Thompson (Norman: University of Oklahoma Press, 1979), 174–175.

40. Lewis, *West to Far Michigan*, 56–58. Contemporary works stressed the advantages of farming open lands. See James H. Lanman, *History of Michigan, Civil and Topographical, in a Compendious Form, with a View of the Surrounding Lakes* (New York: E. French, 1839), 234, 324; *Western Travelers' Pocket Directory and Stranger's Guide* (Schenectady, NY: S. S. Riggs, 1834), 52–53; John Mason Peck, *A New Guide for Emigrants to the West* (Boston: Kendall and Lincoln, 1837), 185–186; John T. Blois, *1838 Gazetteer of the State of Michigan* (Knightstown, IN: Bookmark, 1979), 22–28. See also Albert F. Butler, "Rediscovering Michigan's Prairies," *Michigan History* 31 (1947–1948): 267–286; 32 (1948): 15–36; 33 (1948): 117–130, 220–231.

Joseph River drainages, a countryside dominated by oak openings. Here they saw lands particularly favorable for agriculture that could easily be placed in production. Even the forested lands along riverine wetlands were deemed generally superior to those farther east. The positive image of environments in southwestern Michigan made the region attractive to settlers, and an investment in lands there a lucrative endeavor.[41]

Henry's travels beyond Michigan often led to regions far different from those he had previously known. His visit to the lead-mining district of Illinois presented a hellish and polluted landscape created by the extraction and processing of ore on a massive scale. Centered in the market town of Galena, mining expanded in the 1830s as immigrants poured in and camps sprang up across the region to mine and smelt lead to be shipped on the Mississippi River to St. Louis and New Orleans or to New York via the Great Lakes.[42] When Henry visited the Fever River region in Illinois and the diggings farther west in the vicinity of Dubuque, Iowa, the mining boom was well underway and presented an irresistible attraction to the young explorer. Soon he became acquainted with operators of substantial mines and examined their diggings in detail. Young Sanford's investigations provide not only a description of the mines themselves, but a broader picture of a boom area and the behavior of its colorful inhabitants.[43]

Henry Sanford's expedition of 1846 took him even farther afield, a grand venture by water and land to the far West of antebellum America.

---

41. Bernard C. Peters, "Pioneer Evaluation of the Kalamazoo County Landscape," *Michigan Academician* 3 (1970): 22–25; Lewis, *West to Far Michigan*, 189–191.

42. Ingalls, *Lead and Zinc*, 120–131; Henry, "Galena, Illinois," 52–58; *History of Jo Daviess County*, 245–246.

43. The lead ore deposits in northern Illinois, southern Wisconsin, and Iowa had been mined successfully since the late eighteenth century, and production there expanded rapidly in the 1820s, particularly following the acquisition of Indian lands at the close of the Blackhawk War in 1832. The federal government, aware of the value of these deposits, reserved the mineral lands from sale and managed them through leases to individual miners. Murphy, *A Gathering of Rivers*, 105–110; Ingalls, *Lead and Zinc*, 120–131; Henry, "Galena, Illinois," 52–58; *History of Jo Daviess County*, 245–246.

From Mackinac Island, the site of his short visit of the previous year, he set forth across Lake Superior, an immense inland body of water impressive in its vastness as well as its pristine beauty. But evident here also was the impact of Euro-American expansion. On Michigan's Keweenaw Peninsula he explored the copper-mining activities and described the mines, the processing facilities, and the inhabitants, as well as the landscape of this industrial frontier. Ever vigilant for investment opportunities, Henry paid close attention to the potential presented by this mineral resource.[44] Although Sanford had encountered Native Americans previously at Sault Ste. Marie, he now ventured into their country for the first time. In Wisconsin he witnessed the interaction between visiting Chippewas at La Pointe. Fascinated by these strange new people, Henry observed their appearance, behavior, and customs, as well as their interaction with whites and métis. Similarly, he noted the presence of Indian agents, traders, lumbermen, millers, and missionaries, the vanguard of western colonization, and their impact on the land and its inhabitants. Fascinated by this alien country and the people he encountered, Sanford carefully described the land's appearance as well as the characteristics and habits of those who lived there. As

---

44. Drift copper had been mined on the Keewenaw Peninsula since ancient times, and for thousands of years artifacts made from this source found their way across Native North America. European explorers reported copper deposits as early as the late eighteenth century, and evidence presented by Michigan's state geologist Douglas Houghton in 1841 encouraged efforts by the state to acquire the copper lands from the Chippewas by treaty the following year. This made possible the opening of mines in the Keweenaw, and the Copper Rush of 1843 attracted thousands to the area. Soon the towns of Copper Harbor, Eagle Harbor, and Ontonagon sprang up in sheltered locations along Lake Superior. Between 1844 and 1850 investors formed twenty-four companies, only six of which were successful enough to pay dividends. By 1846 only the Lake Superior Copper Company and the Pittsburgh and Boston Mining Company, operators of the rich Cliff Mine, remained in operation. John R. Halsey, "Copper from the Drift," *Michigan Archaeologist* 56 (2010): 2–7; F. E. Richter, "The Copper Mining Industry in the United States, 1845–1925," *Quarterly Journal of Economics* 41 (1927): 236–239; Helen Hornbeck Tanner, *Atlas of Great Lakes Indian History* (Norman: University of Oklahoma Press, 1987), 159–160; "A Short History of Copper Mining," Exploring the North, exploringthenorth.com.

he made his way westward he witnessed an amazing transformation of the land as the woodlands transitioned into prairies and finally became the Great Plains. The contents of Henry Sanford's final western trip provide a compelling personal account of a land and its people.

Throughout his life Henry Sanford retained the perspective of a member of the eastern elite. Despite his experience as an international traveler, he disdained association with working-class Europeans and Americans, who were largely his servants and employees; but he distanced himself from nonwhite groups as well.[45] This attitude is reflected in his view of Native Americans. Passages in his journal largely express the contemporary image of the Indian as a noble savage trapped by the inertia of a time-bound traditional culture that was changing in response to the overwhelming impact of Euro-American contact. Thus he saw their exotic and sometimes violent behavior as a consequence of both their distinctive nature and their current circumstances. In his narrative he saw them as an alien people that formed a collective other, whose members lacked individual personality and generally remained anonymous with the exception of a few well-known leaders.[46] Similarly, Sanford's statements imply that he shared antebellum perceptions of the inherent inferiority of black people, a belief that justified their treatment as a class below whites and a group in need of supervision. On the eve of the Civil War, he remained lukewarm to the idea of abolition, believing that the question of slavery would be handled peacefully. During the war Sanford recognized the political advantages of emancipation and urged the issuance of Lincoln's proclamation, but supported the moderate wing of the Republican Party that opposed efforts that promoted racial equality and policies that benefited African Americans. Although he assumed African Americans' loyalty to the party,

45. Fry, *Henry S. Sanford*, 6.

46. For the development of this perception, see Bernard W. Sheehan, *Seeds of Extinction: Jeffersonian Philanthropy and the American Indian* (New York: Norton, 1973), 102–105; and Robert F. Berghofer, *The White Man's Indian: Images of the American Indian from Columbus to the Present* (New York: Vintage Books, 1979).

he mistrusted their judgment and sought to limit their political role in the postbellum South. His naive support of purportedly philanthropic schemes in Africa further reflected this subservient image of black people requiring guidance.[47]

Our travelers' observations were not confined to places visited and activities encountered in the far reaches of the West. They also recorded the eastern landscapes through which they traveled and included descriptions and interpretations of places and people encountered. Both Nehemiah and Henry commented upon places they viewed en route to the West as well as the modes of transportation that took them on their journeys. The father's 1839 travels with his wife not only bring us images of travel by canal, stagecoach, and steamboat, but also describe Mackinac Island and the fishing industry on the Great Lakes, and relate his feelings upon a visit to a War of 1812 battlefield. Henry's journals of his eastern travels in 1844 include his impressions of New York City, the military academy at West Point, and the gardens of noted landscape architect Andrew J. Downing at Newburgh, as well as the spa of Saratoga Springs, Buffalo, and other points in New York. His 1846 journey offers an extensive tour of major cities on the East Coast. His journal and letters record his activities in New York, Philadelphia, and Baltimore, studying their character and points of interest as he proceeded southward by rail. Turning inland, he passed through Maryland and Pennsylvania to Pittsburgh and on the Ohio River to the western metropolis of Cincinnati, where he paused briefly before continuing his progress to the Great Lakes.

Henry's journey across the Great Lakes captured his impressions of a wilderness in transition, a region opened by new technologies to exploitation and settlement. Traveling by steam and sail, he surveyed the vast openness of Lake Superior, the strange and fascinating features

---

47. Fry, *Henry S. Sanford*, 31, 82–83, 124, 126. For antebellum attitudes toward African Americans, see Ira Berlin, *Many Thousands Gone: The First Two Centuries of Slavery in North America* (Cambridge, MA: Belknap Press of Harvard University Press, 1998), 363–365.

of adjacent lands, the great fires that ravaged the seemingly boundless forests, the curious immigrant settlements that grew up around exploitable resources, and finally the ocean-like prairie that led to the western lands along the Missouri River in the Dakotas. As he returned to the East, his travels took a more familiar route along the major rivers to St. Louis and Louisville and overland through the state and then continued on into Virginia (now West Virginia) and points farther east. Ever the careful observer, his descriptions of rivers, cities, plantations, scenery, and other elements of the landscape through which he traveled paint a vivid picture of a region whose wild elements persisted amid antebellum development. Henry was clearly interested in the places he visited and carefully recorded his perceptions of settlements and their inhabitants as well as the character of the country itself. Through his eyes we see those portions of antebellum urban American with which he was certainly familiar, but we also share his discovery of new places and his desire to examine and understand them.

On a more personal level, both Nehemiah and Henry recorded their interactions with individuals they encountered and the relationships that developed between the eastern travelers and those they met on travels to the frontier. Both Nehemiah and his son possessed the gregarious nature and presence of mind that allowed them to make acquaintances and find friends among strangers and develop personal networks useful in conducting business and developing social alliances necessary for conducting exploration and traveling on the western frontier, where formal institutions were weak or absent. Henry's success in forming ties with such influential contemporaries as publisher Horace Greeley and Minnesota politician and military leader Henry H. Sibley presaged later associations with notable figures such as Abraham Lincoln and William H. Seward.[48]

---

48. Walter Starr, *Seward: Lincoln's Indispensable Man* (New York: Simon and Schuster, 2012), 255; Harriet Chappell Owsley, "Henry Shelton Sanford and Federal Surveillance Abroad, 1861–1865," *Mississippi Valley Historical Review* 48 (1961): 212.

The Sanfords' movements brought them into contact with fascinating and notable people and interesting places worthy of description, and the Sanfords' accounts provide an intimate picture of people and events of a distant time and place. Whether relating chance meetings with the famous and near famous, negotiations with agents or businessmen, confrontations with recalcitrant providers of services, adventures traversing land and water, encounters with interesting and often colorful characters engaged in making a living in a land of transition, or Henry's infatuations with young women he met in his journeys, the journals bring to life the world of the antebellum West through which they traveled. They take the reader on the steamboats, railroads, and stagecoaches that linked the settlements of America during the second quarter of the nineteenth century and by horseback, canoe, and foot into the cabins, boardinghouses, mining camps, trading posts, barrooms, and forts of the frontier, as well as the hotels, restaurants, and entertainment establishments of the eastern cities. Henry's 1846 journal occurred as the United States mobilized for war with Mexico, and his encounters with troops at western posts and those moving along the riverine highways that led southward offer a glimpse of the conflict's impact on the still young nation. Although membership in the elite class of successful industrialists undoubtedly biased the interpretations of our diarists, their observations are nonetheless valuable as contemporary travel accounts and worthy of our consideration as historical sources.

∎   ∎   ∎

The Sanfords' travels to and in the western states and territories would have been impossible without avenues of access. Without routes to move people and goods into the new country and a transportation system capable of moving produce to eastern markets, the settlement and economic development of Michigan and surrounding areas could not have taken place. In the second quarter of the nineteenth century growing external demand for foodstuffs together with changes in transportation technology facilitated movement into the Old Northwest. The waters of the Great

Lakes allowed direct entry into a vast territory, connecting points along their shores with markets in the East. Although immigrants could travel to Michigan overland through Canada or Ohio, travel over unimproved roads was difficult, and movement via the lakes offered a more direct route of access. Two developments in the 1820s facilitated a rapid increase in traffic on the lakes. First, the completion of the Erie Canal in 1825 connected Buffalo on Lake Erie with the Hudson River and New York City and offered a water link to the lakes, promoting both immigration and trade with the West.[49] Second, the application of steam power to watercraft at the turn of the nineteenth century introduced a form of mechanical propulsion that transformed travel on America's lakes and rivers in the years following the War of 1812. Scheduled steamboat travel began on Lake Erie, in 1818, connecting Buffalo and Detroit via intermediate ports. It soon expanded to offer passage to the Straits of Mackinac, the growing port of Chicago, and other points on the upper lakes. By the time Nehemiah and Nancy Sanford ventured to Michigan, the lake routes were well established, and they traveled extensively by water as far west as Chicago.[50] Henry also came to Michigan by steamboat, but the five years that had passed since his parents' trip had witnessed wider developments in steam technology that made significant changes in his mode of travel.

Steam-powered railroads revolutionized overland transportation in the second quarter of the nineteenth century, dramatically transforming the shipment of goods and the movement of people in the expanding United

---

49. Ronald E. Shaw, *Canals for a Nation: The Canal Era in the Unites States, 1790–1860* (Lexington: University Press of Kentucky, 1990), 30, 44–45; Caroline MacGill, *History of Transportation in the United States before 1860*, Prepared under the Direction of Henry Balthasar Meyer (New York: Peter Smith, 1948), 16–17; George Rogers Taylor, *The Transportation Revolution, 1815–1860*, vol. 4 of *The Economic History of the United States* (New York: Rinehart, 1951), 33–38, 61–63. For the economic impact of the Erie Canal on the growth of New York City as the dominant center of trade on the Eastern Seaboard, see Robert Greenhalgh Albion, *The Rise of New York Port [1815–1860]* (New York: Charles Scribner's Sons, 1970), 86–94.
50. Stone, *Floating Palaces*, 33–36, 74–75.

States. Contemporary observers were well aware of the savings in time resulting from increased speed as well as the comfort and convenience wrought by the new mode of transport. Many, including Henry Sanford, expressed their amazement at the ability of the railroads to "annihilate time and space." Railroads emerged as a viable form of land transportation following successful experiments in England in the 1820s. As early as 1826 the State of New York chartered its initial railroad, the first in the United States, to compete with the Erie Canal. The Mohawk & Hudson began operation in 1830 and ran its first trains between Albany and Schenectady the following year. It expanded with the completion of additional segments during the next decade, and by 1843 the line was complete all the way from Albany to Buffalo on Lake Erie.[51] In 1839 the railroad's scattered segments were yet to form a completed network in New York, limiting the extent to which Nehemiah and Nancy Sanford could travel by rail.

Railroad construction in Michigan began even more slowly. By the time of Henry Sanford's visit, separate lines connected the port of Toledo with Adrian and Tecumseh in southeastern Michigan, and branched northward and southwestward from Detroit, the state's capital, to link it with the settlements of Royal Oak and Ypsilanti. Despite difficulties resulting from inadequate funding and poor planning, the next five years witnessed the growth of rail lines in Michigan, and in the summer of 1844, Henry Sanford rode the state's most successful railroad, the Central, all the way to Marshall. Two years later he traveled by train as far west as Kalamazoo.[52] On

---

51. Alvin F. Harlow, *The Road of the Century: The Story of the New York Central* (New York: Creative Age Press, 1947), 25–59; Stewart H. Holbrook, *The Story of American Railroads* (New York: Crown Publishers, 1947), 22–23; Oliver Jensen, *The American Heritage History of Railroads in America* (New York: McGraw-Hill, 1975), 12–17.

52. Robert J. Parks, *Democracy's Railroads: Public Enterprise in Jacksonian Michigan* (Port Washington, NY: Kennikat Press, 1972), 224–225; Graydon M. Meints, *Michigan Railroads and Railroad Companies* (East Lansing: Michigan State University Press, 1992), 2–4; Graydon M. Meints, "Michigan Railroad Construction, 1835–1875" (Ann Arbor: Transportation Library, University of Michigan, 1981, typewritten), 2–10.

his last western trip, Sanford journeyed extensively by rail along a growing network of lines in the states along the Eastern Seaboard from New York to Philadelphia and Baltimore and as far west as Cumberland, Maryland, and later rode railroads from the port of Cincinnati into Ohio's interior.

·　　·　　·

Despite advances in steam technology, most travel in the West was overland. In Michigan, for example, roads extended across the southern Lower Peninsula by the 1830s to facilitate immigration and travel. The Chicago Road connected Detroit with settlements along Michigan's southern boundary, and the Territorial Road, farther north, linked the capital to points along the lower drainage of the Kalamazoo River. Elsewhere roads penetrated the Grand River Valley and expanded into the Saginaw drainage. The network also provided access by stagecoach to settlements in the neighboring states of Ohio, Indiana, and Illinois, connecting new settlements there with Chicago, Michigan City, and South Bend as well as points farther west. Roads between the principal routes developed much more slowly and unevenly, limiting travel in some portions of the interior to little more than trails. The overland network nevertheless tied together the state's nascent settlements in rapidly growing southwestern Michigan and provided access for immigrants as well as speculators. The Sanfords employed it extensively in their search for lands.[53]

Although overland routes supported regular stage and mail service between major settlements as far west as the Mississippi River, many areas remained inaccessible, and road conditions did not always afford easy or direct movement. In Michigan and elsewhere roads generally remained unimproved. The Sanfords and other travelers found thoroughfares rough and often in horrible condition, especially where they crossed low, wet

---

53. Lewis, *West to Far Michigan*, 195–199, figs. 9.15–9.18; Douglas Waitley, *Roads of Destiny: The Trails That Shaped a Nation* (Washington, DC: Robert B. Luce, 1970), 299–303.

ground. Roads stabilized with logs soon deteriorated and became nearly impassible. Stages and wagons sank in bogs and sloughs along the main roads, often requiring passengers to proceed on foot or to resort to riding on lumber wagons capable of negotiating rough terrain. On secondary roads stumps and uneven ground frequently made progress even more difficult.[54] Seeking out tracts in ever more distant locations, the Sanfords encountered the trials and travails of overland travel in their journeys in southwestern Michigan and surrounding areas and employed various means of conveyance in their travels. Crossing the countryside by stage, horseback, and wagon and on foot, they recorded in their journals a vivid account of conditions there during the settlement period.

West of the Great Lakes overland travel was still difficult at the time of Henry Sanford's visits in the 1840s. Uneven settlement left many portions of Wisconsin and Minnesota without direct links to one another or to population centers farther east. Northern Wisconsin, in particular, lacked roads leading southward from Lake Superior, and access to the interior was largely via Indian trails and the numerous watercourses. Elsewhere those roads that existed were unimproved and especially difficult to traverse in wet weather. Only by the following decade were most of the leading towns of Wisconsin's interior connected by roads, yet improvements to make its interior rivers navigable were still incomplete.[55] Farther west in Minnesota similar conditions on the roads south of St. Paul impeded

54. Lew Allen Chase, *Rural Michigan* (New York: Macmillan, 1922), 238–241; Carl E. Pray, "An Historic Michigan Road," *Michigan History* 11 (1927), 335–336; H. Huntington Lee & Co. and James Sutherland, *State of Michigan Gazetteer & Business Directory for 1856–57* (Detroit: by the authors, 1856), 97–100. Traveling by stage through southern Michigan, Harriet Martineau recalled that "the road was more deplorable than ever today. The worst of it was, that whenever it was dangerous for the carriage, so that we were obliged to get out, it was, in proportion, difficult to be passed on foot. . . . Three times this day was such a scene enacted." "Harriet Martineau's Travels in and around Michigan, 1836," *Michigan History* 7 (1923): 55–56.

55. *History of Northern Wisconsin, Containing an Account of Its Settlement.* (Chicago: Western Historical Co., 1881), 455, 618; John Warren Hunt, *Wisconsin Gazetteer, Containing the Names, Locations, and Advantages of the Counties, Cities, Towns,*

movement, although the higher, smoother terrain of the prairies west of the Mississippi permitted easier passage for stage and wagon traffic. Mail routes connected the growing settlement at the Falls of St. Anthony (present-day Minneapolis) with points to the east and west of the river. Steamboats began navigating the Mississippi River from St. Louis as far as Mendota in 1823, and by the time of Henry Sanford's 1844 visit, regularly carried freight and passengers to St. Paul. The garrison at Fort Snelling as well as settlers and traders in the region depended largely on the river for transport and supply well into the 1840s.[56] Beyond the Mississippi River, all overland travel followed the trails established by Native peoples and were used by the traders, missionaries, and soldiers whose business took them to the Far West. The Missouri and other major western rivers penetrated well beyond the Euro-American settlements, but travel on these navigable waterways afforded access only to those points along their courses.[57]

■　　■　　■

Chicago was an important stop in both the Sanfords' itineraries, and their visits there reflected the growing importance of this city in the development of the Middle West. Nehemiah traveled there to investigate a possible land deal with a prominent speculator as well as to visit two friends who

---

Villages, Post Offices, and Settlements . . . in the State of Wisconsin (Madison, WI: Beriah Brown, 1853), 28.

56. J. Fletcher Williams, *A History of the City of St. Paul, and the County of Ramsey* (St. Paul: Minnesota Historical Society, 1876), 250; Edward D. Neill, *History of Ramsey County and the City of St. Paul* (Minneapolis: North Star Pub. Co., 1881), 299, 335–336.

57. The route followed by Henry Sanford's 1846 journey closely approximated that taken the previous year by another easterner whose interests differed from Sanford's. Asa Whitney, a successful merchant long obsessed with promoting the construction of a transcontinental railroad linking the eastern United States with its soon-to-be-acquired territories of Oregon and California, led an expedition that explored a route westward from Lake Michigan to the upper Missouri River in hopes of obtaining congressional support for such a project. David Haward Bain, *Empire Express: Building the First Transcontinental Railroad* (New York: Viking, 1999), 20–22.

intended to go into business there. Henry also passed through Chicago on his way to look over lands in Illinois and on both voyages to the upper lakes. Both Sanfords noted the city's growth and its emerging role as the focus of trade for the surrounding states. Like other western cities that emerged with the vanguard of settlement, Chicago's rise was tied to its commercial potential.[58] Chicago's remarkable flowering in the 1830s and 1840s was a result of the natural advantages of its lakeside location, but also of the investment of both private sources and government capital. This influx of investments brought modifications that produced an altered landscape that historian William Cronon called a "second nature," one designed by people that incorporated physical improvements intended to facilitate the growing settlement's ties to western producers and eastern markets. The development of Chicago's harbor, and eventually the construction of railroads, linked the city directly to New York and the industrial Northeast and enhanced its potential as a western transportation hub. As such, it attracted immigrants and business that expanded its commercial role as the central market for a wide region.[59]

By the time of the Sanfords' visits, proximity to this western metropolis had already begun to draw Illinois, Indiana, Wisconsin, and southern Michigan into the larger national economy. The extensive inflow of wheat and other crops from these surrounding areas had already made Chicago the center of regional trade, although the older pattern of grain marketing

---

58. Richard C. Wade, *The Urban Frontier: Pioneer Life in Early Pittsburgh, Cincinnati, Lexington, Louisville, and St. Louis* (Chicago: University of Chicago Press, 1959), 29–30.
59. William Cronon, *Nature's Metropolis: Chicago and the Great West* (New York: Norton, 1991), 52–63. Chicago's rapid antebellum growth is reflected in the exponential increase in its population. From a settlement of 60 or 70 inhabitants in 1823, it grew to 250 in 1832. Chicago was home to 4,479 people in 1840, 29,964 a decade later, and in 1852, 38,733 persons called the city home. J. R. McCulloch and Daniel Haskel, *McMulloch's Universal Gazetteer* (New York: Harper & Brother, 1845), 617; *Fanning's Illustrated Gazetteer of the United States* (New York: Ensign, Bridgman & Fanning, 1855), 78.

still restricted trade by delaying its commercial sale. The shipment of grain in sacks left ownership in the hands of original shippers until sold in eastern cities. Passing slowly by water, grain moved eastward until purchased at its final destination. Only then did it become a commodity. The introduction of the elevator in ports like Chicago in the 1840s altered this process by allowing grain to be purchased and graded in the West and stored in structures prior to subsequent bulk shipment to market. Elevators appeared early in Chicago, and Henry Sanford noted their presence during his first visit together with the harbor improvements that facilitated the grain trade. The coming of the railroads to Chicago later that decade provided year-round transport by the carload that completed the transition in the scale of shipping, but already changes in the infrastructure of trade were in place to bring this about.[60] The increased volume of shipping favored the expansion of farm production as well, and the second quarter of the nineteenth century saw not only a growth in the amount of land devoted to agriculture, but the enlargement of individual tracts, as farmers adopted new implements and labor-saving machines to help them achieve these ends.[61] As he traveled through southwestern Michigan, Henry was amazed by the efficiency of farmers working lands and noted how mechanization enlarged the scale of western farming compared to that in the East. Before his eyes, the new specialized plows cultivated deep, heavy prairie soils, and mechanical reapers and threshing machines produced a flood of harvested grain that dwarfed eastern farmers' traditional methods. Chicago's rise and rapidly changing technologies of production, processing, and transportation allowed commercial production to dominate agriculture in southern Michigan and surrounding states. By midcentury the region stood on the verge of full participation in the larger economy of antebellum America.[62]

---

60. Cronon, *Nature's Metropolis*, 104–113.
61. Lewis, *West to Far Michigan*, 258–262.
62. John C. Clark, *The Grain Trade in the Old Northwest* (Urbana: University of Illinois Press, 1966), 202–206.

▪ ▪ ▪

After his 1846 journey, Henry Sanford never returned to the Far West. Nevertheless, he maintained an interest in the family's land business in the West. His papers do not reveal the extent of his total holdings or sales; however, the Sanfords' lands numbered in the thousands of acres in southern Michigan, Indiana, and Ohio.[63] Working through a number of agents, he continued to manage the land business long after his western trips and held title to properties in the West until 1880.[64] Throughout his adult life, Henry was always on the lookout for investments, and the West offered opportunities beyond the sale of real estate. In addition to placing substantial capital in eastern industries, he also bought stock in western companies. In the 1860s he invested in coal mines in Minnesota, a zinc company in Arkansas, and a Nevada silver mine. Western railroads offered further opportunities, and Sanford speculated in the Illinois Central, the Lake Superior & Mississippi, and the Northern Pacific. Both the mining and railroad ventures failed in the volatile postwar economy and resulted in losses made up only by his income from other sources.[65]

Henry maintained a sentimental attachment to the West, particularly the state of Minnesota, which he visited twice in his travels. Years later, while serving as the US minister resident to Belgium during the Civil War, he made the extraordinary contribution of a battery of three rifled cannon to the First Minnesota Volunteers, a unit then serving with the federal army.[66] On this occasion he expressed his lasting interest and feelings toward the state despite the many years since his last visit.

---

63. List of Michigan Lands, 1840–1866, HSSP, Box 64, Folder 13.
64. Amundson, "American Life of Henry Shelton Sanford," 71–72.
65. Fry, *Henry S. Sanford*, 78–80.
66. The First Minnesota Regiment played an active role in the American Civil War, participating in a number of major engagements, including First Bull Run, Ball's Bluff, and Gettysburg, as well as the Shenandoah Valley Campaign. Hazel C. Wolf, "Campaigning with the First Minnesota: A Civil War Diary," *Minnesota History* 25 (1944): 16–17. Henry Sanford's gift of three "steel cannon" represented a contribution to the regiment's arsenal substantial enough to be noted by its commander, who had

I have watched the development of your state with more than ordinary interest. Near twenty years ago I made on the steamboat *Otter* a trip from Dubuque to that little known region, and in 1846 I crossed over from La Pointe to revisit those lovely scenes which had deeply impressed me. I stopped at the present site of St. Paul at the only tenement then visible—a log cabin where a man named Jackson kept what is called a free tavern. I also spent a few days at Fort Snelling with Major Clark, and proceeded thence, with the aid of Mr. Sibley, to Petit Rochero, where I found my old friend La Framboise, and whence I started on a buffalo hunt across the plains to the upper Missouri. These events have left a profound impression upon my mind, and naturally, lead me to follow with special attention and interest the wonderful progress of your beautiful state.[67]

The state acknowledged its appreciation and recognized his long affiliation by making him a major general in the Minnesota militia, a title he retained through the remainder of his life.[68] Perhaps more significantly, he was proclaimed a "pioneer in Minnesota" and an honorary member of the state's Old Settlers Association. Henry Sanford's eventful life would lead him far from the western frontier of the 1840s, but the thrill of that great adventure remained with him and forever connected him to the region and its history.

---

notice of the acquisition read to his troops on the morning of May 31, 1862. Although the guns survived the actions of three more years of war, their ultimate fate was much more mundane, though perhaps no less noble. The guns remained in the possession of the State of Minnesota, which displayed them as memorials to the late conflict.

> The cannons stood on the grounds of the Old Capital in St. Paul for many years; later they were placed in front of the State Office Building, and about 1931 they were sent to Fort Ripley, near Little Falls. There they were delivered to the Salvage Officer of the Regular Army . . . in the first scrap drive conducted . . . in the Second World War. (135)

67. H. S. Sanford to Alexander Ramsey, Feb. 22, 1862, quoted in Neill, *History of Ramsey County*, 425.
68. Fry, *Henry S. Sanford*, 67.

CHAPTER 1

Nehemiah Curtis Sanford Journal, Connecticut to Michigan and Chicago, May 29 to July 10, 1839

Nehemiah and Nancy Sanford's journey marked the beginning of several epic family travels to the western frontier. Although ostensibly conducted for the purpose of overseeing his speculative venture in Michigan lands, the trip combined business with a sightseeing voyage around the Great Lakes. In the late spring of 1839 the Sanfords left their home in Derby, Connecticut and traveled up the Hudson by steamboat, across New York State by rail and the Erie Canal, and to Detroit by steamboat on Lake Erie. They departed the city by rail, but crossed Michigan's Lower Peninsula by stagecoach, the era's ubiquitous form of overland transport. After spending time in the state's southwestern quarter to investigate its real estate market, our travelers proceeded to Chicago by steamboat. Then, after visiting associates, they returned via lakes Michigan and Huron, stopping briefly to conduct business at Detroit. Their return

---

All of the journal entries in this chapter come from Nehemiah C. Sanford, "Journal: Western Trip, May–July, 1839," HSSP, Box 2, Folder 7.

trip through New York by rail and water brought the Sanfords to the home of relatives in Auburn, New York. Their arrival closed the circle of an adventure that introduced Nehemiah and Nancy to a new, distant world in the midst of rapid and continuous change. The journey exposed them to people, places, and situations that differed markedly from the familiar experiences of their eastern home. Although Nehemiah's journal carefully recorded his examination of lands and dealings with agents and others in his efforts to exploit economic opportunities presented by the growth of antebellum America, his observations were not limited to business matters alone, and his perceptions of the country through which the couple traveled, the incidents they observed, and the individuals they encountered provide a fascinating picture of this lost world.

Journal

Start from home, Birmingham, Ct. on Wednesday, 29 May 1839 & bound for Michigan & Chicago. A cloudy & unpleasant morning, but clear & prospect of a fine day on our arrival at Bridgeport [Connecticut]. A pleasant enough passage to New York, where we arrive at 2 o'clock & stop at Mrs. Shepard's. Thursday, 30th May. Engaged passage on board the p/b [packet boat] *Rochester*, secured births 54 & 41. Arrive at Albany Friday morning, take the cars to Amsterdam, where we arrive about 10. Go out myself with brother to his stone quarry.[1] Leave Amsterdam at 10 Saturday night &

---

1. One of the earliest interior colonial settlements, Albany was occupied by the Dutch in the seventeenth century. A manufacturing, commercial, and cultural center, as well as the seat of Albany County and the capital of New York State, Albany was the eastern terminus of the Erie Canal and the Mohawk & Hudson Railroad as well as a major river port on the Hudson. The village of Amsterdam was situated on the Mohawk River that provided waterpower for grist and sawmills as well as a woolen factory. The Erie Canal and state turnpike provided outlets for the products of its industries. Thomas F. Gordon, *A Gazetteer of the State of New York* (Philadelphia: T. Belknap, 1832), 341–346, 536–537.

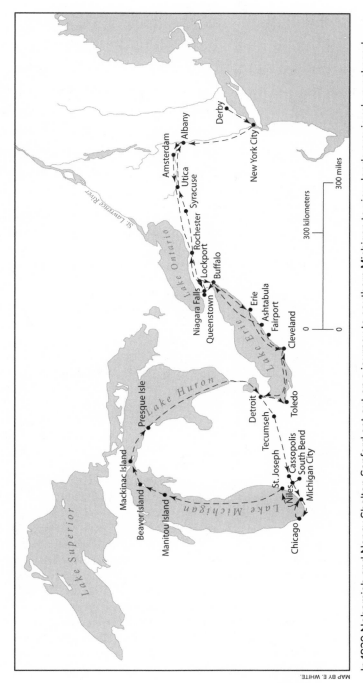

In 1839 Nehemiah and Nancy Shelton Sanford set out on a journey to southern Michigan to view lands previously purchased, conduct family land business, and explore potential investment opportunities in the West. Their route took them far from their Connecticut home and traversed three of the Great Lakes.

MAP BY E. WHITE.

arrive at Utica at 3 o'clock PM.[2] Leave Utica at 4 in packet boat *Rochester*, Capt. Conky. Arrive at Rochester Monday morning, 3 June, go to the Eagle Hotel for breakfast.[3] Leave Rochester at 8 for Buffalo, where we arrive on Sunday the 4th at 6 o'clock AM. Stop at U.S. Hotel, where we spend the day.[4] Engage passage on board S/B *Buffalo*, which leaves at 9 this evening.[5]

Just as we are leaving the hotel to go on board I go to my trunk for some money & find my pocket gone. Can have no doubt in my mind but it was stolen by some of the hands while on board the packet *Rochester*.[6] Advised

---

2. Nehemiah and Nancy Sanford traveled on two of the earliest railroads in New York. They rode the Mohawk & Hudson from Albany to Schenectady and the Utica & Syracuse to Utica, where they boarded a packet boat on the Erie Canal. Alvin F. Harlow, *The Road of the Century: The Story of the New York Central* (New York: Creative Age Press, 1947), 27–29.

3. The city of Rochester lay on both sides of the Genesee River, which provided the water power that supported the growth of manufacturing. Connected by a feeder to the Erie Canal, Rochester grew as a commercial center and the seat of Monroe County, New York. The Eagle Hotel was reputed to be one the finest hotels in the city during the 1830s. Gordon, *Gazetteer of the State of New York*, 528–529.

4. The city of Utica was the seat of Onondaga County and a hub of milling and diversified industries. Access to the Erie Canal and the Utica & Syracuse Railroad contributed to its commercial growth. Located at the outlet of Lake Erie at the head of the Niagara River, Buffalo was the western terminus of the Erie Canal and New York's entrepôt to Upper Canada and the western states bordered by the Great Lakes. Its improved harbor registered 3,280 arrivals and departures in 1835, and by then Buffalo, incorporated as a city in 1832, had become a center for milling and manufacturing. Its population had grown to about 18,000 by 1836. Ibid., 441–444.

5. The steamboat *Buffalo* was built by John Carrick at Buffalo in 1836 and offered passage on the Great Lakes. Charles Manning Reed' s company owned an interest in the vessel, which remained in service in the summer of 1843. Joel Stone, *Floating Palaces of the Great Lakes: A History of Passenger Steamships on the Inland Seas* (Ann Arbor: University of Michigan Press, 2015), 72; J. B. Mansfield, *Great Lakes Maritime History*, vol. 1, *1831–1840* (Chicago: J. H. Beers & Co., 1899), chapter 35; *New York Daily Tribune*, June 26, 1843.

6. Completed in 1825, the Erie Canal promoted agricultural production in western and central New York. By 1832 nearly a half million barrels of flour and 146,00 bushels of wheat reached its eastern terminus at Albany. Expanding Great Lakes commerce during the next four years nearly doubled these figures. The number of packet boats on the canal rose from 14,300 in 1832 to 18,850 two years later, and in

with the landlord about what way it was best to proceed. He advised me to write to the Capt. Conky describing the p[ocket] book & contents, which I did & sent the letter by the return packet to Rochester, informing the capt. of the contents of the letters & requesting his good offices. Those I have informed of the loss seem to believe that any efforts which I may make for the recovery would be hopeless. The only chance will be to watch for any bills which may be paid by any of the hands which are [the] F[armers] & M[echanics Bank of] Hartford & M[echanics] B[ank of] New Haven.[7]

Leave Buffalo at 9 in the evening of the 4th. Should be in very good spirits were it not for the loss of p[ocket] book, which I regard almost as much as the money it contained, it heretofore having stuck by me more than 20 years, being my constant companion at all times & I do not remember that I never before intrusted it to a trunk when traveling. There

1836 the state began reconstructing the canal to accommodate the increased traffic. Ronald E. Shaw, *Canals for a Nation: The Canal Era in the United States, 1790–1860* (Lexington: University of Kentucky Press, 1990), 44–47. Packet boats were the standard passenger vessels employed on the Erie Canal. Generally, they were sixty to eighty feet long and fourteen feet wide. Drawn by horses along the canal, they featured a multipurpose lounge, a dining room, a kitchen, and a sleeping room divided for men and women. "Boats in the Erie Canal," The Eerie Canal, eriecanal.org.

7. Banknotes were the most common form of circulating currency in antebellum America. Unlike specie, they were not a national currency and possessed no intrinsic value. They were issued by the Bank of the United States, private banks, and other financial institutions as promissory notes payable in specie to the bearer on demand. Because of the absence of cash, especially in the West, most banknotes remained unredeemed and circulated as paper money. Their value in exchange rested solely on the reputation of the issuing institution, so all were not of equal worth, and their value as cash could be discounted when exchanged for other currency or merchandise. Edward C. Kirkland, *A History of American Economic Life* (New York: F. S. Crofts & Co., 1939), 240–241; Susan Previant Lee and Peter Passell, *A New Economic View of American History* (New York: Norton, 1979), 125–126. Banking in New England expanded rapidly in the early nineteenth century with the emergence of industry and increasing demands for capital. Characterized by a conservative prudence, Connecticut banks like those drawn upon by Nehemiah Sanford provided a sound currency for exchange in the West. Howard Bodenhorn, *State Banking in Early America: A New Economic History* (New York: Oxford University Press, 2003), 72–73, 86.

was from 200 to 240 dollars in it. The loss is something, but no worse than many have met with & is something consoling that I followed the old adage to not carry all my eggs in one basket, but that I have enough in my wallet to yet bear my expenses around should we have the blessing of health during the journey.

We found a Mr. and Mrs. Stevens of Danbury [Connecticut] at U. S. Hotel who were going to visit the falls. A Mr. Wing & wife & a Mr. Noble of Monroe, Michigan, who have been to attend the convention of Presbyterians at Phila[delphia], and a Mr. Stanley of Ind[iana], whose passages with us from Rochester, likewise a Mr. Ord of Washington City, all of whom go on with us to Detroit. Arrive at Erie about daylight on Wednesday the 5th of June, but do not go on shore there not being time.[8] Said to be improving fast, Mr. Cary from Poughkeepsie is a fellow passenger. He went round the lake in the *T. Jefferson* with self & Edward in 1835. 2 gents with him from Poughkeepsie, a Mr. Williams & [blank].[9]

We have stateroom No. 11 & take as much comfort as can be expected in a crowded tho good boat & filled with every kind of men & waggons & 10 horses besides. We arrive at Cleveland at 4 o'clock & are told the boat will stop but ¾ of an hour. Nancy & myself set on a quick walk to call on Miss. E. Hull, found she had gone into the country, and we hurried back to the

---

8. Erie was the seat and port of entry for Erie County, Pennsylvania, situated on a bluff above a bay formed by a peninsula extending into Lake Erie. The village had a population of 1,451 in 1832. Occupied by Europeans since the middle of the eighteenth century, Erie served as a military garrison through the War of 1812. Although it had grown little by the 1830s, Erie would expand during the following decade with the completion of the Beaver and Erie Canal, linking it with the canal network of Ohio and Pennsylvania. Thomas F. Gordon, *A Gazetteer of the State of Pennsylvania* (Philadelphia: T. Belknap, 1832), 161; Shaw, *Canals for a Nation*, 77–78.

9. The *Thomas Jefferson* was built at Erie and finished at Buffalo in 1834. It was a low-pressure steamboat of 428 tons and was part of large fleet of passenger steamers owned by Charles Manning Reed. Stone, *Floating Palaces*, 71–72; Mansfield, *Great Lakes Maritime History*, chapter 35.

boat walking as fast as our feet would carry us. Our haste was needless for the boat did not leave till near an hour after we arrived on board.[10]

My ideas of Cleveland are confused enough for my head was turned while there, north being south & east west, & though I had a recollection of what it was in 1835, I could not make it appear the same place now, though there were some few places I recognized. Mr. Baldwin of Syracuse, & of life preserver memory, came on board, informs me that he has been out of health & has just returned from Texas very much recovered. Says he saw Mr. Blackman at Havana [Cuba] & should think he, Mr. B., had recovered his health entirely. Mr. Baldwin says he speculates some in goods which he carried between Texas & Havana & should come out minus he did not know how much, but that he had bought some Texas land which he was in hopes would make him good.

We arrived at the mouth of Detroit River about sunrise & had a delightful sail up the river to Detroit, where we arrived at 8 o'clock Thursday morning, the 6th of June. Both sides of the river from the lake up to Detroit are cultivated, some handsome dwellings & the farms very beautiful large orchards & fruit & shrubbery & gave every appearance from the boat of being as finely cultivated as the shores of the Delaware between Trenton & Phila[delphia]. We had with [us] a passenger of Phila[delphia], who had with him his wife & heir, who was traveling to see the wonders of the West. He expressed himself much, surprised at seeing grounds so highly cultivated & such an air of comfort about them where he full expected to find a wilderness.[11]

---

10. Cleveland, Ohio, was laid out at the mouth of the Cuyahoga River in 1796 to form a central settlement in the Connecticut Western Reserve. Incorporated in 1816 and becoming a city in 1836, it grew rapidly once the completion of the Ohio and Erie Canal in 1832 made it a key link in transportation between the Ohio River and Lake Erie. As the seat of Cuyahoga County, Cleveland had a population of about seven thousand in 1837. Warren Jenkins, *The Ohio Gazetteer and Traveler's Guide* (Columbus: Isaac N. Whiting, 1839), 125–126.

11. Detroit emerged as a settlement in 1701 with the expansion of French strategic interests into the Great Lakes and became a supply center and focus of the Indian

We stop at the National Hotel kept by Mr. Wales, and as most of new acquaintances do who on in the *Buffalo*.[12] Mr. Wales was himself a passenger with us & of course managed to form acquaintance with those who were visiting Detroit, very disinterested no doubt. His house is large and commodious & is said . . . We were told by a passenger, Mr. Noble, that his sales of champaign alone was over $2,000 the past year. Luxury extravagance of every kind finds its way to the far West almost as soon as New York & the champaign & extravagant luxuries are paid for with creditors' money as much here as at other places. I learn that Romaine, an extravagant fellow as I thought, who went round the lakes in 1835, being

---

trade. The region passed into British hands in 1763 and was ceded to the United States in 1783. American troops occupied Detroit in 1796, and Michigan Territory was created in 1805. The small settlement burned the same year. Although American immigration had begun in the 1790s, active settlement did not begin until after the War of 1812. Situated on navigable water and lying at the confluence of major overland routes into the interior, Detroit became the territory's capital and principal port. A carefully planned city of perhaps 9,300 inhabitants at the time of Nehemiah and Nancy Sanford's visit in 1839, Detroit had with extensive blocks of stores as well as churches, banks, markets, the houses of government and many other public buildings. The city had already become a retail and manufacturing center that drew produce from Ohio, Indiana, and Upper Canada. Detroit was the focus of the overland network of roads in southern Michigan and the primary entrepôt for immigrants entering the state. John T. Blois, *1838 Gazetteer of the State of Michigan* (Knightstown, IN: Bookmark, 1979), 270–280; Almon Ernest Parkins, *The Historical Geography of Detroit* (Lansing: Michigan Historical Commission, 1918), 46–50, 62–63, 130–131; Kenneth E. Lewis, *West to Far Michigan: Settling the Lower Peninsula, 1815–1860* (East Lansing: Michigan State University Press, 2002), 193–197.

12. The Sanfords stopped at the National Hotel, located at the junction of Woodward and Michigan Avenues. The hotel was opened on December 1, 1836, under the proprietorship of S. K. Herring, and by 1837 Austin Wales had taken over its management. An enterprising hotelier, Wales also oversaw the American House on Jefferson Avenue, which he later extensively refitted as the Wales' Hotel. He also briefly managed the Michigan Exchange, a hotel owned by E. A. Wales, in 1837. Silas Farmer, *History of Detroit and Wayne County and Early Michigan* (Detroit: Gale Research Co., 1969), 481–482, 493; Clarence M. Burton, *History of Detroit, Financial and Commercial* (Detroit: By the Author, 1917), 161.

on a wedding excursion at the time, having his wife & his wife's sister with him & who drank champaign for common drink at dinner, was now living at Detroit. That he had built the finest house in the city, gave the most expensive parties, was implicated in some way respecting the money borrowed by the state from the Michigan Canal Bank, which it was said did not hold out count when it arrived at Detroit, was principal in two wildcat banks which spending is now stopt by the legislature, & I should believe he would after this would find himself willing to be content of good wholesome water.[13]

We left Detroit on Friday morning the 7th of June by r[ail]road.[14] [At] Ypsilanti where we took the stage for Niles at 4 o'clock & arrived [at] Tecumseh where we had our stage at 6 PM, passing through Clinton, the land & scenery fine, the crops of wheat & oats looking very fine & most of the land from Clinton to Tecumseh under cultivation.[15] I was told the

13. A Detroit attorney, Theodore Romeyn was involved with the difficulties that arose when the state of Michigan found itself unable to raise the money to pay the $5,000,000 that it had obligated to fund internal improvements. In the wake of the disastrous Panic of 1837, banks all but ceased making loans, obliging the state to make other arrangements. The following year Governor Stevens T. Mason negotiated with the Morris Canal & Banking Company to dispose of the bonds at a commission of 2½ percent on the proceeds. Theodore Romeyn played a key role in advising the governor in drawing up this contract, which resulted in the state receiving a smaller amount of cash in return and the payment on the bonds being spread out over four years. By the spring of 1839 the state's difficulty in paying contractors and a growing belief that the program would collapse and bring Michigan financial ruin created a public scandal and a political issue that would not be resolved for several years. George N. Fuller, *Michigan: A Centennial History of the State and Its People*, vol. 1 (Chicago: Lewis Publishing Co., 1939), 285–293.
14. The Central Railroad of Michigan reached Ypsilanti and began service on February 3, 1838. Graydon M. Meintz, *Michigan Railroads and Railroad Companies* (East Lansing: Michigan State University Press, 1992), 3. In 1838 Ypsilanti was a village of about one thousand souls. Situated on the Chicago Road, it occupied an excellent site for water power, and four mills, a woolen factory, an iron foundry, and a tannery had been erected there, as well as a number of retail stores. Blois, *Gazetteer*, 383.
15. Formerly the seat of justice for Lenawee County, Tecumseh possessed a courthouse and jail as well as a bank, several churches, mills, and stores. The village was situated

school lands not cultivated [were] sold by the state that spring at auction on a credit of 10 years with int[erest] at from 20 to 30 dollars per acre. They are mostly or all oak openings.

From Tecumseh we traveled all night & saw but little of the country, there being no moon, & breakfasted at Coldwater at about 8 o'clock Saturday mor[ning], pretty well fatigued by traveling 24 hours, Nancy somewhat feverish & both almost concluding to rest thru the day & get recovered before another ride of 24 hours on the stage.[16] After resorting to the contents of a champaign basket to increase an appetite & eating our breakfast we concluded to keep on, which we did, passing thru Sturges Prairie to the beautiful White Pigeon Prairie, where we took our supper. White Pigeon Prairie is very handsome & [a] great part of it has crops of wheat upon it, which looks very fine, which it is certain will yield from 35 to 40 bushels the acre. Probably 10,000 or more acres in this vicinity are now covered with wheat. Here again we found the contents of our champaign basket very useful in reviving our spirits & giving us strength to continue the journey thru the night. We set off from White Pigeon about 7 in the evening. Not many hills but some deep hollows to go over which made it slow traveling, it being steep to descend into the hollows & again very hard for the stage to get out of them & up again on to the high ground. The horses all the way thru were fine ones & the drivers seem disposed to keep them so, for they drive very slow, not averaging 4 miles the hour. We passed the night much better in the stage than we did the first night, the stage not being so full & then again by becoming

---

on the River Raisin, and the Chicago Road passed through the village. It had a population of about one thousand. Situated nearby, also taking advantage of the hydraulic power of the Raisin, the village of Clinton was home to a population of about six hundred. It possessed several mills, a bank, a church, and several stores. Blois, *Gazetteer*, 265, 372.

16. Also situated on the Chicago Road, Coldwater was a fast-growing village that would soon become the seat of Branch County. Its sawmills utilized the power of the river of the same name. Ibid., 266.

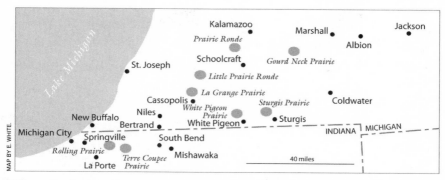

Henry Sanford and his parents visited a number of locations in southwestern Michigan and northern Indiana in connection with the family land business.

more accustomed to it we were enabled to sleep much more than the first night.[17]

We arrived at Niles at 6 o'clock Sunday morning the 7th, pretty well fatigued & sought again for the contents of our champaign basket, but found we had been anticipated. The driver or someone had broken it open & supposing no doubt it was a subtreasury & had appropriated the contents to their own use. It would have done no good to complain, so we put up with the loss with as much composure as possible & went to bed where we slept till nearly 12 o'clock, when we soon cleaned ourselves & eat our breakfast & dinner at the same time, about 1 o'clock. Thought of attending church in the afternoon, but there was not an Epis[copal] church & upon the whole felt too stupid & languid to attend any. After tea I called upon Mr. P. Lyon with a letter & was received very cordially, & on

17. Both Sturgis Prairie and White Pigeon Prairie lay on the Chicago Road in St. Joseph County. Established in 1830, the village of White Pigeon was situated on the prairie of the same name. A small settlement, it contained a few stores, shops, and churches. It was the location of the land office for the Western District of Michigan from 1831 to 1833. Ibid., 364, 381; George N. Fuller, *Economic and Social Beginnings of Michigan: A Study of the Settlement of the Lower Peninsula during the Territorial Period, 1805–1837* (Lansing, MI: Wynkoop Hallenbeck Crawford, 1916), 272–273.

Monday morning after breakfast walked down with Nancy to Mr. Lyon's, where she concluded to stay while I travel to Prairie Ronde.[18] Mr. Lyon offers to find & furnish me with a horse & waggon & I propose to sett out on Tuesday morning.

Tuesday, 11th June. It thunders & rains hard & the prospect is shall have to delay my journey another day. I start Tuesday afternoon for Cassopolis & am caught in heavy thunder shower about 4 o'clock, which I keep off with my umbrella and cloak, which wrapt close around me & kept myself erect as a duck. I arrived at Cass[opolis] just at sundown & after supper went over to call on Mr. [Elias B.] Sherman, where I stayed till something after 7 when I was reminded by the thunder that it was time for me to return to my tavern, which [I] attempted to do but could only find my way while the flashes of lightning lasted, which were very vivid & answered very well for light. But when I arrived at the tavern I found they were lockt up & gone to bed, & at this moment it commenced raining in torrents & I became pretty well drenched before I could get the landlord to let me in. I had my clothes hung up by the kitchen fire & went to bed, where I slept very well.[19]

---

18. Linked to the port and river settlements in Michigan and Indiana, Niles expanded as a regional commercial and transportation center. "It was the most business point we had found after leaving Detroit," commented an 1834 visitor. Enos Goodrich, "Pioneer Sketch of Moses Goodrich and His Trip across Michigan in February 1836, with His Brother Levi," *Michigan Pioneer and Historical Collections* 17 (1890): 230. Although not a political center, Niles became a focus of social and religious institutions that promoted its rapid growth, and by the late 1830s about four to five hundred lived there. *Niles Gazette and Advertiser*, Oct. 10, 1835, Mar. 5, 1836; Levi Bishop, "Recollections," *Michigan Pioneer and Historical Collections* 1 (1877): 125; Blois, *Gazetteer*, 332–333; Harriet Martineau, "Harriet Martineau's Travels in and around Michigan, 1836," *Michigan History* 7 (1923): 58; William C. Hoyt, "Early Recollections," *Michigan Pioneer and Historical Collections* 5 (1884): 62. An attractive tract well known for the fertility of its soil, Prairie Ronde was in the southwest corner of Kalamazoo County. In its center lay a grove of timber about a mile in breadth. Blois, *Gazetteer*, 347.

19. The seat of justice for Cass County, Cassopolis lay at the center of an extensive network extending from Niles and the Berrien County settlements east along the

In the morning, Wednesday the 12th, I concluded as the roads were very bad, occasioned by the rain, & as I had found by my journey the day before how difficult it was to find the road, I hired a man & 2-horse waggon to go with me & be my driver & pilot. We drove hard thru Wednesday, which [was] an extreme warm day, & arrived at Schoolcraft between 4 & 5 & found our horses very much fatigued as well as ourselves & concluded to spend the night there. In the morning, Thursday, I went down to see our land & was some disappointed to find less wood on it than I expected & less meadow. But it is an excellent lot of land, lying just 4 miles south & one east of Schoolcraft, & the land improved, almost all of it, from Schoolcraft to it, & buildings & families, quite a neighborhood with a distillery within ½ a mile. I do believe it worth $10 the acre, tho at this time it would not bring but $5, which [I] am offered for 160 acres. But [I] cannot see why it will not be better to keep it for the present. What a grain farm it would make for some industrious Yanky. He might raise wheat & corn enough upon it to supply a whole town.[20]

Letter

Nancy Shelton Sanford to Sister [Elizabeth Shelton],
Jun. 13, 1839, Niles, Michigan[21]

Dear Sister,

It is now Thursday. I have been here since Sunday morning, but that I would

---

Chicago Road and north to Paw Paw, as well as to those lying between Kalamazoo and White Pigeon. Fuller, *Economic and Social Beginnings*, 334; Blois, *Gazetteer*, 261.

20. Situated in the southwestern portion of Kalamazoo County, Schoolcraft was primarily a small farming community near the center of Prairie Ronde. Nevertheless, it was the marketing center for the surrounding countryside. Blois, *Gazetteer*, 261; E. Lakin Brown, "Autobiographical Notes," ed. A. Ada Brown, *Michigan Pioneer and Historical Collections* 30 (1905): 457–458.

21. HSSP, Box 69, Folder 10.

not write till I have heard from home. Mr. S. Has gone to view his lands, so I watch the mail daily. We sent a paper from Buffalo and another from Detroit with a few lines written upon each so you might know how we progress. But to go back to our journey, we spent one day at Amsterdam, found all well, arrived at Rochester on Monday AM early. All hands had to leave the boat and breakfast on shore, so in the first place we took a look at the <u>Genesee Falls</u>, came back and breakfasted at the Eagle, kept by Mr. Hall, and a very good house. A fine, beautiful morning, the only pleasant one we have had. I really thot I should by way of change like to stage it a little while, had got rather tired of <u>canalling</u>, but that I would say nothing either way but let the good man manage as he thot best. So we took the boat again between 8 and 9 for Buffalo, had some of the same passengers all the way with the addition of some more who were going to Monroe. We reached B[uffalo] on Tuesday morning, again early, cold and rainy, went on shore for breakfast, found there were boats to leave at 9 and 1 o'clock. But our fellow passengers, who were accustomed to cross the lakes say they should not leave in them [because] they were <u>second </u>rate boats, but the *Buffalo* of B[uffalo] would leave at 9 in the eve, a first rate boat. So we passed the day at B[uffalo]. After it cleared up. The rather [illegible] we took a walk thru the city.

At evening took our departure for Detroit in a boat they say far superior to any on the North River. Beside gentleman's & ladies cabbins we have a ladies' saloon with mahogany chairs, mirrors, etc., etc., and staterooms for all who wished. We went ashore at Cleveland, called to see Miss Hull, but found her out. The only place we went on shore. At Erie it was early in the morning and rainy at Huron. It was in the night we arrived very early that we arrived at the mouth of the Detroit River, where all hands [illegible] to the upper deck a fine, lovely morning, and so was the previous evening. Nothing could been more lovely. The sail up the Detroit River at such a time was worth enjoying. It is a beautiful river, the water very like Seneca Lake. At the entrance is Fort Malden on the Canada side and fine, cultivated farms on the Michigan. The banks are here like the Delaware, but higher and the country much more beautiful.

We reached Detroit soon after breakfast. Thursday one of our passengers all the way from Attica was a Mr. <u>Wales</u>, who kept the Nation[al] Hotel here (the best house) and we had by this time got quite acquainted. So most of the passengers who stopped at D[etroit] went there. The cars for Ypsilanti were to leave at 10 and I felt quite disposed to proceed, but that I would let the good man manage. He said very likely on our return our stop might be in the night, so that we might as well pass the day and the landlord said he would give us a ride and show us D[etroit]. So we concluded to remain. He gave us the best dinner I have seen this trip. We had <u>soup</u>, <u>napkins</u>, <u>etc</u>. He sent the waiter with a bottle of wine and his compliments to all his fellow passengers, and there were two or the gentlemen and there and wives of our party. So we had a very pleasant day.

We left there on Tuesday at 10. On getting into the stage at Ypsilanti at 1 o'clock we found we have got to travel night and day till we reach Niles. We had the privilege of stopping a day, but must take our chance for seats the next as there was only one stage a day that carried the mail, as good coaches as we have east. We took tea at Tecumseh at 6, rode all night till nearly 10 in the morning before we got any breakfast. There was an abundance of eatables, but of all the dirty places that existed. But it was the same all the way. We reached here Sunday morning at 6 o'clock, went to bed, and lay till near noon. Got up and dressed with the intention of going to church, but found there was no E[piscopal] church and felt so tired. I concluded to stay indoors. On Monday we came to Mr. Lyon's, where I now am and feel at home as much as if I was at an aunt's.

Yours always,
Nancy

Journal

I directed Mr. James Smith, Jr. to continue to pay the taxes upon it & went on to Kalamazoo where I got the patents for the land we had purchased. I find Kalamazoo, which was formerly called Bronson, very much improved. Should judge there were 100 dwellings in al, perhaps more, & a state of comfort & neatness about which reminds me of our New England manufacturing village. Most of the buildings are on one street, tho it is layd out into squares for a city & is as most of the county seats in Michigan. I left there about 4 on my return to Cass[opolis] by way of Little Prairie Ronde & put up for the night at a little log tavern where they had plenty to eat & a bottle of whiskey on the table to cheer the weary.[22]

I spent the night very comfortably & after breakfast of fried pork, eggs, warm bread & an abundance of strawberrys started on the journey. Stopt at Little Prairie Ronde, gave the horses some oats, but found little fit for men to eat. A fine prairie, some 1,500 acres or more, but settled should think by Hoosiers of a contracted spirit & sordid spirit with no more ideas of comfort & publick feeling than so many horses. Stop a while at La Grange Prairie, go into Spalding's flour mill, who put up about he told me 100 barrels of flour a day [and] could do more. La Grange Prairie

---

22. Kalamazoo was the seat of Kalamazoo County and the site of the land office for the Western District of Michigan. Situated on the Territorial Road, it became a milling and regional commercial center with extensive road connections in western Michigan and was home to a number of social and religious activities. A. D. P. Van Buren, "Some Beginnings in Kalamazoo," *Michigan Pioneer and Historical Collections* 18 (1891): 605; Abraham Edwards, "Sketch of Pioneer Life," *Michigan Pioneer and Historical Collections* 3 (1881): 150; Mary V. Gibbs, "Glimpses of Early Michigan Life in and around Kalamazoo," *Magazine of American History* 24 (1890): 459–460; Blois, *Gazetteer*, 306–307; Douglas H. Gordon and George S. May, eds., "The Michigan Land Rush in 1836, Michigan Journal, 1836, John M. Gordon," *Michigan History* 43 (1959): 283, 448. Little Prairie Ronde lay in Volina Township in the northeast portion of Cass County, and its open environment attracted the earliest settlers in 1828. L. H. Glover, *A Twentieth Century History of Cass County, Michigan* (Chicago: Lewis Pub. Co., 1906) 11, 19, 51–52.

is fine, as are all the prairies, & to a man just from Conn't [Connecticut] to pass thru them at this season & see them covered with fine crops, as I believe they always are, will have no fears but his country will have a supply of bread.[23]

I arrived at Cass[oplis] between 5 & 6, feeling quite satisfied with our land in Cass & St. Joseph [Counties]. Settled accts. with Mr. S.[mith] & left $250 which Mr. S. is to use to buy lands sold for taxes on our joint acct., the lands to be bought in my name & he to get for his time as agent the use of the money. Saturday 15th arrive at Niles & find Nancy well & in good spirits.

Letter

Nehemiah C. Sanford to Brother [John Sanford],
June 16, 1839, Niles, Michigan[24]

Dear Brother,
We arrived here a week ago this morning in good health & spirits & Nancy has spent the week with the family of P. Lyon while I started on Tuesday last to Cassopolis & Bronson (which by the way is now called Kalamazoo) & returned here last evening. The week has been very rainy, which makes the travelling very bad & slow. The country has improved as much as [can] be expected in the four years since you & I was here. Indeed there is, I should think, far more land under the plough through Michigan where I have traveled than there is in some extent of country in Con[nectic]ut.

---

23. Situated in the center of LaGrange Township, in Cass County, LaGrange Prairie occupied a considerable area containing millstreams. In the early 1830s William Renniston constructed a gristmill where the road to Cassopolis crossed Dowagiac Creek. The mill later became the property of Erasmus H. Spalding, who expanded the business to include a general store at the location, which became the site of the Dowagiac village. Glover, *History of Cass County*, 133, 154, 156, 160; Mae R. Schoetzow, *Brief History of Cass County* (Dowagiac, MI: A. Castle, [2000]). 24.
24. HSSP, Box 69, Folder 10.

Their crops of wheat, corn & oats looks very well, but the farmers say there will not be more than ⅔ as much wheat as last year, which is from two causes. First, the sickness during the fall prevented it being sown & what was sown by reason of the drouth did not come up til this spring & some not at all, so that the stalks stand much thinner in the field than usual. Still, the crops will I think be good & a large surplus for export. There is yet a great deal of old wheat in the country, many large stocks I have seen not yet thrashed out, and every vessel that leaves loaded with as much as she can carry & the mills of which there are many fine ones making all flour they can. This country must lower the price of flour at the East, as it will be the staple here and the land capable of producing any quantity that [these] can be a market for. All that is wanted here is an industrious & virtuous people to bring out the resources of the country & the laboror here is abundantly rewarded for his toil.

The prospect for our land here is good so far as I have yet examined as anticipated & as good. Mr. Sherman has sold between 4 & 500 acres & toward [illegible] there will probably be 400 [lots] of 80 acres each more sold within a few days at 5$ the acre. It would seem as if the land ought to be worth more, but others are offering at that price without selling very much & ours seems to be chosen on acct of the neighborhood by people from N[ew] Hampshire who like to settle together[. T]he land is delightful. The section near Schoolcraft is good, but nearly destitute of timber & coming up over a great deal of it thick with white oak. I might have sold by staying a day or two ¼ of it at $5 per acre. I offered to take the 5$ if they would take the whole section one fourth cash down, but money is so scarce here now that it could not be raised although [for] all that it was cheap at that price. That section is worth more than we had anticipated & Mr. Smith says he might have sold it two years ago at $10 the acre. Whether it will ever bring that again is uncertain, but I cannot see why it should not for the school section on the prairie brot at auction from 20 to 25 per acre & an unimproved state & this of ours must certainly be worth half as much. It would make a grand farm for Edwin Shelton to go onto & in 10 years he would make it worth $15,000 & fetch it too. The land is improved all about it & good frame dwellings within 50 rods of it & Prairie Round [Ronde] just above it all divided off into half mile squares & fenced & fine[r] crops were never seen anywhere. Mr. Sherman, our agent, I believe to be a very fine man, plain, industrious & honest, a 3d rate lawyer, the district attorney & will probably become a rich man. He came to this country 9 years ago poor & studied his profession here. His business is such that he will be likely to see that our land is not sold for taxes & shall hereafter feel very safe on that score.

I learn nothing very encouraging about New Buffalo. Mr. Green is at the East, but by what I do learn New Buffalo is on the wane, which Sherman thinks it will rise again after awhile. They think here at Niles that it will. I am surprised to learn that you did not get your bundle. The last thing that I did before leaving NY was to go and leave it as directed. I sent the collar[,] a ring I paid $4 for and two pairs of stockings. And they directed of you as they said I should see Dr. B. in the course of the day and would have it to him. I requested him to put on a larger rapper and seal it, but be that it is unnecessary first tied a string around it in case it moves.

Journal

On Sunday [I] loiter about & waste the day & on Monday Nancy, myself and Mr. Lyon go to Mishawaka [Indiana], passing thru Bertrand & South Bend, all very pretty villages with perhaps from 800 to 1,000 inhabitants each, many of which [I] should believe would be better employed if they were cultivating the soil than now are.[25] We returned to Niles in the evening

---

25. Bertrand lay on the east bank of the St. Joseph River in the southeastern corner of Berrien County. Situated on the Chicago Road, it was said to have been "a place of considerable business [that was] fast increasing in wealth and population," the latter estimated to be six hundred in 1838. Blois, *Gazetteer*, 255. Situated on both sides of

& arrived at Mr. Lyon just in time to save being out in a thunder shower. Got sprinkled some as it was. Nancy rode with a sick headache most of the way. Tuesday morning hesitate about starting for N[ew] Buffalo, Mr. L.[yon] thinking it will rain & I concluded upon the whole to stay in order to learn mor about the property left by Mr. Nant, who died at St. Jo[seph] some years ago.[26] Get but little information as Mr. Fitzgerald, who knows the most about [it], is gone but is expected home tonight.[27] [I] learn from Jewel, the former district attorney, that he has left lands, he thinks 160 acres besides city lots in St. Joseph, that the property was represented to him to be worth 800 or 1,000 d[ollars], that it had probably been sold for taxes but was of opinion that the sales were void & that the land might be regained.[28] Wednesday, 19th June, got Mr. Logan to take us to N. Buffalo

the St. Joseph River, Mishawaka, Indiana, was settled in 1832. The St. Joseph Iron Works, erected three years earlier, became the basis for manufacturing there, and the river provided hydraulic power for mills. At the close of 1837, 1,000 people lived there, and a dozen years later its population had increased to 1,300. Immediately downstream, South Bend, Indiana, was also a center for milling and manufacturing. Laid out in 1835, South Bend had 728 inhabitants in 1840 and 1,600 in 1849. T. G. Turner, *Gazetteer of the St. Joseph Valley, Michigan and Indiana* (Grand Rapids, MI: Black Letter Press, 1978), 51–54, 56–61; E. Chamberlain, *Indiana Gazetteer, or Topographical Dictionary of the State of Indiana* (Indianapolis: E. Chamberlain, 1849), 319, 388.

26. New Buffalo was situated at a point of land extending between an estuary made by the Galien River and Lake Michigan in Berrien County. Settled in 1835, the village contained, by the time of the Sanfords' visit, a mill as well as a number of stores and other buildings. New Buffalo became a minor port, linked by water to Chicago, and the federal government erected a lighthouse there in 1839. Blois, *Gazetteer*, 331; *Niles Gazette and Advertiser*, Jan. 9, 1836; Franklin Ellis, *History of Berrien and Van Buren Counties, Michigan* (Philadelphia: D. W. Ensign, 1880), 44, 272.

27. J. B. Fitzgerald was an attorney and councilor who lived in the First Ward of Niles. D. J. Lake, *Atlas of Berrien County, Michigan* (Philadelphia: C. O. Titus, 1873).

28. St. Joseph, the seat of justice for Berrien County, was located at the outlet of the St. Joseph River on Lake Michigan. Its harbor, one of the few anchorages on Lake Michigan's eastern shore, made it a major stop for steamboats. The addition of federally funded improvements, including a wharf and pier, accommodated shipping and made the village an ideal lake port. One of the few harbors on Lake Michigan's eastern shore, it was a major stop for steamboats on the lake. As a county seat and

& started about 6 in the morning. Past the Terre Coup Prairie some 8 or
10 miles, all finely cultivated & crops looking well & stpt at Mr. Harman's
tavern to dinner about a mile from Springville.[29] After dinner we went
back some ½ a mile by being told that we could reach N[ew] Buffalo some
miles nearer than by going to Springville. Was induced to take that road
because it led thru some of our land in Berrien [County]. We found the
road bad, being thru a timbered country & the roads most of the way only
blazed or markt out & markt only on the marshes & then only by brush &
logs being thrown in. We could only walk the horses & progress only 2½
miles the hour & arrived at N[ew] Buffalo about 6 o'clock. Found there was
no tavern in the place & had to apply to a private home for lodgings. We
enquired for Capt. Whitaker, who kindly offered to keep us, & we should
hardly have felt as much at home at any tavern as we did at his house.[30]

In the morning he got horses & went with me to see the land we own [in]
Township 7, but we was not able to see it as we could not cross the south

---

trading center, St. Joseph contained governmental buildings as well as forwarding
and commission stores, retail establishments, churches, and other businesses. Blois,
Gazetteer, 368–369; Gordon and May, "The Michigan Land Rush in 1836," 292–293.
Hiram Jewell emigrated from New Jersey to LaGrange Township in Cass County in
1830 and became a prosperous farmer. Glover, *History of Cass County*, 236; Alfred
Mathews, *History of Cass County, Michigan* (Chicago: Waterman, Watkins & Co.,
1882), 230, 236.

29. Measuring three by five miles, Terre Coupe (or Coupee) Prairie was the largest
prairie in St. Joseph County, Indiana, and contained a small village of the same name.
Springville, in neighboring La Porte County, Indiana, lay just east of Michigan City.
J. Calvin Smith, *The Western Tourist and Emigrant's Guide . . . of the States of Ohio,
Michigan, Indiana, Illinois, and Missouri* (New York: J. H. Colton, 1840), 101, 118–119;
Turner, *Gazetteer of the St. Joseph Valley*, 37, 46–47.

30. Capt. Wessell Whitaker was one of the early settlers and developers of New Buffalo.
He first visited the site in 1834; the following year he formed a company to acquire
and survey the town site and market the lots. He also owned an interest in a store and
warehouse as well as two mills. As discovered by the Sanfords, "His house furnished
a home for all it could hold." Ellis, *History of Berrien and Van Buren Counties*, 44,
271–272, 274.

branch of the Galien [River], a stream on which he [Capt. Whitaker] has a saw mill, & he thinks there is [an] abundance of water for a grist mill of 10 run of stone. The falls at his dam is 6 feet. As I could not see the land, I took a description from him. He says that Sections 29 & 32 are good timbered land, say at least ten acres of bottom land to the lot of 80 acres. The timber is oak of a good kind, considerable white [illegible] & some sassafras. He says there is one tree, a sassafras, on his land about 20 rods from the line of our land, which is at least 60 feet high without a limb and measures 10 feet 4 inches in circumference. There are clearings at a number of places about it & his saw mill is one mile south and west from our land. Mr. Bennet has cleared 10 acres & Mr. Pinkerton has cleared adjoining to it.[31] Dr. Pierce, who entered the land of the 2 sections which we do not own, which he did in April 1835, he sold to a man by the name of Williams for 10 d[ollars] the acre. Our land in Town[ship] 8, being in Sec[tions] 13–24 & 23, is good, fair land, thickly timbered & will some time or other be very fine grazing land. It lies handsome, a little rolling, and good soil. In Section 13 the stream called Red Run passes through it & perhaps one third of the section is something marshy & there can be no doubt but the marsh all the way contains iron ore, Section 23 the same. The same stream passes through it.

It will probably be some time before New Buffalo & land in [its] vicinity become very valuable in market, but that N. Buffalo will be something of a place in time can hardly have a doubt. Everything by the way will depend upon an appropriation from Congress towards building a harbor. A lighthouse will be built this summer, [$]5,000 being appropriated for it & the harbor bill, which passed one house & [has] not reacht or [been] neglected by the other, had an appropriation for the harbor at N. Buffalo.

---

31. Alonzo Bennett, born in Addison, Vermont, in 1807, settled in Niles in 1833. Three years later he moved to New Buffalo. Although admitted to the bar, Bennett was a merchant and served as a representative in the Michigan legislature in 1842. Ibid., 133, 145; Orville William Coolidge, *A Twentieth Century History of Berrien County, Michigan* (Chicago: Lewis Pub. Co., 1906), 227.

Friday morning, 21st June, was carried by Dr. Pierce to Michigan City twelve miles, the road not the best thru openings & sandy soil. We arrived at M[ichigan] City at about 11 o'clock & stopt at the exchange kept by Doc[to]r. Shelford.[32] We had been in hopes of crossing immediately over to Chicago, but the tide was so high that no boat could come into the harbor which, by the way, they have got none but an artificial one which has cost government some 50,000 d[ollar]s & will [cost] at least 500,000 more before they make a tolerable harbor of it. They propose building a breakwater out some 80 rods in the lake & extending their piers some 20 rods further. Should this ever be done it would prove a great protection to vessels on the lake. As it now is, vessels at the head of the lake in a hard northerly wind must hold on by their anchors or go on shore, very frequently the latter, & fortunately they have a low, sandy shore to drive upon & are usually driven so close on that few deaths occur by shipwreck here in warm weather & the vessels are frequently got off with little damage.

Saturday, here we are. The stage could not take [us] as they carry the mail & with only 2 horses & are not allowed to take more than 2 or 3 passengers. The wind northerly & no prospect of a boat landing today. Nancy grows fidgety, a little petulant & I suspect a little homesick & is in a great hurry to get on. I feel something impatient myself, for tho we have a pleasant landlord & lady, the eternal sands of M. City, filled as they appear to be with fleas, & straw & manure thrown in the streets to keep persons from sinking over their boots in the sand while crossing the streets is anything but pleasing to the stranger. And then when he reflects that almost the whole population

---

32. In 1831, the proprietors of Michigan City, Indiana, situated the settlement at a location convenient for the storage and shipment of wheat on Lake Michigan and anticipated that it would become "the great emporium of the northern trade of the state." The expected trade failed to develop because the contemplated harbor improvements did not materialize. Vessels could not dock there and could only be loaded from lighters. Although warehouses and stores testified to its role in trade, Michigan City remained relatively small, with a population of about nine hundred in 1849. Chamberlain, *Indiana Gazetteer*, 317.

was prostrated by sickness last fall and that one in 10, some say one in 7, died & that even most conversation is interluded by something about chills & fever, & if any complaint or headache is mentioned you are told at once you are going to have a chill is rather calculated to chill one's spirits.[33]

Sunday, now here we are yet, Nancy in better spirits, the day fine & a prospect that the boat will call in the afternoon & we shall be enabled to get out of this purgatory of sand & fleas. Attend church in the morning & hear the Rev. Mr. Johnson preach. Probably 100 attended, all of whom appear devout, & should Mr. Johnson have health & continue at this place he will doubtless build up a good congregation. The people appear to be much attached to him & well they may, for I should think from his sermon he was a man of talent & very devoted & might command a much pleasanter parish & larger salary than they can here afford to pay him. In the afternoon we staid at a tavern, expecting every moment the boat would come, but we might have as well attended church, for no boat came till nearly 10 o'clock & we got on board about 11 by being carried out the harbor in a small boat to the steam boat *James Allen*, where we at once turned into our berths, disturbing as little as possible the comfort of J. Orville Taylor & his wife who had taken possession of the ladies cabin & taken some ½ dozen or more mattresses which they had spread upon the floor & had snugged themselves quite comfortably upon them, locking the cabin door.[34] We were under the necessity of disturbing their snoozing & by the capt's. knocking upon the door they felt obliged to get up & let us in where we

---

33. A widespread disease in the Old Northwest, malaria was caused by several species of protozoa, carried from an infected to a noninfected host by the anopheles mosquito. Despite its debilitating symptoms of chills, rapid rise in temperature, headaches and myalgia, and profuse sweating, the disease was usually not fatal, leaving its victims fatigued but otherwise healthy between attacks. David Charles Nutter, "Malaria in Michigan" (master's thesis, Michigan State University, 1988), 9, 14–17.

34. A relatively new steamboat, the *James Allen* was built in Chicago in 1838 and sailed under the command of Capt. James Stuart. Weston A. Goodspeed and Daniel D. Healy, *History of Cook County, Illinois*, vol. 1 (Chicago: Goodspeed Historical Association, 1909), 136.

took separate berths notwithstanding the exemplary sample of comfort we had before our eyes in the persons of the lecturer on common schools & his wife upon the floor together.

At daylight we found ourselves at Chicago & put up at the Lake House, kept by a Mr. Shelly. We found ourselves very comfortable here. The house is well kept, god & attentive servants & perhaps kept with as much elegance of taste & fashion as the Tontine at N[ew] Haven, & the charges we considered very moderate, $1.50 per day, after the heavy bills we has paid at some houses thru Michigan without any of the comforts which this house afforded. The inhabitants appear to feel proud of the house & like to have strangers praise it.[35]

The city of Chicago is very much improved since I was there in '35. The buildings look much more permanent & there are quite a number of fine three-story brick blocks of buildings[. T]he streets are all through turnpike fashion and descent enough given to carry off the water, & there is now but few of the ditches that have any water in them. The sidewalks are laid with plank or raised by gravel so that the pedestrian can walk about thru any of the streets without being incommoded with mud or sand. The fine green grass and white clover that is growing in the yards & about the city give it a very pleasant appearance & appreciation in the minds of those who like us have been shut up in some 3 days & seen nothing but the white sands of Michigan City.[36]

---

35. David Hoadley, a well-known self-taught architect who designed a number of churches, as well as prominent residences, and public buildings in New Haven County, Connecticut, constructed the Tontine Hotel about 1824. The hotel was a large four-storied structure on the corner of Church and Court Streets. George Dudley Seymour, "David Hoadley Architect," *Art and Progress* 3 (1912): 545–546. The Lake House opened in 1836 across the Chicago River from Fort Dearborn. This elegant brick structure that cost $90,000 was a center for social and political activities in the city. Molly W. Berger, "Hotels," Encyclopedia of Chicago History, http://www.encyclopedia.chicagohistory.org/pages/603.html.
36. Chicago, the seat of justice of Cook County, Illinois, expanded rapidly during the

I did my business with Mr. Kensie & felt a little disappointed in hearing him offer his intent in NB [New Buffalo], it being just double to ours at 1,200$. [I] felt almost disposed to make the purchase, but concluded upon the whole to refrain, tho I cannot but believe it would be a good speculation.[37] Mr. Kensie was about to leave the city on business, so that I did not have the time with him I should have been glad to have. He promises to pay the taxes on our NB purchase equally with his own & when even it comes to enough with drawings for to draw on us for it. He is said to be a high minded & honorable man, & is reputed to be rich, tho he is hard run at this time & I take it there are but few businessmen west of Lake Erie but what are. I saw John Phelps & F[rank] Marshal; both appeared

decade of Nehemiah Sanford's visits. From a town of perhaps two hundred residents in 1833, Chicago had grown to become an incorporated city with a population of 4,170 in 1837. As the principal port on Lake Michigan, the city attracted a growing volume of trade facilitated by harbor and transportation improvements and had become the distributing point for the surrounding country. Chicago claimed one hundred merchants, thirty lawyers, twenty physicians, as well as mechanics and laborers, and its "stately blocks" contained fifty business houses, four large forwarding houses, eight taverns, two printing houses, two bookstores, one steam sawmill, one brewery, one furnace, and twenty-five "mechanic shops of all kinds," in addition to five churches. J. M. Peck, *A Gazetteer of Illinois* (Philadelphia: Grigg & Elliot, 1837), 179; A. T. Andreas, *History of Chicago, from the Earliest Period to the Present Time* (Chicago: A. T. Andreas, 1884), 141–143.

37. John H. Kinzie was the son of John Kinzie and Eleanor Lytle McKillip, who were married about 1800. John, an Indian trader, settled in Detroit, where he also served as a justice of the peace, but in 1804 moved with his family to the St. Joseph River, near the site Bertrand in western Michigan. He purchased a trading establishment at the mouth of the Chicago River the following year. John H. Kinzie was born in Canada on July 7, 1803. Following their capture and internment in Detroit during the War of 1812, the family again returned to Chicago. John H. served as an agent the American Fur Company from 1816 until about 1824, when Lewis Cass, governor of Michigan and superintendent of the Northern Division of Indian Tribes, acquired his services as agent to several Native groups in the Great Lakes. He married Juliette A. Magill in 1830 and four years later brought his family to Chicago, where he became a merchant and held a number of public offices. He died in 1865. Andreas, *History of Chicago*, 97–99; F. Clever Bald, *Detroit's First American Decade, 1796–1805* (Ann Arbor: University of Michigan Press, 1948), 12, 232; Farmer, *History of Detroit*, 179.

to be well suited with Chicago & think they shall call it home there while they live. They are receiving 35$ per month & their board, which ought to enable them each to lay up 300$ per year. They intend, I believe, to go into business together as soon as they think their capital will admit. Frank has bought a lot for which he paid over 300$ for it & it was thot by Mr. Beers to be a good bargain.

We left Chicago on Tuesday even[in]g, the 25th of June. John & Frank called on board to see us off & took seats in the ladies' cabin where we chatted of old Lang Sine, & they forgot that it was time for the boat to be starting until by the motion & that we were off & went out on deck to see and found that we were half way down the harbor. J. & F. concluded they would have to cross the lake with us, at first, but the boat ran up beside a schooner, which enabled them to jump from our boat to that & from thence onto the pier, but in doing it the boat almost caught the schooner, staving in her bulwarks & railing. Just so it often happens, a little thought-lessness causing more damage than could be repaired in weeks. Our boat is splendid and the largest upon the lakes, being, the capt. says, 780 tons burthen, two tiers of decks & staterooms all round the ladies' cabin both on the hurricane & lower decks, and staterooms, some 10 or 12 of them forward for steerage passengers. Capt. Walker says he can accommodate 400 passengers with little inconvenience & the dining room enables 140 to sit at table at the same time. She is so large that one feel the motion but trifling when compared to a small one.[38] The *James Allen*, for instance, in which we crossed over to Chicago on Wednesday morning.

---

38. The Sanfords sailed on the *Great Western*, a lake steamer built in 1838 and launched in August at Huron, Ohio. A vessel of 781 tons burden with a length of 183 feet, the *Great Western* was one of the largest boats on the Great Lakes. The boilers and holds for freight and wood occupied the entire hull, and the ladies' cabin was situated on the main deck aft. The main cabin extended almost the entire length of the hurricane deck and contained sixty staterooms containing about three hundred berths, the dining room, saloon, and ladies' saloon. Capt. Augustus Walker built and commanded the *Great Western* during this time. Barely two months after the Sanfords' voyage, a fire

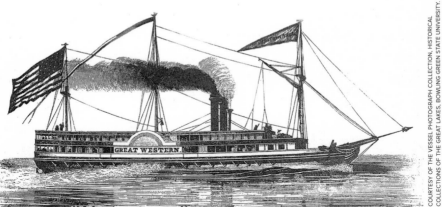

The steamboat *Great Western*, one of the largest steamers on the Great Lakes at the time of Nehemiah and Nancy Sanford's western journey in 1839. They traveled on the *Great Western* via Lakes Michigan, Huron, and Erie from Chicago to Buffalo, New York.

We found ourselves off M. City & the hands busily engaged in landing & taking in freight & noon brought us to St. Joseph, where we took in wood & landed some freight. We spent an hour or more running about the place. Their harbor will make St. Jo[seph] an important point & the bluff where the principal business must be done being small, will probably make building lots situated upon this point always to bring a high price. I enquired after a Mr. Nevel, who died here some years since, & found a Mr. Hoyt, a merchant of this place, who was administrator with Mrs. Nevel in selling her husband's estate. He says there was personal property enough

at Detroit destroyed the vessel's cabins on Sept. 1, 1839, but the *Great Western* was later rebuilt at Huron, Ohio and continued in service until 1855. "New Steamboats," *Buffalo (NY) Commercial Advertiser*, Aug. 13, 1838; "Captain Walker's Great Western," *Cleveland (OH) Daily Herald & Gazette*, May 10, 1839; Sept. 3, 1839; "Burning of the Great Western of the Lakes," *Cleveland (OH) Daily Herald & Gazette*, Sept. 3, 1839; "Riverboats," Riverboat Dave's Paddlewheel Site, riverboatdaves.com; "Great Lakes Vessels Online Index," Historical Collections of the Great Lakes, http://greatlakes. bgsu.edu/vessel/view/002486; Goodspeed and Healy, *History of Cook County*, 1: 162; Stone, *Floating Palaces*, 80.

to pay all his debts & he doesn't know but something more & that Mrs. Nevel found among her husband's papers a deed of one half of the mansion house & lot, it being his whole interest in it at that time, which was signed but not acknowledged & witnesst by 2 witnesses, that Mrs. N. took means to prove by the witnesses the signing of the deed & then sold the property & left the place. Mr. Hoyt seems to think himself that the deed was a fraud, but he said he did not trouble himself about it, supposing the widow to be the only heir & let her do as she pleased with it. The mansion house & lot, the whole of it he said was now worth some 3 or 4,000$, but there had been considerable addition to the building since the sale by Mrs. Nevel.

At evening we arrived at Grand River, where the boat took in wood & stayed most of the night, it being foggy & the morning of Thursday 27th June found us coasting along in sight of the shore of Michigan & in sight of the Manitou Islands & passt the Fox & Beaver islands just at dusk & arrived at Mackinaw Island at about 10 o'clock and traveled about by moonlight on to the hill back of the fort & back again & through the village which is situated, or located, in two streets running parallel with the water. We went into a store & Nancy bought some Indian pin cushions & we went again on board & into our berths at about 12 o'clock.[39]

---

39. The North and South Manitou islands in Lake Michigan lay west of the Leelanau Peninsula. The settlement of South Manitou island began in the 1830s to provide cordwood for steamboats on the lake, and construction began on a lighthouse there in 1839. Farther north, the two Fox Islands were situated northwest of Grand Traverse Bay. Beyond them lay Beaver Island, the largest of a group of five islands. Native Americans had occupied the island for more than two thousand years. The Ottawa people arrived there in the mid-1700s and Father Baraga established a Catholic mission on Beaver Island in 1832. Trappers, traders, and cordwood cutters also inhabited the island at the time of the Sanfords' travels. Mackinac Island was situated in the Strait of Mackinac immediately east of St. Ignace. Occupied and fortified by the British in 1779–1781, the island was transferred to the United States in 1796, captured by the British in the War of 1812, and returned to the United States by the Treaty of Ghent in 1815. The village, situated on the island's southeastern extremity, was the seat of Mackinac County and contained the public buildings, retail establishments, and two missionary schools. The American Fur Company maintained a subagency here, and the inhabitants of Mackinac Island derived subsistence from the fur

Friday morning the 28th found us steering along Lake Huron & we stopt at Presque Isle about 9 o'clock. While they were taking in wood I strolled along the beach endeavoring to get some shells, which failing in I selected some petrified stones & went on board.[40] There are some 8 or 10 log houses here the men engaged in cutting wood to supply boats stopping here, and our capt. says they make it very profitable & the fishermen I am sure must, for our capt. enquired of them for fresh fish which they said they could supply him with if he would wait till they could go to their hooks for them & they started, 3 men off in a boat, to their hooks. After they had completed wooding, the boat started & [we] began to conclude we should have no fish. But after passing some distance I saw the fish boat, which we made for, & when near enough could be seen one of the men hauling in the lines while the other two rowed the boat, which danced about in the waves in a manner that would have destroyed the feelings of safety in any other but a fisherman or lobsterman. Our capt. call them alongside when they said

---

trade as well as its fisheries. The island's population fluctuated with the continuing movement of traders and Indians. "South Manitou Island," National Park Service, https://www.nps.gov/slbe/planyourvisit/southmanitouisland.htm; "An Overview of Beaver Island's History," Beaver Island Historical Society, beaverisland.net/beaver-island-history; James H. Lanman, *History of Michigan, Civil and Topographical, in a Compendious Form with a View of the Surrounding Lakes* (New York: E. French, 1839), 311–312; Tanner, *Atlas of Great Lakes Indian History*, 131; Blois, *Gazetteer*, 252, 317–318, 322–323; Phil Porter, *The Eagle of Mackinac: The Establishment of United States Military and Civil Authority on Mackinac Island, 1796–1802* (Mackinac Island, MI: Mackinac State Historic Parks, 1991); Keith R. Widder, *Battle for the Soul: Evangelical Protestants at Mackinaw Mission, 1823–1837* (East Lansing: Michigan State University Press, 1999); Craig Wilson, "What Is Gained but Mackinac? The Battle of Mackinac Island," *Mackinac History* 4, leaflet no. 5 (Mackinac Island: Mackinac State Parks, 2014).

40. Presque Isle lies on the eastern shore of the Lower Peninsula, an area traditionally occupied by the Ojibwas and the site of a reservation established for them in 1836. Traders visited the area, and later its forests became a source of cordwood for lake steamers that stopped there to take on fuel. Work Projects Administration, *Michigan: A Guide to the Wolverine State* (New York: Oxford University Press, 1941), 484; Tanner, *Atlas of Great Lakes Indian History*, 163–166, maps 29, 31.

they had not had time to examine near all their hooks, but as it was they threw on board of us upwards of 41 salmon trout, for which our capt. said he paid them about 4/ [shillings = forty-eight cents] each, coming to more than $20. These fish abound here in great quantities. One of the fishermen said he visited his hooks, 240 in number, & had 210 trout caught. Some of these thrown on our deck should think would weight 50 or more pounds. The fishermen salt them in barrels & they are sold all over the western country, brining about the same price per barrel as shad or mackerel at the East. We had salmon trout served on the table for dinner, having it boiled, broiled & baked & fried. Everyone could have it in his own way of cooking & dinner appeared to be taken with a very good relish.

Saturday morning found us entering Lake St. Clair, having gone thru most of the strait connecting [lakes] Huron & St. Clair during the night. The lands on the shores of St. Clair River are beginning to be thickly settled & along Lake St. Clair, but should fear the ague & bilious fever to[o] much to desire a residence among them. It is expected there will eventually be a railroad from Buffalo thru Canada to Palmer or some place on the St. Clair River & canal or railroad or both across Michigan to Grand River Rapids, from whence steamboats would take passengers & freight to Chicago or any place on Lake Michigan.[41] A railroad would connect Palmer with Detroit when these complicated improvements are all finished. A journey

---

41. Nehemiah Sanford's prediction of a through rail route from Buffalo to Detroit and Grand Rapids eventually came to pass with the 1866 cooperative agreement between the New York Central and the Great Western Railway to run trains from Niagara through Canada to Windsor, Ontario, across the Detroit River from Michigan's entrepôt. The extension of the Michigan Southern and Michigan Central lines to Chicago in 1852 and the completion of the Detroit, Grand Haven & Milwaukee to Grand Rapids in 1858 provided direct rail access to both cities from Detroit. Harlow, *Road of the Century*, 225–229, 234–235; Meints, *Michigan Railroads*, 5–6. Although the state of Michigan initially planned two extensive canal projects to link the Clinton River on Lake St. Clair with the lower Kalamazoo drainage and the Saginaw and Grand rivers, insufficient funding and the development of the rail network doomed both projects. Hannah Emily Keith, "An Historical Sketch of Internal Improvements

to what is now called the far West will be performed in a few days to almost any prominent place between Detroit & the Mississippi. Michigan will be the thoroughfare for N[ew] York travelers, all crossing it on their way west & though Toledo may strain every move with the state to back them thru shallow waters of their bay, the sickly hue of its yellow waters & flat country with its heavy timbered land about it & then again the bad harbor on the other side of the peninsula of Michigan City will never or at least not very soon attract the travel to Chicago or divert it from going by way of Detroit.[42] All the roads across Michigan will have connecting links with the road from Detroit, & beside Detroit is on the way to the upper lakes & no boat bound up has to go one inch out of her way to stop there, & all do stop. Event [*sic*, Even] the inhabitants of Monroe frequently take passage from Buffalo to Detroit & then go back & up the bay in boats running between the places.

We arrived at Detroit around 7 o'clock Saturday, 29th June where [we] spent about 2 hours. I made my way at once to the office of the Auditor General to see if he had any land returned for taxes, which by the law of 1838 all taxes not paid on the 1st of March shall be returned to him whose debtors may pay at any time with interest computed from the time they are returned at 15 per cent per annum. I found our N[ew] B[uffalo] lands returned and paid them & found there was some from Cass Co. likewise returned, which as I had not time to examine them all through & as Mr. Sherman told he believed he had receipts for all the taxes that had become

in Michigan, 1836–1846," *Publications of the Michigan Political Science Association* 4 (1902): 36–39.

42. The infamous Black Swamp was the principal impediment to overland travel to Michigan through northern Ohio. Stretching south from the Maumee River, the Black Swamp stretched over some fifteen hundred acres in Indiana and Ohio and consisted of swamp and marshland of varying degrees of wetness. Despite the construction of a road through the swamp during the War of 1812, travel was so difficult that it continued to hinder travelers and retarded settlement in the region as late as the 1840s. Martin R. Kaatz, "The Black Swamp: A Study in Historical Geography," *Annals of the Association of American Geographers* 45 (1955): 14–19.

due, I concluded to write him, which I did saying on what lands I had paid in Detroit & informing him that some was returned which he supposed he had paid & requested him to be sure of attending to it. I believe I forgot to mention in my hurry of writing, but am not positive that I had paid the highway tax on the 800 acres of land in N. B. for 1839 in advance to enable them to open the road from N. B. to Rosling [Rolling] Prairie.[43] The day was quite hot in Detroit & though I got on a thin boat to go on shore, my hurry & anxiety & fear of being left by the boat got me pretty well heated by the time I got back to the boat, where a glass of rum cooled by some ice water tasted as refreshing as any beverage that might be mixt by old Nestor himself.

We left same at 11 o'clock & proceeded to Toledo passing Malden, Brest, Monroe & many other places that on speculators' maps are fine cities that are to be, & arrived at Toledo at _ o'clock.[44] Toledo has a place called Manhattan, which I suppose being built in opposition to it, a mile or more below, & then again Perrysburg further up the river disputes the claim with the town for which Ohio & Michigan contended for & for which each raised armies to defend it for self.[45] Ohio conquered, having the most influence

---

43. Rolling Prairie is situated in the eastern part of La Porte County, Indiana. Deriving its name from the undulating surface of the land, Rolling Prairie contained nearly thirty sections. Chamberlain, *Indiana Gazetteer*, 376–377.

44. Toledo, the seat of Lucas County, Ohio, was located at the confluence of the Maumee River and Lake Erie. Already a substantial port city and center of trade on the Great Lakes at the time of Nehemiah Sanford's visit, Toledo had a population of 2,072 in 1837 and saw as many as 390 steamboat arrivals annually as well as 211 schooners. Jenkins, *Ohio Gazetteer*, 429–431. Situated on the River Raisin, it was originally known as the Raisin River settlement when French farmers occupied the area in the 1770s. As the seat of Monroe County, Michigan, Monroe had grown into a substantial city by the late 1830s, with a population of about 2,595. It was the site of the federal land office for southeastern Michigan. Blois, *Gazetteer*, 327–328.

45. Situated at the head of steamboat navigation on the Maumee River, Perrysburg was the seat of justice for Wood County, Ohio. A center of trade and manufacturing, Perrysburg had a population of about fifteen hundred in 1839. Jenkins, *Ohio Gazetteer*, 357–358.

with the powers that be & Toledo is now a city of Ohio containing some 1,000 or 1,500 inhabitants.[46] If the lake should fall back to its former level of say 10 years ago, she will have to be content to have steamboats of the 2nd or 3rd class in point of size only to visit the city. Capt. Walker says the waters of the lake have been increasing ever since he has known them, say 20 years, perhaps one year falling back some inches or a foot & the next bringing it still higher than they had ever before known it. Whether this rises from colder summers then formerly, causing less evaporation, or from what cause I should like to be told by the curiously learned philosophers of the age.

Sunday morning the 30th found us approaching Cleveland, the boat having stopt at Huron in the night so, that in going & returning altho we have stopt here both ways, have had no opportunity of seeing the place on acc[oun]t of its being in the night. I am told it is a flourishing place, having one of the finest hotels in the West & is something noted for ship & steamboat building. The fine boat in which we are on was built in Huron & her Capt. Walker resides there. We arrived at Cleveland at say 8 o'clock, but had no time for a ramble on shore. The place from the boat lookt much better to me than when we went up, for at that time my head on the wrong side & there is no seeing or forming any correct ideas of a place when the south side points to the north[.] Ohio City, tho belonging to the same corporation, is on the west side of the river & causes great

---

46. The "Toledo War" refers to the dispute that arose between Michigan and Ohio over the location of the boundary between them. Ohio's northern border had been poorly defined in the Northwest Ordinance and following its admission as a state in 1803, attempts to establish a line resulted in conflicting claims of ownership of the valuable port of Toledo. These erupted into open political conflict when Michigan applied for statehood in 1835 that was settled the following year when Congress awarded the harbor to Ohio and statehood as well as the Upper Peninsula to Michigan. George J. Miller, "The Establishment of Michigan's Boundaries: A Study in Historical Geography," *American Geographical Society Bulletin* 43 (1911): 340–346; Don Faber, *The Toledo War: The First Ohio-Michigan Rivalry* (Ann Arbor: University of Michigan Press, 2008).

rivalry between the property holders of the two places.[47] Then we saw expensive buildings in each & a heavy business must necessarily be done here, having a fine back country & a canal through which a considerable portion of their supplies & thru which the products of their farms must pass, being mostly transshipped at Cleveland. I saw a s[team]boat going in having 3 canal boats in tow from Buffalo, thus saving unloading & loading. The boats can be loaded at Albany or New York, pass through the Erie Canal to Buffalo, from thence be towed to Cleveland, pass up the Ohio Canal & go on to Portsmouth [Ohio], Pittsburgh or N[ew] Orleans if they please.[48]

We stayed in Cleveland but a short time & again stopt at ½ past 10 at Fairport, where our boat wooded, giving us time to ramble some on shore. This place stands at [the] mouth of Grand River & was built to rival Richmond, which one or two miles up the river & in sight & which is again is rivaled by Zainsville [Zanesville, Ohio] some 4 or 5 miles back. There is a cheap railroad from Zainsville to Richmond thru Fairport[. H]aving wooded rails gives them a cheap conveyance of good[s] & produce to & from. We went to the lighthouse, which stands on the north side & in the village, the keeper of which keeps likewise the post office. The garden back of the house was stockt with fruit. We got the privilege of picking cherries

---

47. A rapidly growing lake port with an artificial harbor, Huron, Ohio, had become a center of shipbuilding, constructing more steamboats and lake vessels than any other port on the western end of Lake Erie. Jenkins, *Ohio Gazetteer*, 234. Located across the Cuyahoga River from Cleveland, Ohio City was a commercial rival of its neighbor. It had about two thousand inhabitants upon its incorporation in 1836 and was annexed by Cleveland eighteen years later (343–343). "Ohio City History," Ohio City, http://www.ohiocity.org/history.

48. Archaeological evidence testifies to the use of shallow draft canal boats towed by steamboats to haul lumber, wood, and other heavy cargos on the lakes and other waterways. Underwater archaeologists have recorded the remains of such boats that sank in Lake Ontario and in the Oswego River and Cayuga Lake in New York. "2 Sunken Canal Boats from Mid-1800s Found in Lake Ontario," *MSN News*, http://www.msn.com; Debra J. Groom, "Rochester-Area Men Find Sunken Erie Canal Boat in Oswego River," *Syracuse (NY) Post Standard*, December 8, 2010; Andrew Casler, "Mystery at the Bottom of Cayuga Lake," *Ithaca (NY) Journal*, October 7, 2014.

from the trees, which were of the red sour kind & hardly ripe enough to be good. The trees hung very full as did the apple & plum trees. I ventured to eat but few of the cherries, fearing the consequences if I ate much of unripe fruit.[49]

We left Fairport at between 11 & 12 & stopt again at Ashtabula about 1 o'clock where we staid but a few minutes, taking in some passengers & again proceeding on. The day is very fine & lake almost as smooth as a millpond. We pass a steamboat about every hour & many schooners & vessels are to be seen at all times in sight. The steamboat *Perry*, which left this morning, is constantly tugging at our heels & appears to strain every nerve to keep up or at least to keep in sight of the *Great Western*, & so far has sustained herself nobly.

Our next stop was at Ashtabula & again at 3 o'clock [in the] afternoon we stopt at Coneat [Conneaut], the last stopping place in Ohio, & kept in sight of Erie.[50] At 5 o'clock it is said that we are now just 90 miles from Buffalo. Of course, if nothing unfortunate happens to us we shall be in Buffalo when we wake up tomorrow morning. I find I am mistaken in our boat not stopping at Erie as she past by the island in front, I supposed she was going to continue on, but on looking out found the boat headed round & making for Erie & on enquiry learn that its only approacht from the north part of the island which with the work of art done by Uncle Sam makes this one of the most safe & commodious harbors on either of the

---

49. Fairport, Ohio, lay on the east bank of the Grand River on the southern shore of Lake Erie, thirty-two miles east of Cleveland. Its lighthouse and harbor made it regular place of landing and embarkation for travel between New York and the western country. One mile and a half upriver, the new town of Richmond City had expanded rapidly as a center of trade. Jenkins, *Ohio Gazetteer*, 170, 382.
50. The town of Ashtabula, Ohio, was situated on both sides of the Ashtabula River two miles below its month on Lake Erie. Farther east, Conneaut was a commercial center located on the lake just west of Ohio's border with Pennsylvania. A major lake shipping port, Conneaut, Ohio, was also home to milling, manufacturing, and boat-building industries. Ibid., 144–145.

lakes. We stopt about one hour & we had some little time to run up to the city which is reacht by crossing a bridge from the s[team]b[oat] landing. The town stands upon a high bluff & is beautifully situated & fast improving in business & number of its inhabitants. It is handsomely laid out, streets crossing each other at right angles & contains some very handsome buildings. The Bank of the United States are putting up an elegant banking house at this place, with marble front with a portico on the whole length of the front & Grecian pillars of solid marble some 4 feet in diameter. It must be very handsome when finisht.[51]

The passengers have just signed a card expressive of the kindness of Capt. Walker & the excellent deportment of his servants & hands on board, as well as their satisfaction in the good qualities & roominess & finish of this fine boat. Sat up late conversing with passengers to most of which we have become much attacht & the anticipated parting in the morning all seem to be regretting. This shifting of baggage & change and bustle & elbowing your way thru the crowd may be ex[c]iting for a time, but it will soon tire & make one long for rest.

Monday morning, 1st July, found us in the harbor of Buffalo & we were obliged early to leave our berths & with less than our customary sleep as all was bustle in the hands to get the boat clean'd up & ready for visitors and their linen from the berths sent to be washt. We were obliged to turn out however reluctant, pack up & be off, which we did & again sought our old stopping place, the U. S. Hotel, where we got our breakfast & then took the cars to the falls [Niagara Falls]. Stopt at the Eagle & then rambled to the ferry to view the world of waters tumbling over the falls with its endless din. Again climbed up the stairs & made our way to

---

51. The seat of justice of Erie County, Pennsylvania, the village of Erie was largely dependent on the lake trade. It was an important naval base during the War of 1812. Commodore Oliver Perry's fleet was constructed in its harbor, which now formed a protected anchorage for lake vessels. Gordon, *Gazetteer of the State of Pennsylvania*, 161.

Goat Island & then down the wide staircase & went out to near the place where Doct[or] [blank] of Troy, [New York] was killed & back & up the stairs & out to the lighthouse, so called, & up to the top of that & after seeing the falls from every point on the American side took passage to Lewistown same afternoon, where we arrived as thoroughly fatigued as going up & down stairs in a very hot day could make it.[52] We slept at the Eagle, where we got our supper at about 6 & felt more resting than viewing curiosities.

Tuesday morning, the 2nd July, found ourselves rested from our fatigues of yesterday and walkt out to see the Lyons[?] of the place of which not many were to be found in Lewistown, tho I should feel disposed to call it a very pretty & pleasant place for a residence, the land good about & well cultivated & the crops on the ground look promising. Myself, Nancy, Doc[to]r Hatch & Mr. Cox & wife crosst over to Queenstown, Ontario & went on the heights to Brock's Monument of which we ascended through the winding stairs to the top where the delightful view will replace the fatigue of ascending.[53] Lake Ontario was in sight & forts Niagara & George

---

52. Niagara Falls, New York, was a village situated on the American side of the Niagara River above the falls. Linked by the river to Buffalo, it gained a rail connection via the Lockport & Niagara Falls Railroad in 1838. Goat Island lay in the channel of the Niagara River opposite the village and bordered the American side of the falls. Gordon, *Gazetteer of the State of New York*, 560–561; Harlow, *Road of the Century*, 59. Located on a high bluff at the head of navigation on the Niagara Gorge, Lewiston was an important portage around the falls during the eighteenth century and was destroyed during the War of 1812. Following the war it emerged to become the "Gateway to the West," and prior to the opening of the Erie Canal was a major transportation hub on the route into Canada and the social center of the Niagara frontier. Home to several mills, its primary export was lumber. Gordon, *Gazetteer of the State of New York*, 558; "History of Lewiston, New York," Historic Lewiston, New York, http://historiclewiston.org.
53. Queenstown, now Queenston, lay on the Canadian side of the Niagara Escarpment opposite Lewistown (now Lewiston), New York. It arose in the 1770s at the north end of the Niagara portage and later prospered in trade as a ferry crossing to the United States. An American army attempting to invade Canada was defeated on the heights above Queenston in October, 1812. "Queenston," The Canadian Encyclopedia, www.

Connecticut to Michigan and Chicago | **75**

could be seen by those who had better eyesight than myself.[54] The plains to the north & west of Queenston appeared beautiful. The ground where not cultivated all the way from the landing to the monument is finely ornamented with sweet brier, which grows spontaneously over the ground which are now large & in full bloom & seem to grow very luxuriantly all over the ground where so many Americans fell in the death struggle to gain & retain the heights by our army in Oct. 1812. The clusters of sweet brier are scaterd over the ground, being on the brow of the hill & at its foot in bunches some rods apart, but at the place where our troops landed on crossing the river & where the British barracks & redoubts stood & where the greatest carnage was made they grow quite thick & very luxuriantly. On standing on Brock's Monument & looking down to where the scene of blood & slaughter took place it requires but little stretching of the

---

thecanadianencyclopedia.ca/en/article/queenston/. Maj. Gen. Sir Isaac Brock was commander of all British forces in Upper Canada when the War of 1812 began. Following his successful campaign to capture Detroit and secure the Michigan Territory in the summer of 1812, Brock traveled to the Niagara frontier to face a new threat posed by an American force under Gen. Stephen Van Rensselaer. During the Battle of Queenston Heights he led a counterattack that eventually drove back the invaders. Leading his troops, Brock was shot and killed. Robert S. Quimby, *The U.S. Army in the War of 1812: An Operational and Command Study* (East Lansing: Michigan State University Press, 1997), 68–74. In 1824 Brock's remains were moved to the site of a monument that overlooked Queenston Heights., "Brock's Monument, Queenston Heights," The Canadian Encyclopedia thecanadianencyclopedia.com/en/article/brocks-monument-queenston-heights/.

54. Fort Niagara, situated at the mouth of the Niagara River, has been the site of fortifications since 1679, when the French established a garrison there. During and after the battle of Queenston Heights in 1812, American artillery at Fort Niagara bombarded the British Fort George across the river, and an American invasion of Canada eventually brought its abandonment in 1813. Fort George, constructed in 1796–1799, served as the headquarters for troops under Gen. Brock's command. Following the American withdrawal in the autumn of 1813, the British reoccupied Fort George and later captured Fort Niagara, which they held until 1815, when the Treaty of Ghent returned it to the United States. "History of Old Fort Niagara," Old Fort Niagara, http://oldfortniagara.org/history; "Fort George National Historic Site of Canada," Directory of Federal Heritage Designations, www.pc.gc.ca/apps/dfhd/page_nhs_eng.aspx?id=432.

imagination to see the sweet brier grown upon each spot where a human being fell & and representing the once animated being who there lost his life blood, enriching the soil which nourishes the rose.

There are barracks here at the landing & a company of soldiers in the Queen's pay, which the unsettled state of the inhabitants of Canada render necessary for her to keep at all the principal places & especially at the ferries to prevent & guard against citizens of the United states crossing over with arms to commit depredations. We returned to our tavern, the Frontier House, in time for dinner, after which I took the cars for Lockport, [New York], leaving Nancy in the care of Doc[to]r Hatch to go down Lake Ontario to Oswego, [New York] in the steamboat which leaves here at 4 PM.[55] I arrived at Lockport between 4 & 5 & took packet boat for Rochester, where on waking on Wednesday morning, the 3rd of July, I find myself & repair to the Eagle Hotel.

I have been thru the day endeavoring to get some clue to my lost pocketbook, but have little hopes of success. Capt. Conky is absent & is not expected until the 5th. I have been endeavoring to learn whether there has been any bills of the F[armers] & M[echanics] B[ank] past here by any of the boatmen & learn by one of the brokers that he had taken some of one of the banks. Go there & enquire how they came by them & am told that a man exchanged them there some 4 weeks ago, but they did

---

55. The "Frontier House," in Lewiston, considered by some to be the "finest hotel in the United States west of Albany" upon its completion in 1825, was a landmark on the stage routes. Town of Lewiston, "Historic Lewiston." Lockport, New York, was an industrial village and the location of a series of locks on the Erie Canal that allowed the artificial waterway to ascend seventy feet to pass through a mountain ridge. The Tonawanta Creek that fed the canal also supplied industries at Lockport, which produced lumber, flour, and manufactured goods. Oswego, New York, spanned the Oswego River at its outlet on Lake Ontario, possessing a fine harbor protected by a mole. The seat of Oswego County, New York, the village was a major lake port through which passed grain, salt, and merchandise. It was also a manufacturing center. Gordon, *Gazetteer of the State of New York*, 557–558, 616–618.

FREDERICK G. MATHER, "WATER ROUTES FROM THE GREAT NORTHWEST," HARPERS 63 [1881]: 429.

Although railroads were rapidly linking the interior of New York, the Erie Canal remained the principal thoroughfare for freight and passenger traffic between the Hudson River and Lake Erie in the 1830s. The combined five locks at Lockport allowed boats to surmount the Niagara escarpment near the western end of the canal.

not know who it was, but know it was not one of their customers. They think it was about $200. That agrees with the amount I had of those bills so well that I have little doubt but it was the same money. I got the clerk who took them to examine the hands on board Dicky's boat in hoping he might know the man on seeing him again, but he does not recognize any among Capt. Dicky's hands as the man.

I have strong hopes that when Capt. Conky arrives he will see &

recognize one of his men. I have no doubt it was taken while on board his boat & by one of his men. A man by [the] name of Levy Neely has been mentioned to me as something suspicious from the circumstances of his boarding in the winter in an expensive house & that he has bought land in Michigan for which he has paid & it does not look probable that his wages would pay [for] his expensive clothing & board, but that he must have some other way not known to obtain money.

July 4th, the nation's birthday commences with rain which bids fair to mar the pleasures of the anniversary, which would seem a pitty for it seems they have made a good deal of preparations for celebrating it. The boys are not to be disappointed in their sport for they are filling the street notwithstanding the rain & cracker & fireworks are popping on all sides. About 10 o'clock the weather became clear & the whole city seemed to turn out the inhabitants, the streets being filled with men, women, boys & children. All sorts of people are to be seen walking the streets, Dutch with their pipes & wife & children, Irish & Irish women & many carrying infants who are not Irish all determined to enjoy the 4th of July. There is an oration to be delivered at the Methodist church, but learning it was filled to suffocation I did not attempt to hear it, but rambled about the falls & viewed the mills, &c.

The number of flour mills here are astonishing enough to make some 5,000 bbls. of flour per day & there is more flour made & sent from here than from any other place in the world. The military made quite a display & citizens by their numbers still more & in the evening the boys had their fun by building bonfires, burning crackers & powder in every way it could be fixt. They have here a kind which when lighted would run all about the street spitting fire at a great rate & setting men, women & children to running too when it came near them, & the boys seemed to take great pleasure when they could direct one of them among the thickest of those standing on the side walk to see the fun. About 9 of the boys collected all the old barrels they could & piled them in the middle of the streets cross each other & set them on fire, making a great blaze by the light of which I retired to bed & slept soundly till morning notwithstanding the hubbub & din that was kept up till 12 o'clock or later.

Friday the 5th. Our breakfast is later (& hasty) than usual & those of the lodgers which I found up when I went below showed symptoms of having kept late hours or of sucking t[oo] much punch thru a quill, a way of drinking which was quite new to me. The punch was made, adding to it mint & pine aple cut in pieces & [a] person suckt it thru a pipe which would take him some time to exhaust a glass, & of course would have it taste good much longer than in the usual way of drinking. It certainly lookt very tempting & the drinker much at his ease when quaffing the contents of his mint glass. But I did not try the new way myself, tho had intended to do, but waited to feel the want of some stimulus which did not happen to come upon me. Therefore cannot speak from experience of the excellency of the new way of drinking.

----

9 o'clock & Capt. Conkie has arrived but get no further clue to my lost money. He says he saw my wife at Syracuse yesterday & that she would take the boat to Utica. Of course she is safe at brother John's by this time. Spent the day going from the boat to the Bank of Western N[ew] York & back again, having the clerks see the hands on board to see if they could recognize the person who paid them the F. & M. Bank bills, but elicited nothing by it. I insisted to the agents that they should be responsible to me for the loss, but they say that I cannot hold them responsible without I can prove that it was lost on board of their boat, & even then doubtful unless I could show that it was through their negligence that it was stolen. I see not how I can prove either, though I feel little or no doubt in my own mind but that it was taken on board the *Rochester*, Capt. Conky's boat & by his own men. I shall take my passage with him to Syracuse & he offers to give me my passage. We left Rochester about 9 in the evening & am disappointed in not having Conky to accompany me, for I had intended to have consulted him as to [the] propriety of charging the crew with it one

by one & offering each a large reward to bring out the other or give [an] impression that would lead to detection & finding the money.

Saturday the 6th. On board the boat on my way to Syracuse. The hands either do, or I imagine it, look guilty & have seen them two or three times conversing together & looking towards me. Capt. Conky says he has said nothing to any of them about it except the steward & enjoined him not to mention it. His object is to keep watch & see which appears more flush of money than usual. I have converst with the steward about it today & am satisfied that I shall learn nothing by him. He affects to believe it could not have been taken on that boat, but must have been done somewhere else. He is young & volatile & I should as soon distrust him as any of the crew. The one on which suspicion rests I should not suspect from his appearance or behavior to be more likely to be guilty than any of the others. He is said to be an arch one & if he has got the money he has got it alone & has no accomplices.

I arrived at Syracuse about 6 & should have had some time to run about, but it raind & the weather quite cold.[56] As it was, I only went into one of the salt works & found but one man at work keeping fire under two rows of potash kettles, 15 in a row. He told me two men did the whole of the boiling & taking out of the kettles the salt when made, & again filling them, each working six hours at a time & then resting six, & that they made 150 bushels of salt in the 24 hours. There are a vast number of vats for saline evaporation, covering a great many acres of ground & the number of works for boiling here & at Onondaga & Salina are very great, causing a cloud to rise, looking from a distance, like the smoke of a coal pit extending in a circle from Onondaga to Syracuse & Salina.[57]

---

56. Situated at the junction of the Erie Canal and the state turnpike, Syracuse, New York, was a major thoroughfare to Canada and a center of trade, milling, manufacturing, and salt-making. The city was the seat of Onondaga County, New York, and had a population of 4,103 in 1836. Ibid., 584.

57. To the south of Syracuse lay several small communities that comprised Onondaga, New York. They included the reservation of the Onondaga Indians and the village

Sunday morning, the 7th July. Was called at 4 o'clock to take the cars for Utica & waited until after 5 for them to arrive from Auburn. The cars started sometime after 5 & went very slow across the low ground over which the rails are laid on spikes driven into the mud, & by the time we got onto good & firm ground the fire in the boiler had got so low that they could raise steam only enough to just move & finally came to a standstill where we stood for 15 or 25 minutes when they made out to get up steam & we went on at a brisk pace, arriving at Utica about 9'oclock when we got our breakfast. Very few passengers take their meals while riding on railroads for a day, there being every 15 or 20 miles houses of refreshment where the cars stop some 10 or more minutes & the tables are coverd with hot coffe, pies, cake &c., which together with the young girls which deal these luxuries out make it very tempting & few can look on without partaking of a sixpence or shilling's worth of the dainty things set so neatly & in so good style before him.[58] I held my watch & counted the number of minutes we were going a mile & found them to average not far from 3, some miles only 2½ & arrived at Amsterdam at one o'clock & found N[ancy] & Eliz[abeth], both at my brother's [John Sanford] & well. To please N. & E. I went to meeting that afternoon, when I thought I would have enjoyed a snooze much better, & again at 5 o'clock went with them to church where an Englishman officiated & who might have so well spoke in Greek as English & I should have understood him in one language as

of Onondaga Hollow, as well as Onondaga West Hill, the former county seat. Salina lay on a level plain rising from the center of a marsh at the northern side of Syracuse. It was a chief producer of salt, which was pumped from a great salt spring and distributed via subterranean log pipes. Salina's seventy-seven factories manufactured coarse salt by solar evaporation and fine salt by boiling. Ibid., 581–584.

58. Nehemiah traveled eastward to Amsterdam on the Utica & Schenectady Railroad, about which a contemporary observer wrote, "If the cars breathe a minute or two or take in water, the traveller can spring out and enter the restaurants for hot coffee and refreshments, that opportunely occur at intervals of about twenty miles." J. Disturnell, *The New York State Tourist*, quoted in Harlow, *Road of the Century*, 28–29.

another. I never before heard the beautiful epic service so murdered. As all things finally come to an end I knew his sermon would too & sat with patience till he finished & whether I felt very devout or not am certain I exemplified one of the Christian virtues—self denial, in not going to sleep during his sermon.

Monday the 8th. We started for Saratoga at 10 o'clock. Stopt an hour at Schenectady & called on Mrs. & Caroline Walter & arrived at the U. S. Hotel where we stopt between 5& 6, the weather showery & no time for promenading or looking for the Lyons.[59] After tea looked on to see dancing in the parlor, which was commenced but for a short time for the want of dancers, there being not yet company enough to make dancing very enticing & at an early hour for the place retired to bed and had a comfortable night's sleep.

Tuesday the 9th. Breakfast at 8 o'clock after a walk to the spring & taking myself 3 glasses of C[ongress Spring] water, after which went to the Pavillion [Spring] garden & to High Rock [Spring] & to a new spring but just found or again recovered, which should judge from the taste of the water to be stronger or more impregnated with soda than the Congress or either of the other springs.[60] It is not so conveniently located in respect

---

59. The United States Hotel was centrally situated between Washington and Franklin streets on Broadway, the principal thoroughfare in the village of Saratoga Springs. The first portion was built in 1825 and later enlarged until it occupied the entire block. A large, commodious structure with first-class accommodations, the United States was one of the most renowned hotels at the springs. The original hotel burned in 1865 and was replaced by a new building nine years later. Nathaniel Bartlett Sylvester, *History of Saratoga County, New York* (Philadelphia: Everts & Ensign, 1878), 166–167.

60. Discovered in 1792, Congress Spring became the most celebrated spring at Saratoga Springs. In the 1820s its owner, Dr. John Clarke, developed the swamp surrounding the spring as a park, complete with streets and houses. Because of the spring's popularity with visitors, demand for its water increased and led its owners to direct its flow into a well from which the water could be drawn. Later they also bottled the water for sale. The High Rock Spring was known to the Mohawks traditionally as the "medicine spring" and Euro-Americans recognized the purported curative properties of its waters as early as the 1740s. Formerly known as Flat Rock Spring, Pavilion Spring was surrounded by walks and gardens as well as its namesake pavilion. Also

to the fashionable publick houses, & the waters of course will be drunk but little for it is not to be supposed that people come here solely for the purpose of recovering health, & it is certain that many do not & probably as many constitutions are injured here by champaign & other liquors, high living &c as are bring mended by the medicinal powers of the water. We had our dinner at the publick table in a style I should always like to have & just such a dinner as I would like every day to have, especially when I feel as well as I now do. No hurry in the eating, but the dinner partaken of by most just like persons having their reason & governd by the common sense of civilization & not in the hurlyburly of some tables where the meals are eaten with the appearance of a strong fear they should not get part of the luxuries.

A show after dinner keeps all quiet in the house & it is fortunate we made good use of our time in the forenoon for the prospect looks not favorable for walking this afternoon. There is not company enough here now to entirely keep off ennui from all & the want of excitement is hurrying many off to the [Niagara] falls, Lake George & other places, expecting to return & meet more company than at present. Those that remain here just now appear to be staid & steady common sense people such as I most admire & upon the whole think we hit on a fortunate time of coming here. Tho to see all the follies of the fashionable should not have come here before 6th of August. They give us this time a good supply of straw & raspberries at tea, which with their excellent biscuit made with congress water without yeast endangers the quiet sleep of the boarding.

Wednesday, 10th July. Had to hurry to get dresst for breakfast at 8 o'clock & had slept from eleven the night before, which apparently gives evidence of a quiet conscience of a mind much at ease. I begin to be fond of traveling & finding a home wherever I happen to be, having no thought

---

recognized early, its waters were considered among the best at Saratoga. Gordon, *Gazetteer of the State of New York*, 675–676; Sylvester, *History of Saratoga County*, 156–160, 163.

for the morrow and trusting the landlord to supply all my wants at the word of command, giving him his revenge by paying his bills which he makes larger than the earnings of many. The traveler for pleasure must count money but as a cross. If he feels miserly he had better stay at home, and then his creditor will spend it for him. The answer to the question where so many find money to pay the expenses of traveling, which use of it their creditors' money, which they spend is no doubt in many cases correct, yet there are many who spend their sum but are rather lookt at as rather vulgar & miserly by the affected great & their servants.

CHAPTER 2

Henry S. Sanford Journal, Connecticut to Michigan, July 9 to September 6, 1844

When Henry Shelton Sanford set forth on his journey in 1844, much had changed in the five years since his parents' return from the West. His father's untimely death in 1841 had placed the family's land business in the hands of his brother-in-law Edward Shelton, who was obliged to conduct affairs from afar awaiting the majority of his nephew. Now a full partner, Henry assumed responsibility for managing the far-flung western properties and soon embarked on an extended trip to contact agents, examine properties, and arrange affairs in southwestern Michigan. Accompanied by family members, he spent the first week visiting relatives and touring sights in New York before setting off alone. Henry's journal records the adventures of a young man in an unfamiliar, new land as he encountered and interacted with its inhabitants on business and pleasure. Unlike his father, Henry Sanford often viewed the world

All of the journal entries in this chapter come from Henry Sanford, "Journal: Connecticut to Michigan, July–September, 1844," HSSP, Box 3, Folder 1.

with the eye of a romantic, rhapsodizing in the magnificence of as yet unspoiled nature and the heroic role of those who made it their home. As he traveled he also took time to describe his surroundings, often with great detail, illuminating the countryside, its settlements, and those who lived there. Seeking to explore farther west, Sanford's travels took him beyond Michigan and the realm of the family land business. He retraced his parents' route to Chicago, but then struck out to examine the lead-mining region of Illinois and Iowa and visit points farther west. Henry's journal stopped at the Mississippi River, a point to which he would return on a later trip. Throughout his journey the young adventurer's observations present us with both an objective and subjective evaluation of the frontier through the eyes of an eastern traveler and investor, offering a unique perspective on the region's development and providing a picture of a land undergoing rapid change.

Journal

Tuesday, 30th July. Got into New York this morning about 4 o/c, after which of course sleep was impossible as it indeed was. To many riding the whole night who were not accustomed to noises, jarring, &c; however had a good night's rest. New York seemed hot and insipid enough after the pure air and refreshing scenery of the country. The brick walls seemed fiery red and together with heat, noises, rolling of carts, unpleasant and odious dust and dirt seemed to have increased ten fold and I felt that a twelve hour stay there was twelve hours too long; however, I had many purchases to make and was busy the whole day. Called on Mr. Cook who went with

(*Opposite*) Henry Sanford's 1844 western journey took him over familiar territory in southwestern Michigan; however, he also extended his explorations to visit the lead district in Illinois and Iowa. Although his journal ended on the Mississippi, he continued on to St. Paul and then down the great river to St. Louis, before returning to the East by an unknown route.

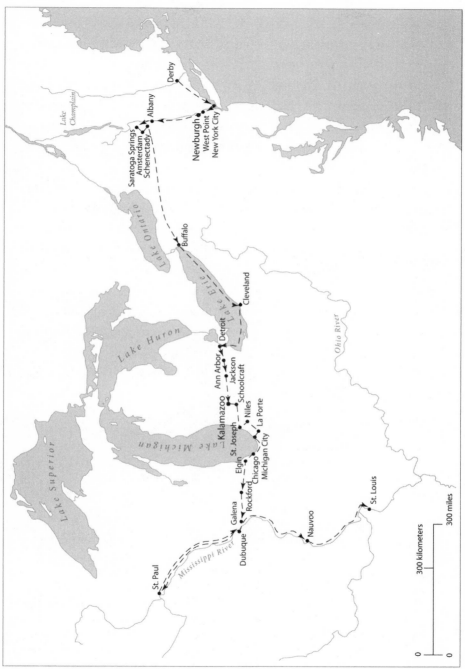

me to his friend Mr. Webb to whom I think I shall owe a good part of the pleasure I may experience in my intended trip. He immediately set about giving me directions, advice &c. & promised to furnish me letters by 4 PM to different points in the Great West. How well he fulfilled his promise I can bear grateful witness while I found at the time near a dozen letter of introductory for me and a request from Mr. Webb that should I at any time get out of friends on my trip to draw on him. I owe Mr. Cook much for his introducing me to Mr. Webb.

Gilead Smith dined with me at the City Hotel.[1] Capital dinner. We then started for the boat, he going to Newburgh as well as ourselves the evening. Found my mother and aunt [Lizzy] agreeably to appointment and boarding the *North America* steamer found ourselves ready for a start.[2] Punctual at 5 we started only to stop at a wharf a short distance above and crowd our desks with German immigrants & their luggage, whose embarkation occupied half an hour. I had forgot to mention the manner Gilead and myself rode down to the boat. We could find no cab and were forced to put our luggage on a dray cart & ourselves on top, and so proceeded in state jolting beautifully from the Naugatuck to the *N. America*. Our car man was a jolly fellow enough. I shall not soon forget his definition of the

---

1. A friend of Henry's from their days at Washington (Trinity) College in Hartford, Gilead A. Smith was then a merchant and businessman in New York. Harriet Chapell Owsley, *Register: Henry Shelton Sanford Papers* (Nashville: Tennessee State Library and Archives, 1960), 71. A contemporary gazetteer described the City Hotel in New York City as a structure "built of brick, 7 stories high, has a fine assembly room, and more than 100 parlours." Thomas F. Gordon, *A Gazetteer of the State of New York* (Philadelphia: T. Belknap, 1832), 547.

2. The steamboat *North America* was a large, well-known passenger boat on the Hudson River between New York and Albany. Built in 1840 by Devine and Burtis for the People's Line, it was a fast boat, cutting the running time between the two cities to ten hours, and often raced other steamboats on the river. Subsequently operated by the New Haven Steamboat Co., the *North America* was chartered by the US government in 1862 as a troop transport. Employed on the Mississippi and Red Rivers, it was destroyed by fire at Baton Rouge, Louisiana, in October 1863. David Lear Buckman, *Tales and Reminiscences of the Stirring Times That Followed the Introduction of Steam Navigation* (New York: Grafton Press, 1907), 21, 65, 66, 68.

origin of the Paddies. We were passing through a rowdy set of them when he called to our remembrance the account of the Devils having been cast into service & who ran into the Dead. All were drowned he said, but one which swam to Ireland & there littered.

We finally started off to our great satisfaction and now had ample time and opportunity to scan the faces of our fellow passengers, including the emigrants on the decks below, the river craft with their glistening white sails moving here and there, the steamers plowing the waters in all directions, and the scenery around. Our emigrants were in their own costume. All were tow headed, all were dirty, all the men had their pipes, all the women their children. I observed one child of about two years that attracted much attention, of which the father seemed very proud. A bright eyed, handsome boy he was, but with a head, absolutely a deformity so was it being full a third larger than those either its father's or mother's. There was much grunting of German and whiffing of pipes and I felt on the whole much better pleased with looking at the faces on the Promenade Deck. There were few interesting ones there, even among the females. The most so was Miss Platt of N. Y[.], an Heiress and who had just received the Gold Medal at Rutgers Institute in French. She was not beautiful, but of an interesting & pleasing countenance.

The steamer *South America* passed us going down, in an excursion.[3] She had a band of music, etc on board & was crowded. We saluted her, which she returned & her band struck up "Life on the Ocean Waves." We passed through the Pallisaides, admired the beautiful scenery of the Hudson, and paced the deck, watch each new scenery that came there with interest. The sun set beautifully and presently, the moon appeared, first a light just discernable over the Eastern Hills, which grew more and more distinct,

---

3. The *South America,* also built by Devine and Burtis and launched in 1841, was another prominent passenger steamboat of the People's Line operating on the New York to Albany run. It was dismantled in 1863. Buckman, *Tales and Reminiscences,* 21; "Oldtimers: Boats on the Hudson."

till finally it had the appearance through the clouds of a column of fire & presently the round, full moon peered out from among the clouds and showered its silvery light upon us.[4] Twas beautiful, a time for pleasing thoughts, delicious musings, soft whispering with fair girls. And so seemed to think a pair leaning over the top rail under the Promenade Deck—a dark haired girl the one, a fine looking & older man the other. She hanging upon his arm and leaning so that her face almost touched his—looking into his eyes so earnestly & so trustingly—and their few works sounded so soft & so confidential. Oh, twas a time for love! The dark wooded shores around, the swift foaming waters washing by beneath, the pure Heaven above, radiant in the moon's beam.

————————

Wednesday 31st, West Point. We started for Newburgh, but in account of the detention of the boat found we were going to arrive there at such a later hour in the evening as would inconvenience our friends there who were not expecting us. So we concluded to stop at West Point where none of us had yet stopped. So we did—and giving our luggage in charge of the porter of the hotel wound our way up by the fine but circuitous road which climbs up to the hotel. Twas a fine evening and we enjoyed the walk. I shouldered my gun and with my aunt on one arm went at the hill admiring everything, for the moonlight made all objects distinct. Gil followed with my mother. We arrived at the hotel, which is charmingly situated, registered our names at the office for the edification of the officer whose business it is to see who arrived, found our rooms, and then Gilead and myself started for a cotillion party which was across the parade ground. We however did not find it—not knowing the localities and so walked through and around the

————————

4. The Palisades are basalt cliffs bordering the Hudson River on its western bank, stretching from Jersey City to near Nyack, New York. A romantic contemporary account noted that the Palisades' summit was "even and regular as the cornice of a house, the entire facade like the ruins of an ancient feudal castle, ornamented with the moss and hue of antiquity." *The New York State Tourist* (New York: A. T. Goodrich, 1842), 13.

encampment. The cadets are all compelled to encamp during the summer months and there were their tents, each holding three, to the number of 80 or more arranged in regular rows, with sentries pacing their rounds around the square. It looked quite en militario. We then returned, looked at the faces in the parlour. Soon we heard the tattoo and presently came flocking in those who had been to the cotillion. If they are in the middle of one, it ceases immediately at drum beat, which is at 10.[5]

Gill and I sat on the piazza looking down upon the Hudson below us, with here darkness by the deep shadows of the mountains and there bathed in the moon beams—till midnight when the steamer appeared in light from Albany or rather her lights far distant up the river. Then we shook hands and separated, he for New York, I for bed. I slept soundly and waking up next morning found our anticipations of a fine stroll through the grounds quashed; it was raining hard. I sought my mother and aunt. They were disconsolate. We seated ourselves in the parlour & looked out through the storm upon the scenery around us and sighed for breakfast. That disposed of we felt better and resigned to our lot and proceeding to the observatory looked out through the dripping glass upon the country around us. Kosciuszko's monument was hardy & composed by the beatings of the rain.[6] The cannon upon the parade ground was in mourning, covered in black oilcloth. The hills veiled their heads with mists which hovered around their summits & clung to their sides. The trees weeped watery traces plentifully, so did the clouds. The white tents of the cadets looked disconsolate & dripping. Still more so appeared the

---

5. West Point, home of the US Military Academy, founded in 1802, included a landing for boarding and discharging boat passengers. The bivouac Henry observed there occurred after the yearly examination in June, after which "the cadets are encamped on the plain for a certain period, when the drills and parades are worth seeing." The Sanford party presumably stayed at the Capital Hotel, situated on the brow of a hill that offered an excellent view of the Hudson Valley. Ibid., 24.

6. In 1828 the cadets at West Point erected a monument as a memorial to the Polish hero of the American Revolutionary War, Gen. Thaddeus Kosciuszko. It consisted of a classical marble cenotaph surrounded by an iron railing. Ibid., 23.

sentries pacing their rounds or cuddled in their sentry boxes—all did no good. It would rain & did so as long as we stared. Still the view was fine & we enjoyed it.

At ten ourselves and luggage were transported together with a number more by means of the omnibus & baggage waggon to steam boat house at bottom of the hill where we waited patiently the coming of the boat. Finally the *Empire*, one of the finest boats our country can boast of, rounded the point and stopped at the little wharf. There was the usual bustle and hurry in getting passengers off, & on and in a few minutes we were speeding through the waters a twenty mile per hour pace. This boat and the *Knickerbocker* may well be called floating palaces.[7] The sun came out before we reached Newburgh where we stopped, put o[u]r luggage in charge of a lame man on crutches who called himself public porter & climbed up the hill to my aunt's, whom we were giving a visit. Newburgh has some fine situations on its outskirts & pleasant places they are. The town itself, situated on a side hill, is nothing remarkable & not a pleasant place of residence.[8] In the afternoon we walked around, visited Downing's

---

7. The *Empire* and the *Knickerbocker* were among the prominent steamboats on the Hudson. Buckman, *Tales and Reminiscences*, 21. The *Empire*, commanded by Capt. R. B. Macey, was built in 1843 for the Troy Line for the Hudson River trade. At the time of its construction it was the largest steam vessel in the world at 936 tons. The steamboat was sunk in a collision at Newburgh, New York, in 1849, raised and repaired, and damaged in a second collision four years later. Also constructed at Albany in 1843 for the People's Line, the *Knickerbocker* featured seventy single rooms and twelve staterooms. It remained on the New York to Albany run until 1848 and again from 1859 until 1862, when it was chartered as a transport by the US Sanitary Commission. It sank in a storm at the mouth of the Potomac River in February 1865. "Oldtimers: Boats on the Hudson."

8. Newburgh was one of the principal ports on the Hudson and an outlet for overland routes reaching central and western New York. A site of manufacturing, milling, brewing, and commerce, Newburgh was a home port for steamboats and sloops on the river as well as whaling ships abroad. Andrew J. Downing, the noted landscape architect and author, was born in Newburgh on Oct. 31, 1815, and maintained a nursery and model gardens at his home on the Hudson. Gordon, *Gazetteer of the*

Nursery <u>Garden</u>, which is well known through the U. S. & which is well & tastefully laid out, with his house, a pretty Gothic building, in the center, looked art [*sic*] the principal country seats around, admired the view from sufficient points and at 9 o'clk went on board the *Columbia* for Albany.[9]

I turned in & was soon sound asleep & in spite of the frequent stopping, slept soundly & did not get up till 6 next morning, two hours after we had got to Albany. I had procured a state room for my mother and aunt—and had the satisfaction afterwards of knowing that they had scarcely slept long, the room being in the middle of the boat, the center of all the noise & clatter during the night, so that my pains to procure them comfortable quarters went for nothing.

<u>Thursday, Aug. 1, Albany</u>. We went up to Congress House and took breakfast, met there some people from the South who had come from West Point then [New]burgh in company with us.[10] I then transacted what little business I had and at ten and a half started for Troy per steamer. Glad to leave a city that seems only to abound in dirty streets, mean houses, and bad smells. Had a pleasant sail up with the *Maria* that used to run from Binghamton to New York—coming down towing vessels on one side of the river. They were grading for a railroad down from Troy to Green Bush on the other side. We admired the arsenal. Stopped at Troy House, a place I like, a clean city, enterprising inhabitants, and some fine buildings &

State of New York, 605–606; *New York State Tourist*, 30–31; A. J. Downing, *Rural Essays*, edited, with a Memoir of the Author by George William Curtis and a Letter to His Friends by Frederika Bremer (New York: George P. Putnam and Co., 1853), xix–xxi, xxvi–xxvii, xxxii–xxxiii, xliv.

9. The *Columbia* was another prominent steamboat traveling between New York and Albany during the 1830s and 1840s. Buckman, *Tales and Reminiscences*, 21.

10. The "Congress Hall" was one of the principal hotels in Albany during the 1830s and 1840s. It was located on State Street across from the Mohawk & Hudson Railroad station near the public square. Gordon, *Gazetteer of the State of New York*, 346; *New York State Tourist*, 51.

pleasant situations around it.[11] Dined here and at four PM took the cars
for Saratoga Springs. I had a pleasant gentleman for companion as far as
Ballston—who served as chaperone for the different places of interest.
Ballston Spring it seems is lost and its boarding houses & hotels remain,
but no mineral waters. It's a pretty place and some few stop here to rus-
ticate, but a droplet, the great stream runs on to empty itself at Saratoga.
This railroad is poor stock. The citizens invested $300,000 for stock and
the company borrowed the rest of the balance. It proved a failure. The
$300,000 was lost and the banks took the RR for their debt. It has never
paid a dividend. During the months of July and Aug. there is much travel
over the road, in winter none, & it is laid for a few months. The first dozen
miles lay along the Hudson & Mohawk rivers & was rather interesting. The
rest of the way was through pine woods, swamps & barren country, & we
were glad after three hours to have got to Saratoga, 28 miles.[12]

We had written on from NY for rooms and as soon as the cars arrived I
hurried up to the United States to get our names down first. How cool
everybody seemed & how freshly did the trees & gardens look around
the hotels! There were many people in the piazza of the hotel, all taking
huge comfort, ladies and gentlemen by quantities promenading the long
extent of the front piazza and plenty smoking already at there ease on the
back piazza, and thirsty and heated passengers presented quite a contrast
to the well dressed crowd around me. I had however the satisfaction of

---

11. The city of Troy was the seat of Rensselaer County, New York. A milling and
    manufacturing center and home to diverse heavy industries, Troy lay on both sides
    of the Hudson River above Albany. The Schenectady & Troy Railroad terminated
    there and connected the city with points west. The Troy House was one of Troy's
    most distinguished hotels. The village of Greenbush, New York, was situated on the
    east side of the Hudson opposite the southern part of Troy. Gordon, *Gazetteer of the
    State of New York*, 643, 646–650.
12. The Rensselaer & Saratoga Railroad, completed in the mid-1830s, crossed the Hudson
    and spanned the twenty-four miles from Troy to link Troy to the resorts of Ballston
    Spa and Saratoga Springs. Ibid., 650.

finding my name upon the card & rooms reserved for us and went back trifling some equanimity. Saw our luggage placed under the sign of the US Hotel. (Each hotel here has a window in the car house over which is its sign, and the luggage for each hotel is placed under its corresponding sign & handed out to the porters who are not allowed to enter.) This done, I escorted our ladies to their room, saw their luggage sent up there and then gladly betook myself to my own to get a cool wash & clean clothes before tea. The tea bell rang just as we came to the hotel and crowds were hurrying to the supper room. And here I found myself after going up flights of stairs & threading long passages full of doors only numbered like cells in a prison in No. 10, 3d story, a little room with one window, white walls, no carpet, a bed, wash stand, six by nine mirror & three little shelves & 2 chairs duly domiciled in Saratoga.

Oh, the luxury of clean, cool clothes after a journey on a hot day! One feels a new man and his confidence in himself is redoubled. At 8 I found our ladies ready & we proceeded to the supper table. We had arrived too late for a servant and we found the almost utter impossibility of getting anything to eat. Not a servant but seemed too intent to notice us. I could not catch the eye of one of them. Fellow finally gave two plates for them & without knives & so we waited. Finally the fellow coming near again was met by a word and a look that showed there was to be no trifling about it and proved attentive enough for the rest of the meal, and we managed thus to get what we wanted. I would be ashamed to admit being out of temper with a servant, but I felt completely so.

Tea being finished, we went to the drawing room; a noble room it is and was filled with ladies and gentlemen all looking their prettiest. In the piazza too were many promenading up & down & knots of ladies & gents seated around. All was gaiety & animation. All the world seemed to have been imported freshly in band boxes to Saratoga and just let out unsoiled.

There was a dearth of familiar faces and we felt very happy in finally seeing someone we had known before. We saw Mrs. Selliman, mother of the

Professor and Mrs. McGregor. These had been here a fortnight and knew most of the distinguished characters around us. I was disappointed in the dearth of pretty faces. The belles were those that had been such but had surely the qualifications though still the name Mrs. The most distinguished one perhaps was Mrs. O'Donnell from Balt[imore], a fine looking woman of 50 with two pretty daughters whom she surpassed in beauty. Mrs. Meredith of same place attracted some attention. She it was who treated her lover so badly (a Navy officer) that he shot himself. She of course became a lioness by it & is so now. One of the prettiest faces there was that of Miss Bayard of [*sic*] daughter of the Hon., a lively light haired girl.

I went into some of the hotels in the course of the eve[ning], but none would compare with the US either in style of occupants. The drawing room of the US is a very fine one & presents a beautiful appearance in the evening when filled with well dressed ladies and gentlemen. A noble piazza runs around the House and was full of promenaders walking by the light of the moonbeams.

And here is Saratoga, filled with aspirants for matrimony & renown, anxious mommies and their still more anxious daughters, the fashionable & the would be fashionable, the beauties and the would be beautiful, the rich and the would be rich. Verily this is the place of pretension. Everybody are "fortunes" and "rich as Croesus." Everybody are "good matches." The US is crammed from 500 to 700 due here daily and the places of the outgoers are supplied by two newcomers immediately. Loads of passengers are sent out from here daily, having no accommodations. In the same yard with the US are a few cottages where a few families from the South take up their abode, having appointments and happy are those who get such[. T]hey must speak the year beforehand. Bishop Heyes[,] Francis Granger, N. P. Willis, Ole Bulls [*sic*], Burgess, Chester Carter &c&c&c, and a host of smaller fry who would be distinguished.[13] Miss Sedgwick & Miss Brownell have just left.

---

13. As a popular antebellum resort, Saratoga Springs attracted many public celebrities as performers and guests. Among them were several notable individuals who resided in New York during the year prior to Henry Sanford's visit.

Dr. Lardner is here giving lectures on astronomy &c & had this evening 10 listeners, while some thespian performers the same evening had a hall full. Verily talent cannot be appreciated at such a place. Burgess & suite & Ole Bulls are giving concerts, Korphonay is teaching the polka. The dwarf who was our companion on voyages in the st[eam] boat is exhibiting, &c &c.

Friday, Aug. 2 (1844). All manner of attractions are at Saratoga, all manner

---

Born in 1806, Nathaniel Parker Willis was a well-known and successful American author, poet, playwright, literary critic, and editor whose literary career began in the late 1820s. He built his career through a number of publications and worked with a number of notable American literary figures, including Edgar Allan Poe and Henry Wadsworth Longfellow. Although born in Maine, Willis's career was centered in New York, where he established his residence on the Hudson River, where he died in 1864. Cortland P. Auser, *Nathaniel P. Willis* (New York: Twain Publishers, 1969), 19–20, 118, 128–129.

Francis Granger was born in Connecticut in 1792 and followed a career in public service. Graduating from Yale College in 1814, he served terms in the New York state assembly from 1826–1828 and 1830–1832 and the U. S. House of Representatives from 1835–1837 and 1839–1843. In 1841 Granger briefly joined President William Henry Harrison's cabinet as postmaster general. Although he left political office following his last term in congress, he remained active in the Whig Party in the decade prior to the Civil War and actively worked to achieve a compromise to avoid the conflict. Granger died in Canandaigua, New York, in 1868. "Francis Granger (1841) Postmaster General," Miller Center, University of Virginia, http://millercenter.org/president/harrison/essays/cabinet/205.

Ole Bull was a celebrated Norwegian violinist born in Bergen in 1810. He had become a well-known musician in Europe by the 1830s, giving concerts in England, Scandinavia, and throughout Europe. He visited the United States for the first time in 1843 for a two-year tour. Based in New York City, Bull traveled more than a hundred thousand miles and played in more than two hundred concerts in a number of major American cities. During this time he also wrote several important musical pieces. He returned to America in 1852 and purchased land in Pennsylvania with the intent of founding a Scandinavian colony, but lawsuits over land ownership drained his resources and eventually led him to give up the venture. He divided the latter part of his life between Norway and his summer home in Maine. He died in Bergen in 1880. Henry C. Lahee, *Famous Violinists of To-day and Yesterday* (Boston: L. C. Page and Co., 1899), 192–199; George T. Ferris, *Great Violinists and Pianists* (New York: D. Appleton and Co., 1892), 165–168, 171–177.

of ways to observe species. Got up and off to the Congress spring at 7 this morning. Frank Johnson's band was discoursing sweet music from nearby and everybody was crowding to get their allotted no. of tumblers of water. We walked down the street by the principal hotels till we saw the portico under which is the spring and here were crowding plenty of both sexes pressing forward for mineral water. There is a square sunken below the floor around which run counters or tables and inside are three or four bays, each with a utensil in which are placed three tumblers. This by means of a long stick is plunged into the spring in the center of the square & drawn up full of the sparkling beverage & handed thus to those standing around. Thus four or five boys are kept constantly at work dipping up, and then not fast enough to supply the demand. One can readily tell the newcomers here; they take the glass suspiciously—taste it—and finally after two or three swallows, accomplished with wry faces, they have half the water in the glass & go away scowling & making faces. But those who have been here long seem to go at it in a business like manner and tumbler after tumbler is poured down & disappears, till all wonder where they can dispose of it.

The grounds around the spring are very pretty. There are diverse open plats of grass & winding walks. After the first glass or two the people walk around, listen to the music, admire the grounds, perhaps take a ride in a velocipede, a circular r[ail] road, and then, having duly settled their stomachs, return home to breakfast, stopping on their way at the spring for another glass of water. There are many other springs here, the most famous of which are the High Rock, Iodine & Pavillion, but Congress is the favorite and many go to no others. It is customary, I believe, to drink the Congress water before breakfast and the High Rock after ten, the latter is a tonic.[14]

---

14. Visited by Europeans as early as the 1760s, High Rock Spring became known for the curative properties of its waters. Its name derived from the rocky concretion through which its waters rose. The Pavilion Spring lay east of Broadway on grounds developed as a park with a pavilion built over the spring. Gordon, *Gazetteer of the State of New York*, 675; Sylvester, *History of Saratoga County*, 156–159, 163.

Came back to breakfast at 8. I had liked the water our people had. This time we got seats and an attentive waiter. Met Dixon opposite us at the table, was glad to see someone I knew. The breakfast hall is three large halls in succession & will accommodate a vast number. The best seats are always reserved—the way being to free the waiter who keeps the seats for them. I did the same to our waiter (an admirable practice) and hope thus to get at least some attention. So crowded are they that it is difficult to get anything to eat or anyone to get it. I am getting sick of going to a stylish house if it to be as crowded as this, however one sees the house mandatory[.]

Saratoga, Aug. 2d [3rd], Saturday. The day was spent [as] yesterday—doing nothing—staring at the people walking the piazza & writing, dinner being the great thing through which the former is lived for. They would set a fine table at the US, had they half the number of visitors as it is, so many get half served and half that they ought to be. Still they set a very good table. It is curious to be as we were at the end of one of these long tables and look through the long vista till the table seemed converging to a point lined on each side with heads thickly studded & variegated, male and female, curls & plain hair, all opening and shutting their mouths by common consent while the knife & fork of each seemed barely employed in furnishing occupation for said mouths. After dinner, as before lounge, sit in the back piazza & read or listen to Snyder's band discoursing sweet music under the shade or look at the people crowded into the drawing room & on the piazzas.

This night was that of the ball. They had a hop here once or twice a week when the visitors at the US drop in without ball dress and have an unceremonious dance, but this was the great event of the week and had been looked forward to the whole week anxiously by all the belles and beaux. Tea was half an hour earlier than usual in consequence and after that the great hall was cleaned out completely of tables, etc presented a fine place for a dance at 9. Before tea Aunt Lizzy & I had taken a stroll and visited [the] pavilion at High Rock, Iodine, & other springs, but came away preferring Congress Spring to the whole though there is some similarity in all the waters. About half past 8 the drawing room, which before had been quite deserted, began to fill up with young ladies &c. dressed for the ball ad extremum, come down to show themselves before going in and each one was critically admired and envied by the others just in proportion as one excused another. At nine the doors were thrown open—Snyder's band struck up a fine march, and the whole company streamed in and promenaded two or three turns in the hall and left the drawing room almost empty. I did not get in for the first cotillion, knowing noone. Dixon, however, introduced me before the next set to a pretty woman, Mrs. Thatcher of Boston—danced with her—found her very amiable & lively. He then introduced me to Mrs. Harrison Gray Otis of Boston, a woman at present of 50 perhaps, but who has been & still is in part the belle of Saratoga—not so much at present since her personal charms, for she would be able at first from her manners to excite the visible faculties of strangers, as from her good nature & sense and affability. Everybody knows Mrs. Otis and she knows everybody. Noone at Saratoga is better known than herself. She has her rooms engaged at the US the year beforehand—and on Thursdays "receives" and has her receptions in fine style. Oh twas amusing to see the spirit with which she danced. Her whole soul seemed bent upon doing it with spirit, grace, and vigor. But she was very agreeable & we promenaded & walked the rooms some time after the set. She knew everybody & offered to introduce me. So I here found a key to unlock the delights which are unapproachable to a stranger and anticipated some pleasure hereafter.[15]

---

15. Eliza H. Boardman Otis was the widow of Harrison Gray Otis, the son of Boston politician Harrison Gray Otis and his wife Sally Foster Otis. His father Otis served in the Massachusetts House and Senate and the US House and Senate, and as US attorney for Massachusetts, common pleas judge, and mayor of Boston. Eliza and the younger Otis were married May 6, 1817, and he died in 1827. "Harrison Gray Otis, U. S. Senator," Geni, https://www.geni.com; "Eliza H. Boardman," Ancestry Library, https://www.ancestrylibrary.com/.

Herr Korphonay & Sy Burgess danced the polka. So I mounted Mrs. Otis in a chair, mounted another one by her side and she looked on & enticed, and she was skilled for it, for of the last 10 years she has passed it in Europe and knew the polka. I was much pleased with the dance, which was first time I had seen it danced. But I found in walking around with Mrs. Otis, who stopped continually to ask "how do you like it" that the young ladies generally were not much in favour with it. So it was with the waltz, a dozen years since & know [now] its universal. I danced the two following & last sets with Mrs. Wilkinson of S. Carolina, a pretty amiable and agreeable woman in whom I became much interested. We had waltzes ultimately with the quadrilles & I saw some good waltzing. Refreshments of all kinds were handed round plentifully and at ¼ past 12 the ball broke up and I went to bed, tired and pleased there was much elegant dressing and enormous trousseaus, and as Mrs. W. remarked, the young ladies in getting the numbers for the set forgot how much space she occupied running the reals & forgetting the superficial. These balls are got up by one of the waiters carrying around at dinner a sheet of paper on which those who wish to go to the ball put down their names and the cost is jointly paid among them.

We determined today (Saturday) to go to my uncle's in Amsterdam as my mother and Aunt Lizzy have already got tired of Saratoga & so could not stay till Monday next as we had originally proposed, and though I could have enjoyed it well throughout the season over. We made our arrangements for departure by th[e] 5½ p.m. train for Schenectady. After dinner we took a walk through the grounds now familiar to us, heard the last notes from Snyder's band, and at 5½ got into the cars and were soon rattling toward Schenectady. We looked again with interest upon the pretty town of Ballston and saw nothing interesting on our route till just when we entered Schenectady.[16] Here the scenery changed from the rough woody

---

16. Situated four miles from Ballston Spa, the village of Ballston lay on Long Lake. The Renesselaer & Saratoga Railroad passed through the settlement. Gordon, *Gazetteer of the State of New York*, 680–681.

country to the smiling, pleasant valley of the Mohawk. Schenectady is prettily situated, the college buildings having a very prominent place in the landscape. We crossed the river and stopped near the Phoenix Hotel. Here we got out for have we waited for the cars from Albany till 8½, we having got in near 7. Having taken some refreshments we commenced a walk to the college and found the city looked better from a distance, for we went through some very vile, dirty streets with mean houses attached. We finally reached the street which leads to the college and which I believe is their best street. So we it climbed it up and while in the ascent met Mrs. Caroline Walter & sister, formerly of Derby, coming down. They were as surprised to see us as we them and they immediately turned round and accompanied us to the college.[17]

The buildings, two in number, are situated on a commanding situation in the brow of the hill looking down upon the valley below. The entrance to the grounds is by a gate above, and the way extending in front of the buildings and from which is a fine prospect. The two higher classes only are in this college, the two ones being in the Lower College so called. The buildings have residences for the faculty at each end where they reside. We went to the garden of Prof. Jackson, who lives in one of the buildings. It is very tastefully and prettily laid out, with winding paths & flowering walks and has many & beautiful varieties of flowers. There is a wood in one part of the garden on a declivity, and here grow forest trees & plants just as nature left them, while winding walks cut through and in a very pretty manner to the garden below. There is one beautiful shaded bower or nook in the wood with a rustic seat within seeming completely away from anything worldly & a most fit place for moonstruck lovers and is called Lovers' Retreat, or something of the kind, signifying that it is a place to talk soft nonsense.

---

17. Schenectady, the seat of Schenectady County, was a city of around 5,500 inhabitants, known for its foundries as well as its carpet and paper mills. Ibid., 691–692. The Phoenix Hotel was presumably the "good hotel on the main street" observed in 1842. *New York State Tourist*, 54.

It was nearly dark when we came away, or should much have liked to see more of the college grounds which seem very prettily laid out. It is now vacation & save the professors families the colleges are deserted.[18]

We descended the hill, stopped at Mrs. Walter's for half an hour, and then proceeding to the cars at half past eight were again whizzing along on our way to [our] destination. It was near ten when we arrived there, which we did without accident. We fortunately met at the car house cousin Stephen [Sanford], oldest son of my uncle & his assist went soon arrived there. The door was locked & part of the family was in bed, but nevertheless glad to see us, and at eleven all us had retired & I for one was sound asleep.

Sunday, Aug. 4. Was a fine day and some sun nevertheless. I did not see the sun rise. We went to the Presbyterian church in the forenoon, the Episcopal church in the PM & Presbyt[erian] again in the even[ing]. Amsterdam is a growing place, has three thousand inhabitants, and but three churches. The Erie Canal runs through here and, as canal boats do not stop for Sunday, its banks are a scene of business & bustle throughout the day for the canal boats pass very frequently the grog shops and they are many, and all open along the banks and Sunday is perhaps a day of as much discourse as any day in the week.

I took a stroll through the town towards sunset. Nothing remarkable. Uncle John [Sanford] has erected a carpet factory on the creek which runs through the town and which has a considerable fall there, running down a rocky bed and thus forming almost natural dams by means of which water power may be had for but a trifling outlay. He is erecting

---

18. East of town, 250 students matriculated at Union College, built from the proceeds of a state lottery in 1814. Its faculty included a president and seven professors, an instructor, a tutor, and two fellows. The college possessed "a library of 10,000 volumes, a museum, and chemical and philosophical apparatus." Gordon, *Gazetteer of the State of New York*, 691–692; *New York State Tourist*, 54.

a row of houses for his workers and calls the street in which he places them Shuttle St.[19]

———————————

<u>Aug. 10th, Buffalo [Saturday]</u>. This morning at 6 we left Niagara, our puffing locomotive endeavored to drown the din of the rushing waters and we were soon whizzing along having Niagara behind us. Part of our road lay along the banks of the river and we passed some places of interest. Schossler where the *Caroline* was burnt on Navy Island, the principal scene of the Revolution at that time, Chippewa &c.[20] We passed towns and a creek about half way between Niagara and Buffalo, a place as the guidebook says remarkable for catfish . . . which are caught in great abundance. A very good dam for supplying the canal is here. We were nearly two hours in going to Buffalo, a distance of little over 20 miles. Glad were we to reach it for we were without our breakfast and what was more unfortunate, our party did not have time to get any before the cars left for the East. I hurried them to the depot and they were forced to supply the cravings of hunger from a baker's shop on the way. Here I was to bid adieu to Mother, Aunt and the other ladies and hereafter go on my way—long and tedious perhaps—alone. After much crowding & squeezing, I [gave] them their tickets for Auburn whither they go and spend Sunday, for at the hotel there my mother has been unfortunate enough to leave or lose here purse and

———————————

19. John Sanford's carpet factory in the growing village of Amsterdam utilized the hydraulic power of the Mohawk River, as did the village's grist and sawmills as well as its factories. Gordon, *Gazetteer of the State of New York*, 536.

20. Fort Schlosser was a stockade erected by the British on the east bank of the Niagara River during the French and Indian War. Surrendered to the United States in 1796, it later became notorious during the Rebellion of 1837 when invaded by Canadian loyalists who crossed over from Chippewa, Upper Canada (Ontario), to capture the American steamboat *Caroline*, a vessel supplying men and supplies to the insurgents at Navy Island. After taking the ship, they set it afire and cut it loose to drift over Niagara Falls. Navy Island, a Canadian possession lying in the Niagara River between Goat Island and the Falls, was occupied by British forces during the Rebellion of 1837. Carl Wittke, *A History of Canada* (New York: F. S. Crofts & Co., 1941), 110; *New York State Tourist*, 88.

hopes to recover it by stopping there. I saw them safely seated, gave my last adieus not without a mother's regret and soon the cars rolled slowly out of the depot and I was left alone in Buffalo.

I wended my way up to my hotel & breakfast. Everything in the streets was bustle and animation. Large blocks of buildings were being put up, new streets were being paved, new houses built. Everybody seemed on business thoughts intent and were moving backwards & forwards like men who had something to do. I found myself the only saunterer among them all and infected as it were found myself going at a fast walk and like a man who had business towards the American.[21] Carts were rattling through the street every way. Omnibuses loaded with passengers were arriving and departing from the hotels. All manner of people were in the streets, Indians rolled in their blankets and squaws with long hair with children strapped in cradles at their backs were at every corner conversing in their guttural dialect. Immigrants were met at every step, principally Germans, all of course wearing their peculiar costume. One might hear the Indian, German, Dutch, French & English all mixed together as one saw the mass of people moving by, each in their peculiar tongue. This Babel reminded me of some of the ports in the Levant where one sees the costumes & & hears the tongues of nearly every country on the Mediterranean at the same time. The costumes were of course not so varied, though the blanketed Indian & high coiffed German gave some variety to the appearance of the streets.

My breakfast was soon dispatched, everything was cold and the butter was the only thing that ought to have been. The cupola of our hotel presents a fine view and looks over Buffalo and the surrounding country. Up and down the long street (Main St.), which runs from the lake through the town & far out beyond and on which the principal business of Buffalo is

---

21. Benjamin Rathbun built the American Hotel on Main Street below Court Street in Buffalo in 1835. "Benjamin Rathbun in Buffalo," History of Buffalo, http://www.buffaloah.com/h/rath/rath.html.

done, all was bustle and animation of course here. It looked out upon the lake, its green waters lashed and agitated by a strong breeze blowing and on whose surface as far as the eye could reach could be seen vessels arriving and departing, bringing in produce from the shores of these vast lakes and their tributaries and carrying back again the manufactured products of the eastern states or other hemispheres in exchange for their raw materials. On the other side were the barracks over which the stars and stripes were proudly waving, and all around were pleasant country seats and a vast extent of level country.

This hotel and many of the fine buildings were erected by Rathbun, to whom Buffalo owes much & who now just released from a penitentiary where for five years he has been paying the penalty awarded for the crimes of others, is employed to oversee the erection of a new hotel which is building here now. How he must feel his degradation, he who ten years since was the Girard of the West who planned and executed works of improvement which will make his name remembered while those who brand him as felon are rotting and forgot[ten]. Now performing the office of overseer of our building where he was ten years since causing hundreds to be erected, when the streets were crowded with carts, workmen & artisans in thousands looking to him for subsistence, and this man is despised & condemned [and] called felon by those very men whom he has been the means of enriching. Pah, what are the dignities or honors of this world! In prosperity the world fawn upon you & lick your feet. In your misfortunes each throws on his weight & crush[es] you.[22]

---

22. A wealthy developer, Benjamin Rathbun was one of the most influential individuals in western New York and the leading citizen of Buffalo in the early 1830s. His purchase of the Eagle Hotel in 1821 began his business ventures in the city. His mercantile firm soon expanded into construction, an endeavor that boomed in the following decade. He erected ninety-nine buildings, including stores, homes, a theater, hotels, warehouses, and barns, operated machine shops and a tannery, and virtually dominated Buffalo's business. To fund his activities Rathbun formed a private bank that issued its own notes. Caught up in the speculative excess of the rapidly growing city, he borrowed beyond his means, facilitated by his unknowing use of forged notes issued

I took a stroll through the city and went down to the docks. The long mole stretching across forms the harbour and is called the creek. In here are all maritime vessels thickly jammed in. The mighty steamer destined for the upper lakes [is] like a large two-story house floating upon the waters. Though some of these deserve the name of palaces, not the one however that I was destined to go on. Canal craft loading & unloading, square rigged & other craft bound for the lakes, &c. &c. [T]his is the great depot of the West and the quantity of produce & merchandise that passes through here is astonishing. It seems here more busy than the busiest part of South St., N.Y. Canal boats destined to carry their freights to New York are filling up with barrels of flour while the wharfs are crowded with it being inspected. Vessels are leaving the port for the lakes, their decks filled with immigrants and their holds with merchandise. All is life, activity & babel. Goods are being continually to the farthest point in our eastern states and to the farthest point in our western wilds, of all kinds, all sorts. Crowds of immigrants cumber the wharves, standing, lying, eating & drinking, & washing and waiting for the vessel in which they have engaged their passages to start. One of the huge steamers from Chicago comes puffing in with the unearthly bellow of high pressure. A crowd collects around the docks, cabs & hotel omnibuses, each one bellowing out the name of his hotel or carriage or the praises of the line he is runner for, and confusion becomes more confounded. The passengers get out as well as they can, their luggage is seized, hauled & struggled for, rival hotel keepers or dray men shout epithets and abuse upon each other extensively. An unlucky passenger unless he be very thorough in naming his hotel may thus be seized between two of these runners, each claiming him as "my man" and you will see some "green" one in great tribulation

---

by his brother Lyman bearing the names of affluent citizens. The scandal resulted in his arrest and imprisonment for five years, after which he returned to the hotel business in Buffalo. Ibid.; "Far Sighted Builder-Promoter Creates Vast Financial Empire," *Rathbun-Rathbone-Rathburn Family Historian* 2 (1982): 4–8; Gordon, *Gazetteer of the State of New York*, 443.

thus. Add to this, the steamer commences blowing of steam from its brazen throat and nearly drowns out every other sound. But still you can see mens lips & mouths showing evidently that they are being used to their utmost capacity. In coming up I came through one of the most miserable places in Buffalo, where the miserable people were as filthy as they knew how to be though in nothing to compare with some of the filthy streets I have been through in London, Dublin & other cities of Europe.

Buffalo appears like a new city and is one. The houses all appear as if lately made, the signs as if freshly painted & gilded, and so they are 30 years since and where this large city now is there stood scarcely a log cabin and now it numbers a population of [blank]. I took a ride around the city after engaging my [passage] in the Steamer *Bunker Hill* for Detroit, and after dinner, by the way at dinner table and close by me I saw a man that seems determined to be my perpetual annoyance. He is a sharp-nosed, sharp-featured fellow with one sharp eye; the other is extinct, and it seems as if there had not been a hotel on my route from Utica here, but I have not seen his meager face at nor on whose books. I have not seen his name. Wm. C. Boyd, Baltim[ore], confirmed the fellow there, he was close to me that one eye swung sharply around, lighting on me in a manner that showed he knew me while he was bolting his dinner. I went to the books. There was his name in full, just from Niagara. He seems to have come, though not in the same conveyance, and stopped at the same hotels. So it has been with a great many whom I have seen at Saratoga & with whom I seem to have come on in company to Niagara. I felt afraid that this fellow, who reminded me of the story of the Blue Dog, was going too, as far as St. Anthony. I had however the happiness of seeing him get into the omnibus for the eastern cars in the afternoon. I breathed more freely and when after getting on board the *Bunker Hill* and looking among the passengers I did not see his turn-up pointed nose and blind eye. I felt as if a free man again.[23]

------

23. The *Bunker Hill*, a steamboat propelled by a low-pressure beam engine, entered

Well, to my ride. I got a carriage to go up to the barracks where are three or four comp[anies] of infantry stationed and where I hoped to see a review, but was disappointed it was a[t] 7 instead of 9. The barracks are a little over a mile from the American, which is in about the center of the city and are of brick built around a square, in the center of which is the flag staff, and around it a little mound and seats for the band. A few soldiers were on guard in full uniform, but the greater part were in undress. We drove through the gateway around the flag staff and square, at one end [of which] some of the officers have dwelling, and came out again. A great many people were coming down the road on horseback, in gigs, waggons, & carriages. There had been a trotting match half a mile further out and all the idle vagabonds & well-dressed loafers had been there and were now returning.

I came home different way than I came (up the principal route), taking a little circuit and seeing thus some of the pretty country seats around in the environs, of which there are several and with very pretty grounds attached. Came back to tea. Several Locofocos near the hotel were engaged in putting up a huge hickory pole spliced in two places. I observed that all that were collected around it, perhaps 50, were nearly all foreigners and half did not talk English.[24]

---

service on the Great Lakes in 1837. In May of that year it was damaged in a collision with the *Cincinnati*, another steamboat, and towed to Cleveland for repairs. The following year the *Bunker Hill* ran aground on Long Point, Upper Canada (Ontario), but was safely recovered. "Bunker Hill," *Cleveland (OH) Daily Herald & Gazette*, May 13, 1837; "Fright and Valor," *Buffalo (NY) Commercial Advertiser*, Apr. 30, 1838; *Erie (PA) Observer*, May 12, 1838.

24. The Locofoco Party split from the national Democratic Party as a radical left wing. A working-class movement, its members opposed banks, monopolies, tariffs, and financial policies that they considered conducive to special privilege and opposed to laissez-faire and the rights of individuals. Organized in New York as the Equal Rights Party in 1835, the Locofoco Party attracted workers as well as reformers. Its influence peaked in 1840 with the passage of the federal Independent Treasury Act, which separated government from banking. Their influence declined in the following decade and remained largely confined to New York State. Edward Pessen, *Jacksonian*

Just before tea [the] hotel omnibus drove up from the Niagara st[eam]boat. In it was Dr. Webster & daughter, whom I was glad to see, and in company was one, who like the one-eyed man, seemed to have been on my track the whole way from Saratoga even. I had seen Luther Park, Jr's. name in every hotel book I had seen almost, and now Dr. Webster introduced me to Mr. Luther Park, Jr., who was a tall and slender young man apparently very devoted to Miss Webster. Inquiries and answers flowed thick and fast over our tea and their having heard of the welfare of some in whom I felt strong interest. I bid them adieu and with a godspeed was on my way to our steamer at the wharf which already began throwing up large columns of black smoke from her smoke pipes. The wharf of course was crowded with baggage, waggons, drays, carriages & men, women & children, the decks with emigrants & luggage. Bales, boxes, bundles and people were crowding upon the decks & porters were passing up trunks & boxes. Children were squealing & so were some women. Men were calling to each other and the bell was ringing. Dr. Forest was on the wharf and came on board. I shook hands with him.

The bell tolled & boys with apples and papers scampered off, so did men who were not going, the fastenings were thrown off with a hoarse bellow or rather growl, a jet of steam sprang into the air from the steam pipe and floated away in the vapor. The wheels slowly revolved, then another growl and we moved, another as we slowly left the wharf and threading our way through the vessels lying on each side [in] the channel and, with slow motion each revolution being accompanied with a roar of escaping steam, we passed between them, our puffs becoming more frequent & our motion quicker as we neared the outlet. We now rounded the lighthouse and came into the open lake.[25] Our boat commenced pitching in the short

America: Society, Personality, and Politics (Urbana: University of Illinois Press, 1985), 276–279; David S. Reynolds, *Waking Giant: America in the Age of Jackson* (New York: HarperCollins, 2008), 110–111.

25. The harbor of Buffalo lay at the mouth of Buffalo Creek, an outlet originally obstructed

seas that were running and the women already commenced growing pale. Some tried to look unconcernedly as the plunges of our vessel became more violent and frequent, & some tried to laugh & failed signally, and most looked forward to a rough night, and accompanying seasickness. And now our vessel was ful underway. The blasts of steam were regular and quicker and [I] could not help looking wonderingly at the steam pipe through whose brazen throat such strange sounds were emitted. It has something of the sound of a bass drum, though one [that] must be of colossal dimensions to make such a sound. This can be heard for the distance of ten miles and gives warning of the approach of the boat long before her bell could be heard. And now our colors were pulled down. Our yards were also sent down for our steamer (as all of them have) has two masts and sails. Buffalo with its glimmering light was directly in our wake and ahead of us the horizon was bounded by water. The stars glimmering overhead, the sun had set beautifully, seldom if ever have I seen a more gorgeous sunset than that was just above. Left the lighthouse. Heavy masses of dark clouds hung around the western horizon and as the sun set they were tinged with its rays beautifully and they were scattered through that mass of clouds as if the lightning with crimson fire were playing in zigzag course amongst it.

And so I paced the deck. We numbered in the cabin 50 or 60 passengers, none very remarkable for anything, a few women, none pretty and I saw nothing interesting in any of us. We had one or two hundred deck passengers, Norwegians, all of course in costume and chattering in a dialect unknown to me. All seemed to look alike, little bitty tow headed children with fat cheeks. The men with all the same flat caps, the same kind of jacket and trousers, also with red cheeks and tow heads, and goggle eyes trying to

---

by a sandbar. This obstacle was overcome by the construction of a mole and pier of wood and stone, extending fifteen hundred feet into the lake on the south side of the creek. A lighthouse at the head of the pier and a ship channel eighty feet wide and thirteen feet deep were completed by 1833. Gordon, *Gazetteer of the State of New York*, 441.

look over their fat cheeks. The women too have the same kind of uniform cap or headdress, the same jacket & buttons and same gowns whose waist reaches up to their armpits almost, huge shoes thickly studded with clout nails. And they stand on the lower deck all gazing & staring up at the steam pipe and wondering at its belching off steam in such a thunderous manner.

<u>Aug. 11, Sunday</u>. Here we are, out on Lake Erie. Out steamer goes roaring, grumbling & steaming onwards. There is a little motion, but not enough to make the women sick, though most of them were last night. I believe the day is fine, but appears little like Sunday. Some of the passengers talk politics, more read novels and a great many are talking & laughing in squads around and two are playing backgammon. I find we are miserably deceived in our boat. She is about a 4th class one, is old and this is her last trip before laying up for repairs which are much needed, her boilers being considered unsafe. This is a comfortable thing to know after getting away from port. We had a miserable breakfast and an equally miserable dinner, what they had bring ill cooked & ill served, cleanliness not being very apparent in any of it.

The passengers that I conversed with were to a man as dissatisfied as myself. Here we were, paying the same fare as in a first class boat and not being half as well accommodated [in] any way. About 12 n[oon] we went into Fairport for wood and I put my foot for the first time on the shores of Ohio. The *Illinois* was lying there for the same purpose as ourselves, bound for Buffalo from Chicago.[26] I went aboard of her & was much struck with the differences of her accommodations as compared with our own, everything showed neatness & taste & splendor even. She had apparently a good compliment of passengers. Fairport is a place of no note, there

---

26. Built in 1837, the *Illinois* was comparable to the *Great Western* on which Nehemiah and Nancy Sanford sailed in 1839. Both steamboats were considered the largest and finest of their day on the Great Lakes. "Passenger and Package Freight Steamers," Riverboat Dave's Paddlewheel Site, riverboatdaves.com.

being perhaps ten houses and two lighthouses here, one half of the former being taverns, which they call hotels, and nearly the other half stores. The wharf had many idlers upon it and many boys selling large, sweet apples & peaches. I walked up to a nice hill near to get a view of the country. I looked over the lake, but not much country, the woods bounding the prospect. There was a kind of brick school house where was a man in a black coat exhorting, very earnestly if one might judge from his voice, which was strong at about its highest pitch. We stayed here about an hour and then started off again, leaving the *Illinois* still lying at the dock.

We now coasted along the shores of the lake. The scenery is not very striking, sand banks stretching along the shore as far as the eye can reach, crowned with woodlands, a few such are seen here and there. We have had the wind fair enough part of the way to have sails out. Our captain is a short fellow with a glazed cap grey oval with huge pockets in it, who says nothing to anyone & does not even appear at dinner table. Above [the] end of our cabin is a room labeled "saloon." Here is a bar and a banker's chair and a black fellow, a barber, and a white one for bookkeeper, and also a wash stand where passengers may wash. This is our upper cabin and has staterooms with 8 berths each all around it. This enters into a kind of hall, or passageway, & then there is a ladies cabin, also with staterooms, and beyond that is the stern. Below is another cabin and the main deck. So we are literally two stories high above our main deck.

At 5 PM we reached Cleveland and remained there two hours, so that I had time to look over the city a little. The harbour, like Buffalo, is formed by moles or piers projecting out into the lake.[27] On the extremity is a light-house and on the hill is another. There were several square rigged vessels in port, principally hermaphrodite brigs. I saw one with British colours flying which [seemed] strange to me at such a place, though I suppose they

27. Cleveland's harbor, at the mouth of the Cayahoga River, was protected by piers extending twelve hundred feet into the lake. Warren Jenkins, *The Ohio Gazetteer and Traveler's Guide* (Columbus: Isaac N. Whiting, 1839), 126.

may have considerable trade with Canada now that their [goods] can be shipped through the Welland Canal.[28] Cleveland is perfectly situated on a bluff rising from the lake and which runs back till it meets the valley in which is the creek which forms partly their harbour, and their canal. It is laid out with broad streets, which are planted with trees. Their principal street is called Superior St. and is indeed so, having many fine buildings upon it. In the outskirts are many extremely pretty countryseats and an air of taste and neatness pervades the whole city. There are several squares, or greens, filled with trees and I observed many that I should suppose were vacant lots left open to the street and in which were growing plentifully the forest trees as nature had planted them, principally oak. These seen in different places gave an appearance of freshness & of something rural that was delightful. None of the houses seemed to be crowded together, but each had generally its little yard in which were growing fruit & shade trees. This was more especially the case with the largest residences and some of them were almost concealed amongst the trees and flowers which surround them.

We left Cleveland at 7, I certainly being much pleased with it. I observed in one part of it a large circular brick building & inquired what it was. It was the Millerite Tabernacle, its only light being from the top and was no means a contemptible building. Brothers Miller & Hine I saw advertised to preach, so it seems that their furor respecting 2nd Advent is not yet over.[29] A lank haired, ill-looking sort of fellow rejoicing in the name of

---

28. The Welland Canal was constructed between 1824 and 1833 through Upper Canada (Ontario) as a water route connecting Lake Ontario with Lake Erie, bypassing Niagara Falls. The St. Lawrence Seaway Management Corporation, *The Welland Canal Section of the St. Lawrence Seaway* (Cornwall, Ontario: St. Lawrence Seaway Authority, 2003), 2–3.

29. The Millerite Movement was a nineteenth-century American Christian sect founded by William Miller, a Calvinistic Baptist who became obsessed with the possible second coming of Christ. On the basis of elaborate calculations he determined that the Second Advent would occur in 1843 and began preaching. In 1840 he met the

Smith left the boat at Cleveland and I found like most downeasters he was much better than he looked, and was a downright sensible fellow. He had been conversing with the interpreter of the emigrants on board and gave me the result of his conference. It seems these are Norwegians, part of a company of two ship loads, which have just come over and who came on in squads of about 200 at a time. Those that we took on board the *North American* at NY were part of these same people. A company of them, it seems, is formed who have sent out agents to this country to purchase land and having purchased one of the most beautiful tracts in Illinois to the number of many thousand acres have gone home again & returned in company with their people. About a thousand have just come over and more are coming, 2 or 3,000 in all, I think. All are Lutherans and they bring out with them their priests and schoolmasters, their interpreters and [assign] one of each to each squad and are going on to make the bone and sinew of our country. All of them, in spite of their squalid appearance, bring money & some of them no inconsiderable an amount and they will all get well & better off. They are, the interpreter says, a very industrious, hard working & saving people. [An] Instance [of] the latter [occurred] at Fairport [where] we should have had to stay one and a half or two hours to get in wood. The interpreter merely pointed with his hand to the wood pile, indicating thus to the emigrants what was wanted, when they set out to, and in half an hour all the wood was on board and we were ready to start. They have bought no provisions he says, since they have left home having brought it with them. He gave me a specimen of their bread. It is a thin cake, say $\frac{1}{16}$ to $\frac{1}{8}$th of an inch thick, made from oats ground straw

---

Reverend Joshua Himes, who became his publicity agent, manager, and promoter. His movement grew as the Millennial year approached, but began to lose favor when the Advent did not occur as predicted. When Miller predicted a new date in October 1844, excitement revived among the faithful, who flocked to the standard of their preachers and awaited the chosen day. When the day passed uneventfully, the movement declined rapidly and its leaders faded into obscurity. Alice Felt Tyler, *Freedom's Ferment: Phases of American Social History from the Colonial Period to the Outbreak of the Civil War* (New York: Harper & Row, 1944), 70–78.

and all, and birch bark, made into a paste, rolled out into thin cakes and lightly baked. They are from the northwestern part of Norway and are accustomed to hard fare. He told of kind of fish that they depended much on for subsistence, the oil being used either for butter on their bread or for burning. Six pence a day here, he says, will give them better fare than they have ever had before in their lives, and what they would consider great luxuries. They will make good bulwarks. I shall preserve that piece of bread as a great curiosity, which it certainly is.

──────────────────

I made a pleasant acquaintance while at Cleveland. I had observed during the day two young ladies who looked as though they might be from some country town down East, one of whom (they were both good looking) had particularly large blue eyes and black hair[,] and very pretty countenances. Just before we left Cleveland I managed to get in conversation with them and got quite interested in the blue eyed one. She was nothing loth & looked at me most bewitchingly with those big blue eyes of hers. I drew out by little and little their account of themselves. They were from New Jersey going West. One of them had lived there several years, the other (my favorite) was going there for the first time in company with three men, their relations, and in a little private conversation with her found that none bore the dearer relation of husband, to my great satisfaction. We got to be, as the evening wore on, great friends and as we leaned over the bulwarks and chatted on all manner of things. I felt like and old acquaintance and made no scruple in taking her hand (twas not small but one of your hearty, good, honest hands) in mine and telling her how much pleased I was in meeting so interesting a young person as herself. She returned the compliment in full, gave me her own story and wanted mine, said she had two brothers and three sisters, no father no mother, should spend a few weeks in Michigan & then return. When she found I had been abroad she was all curiosity, asked about everything, bussed me to the light in order to examine my plaid which I had on, put her arm (I showing her how) within mine in order to see how warm my plaid kept it, and then we sat down and chatted away till the rain commenced, falling from a black cloud which had been rising rapidly, and after the repeated instigation of her companion she wished me good night with a roll of those large blue eyes and a turn that was running in my head & in my dreams (in which she played a conspicuous part) for a good part of the night. She was a most artless, unsophisticated girl, who hearing events on paper and kept her journal, had got two sheets written almost, she said, had a gold watch and seemed well educated in other matters, some knowledge of the world. They were going to, I have forgotten the place, about forty miles west of Detroit and go in the cars tomorrow morning. I wish twas the next day, for I would like those girls well for companions part of the way.

<u>Detroit, Aug. 12</u>. This morning when I woke up we were already in the straits. I hurried on my clothes and went on deck. It was a beautiful morning and the water was like a mirror. The shores narrowed as we advanced and presented a very pretty approach, being lined with houses and cultivated lands. I soon joined my companion of last evening and we leaned over the stern and observed what we passed and chatted away briskly. She wanted my name she said and where I was from. So I took out a card and inscribed "Derby, Ct." under my name, gave it to her and asked her to give me her card and, sitting herself down and making a desk of her lap, she wrote her name and I deposited her card carefully away. Here is her name as write, "Matilda Pharr, Barnegat, New Jersey." But that would not do for her. She took out her little journal, asked me to transcribe there my name & where from & whether going or here coming back. I did so and there it will without doubt be preserved for future generations. I was just telling her here I hoped we should meet again and how interested I had been in her company &c. when the engine stopped and we found ourselves at the wharf in Detroit. Her friends came & hurried her off and I lost what I had been looking forward to with pleasant anticipation, a sweet parting. And here we were at Detroit. Runners from all the hotels were at

the gangway calling out with leathern lungs and brazen throat the names of their respective hotels and all was babel and confusion.

Near us being repaired lay the steamer *Gen. Vance*, which has blown up and the capt[ain] and 3 men killed. A man near me said he was in her, that the boiler burst in the bottom and the vessel sank in five minutes. Her bottom and sides were much shattered.[30] The Canadian side looked very thrifty and well settled. On the wharves on our side were huge storehouses owned by forwarding merchants, by whom & through which a heavy business is done. I went up to the National Hotel—got a good breakfast, met Gen. Gould of Rochester, dressed myself & went out to view the city and deliver a letter of introduction.[31] The city looks thriving, the streets are wide but need keeping in better repair, and being situated low in wet weather are very muddy. Buildings & blocks of houses are divine put up around and the place looks very busy, not so much however as Buffalo. The Cleveland steamer had just got in and I went on board of her, she being, and deservedly so, one of the crack boats.

Thence I went to deliver my letter. Mr. Dorr, to whence it was addressed,

------

30. On June 26, 1844, the steamboat *Gen. Vance* departed Detroit for Toledo via Windsor, Upper Canada (Ontario). Just as the boat stopped at the wharf at Windsor, the boiler exploded and the forward part immediately sank. Four persons were killed, including the captain, S. D. Woodworth. "Awful Explosion," *Buffalo (NY) Commercial Advertiser*, June 27, 1844.

31. Henry Sanford's parents had stayed at the National Hotel five years earlier. By 1844 it was under new management by Edward Lyon, who refurnished the hotel in 1840. Silas Farmer, *History of Detroit and Wayne County and Early Michigan* (Detroit: Gale Research, 1969), 482. Jacob Gould was born in Boxford, Massachusetts in 1794 and came to Rochester, New York, in 1819 as a shoemaker and leather dealer. He was elected a captain in an artillery company of the New York state militia an later appointed a major general by Gov. Dewitt Clinton. He was elected the city's second mayor in 1836 and served in other public offices, including customs collector and US marshal. Gen. Gould was also an officer with several banks the railroads and an associate of Presidents Martin Van Buren and John Tyler. John Devoy, *A History of the City of Rochester from the Earliest Times* (Rochester, NY: Post Express Printing Co., 1895), 151.

I found in one of those large white ware or storehouses before spoken of & who received me very kindly, offered me letters to the other places on my route and, as I had a little business to transact, said he would call in half an hour at my hotel and ride round the city with me.[32] I went thence to the State House, a building looking much like a New England meeting house, to find the Secretary of State to get some patents for lands. I found him inclined in a huge arm chair on one side of which both before & behind were strapped to large horse pistols in cases ready for use. Why then I could not divine as I could not suppose they were the insignia of his office. Mr. Dorr came agreeably to appointment and rode out with me to see the city. The Roman Catholics have now two churches here and he showed me where they were building two more, one of them to be the finest building in all Detroit I should think—a cathedral—for they have [a] bishop here.

Detroit was, as everyone knows, a French settlement. There are many French families here at present and French is very considerably spoken here. The way their land is divided is curious. Each of the settlers had their farms laid out fronting on the river & running back 3 miles. As they have died, they left their farms to their children and when the farms had to be divided into two or three parts, they always divided it in lengthwise so that by continual division some of the farms have very narrow fronts, some of them a front of not more than an acre square, but still running back the original three miles. There are some very pretty country seats around the town. The French ones however not remarkable. The land looks well and yet that which the French still hold is not very productive

---

32. This individual was likely Melvin Dorr, a well-known and influential Detroit attorney. Dorr came to the city as early as 1820, when he was appointed city marshal, Detroit's chief constable, and one of two supervisors of Detroit Township, overseeing roads. He also became clerk of the Territorial Supreme Court, an office he held until 1822. In an attempt to regulate retail sales by individuals, the city appointed him auctioneer in 1823. The following year he was appointed an associate justice of the county court and became its chief justice in 1828. Dorr was one of three property assessors appointed in 1828 and served as a street commissioner for Detroit's Fourth Ward in 1829. Farmer, *History of Detroit*, 142, 164, 192, 186, 202, 770, 933, 935.

& for a very obvious reason. Mr. Dorr says that when he first came here the French would in the winter take the pains to cart their manure onto the ice in winter in order to have it carried off in the spring. The more slack farmers still would, as the manure accumulated around their shanties or barns, move them off to another place and then again in due time move them again.

We passed "Bloody Run," a place known for a most sanguinary battle between Pontiac & some of our troops, in which nearly all of the latter were slain. The Indians lay concealed under and around the bridge and waiting till the troops had marched over, caught them in ambuscade and prevented their escape to the fort & made terrible slaughter and hence the name of the stream which seemed then to actually run blood. It is now nearly dried up.[33] Mr. Dorr pointed out the prettiest residences as we passed on, telling their owners' names. I found that our Army officers had some of the prettiest residences.

On returning, he pointed out Gen. [Lewis] Cass's residence, a good sized wooden two-story house with a pretense to elegance placed sweetly on the street without yard in front. He lives however in great elegance & style and is quite wealthy, owning as he does the original farm of his ancestors, which has now become very valuable. In 1836 he sold a portion running down to the water's edge to a company for $20,000 & they extended some upon it in grading, building wharves, storehouses, &c. and were to pay the interest on the cost & the principal any time in 20 years. When the great crash came on, many were unable to pay the interest and as it had been

---

33. The Battle of Bloody Run occurred on July 21, 1763, at Parent Creek. It involved an attack by forces under Pontiac, an Ottawa leader, on a British relief column sent to break the Indians' siege of Fort Detroit. In the one-sided battle the British were defeated with heavy losses and retreated to the fort. Timothy J. Todish and Todd E. Harburn, *A "Most Troublesome Situation": The British Military and the Pontiac Indian Uprising of 1763–1764* (Fleischmanns, NY: Purple Mountain Press, 2006), 76–84; "Battle of Bloody Run Informational Historic Marker: P25,024, Listed August 23, 1956," Detroit1701, www.detroit1701.org.

divided up among the individuals of the company, many were glad to lose what had been expended and have Gen. Cass take it back. He did so to those who were unable to pay, at the same time holding on to those who were able & who all have been willing to have given up their right. So he has now the best part of the land back with the improvements upon it and is at present well worth all that he sold it for, and what has been laid out upon it. Nearby is seen the old house in which the family formerly lived & which they preserve out of pride I suppose. Mr. Dorr says that when the General left it for his present residence it looked just as old and dilapidated as at present. It is an old, <u>very</u> old-fashioned house more than a century old I should think, and was in those days called a good farm house. But at present I would not put cattle I valued in it for fear that it might tumble down upon them. Gen. Cass is quite wealthy. Think Mr. Dorr estimated his property here at ½ million alone. The street running by his house is called Cass St. He is not very popular in state or city it would seem, as he has not been able to command the vote of either of their elections.[34]

Nearby is the site of the old fort which Gen. Hull surrendered. The people have not so much pride or desire to keep the fort as a memento of past days, and without a guide one could not find the site of it even now. New buildings are covering the ground it once occupied and only one

---

34. One of most important Michigan politicians of the nineteenth century, Lewis Cass served in the Ohio militia during the War of 1812 and rose to the rank of general. In recognition of his military service, President James Madison appointed Cass governor of Michigan Territory in 1813, a post he held until 1831, when he resigned to become secretary of war under Andrew Jackson. During his tenure as governor he successfully negotiated several treaties transferring the lands of Michigan's Native inhabitants to the United States, and his support of removal helped shape American Indian policy. He was also instrumental in the promoting the territory's settlement through the construction of roads, formation of local government in newly occupied areas, and the creation of a public school system. Following an unsuccessful bid for the Democratic presidential nomination in 1844, he represented the state of Michigan in the US Senate from 1845 until 1857, when he became secretary of state under James Buchanan. Willis F. Dunbar, *Lewis Cass* (Grand Rapids, MI: William B. Eerdmans, 1970), 21–39.

building remains of the whole, that one of the cantonments. Mr. Dorr pointed out where was the fort, where the stockades, where the gateway &c. directly on the site of this last is a very pretty residence with yard garden, &c. all very pretty attached built by a late surgeon of the Army.

I went back to my hotel to dinner, found Gen. Gould there again. He introduced me to some of his acquaintances & I had pleasant company. The landlord was obliging again a very good dinner & good rooms. In the afternoon I took a horse and buggy and started for a ride in the other direction than this morning's. [A] very pleasant one it was too, along the banks of the strait or river. On Canada side were apparently pretty residences & wide cultivated grounds, & two or three steeples showed themselves, one old church looking antiquated enough to have built by the first settlers was being supplanted by a fine brick Gothic church erecting nearby. I stopped at Mr. Dorr's residence about a mile or two from the city, the grounds around which are very tastefully laid out & looked very prettily. A pretty child came to the door and showed me in. Mr. Dorr came in, introduced me to his wife & invited me to tea. I took my departure in order to visit a fort which is being erected about two miles below his residence.[35] My ride down was pleasant, laying along the banks of the stream. The fort will be a fine one and is in a good situation so as to command the entrance I should think. The other barracks will be removed when this is finished. It was the intention of the builders to have had the outworks of the earth turfed over & sloping down outwardly, but so sandy is the soil that it was found impossible to keep the earth from sliding down. They are now getting

---

35. As a result of concern regarding a possible invasion from British-controlled Upper Canada following the Patriot Rebellion of 1837, the US government authorized the construction of a series of defenses along the US-Canadian border in 1841. Fort Wayne on the Detroit River, named for Revolutionary War general "Mad" Anthony Wayne, was a star fort begun 1843. Following its completion in 1851, the work remained unused by the military until 1861. Kathryn Bishop Eckert, *Buildings of Michigan* (New York: Oxford University Press, 1993), 95.

large timbers, soaking them in [word omitted], which gives the wood the durability of iron and by this means they will make the walls of sand more stable. There were many shanties for Irish around who were engaged in working on the fort.

After viewing the works and riding on a mile or so, I returned to Mr. Dorr's. Here I met Capt. Hazard & wife & wife's sister and had an agreeable time of it. Mr. Dorr showed me around his grounds, which are in fine order. He has a fine hothouse and showed me more than a hundred varieties of the cactus. They had many fine peach trees, all of which burdened down with fruit, are but five years from the seed. He has fine locusts, on bean trees, for shade to his house & which will near reach to the ridge pole & which were five years ago in the seed from which he plants them. His house is a log cabin that was, but is sided & sealed up so that but for the low ceiling it would be an advantage from its warmth in winter. He has made additions to it & so has [become] a very pleasant and commodious dwelling house. The coffee I drank here showed me, as I told Mr. Dorr, that I was near the French, for it was the hot cup of coffee I think I have drank on of France. Capt. Hazard was of the *Cleveland* st[eam]boat which was to leave at 6_, so we started away early. I went on board the boat, which is low pressure, and a fine one & full of passengers. This is a favorite boat, though some of the other boats excel it in splendor. I then went up to the hotel, left my buggy & got into the omnibus and went down again with Gen. Gould to introduce him to the captain, as he was going off in her. The steamboat was crowded with passengers. Mr. Lyon, our landlord, had never seen it more so. And she went off in gallant style.[36] I walked round the city, bought some fishing tackle, came home and went to bed. I don't see how people can think of putting travelers on feather beds in this weather.

---

36. The steamboat *Cleveland* was launched at Huron, Ohio, on June 24, 1837. Its deck measured 180 feet in length and 28 in breadth. The cabin occupied nearly the entire length of the deck, with accommodations for two hundred passengers. "Another New Steamboat," *Cleveland (OH) Weekly Advertiser*, Oct. 6, 1836; "Steam Boat Launch," *Cleveland (OH) Daily Herald & Gazette*, June 22, 1837.

<u>Aug. 13th, Tuesday.</u> Up and breakfasted at 7 and off in the cars at half past seven. Cars are poor, speed better. Had for companion my roommate on board the *Bunker Hill*. There were few passengers. The road lay through some cultivated lands & through much woods & swampy do. Nothing material happened till we arrived at Marshall, and here our arrival was something material to the town folks. Half the town apparently having assembled to see us come in, this being the second time the cars had come in there. Heretofore they had stopped at Albion, ten miles back, but now they had got their rails laid through to Marshall, or at least part of the way, for part of the distance we came on wood.[37] Fences too were thrown across the track and the conductor would get off, let down the fence & whenever had got through put it up again. Ypsilanti and Ann Arbour are pretty places which we passed though.[38] At the former is I believe an arsenal, at the latter

37. From its beginnings as a sawmill site in 1830, Marshall grew rapidly and became the seat of Calhoun County. In 1836 this milling and retailing center had a wide regional market and was an important dispersion point for immigration in western Michigan. It became a center for missionary activity by several Protestant denominations and was headquarters of the Presbyterian Home Missionary Society. Douglas H. Gordon and George S. May, eds., "The Michigan Land Rush, Michigan Journal, 1836, John M. Gordon," *Michigan History* 43 (1959): 131; George N. Fuller, *Economic and Social Beginnings of Michigan: A Study of the Settlement of the Lower Peninsula during the Territorial Period, 1805–1837* (Lansing, MI: Wynkoop Hallenbeck Crawford, 1916), 340–342; Elijah H. Pilcher, *Protestantism in Michigan: Being a Special History of the Methodist Episcopal Church* (Detroit: R. D. S. Taylor, 1878), 292–293; Daniel R. Campbell, "Village and the World: The Shaping of Culture in Marshall, Michigan" (PhD dissertation, Michigan State University, 1986). Albion, situated on the Kalamazoo River, was a relatively new village with saw- and gristmills, several stores, and about forty dwellings. John T. Blois, *1838 Gazetteer of the State of Michigan* (Knightstown, IN: Bookmark, 1979), 247. The Central Railroad was opened as far as Albion on June 25, 1844, but did not reach Marshall until August 12, the day before Henry's arrival. Graydon M. Meints, "Michigan Railroad Construction, 1835–1875" (Ann Arbor: Transportation Library, University of Michigan, 1981, typewritten), 6. Apparently the railroad operated on the wooden rails before the iron strap rail was installed.

38. Ann Arbor, the seat of Washtenaw County and the home of the University of Michigan, lay on the Territorial Road leading from Detroit to the Kalamazoo Valley.

a university. At Jackson is a prison, at Marshall, which is a pretty town enough, we waited an hour or two without much reason and were finally glad at 6 or 7_ to get under way.[39]

Stages are shameful. In past, passengers were carried through here from Detroit to Chicago for $6.50, thus running serious opposition to the boats. Now the boats are all combined and all called the "Combination," and of course this affected them. So they bought the st[eam]boat running in connection with the stages from St. Joseph to Chicago and warrant the stages 10 passengers each way, or in other words $100, on condition of their charging $10 each way. The consequence has been that travel has been much diminished. When sometimes seven stage loads went through, but one or two go now. The stages have to wait for the mail, the cars taking it no farther than Jackson, so it comes on from there by stage, hence their waiting an hour or two at Marshall and moving slow over the roads to Kalamazoo. The mail however only caught us up at Kalamazoo, 36 miles

---

Settled by the mid-1820s, Ann Arbor grew rapidly to become one of the principal regional centers in eastern Michigan. In addition to milling and retail businesses, it housed public offices, banks, and religious institutions. By 1840 its population was estimated to be two to three thousand. Gordon and May, "The Michigan Land Rush," 265; Ezra D. Lay, "Condensed Early History, or Beginnings of the Several Towns in Washtenaw County," *Michigan Pioneer and Historical Collections* 17 (1890): 462; Lansing B. Swan, *Journal of a Trip to Michigan in 1841* (Rochester, NY: George P. Humphrey, 1904), 18; Blois, *Gazetteer*, 248–249; Kenneth E. Lewis, *West to Far Michigan: Settling the Lower Peninsula, 1815–1860* (East Lansing: Michigan State University Press, 2002), 201, 203, 207, 209–210.

39. The county seat of Jackson grew remarkably as a milling, retailing, and manufacturing center and as the site of the new state prison. It also possessed links to a growing network of emerging frontier settlements. Jackson's growth as an industrial and manufacturing center was further aided by the availability of leased prison labor. *History of Jackson County, Michigan* (Chicago: Inter-State Publishing Co., 1881), 18, 216, 238; Blois, *Gazetteer*, 304–305; Richard Arthur Santer, "Historical Geography of Jackson, Michigan: A Study on the Changing Character of an American City, 1829–1969" (PhD dissertation, Michigan State University, 1970), 75–76, 97, 103–105; Swan, *Journal of a Trip*, 20; James H. Lanman, *History of Michigan, Civil and Topographical, in a Compendious Form with a View of the Surrounding Lakes* (New York: E. French, 1839), 287, 289.

beyond Marshall. The roads were bad, deep ruts & mud holes in them so that very often the stages (there were two) left the road & went through the oak openings, the tree branches rushing into the windows loaded with wet (for it was now raining). The top leaked too. We jolted confoundedly and I made up my mind for a miserable night. Twas impossible to sleep. Toward 9 o'clock we came near to running over an Indian, who naked & drunk was lying across the road. It seems he had been robbed by another Indian with whom he had been traveling in company and was half dead. The other stage, which had less passengers, took him in & left him at the next house. I was glad when we arrived in Kalamazoo. Our stage rattled in, making an infernal racket. The mail came up with us here and each driver, armed with a tin horn, made a music that made me laugh absolutely, sometimes their long winded blasts would accord together and then again make horrible dissonance, & so we rattled through the town & stopped at the Kalamazoo House. Here I gladly left the stage (it was now 3 o'clock AM) and, finding there was one small room in the house, & quickly took myself to it where a fellow traveler & myself each took to bed. They were both feather beds of course and were soon sound asleep.[40]

Aug. 14, Wednesday. Woke up at half past six by their account. Breakfast, which was four times as large as need be, and as I could not get to sleep again got up and eat a poor breakfast and after that walked around the town. Kalamazoo is a very pretty town. It was built upon an oak opening, as they call the land here, which has a moderate growth of oak upon it,

---

40. Erected by Cyrus and Ira Burdick in 1832, the Kalamazoo House was a hotel and boardinghouse that fed the public day and night. Many early residents boarded there upon arrival, and the house was especially crowded when the land office opened. In 1835 Emmor and Caroline Hawley took charge of the Kalamazoo House. David Fisher and Frank Little, eds., _Compendium of History and Biography of Kalamazoo County, Mich._ (Chicago: A. W. Bowen, 1906), 57, 65, 293; Samuel W. Durant, _History of Kalamazoo County, Michigan_ (Philadelphia: Everts & Abbott, 1880), 214; Kalamazoo Ladies Library Association, _Quarter Centennial Celebration of the Settlement of Kalamazoo, Michigan_ (Kalamazoo: Gazette Print, 1855), 48.

which is the prettiest land in the state and the people have good sense and taste enough to leave the oak trees standing in their yards and streets, and it makes a pleasant appearance. I went to the court house on some business & could not help remarking what I have observed in every town in Michigan, that the court house seems built on the same model as their churches. For example, near the courthouse stood a church and both were alike. Had the door of the court house not been open I should have been at a loss to know which was which. I went to the land office on business. What a confusion it puts my head into to talk of towns, sections & ranges by numbers so! Kalamazoo has in front of the hotel and within 30 rods space I should think no less than five so called Liberty Poles, two hickory & two ash & one something else. Politics rage as high here as any where. I observe that the bloated bar room politicians are always Locos. The travelers I have so far met with seem to be Whigs. I haven't found one Loco.

After looking around the town I got a horse and buggy and started for Texas [Township], so called, the residence or rather where resides Mr. Booth, our land agent. My ride was a pleasant one. I turned off the road and then turned off again, each time changing the aspect of the country somewhat, that is from cultivated fields to those just cleared and fenced & presently to those that were in a state of nature. The country was pretty, the houses I passed principally log, though now and then in the more cultivated parts the old log house might be converted into a stable, while the new frame house, painted white and set jauntily near the road side proclaimed in strong terms the thrift and success of the occupant.

My last turn off was through openings where as yet no fences had been placed, where the plow had never been. It was very pleasant riding so and it seemed like riding through the grounds of some gentleman who had bestowed much pains in planting trees and seeking smooth grounds. I could, if I liked and did so some of the time, turn off from the trail and ride over the smooth ground where one would be at some difficulty to find a stone. And under the shade of these fine oak trees, the vista on all sides being of trees throwing up their trunks nobly to form a canopy overhead, no underbrush beneath and no place to be seen where I could not drive easily. I finally, at 7 miles from Kalamazoo, found Mr. Booth's house. This was one of the better sort, a good size (for these parts) frame house, a picket fence stretched part of the way around it and was apparently being continued and finished as the owner had leisure. I went in and was shown by one of the sons into their front room. The threadbare "Brussels" carpet in the passage & rooms, the faded rug & many other things were evidence of former prosperity. The last time I was in his house was in Stratford [Connecticut], where they were living in as good style as anybody in the place, and that was handsomely. I now found him in a wilderness almost, with but one neighbor in ¾ of a mile of circuit, turned farmer and with his boys working grubbing at the soil. He had come here ignorant of farming or work and was now a grey bearded man serving his apprenticeship at it. His wife, brought up amidst refinement, ease & plenty, here found herself exposed to hardships she never before thought of experiencing. Mr. Booth soon appeared while I was thinking over these things and gave me a hearty welcome. Mrs. Booth too came in & glad enough was she to see anyone from so near home and had many inquiries to make. She had much to do & I went out & talked with her as she was cutting up pumpkins to boil for dinner. And here she was with 15 or 20 in her family and no help providing for the whole and doing it in a way as if she had been brought up to it and had never been a fine lady or thrummed the piano or studied French & Italian, &c. Yes, she went right at it & with a will too. Her boys, hearty looking youngsters enough, had grow[n] fat and healthy here, but were nevertheless wishing they were well away from Michigan. "Would you like to go back to Stratford?" asked I of one of the boys. "Yes <u>siree</u>," (the yes siree everybody here understands as the most expressive of all affirmatives). Mr. Booth proposed going around with me to look at our lands and while my horse was feeding took me over his grounds to show me what he was doing. He has been here a little over 2 years and has not yet got very much land under improvement. His corn & oats looked very well, though our farmers would not like so many stumps as one sees in the fields here. These however the farmers here care less for than the "grubs" which they take much pains to eradicate.

———————

But I may as well commence at the beginnings of a farmer's life, viz., he first chooses his land. It has been the <u>fashion</u> among the farmers generally to choose oak openings in preference to any other lands, principally because the land requires less labor to render it fit for cultivation. The soil on the heavy timbered lands is generally stronger & richer, but is of course of much greater toil to clear off. It has always been the custom among the Indians to burn over the prairies & grounds generally every year on account of the ground, I suppose. Hence it is that the oak openings are as free from underbrush, the annual fires destroying all the sprouts and leaving a smooth turf under the trees. The roots of these sprouts, called grubs, nevertheless remain and will continually send forth sprouts unless the fires keep them under, so that in the more thickly-settled parts, where the farmers cannot burn over their openings on account of their fences, the sprouts increase amazingly and would in a few years make a dense forest. After having two or three years' start so they become almost impenetrable, or at least unpleasant for men to traverse and become great places of resort for wolves. Much of the land which in 1830 looked as beautiful to the speculators who were heading here is, now the Indians are away, being covered with sprouts & presents by no means so pleasant a landscape.

These grubs are the bane of the farmer. He has to [go] over the land and carefully exterminate every one, which requires much labor. They were at work here at it now. Two or three other men with axes cut and dig at every grub they could find. A strong team & plow followed to break up the ground and then every root was sought for & pulled up. This probably costs about $3 per acre; cutting the tress costs about $1.50 per acre, so that the farmer requires some outlay to make his farm fit for cultivation. Wood of course is plenty here. Mr. Booth says he would thank any man that would come and cut down trees for him, for the trees, and says he would help him draw them away. Very little of the timber in these openings is good for

anything but rails and ashes.[41] The continual fires that have yearly overrun
the land having made them unsound so that few trees of any size can be
found that are not unsound, and any gale of wind overthrows many which
break off at the roots. Farmers, it is now found, consequently do better in
heavy timbered lands. If the timber will not sell, the ashes alone that he
can get from the trees he cuts will be sufficient to support his family for
the first year, ashes commanding at any of the stores 10 or 12¢ per bushel.
The farmer gets moreover better soil after he gets his land cleared up.
The soil on the openings is lighter [and] sour, the continued burnings &
deposits of ashes forming an alkali that is not of benefit to it. I don't see
how farmers can live here. Wheat brings 37½ or 40¢ per bushel, oats from
8 to 12½¢ & potatoes what you can get for them, which is most nothing.
Corn not much better.

The road had ended at Mr. Booth's house, so we went through a gate and
soon struck a "trail" that led through the openings. The ride was delightful
among those fine oak trees and over the smooth ground below. I know of
nothing that can be more delightful to a lover of nature than a ride through
these openings, the ground gently undulating gives no monotony and then
is a feast for the eyes. Flocks of pigeons would now and then start from the
ground and, alighting on some neighboring tree, watch us as we passed
beneath apparently knowing no fear.[42] A road is very easily made here,

---

41. Settlers from the Northeast brought with them the knowledge of potash making, an
    important forest industry and one of the few marketable products available to pioneer
    farmers while clearing land. As the by-product of clearing hardwood forests, ashes
    were worked up into "black salts," which formed the basic ingredient for potash,
    and its purified derivative, pearl ash. Both were used in soap- and glass-making and
    medicines and constituted the major component of saleratus, a leavening agent.
    Black salts shipped to Buffalo and Chicago to be made into saleratus often returned
    to Michigan to raise the pancakes of frontier residents. Lewis, *West to Far Michigan*,
    163; William Barillas, "Michigan's Pioneers and the Destruction of the Hardwood
    Forest," *Michigan Historical Review* 15 (1989): 15.
42. These were undoubtedly passenger pigeons (*Ectopistes migratorius*), or "wild
    pigeons" that existed in large numbers in Michigan until well after the Civil War,

no stones, no sand, no underbrush, and a person feels at liberty to make a new trail if he likes not the old one. It's like riding over the turf in some English park, only the trees are not so large, the fires not allowing them to grow rapidly. Mr. Booth said by counting the rings he has found some of the trees that I had judged to be 30 or 40 years old to be 100 & over.

We soon emerged from our trail onto the highway for Schoolcraft, which was so designated by the letter A blazed on all the trees on either side of the road and was laid out in a straight line, and all the trees cut down that stood in the way so that we often had to turn around stumps in our path. Mud holes too became frequent and had to be turned out for as their abrupt sinkings in the ground would give one a severe jolt unless prepared for it. Our way lay through Prairie Round [Ronde], the largest one in Michigan, and a very beautiful one it is, all under cultivation, each farm having its neat house attached and everything looked thrifty. The soil here is very rich, absolutely black, as if black paint was a component part of it, and it rears such crops! There was scarce a field laid out that was less than 40 acres and oftener a "Lot" is 80 acres, some 160. There is much good arising from this manner of dividing land here, if it only makes the fields square. One can never find a field in all Michigan where the fences do not terminate at right angled, quite different from what one sees in Connecticut. There is a singular thing in this prairie, it is about 8 miles by 6, perfectly smooth, level & free from trees, but in place just about in the center is a place called the "Island," and well named so. It is about a mile in circumference and is densely wooded. It is a knoll or rising ground and in the center is a beautiful lake. The subsoil in the prairie is clay. In the

---

but human exploitation and habitat destruction resulted in their extinction. Jerome A. Jackson and Bette J. S. Jackson, "Once upon a Time in American Ornithology: Extinction; The Passenger Pigeon, Last Hopes, Letting Go," *Wilson Journal of Ornithology* 119 (2007): 769–770; William Brewster, "The Present State of the Wild Pigeon (*Ectopistes migratorius*) as a Bird of the United States, with Some Notes on Its Habits," *The Auk: A Quarterly Journal of Ornithology* 6 (1889): 286–287; Charles D. Stewart, "The Pigeon Trap," *Wisconsin Magazine of History* 24 (1940): 20–24.

Island it is coarse gravel. Around the prairie are oak openings except in the southwest, where is thick timbered land. This is, Mr. B. says, always the case[—]on the SW of a prairie is always heavy timber.

We stopped a short time at Schoolcraft, which is a pretty village near the center of the prairie. Twas rather bleak here in the winter, the wind having full sweep. The farmers have however long rows of trees, principally the sugar maple, planted around many of their dwellings & lands & will serve a double object, to raise sugar & protect themselves. Some peach trees were seen, but the late frost has spoiled the fruit. The apple trees looked remarkably thrifty. I know not where I have seen more flourishing trees, the bark perfectly smooth and absolutely <u>shone</u> as if soaped. The farmers were busily engaged in threshing & getting in the crops. We passed one 100 acre wheat field where they had just commenced harvesting it, and it would astonish a Yankee farmer to see how expeditiously it was done. They had a large machine drawn by 8 pair of horses. This went round and round the field, the horses going at a fast walk. At the end of this machine, on a platform, stood a man holding bags under a spout into which the wheat was pouring fast enough to fill the bag in a very few minutes, say 5 or less. A team followed behind and took the bags as soon as filled. So here was a machine cutting, threshing & winnowing all alone but at the rate of 400 bushels per day, or over 200 acres of ground! We saw the threshing machine at work around many of the stacks. The grain is all stacked generally near the center of the field. Here the threshing machines come and turned by 4 pair of horses thresh out 400 bushels per diem. I saw another contrivance moving over the fields. This was a large waggon drawn by 2 pair of horses. It moved around the fields taking in bundles of grain. The wheels turned the machinery so that this thing threshed & winnowed its 400 bushels a day. It would astonish our farmers to see the huge stacks of wheat and how they vanish under the power of these machines. The heavy crops too would make him envy these easy farmers, though he probably would think he could take better care of them. The farmers here live very easily, don't consider it necessary to see the sun rise, or take much pains with their ground. Manure is unnecessary. He scratches the ground, throws in the seed and perhaps weeds those crops that require it once. Here one sees high weeds among their corn & potatoes, but the crops overtop them and the soil is strong enough to bear both, and so the farmer does not take it much to heart if his ground is weedy.[43]

We came into oak openings from the prairie, then across a marsh, the road being on timbers or corderoy. They depend on these marshes for hay and hence they are valuable. The wheat lands do not produce a heavy yield of hay. Where the soil is clay they often drain these marshes, should they require it, by sinking wells or deep holes till they touch the gravel which lies beneath the clay, and never far down, and there the water escapes. These marshes yield very heavy crops. We then crossed Goat Neck [Gourdneck]

---

43. Obed Hussey and Cyrus McCormick introduced horse-powered harvesting machines in 1833 and 1834, and by 1844 they were in operation in southwestern Michigan. Mechanical reapers cut grain faster and more cleanly than manual labor, allowing farmers to cultivate greater acreages and to time harvests more accurately. Paul W. Gates, *The Farmer's Age: Agriculture, 1815–1860*, vol. 3 of *The Economic History of the United States* (New York: Holt, Rinehart & Winston, 1960), 287; Clarence H. Danhof, *Change in Agriculture: The Northern United States, 1820–1870* (Cambridge, MA: Harvard University Press, 1969), 243; Calvin H. Starr, "Some of the Beginnings of St. Joseph County," *Michigan Pioneer and Historical Collections* 18 (1891): 515. Horse-powered threshing machines appeared in the 1820s, and farmers in southwestern Michigan had adopted them by the by the 1830s. Percy Wells Bidwell and John I. Falconer, *History of Agriculture in the Northern United States, 1620–1860* (New York: Peter Smith, 1941), 215–216. The third machine Henry described was probably a combine, a machine that combined the tasks of the reaper and thresher. In 1835 Hiram Moore, of Climax Prairie in Kalamazoo County, built the first combine with the financial support of his neighbor John Hascall. Farmers in southwestern Michigan employed the Moore-Hascall combine, a machine that set the stage for the massive machines employed on the large farms in the West. Lou Allen Chase, "Hiram Moore and the Invention of the Harvester," *Michigan History* 14 (1929): 503; R. Douglas Hurt, *American Farm Tools: From Hand-Power to Steam-Power* (Manhattan, KS: Sunflower University Press, 1985), 77–80.

Prairie, which is small but of good soil, then into an opening again.[44] In passing through some rick land we came upon a mound quite different from all around it. It was of sand, soil of course poor on it, while all around was rich, black mould. This mound stretches east & west I believe a distance of many miles, 50 or 60 I think, and preserves the same uniformity in substance & size as here. We passed the Buck Horn, soon a tavern, formerly well known to speculators, and a great rendezvous for them, and stopped to make inquires. Not being satisfied, we stopped at widow Bristol's, a woman who lives above the "Buck Horn," being the only neighbour. She was in a mile's circuit, I believe. She gave us all the information we required. Her land adjoining that we came to see. Here was one of the prettiest farms my eyes almost ever rested upon. It consisted principally of openings, rolling, undulating beautifully. We walked over it and in the center found what the old woman had called the <u>Mash</u>. This marsh was about 150 acres in extent, at its center was a little lake of over 5 acres and two or three streams meandered through the green plain. The openings rose up from the marsh say 20 feet, forming not too abrupt a bank, and in one or two places were knolls thickly timbered. A few tamaracks helped out the scene and all combined to make a delightful prospect. This was the farm I had often thought & talked about, which my father used to call mine, & surely I would not like to live in a more delightful place. I roamed around delighted, completely so, & finally we made our way back to our horse and turned our faces toward Schoolcraft. I saw some stacks of hay in this marsh, the farmer's men thinking themselves at full liberty to cut it if they want it as it was now with cows feeding over it. It would yield a ton to the acre and if enclosed would probably yield two or three. We arrived at Schoolcraft about sunset. Here were to spend the night. We took tea and I went with Mr. Booth to call upon the man who selected this land.

---

44. Gourdneck Prairie and Gourdneck Lake lay east of Prairie Ronde in southern Kalamazoo County. Albert F. Butler, "Rediscovering Michigan's Prairies," *Michigan History* 32 (1948): 28–29.

After that, declining their pressing invitation to spend the night we went home and I for one know that few minutes elapsed before I was asleep after getting there.

———————

Schoolcraft, Aug. 15. We were woke up early this morning as per request by our landlord. I had kicked off their eternal feather bed and slept soundly and woke refreshed. Our route this day lay towards Brady [Township]—easterly where Mr. Booth had entered some land for us. This is part of the Indian Reservation and had been retained for them till they had been induced to sell out, and then the State had selected this land as part of the 500,000 acres given them towards internal improvements, and a splendid selection it was.[45] There is a belt of heavily timbered land, say 12 miles each way, lying in a country of oak openings & prairies where was scarce woo[d] enough found to fence it and where the settlers must depend upon this land for timbers. They had settled too all around it and, as it has just been thrown into market, the land is, as may be supposed, of the wilderness kind. We threaded our way through trees, around & over swamps and mud holes & sinks, and finally came to a log hut with a little clearing around it and, as we could go no further, we stopped. A board was placed across the door, signifying noone was in, so we thought to go on further to another house about ½ mile beyond. Mr. Booth got out & pointed & I drove, and after scaling all perils and feeling that my neck was safe we finally stopped our horse and getting out proceeded to the cabin. To do this [it] is necessary to go through the pig pen. An old woman met us at the door and welcomed us in. So we entered, took a

———————

45. In September 1841 the federal government approved a statute that provided for the transfer of five hundred thousand acres in the public domain to the state of Michigan to be sold to finance internal improvements such as roads, railways, bridges, and canals. In 1842 state agents evaluated federal lands to designate internal improvement tracts, and the first sales took place the following year. LeRoy Barnett, "Internal Improvement Lands: A Down-to-Earth Solution for Developing Michigan Transportation," *Michigan Surveyor* 25, no. 5 (1990): 10–12.

chair, and here I found myself in a veritable log cabin. I had been into Whig ones before, but never into one in as wild a place as this. I looked around while Mr. Booth questioned the old woman. Of course it was one room. I would have been dividing into infinitesimals to have made two of it. Two beds were crowded into the corners. Blankets & bed clothes were piled upon a shelf against the wall. A cupboard, so called, contained what little crockery they had, together with their milk pans & tinware. There were several chests which served for seats and two chairs, a table, a huge fireplace, the smoke from which curled up till it met a projection overhead. And this was their chimney made of sticks piled as children pile corncobs and plastered with mud. The fireplace of logs, also plastered with mud. Last of all was a ladder which served as stairs to admit persons to the loft above. There were also some shelves over head hanging on poles which served as places of deposit for various things. Under one bed was a dog. On a chest near it was a young man, about 20 I should think & who attracted my attention when I first came in.

He was suffering from the chills & fever, or "ague," and I shall not soon forget his miserable, gaunt appearance. Lean and lank his legs protruded through his trousers and seemed to be of one size their whole length, and his long, boney fingers showed at least lack of flesh. He had the shakes & fever every day he said, and in telling of it, one word seemed hardly able to overtake the other as he drawled out his account of himself.[46] I commenced making enquiries respecting our route and he answered a few times and then, taken up a woodchuck's skin which lay near him and rubbing it

---

46. The young man undoubted suffered from malaria, the symptoms of which he exhibited. So common was its occurrence in the Midwest that many settlers perceived it to be an inevitable part of the "seasoning" process of colonizing a wilderness. Nutter, "Malaria in Michigan," 14–17. A resident conveyed the contemporary attitude toward the disease, commenting that, as a factor "in the general health of the country, [malaria] was hardly to be considered." Charles Fenno Hoffman, *A Winter in the West*, vol. 1 (New York: Harper & Brothers, 1835), 153.

through his skinny hands, his eye glistened & his showed animation for the first time as he drawled forth. "That skin will make the first rate of cash." He had interrupted me but I thought best to let him go on. So I asked who tanned it. His father he said, and he guessed was done first rate, and he caught it. So after a time he sank down again into his former listlessness. When Mr. Booth happening to speak of one of his neighbours he roused again and told him that he had accused their dog of killing sheep and had "t'want no such thing," and then he called the dog from under the bed and showed his teeth now that he couldn't bit[e]. And there he was[,] this whole existence turning on such trifles. Knowing & caring nothing of what was going on around here, such a little incident as our visit serving as food for conversation for I don't know how long. He finally got up and showed us where to put our horse the old woman saying that he should have some good <u>tame hay</u>. So we put our horse in the stable, our lank boy showing the way. We then got some milk and started off for Wilcox's, about a mile beyond. The old woman was a good talker and told all about herself, how she had been cheated by one of these rascally land agents, how somebody had girdled the trees in their sugar bush, &c. & so she talked on until we got out of hearing.

I ate some of her bread with my milk. It is called here "salt raising" and is of Indian meal & wheat flour, & very good. A mile's walk through the woods brought us to a clearing, or improvement. In the center was a log cabin, the smoke coming up cheerfully from the low stack chimney. Half a dozen white headed children were playing around the door, who on seeing us ran in to tell mother. Our business was soon told. Mrs. Wilcox, with hair flying every which way, was busy preparing dinner for her husband, who was not home, & welcomed us in. One chair was occupied by the baby, the other two Mr. Booth & I took and commenced making inquires. Their health was good she said. I have been struck with the interest manifested here in their inquiries about health. It shows much more than the ordinary feeling which we show at home in our casual inquiries. Mr. Wilcox soon came in with his two boys. They had been at work in the mash cutting hay and were wet up to their knees. That's the way to catch fever & ague. This now is one of your strong headed, strong minded men, & if he had strong mind enough to resist whiskey would be an honor to his town. As it is, he has represented it in [the] legislature as he has before his town in New York. We told him we wanted him for a guide through the woods. He was engaged, he said, as council to plead one of his neighbour's suits that PM, but he would go.[47]

_____

So off we started. He had great knowledge of the woods. The "blazes" on the trees, perfectly unintelligible to another man, were plain as print to him. So we went on treading our way through the forest, he occasionally telling us where we crossed a section line. I love to go through our forests, and surely there can be no more graceful on[e]s in America. Here were trees running up straight as an arrow 40 to 80 feet without throwing out a limb of all kinds. And noble trees they were, the bass, whitewood, maple, blk walnut & cherry, their trunks forming (except the beech) fluted columns whose shafts ran up beautifully to support the living canopy above and whose capitals were of models formed by the living hands, but fashioned by the Great Architect, then support the ground free of shrubs or bush. And all around the view was enclosed by these living columns, some nearby towering up till man standing beneath feels diminutive & seen (deemed big) off in perspective till man thinks to measure himself with them. And so we went on among their towering shafts till we came to <u>our land</u>.

This, of course, I looked at with more interest and I admired particularly the noble trees around me. Here and there was a clearing where some

_____

47. Nelson Wilcox was an early settler who became prominent in the administration of Brady Township in Kalamazoo County. He served as the first township supervisor upon its organization in 1842 and held the office for the next three years. At the same time he was elected a justice of the peace, school inspector, county commissioner, and election inspector. Durant, *History of Kalamazoo County*, 109, 304, 307, 308; James M. Thomas, comp., *Kalamazoo County Directory, with a History of the County from Its Earliest Settlement* (Kalamazoo, MI: James M. Thomas, 1869), 113.

squatter had settled down & built him a log cabin and waited for the land to be offer [for] sale. But [it] being reserved, he finally got tired & cleared out.[48] I saw several deserted in this manner. One of them was of cherry logs entirely. We found several "sugar bushes" here. These are valuable. They are clumps of fine sugar maples & in the Spring whole families will camp out around theses and make sugar. A rough cabin of sticks and bark is made, places erected for their pan & fires, wooden troughs for sap are made. Slashes are cut in the trees and a little beneath a gouging chisel makes a place for the insertion of a stick with a groove in it on which the sap runs out and so falls into the trough below. The sap each day is emptied into their receivers and thence fed into the pans as required. These pans have only the bottom of iron, the sides being wood, the fire touching only the bottom. These pans have a large surface exposed to the fire, the sap not being more than six inches deep, and as part as evaporated is supplied with more from the receiver till it becomes syrup when it is cooled. Thus, in one camp will a ton of sugar and two or three barrels of molasses & vinegar be made in one season. This sugar sells as high as good brown sugar, say 8 to 10¢ per lb. and is genuinely preferred by the people here. Thus one half of the sugar consumed in the state is of home manufacture. Their method of gashing the trees is ruinous to them however, and if followed long must destroy them.

After looking round as long as we chose we thought to start from here.

---

48. Immigrants without sufficient capital often employed squatting as a means to acquire government land not yet brought into market. Although the practice was illegal, federal officials were reluctant to disrupt western settlement by removing squatters, and Congress passed legislation in 1830 and 1841 to allow preemption for agricultural purposes. Under this provision, squatters could file claims when the lands they occupied illegally came up for sale. To strengthen their claims, squatters often formed claim associations to help regulate the distribution of land among their members and protect their interests at land sales. Benjamin Hibbard, *A History of Public Land Policies* (Madison: University of Wisconsin Press, 1965), 151–152, 198; Roy M. Robbins, *Our Landed Heritage: The Public Domain, 1776–1970* (Lincoln: University of Nebraska Press, 1976), 91; Lewis, *West to Far Michigan*, 121–126.

Mr. Wilcox found a section line. We are, he says, in such and such a town, such and such a section, my house is in such and such a town, such & such section, such a range, one mile & three quarters southeasterly, and off he started in a straight line. I follow him in perfect astonishment at his readiness. He ran a straight and we at length, run up at the bars of the fence at his clearing. I found people get an affection for these fine trees around here, they having cut off many noble trees, principally cherry, for saw mill logs. They don't call it stealing here.

Mrs. Wilcox had got dinner for us, which we dispatched and then, satisfying our host for his trouble, started off for the next cabin & our buggy. These we found together with our lank case of <u>ague</u> & his talkative mother & were glad to seat ourselves once more & drive off. We passed again through Schoolcraft and through the beautiful Prairie Rond[e], soon entered the openings &, taking off onto a faint trail, took the directions of Mr. Booth's house. It was dark when we reached his house. Here I stayed and took tea. The family had all gone to a raising, but returned soon after we got there. After a <u>rest</u> I took my leave of these kind people and started for Kalamazoo. I had to trust to the sagacity of my horse to keep the path & find the way home, for it was too dark for me to distinguish the road. Two miles from Mr. Booth's I overtook his son who was going to a Whig meeting just fledgling as a political speaker. I took him in & we soon came to a log school house from whose open windows I could hear somebody with leathern lungs laying it down <u>hard</u>. I did not stop though would have been interesting to hear how these yeomanry of our country discoursed on its political economy. There were horses & waggons around & without doubt the majority there had come two or three miles, the nearest house being full half a mile off. It was 10½ when I arrived at Kalamazoo & I sought my bed at 11 heartily tired.

<u>Aug. 16</u>. This morning at 3 I was awakened by the stage from Marshall &, but half rested, hurried on my clothes and got aboard. Twas dark and a

sweet voice near me said, "That's my husband's place." I knew there was a female there and thought from her voice it was a young one, but her talking thus of her husband told me that I should not make the agreeable acquaintance I anticipated. Not but married ladies are very agreeable, they <u>are</u> so, but they are too much au fait at everything, & I admire much more the fresh bread & butterishness of sweet 16. So I told my informant that I would by no means occupy her husband's place and, leaving my gun to be taken care of by one of the passengers who enquired anxiously if it would go off, which I assured him it could not do, as he might satisfy himself on inspection that the muzzles were <u>covered</u>, and took my seat on the outside with the driver. Our driver was a jolly, good-tempered fellow with a red face & round sides, [and] was ful of quirks, oddities & information. He had his dog, which accompanied him on all his trips. It would stand, balancing on the top of the stage, looking on every side for game, & if a squirrel or prairie hen started up at our approach, he would jump off regardless of right or left in pursuit, and then run along with the stage for few miles till tired, and then mount again with the assistance of the driver. All the drivers on the route knew the dog and [when] he took it in his head to pay any of them a visit he was always well taken care of. Our road lay principally through oak openings, a house here and there on the road, and the best part of the land under improvement, or at least fenced in. At daylight, or rather sunrise, we stopped at a log house to change horses, and the driver gave me some particulars in the history of its inmates that were interesting. We arrived at Paw Paw at 8 to breakfast.[49]

My driver had been advising me all the latter part of my journey to take a conveyance from there to Cassopolis instead of going on to the station beyond as was my intention, & as I had paid my fare for & I had considered

---

49. A small, recently settled village in Van Buren County, Paw Paw was situated on the head branch of the Paw Paw River. Containing two mills and several stores, its placement on the Territorial Road contributed to its recent growth. Blois, *Gazetteer*, 338.

to do so. On enquiring, however, I found that they asked a higher price for a team as it would take two days from there to go & come. While at Coleman's, whether I had proposed going, it could be done in one day being about 8 miles nearer.[50] I found moreover that if I went on they would have to send on another extra stage on my account, there being just one stage load without me (There were two stages from Kalamazoo). So I concluded that the driver's advice was not quite disinterested and that I would go on, which conclusion made the driver wish me to the Devil. I was strengthened in this by Mr. Dodge, our landlord, who gave us an excellent breakfast after waiting half an hour for it and gave, as I thought & so did I, excellent advice viz. to go on.[51] How good that was will be seen in conclusion. There was a deaf man in the stage who asked [if] he could take my place on the box to smoke. So I got inside and found myself among a very agreeable set of gentlemen. One of them I found was on his way to Niles and we agreed to take a team together from next post if we could get. Concerning the probability of which began to arise some doubts. On

---

50. In 1837 Henry D. Coleman settled in Hamilton Township in Van Buren County, where he built a tavern on the Territorial Road. His efforts to make the tavern a stop on the stage route enhanced his business, as did his opening a mercantile store and a post office. He operated the tavern until the abandonment of the stage route. Active in politics, Coleman was elected an associate judge in 1842 and was later a representative in the state legislature. The organizational meeting for Hamilton Township took place at his tavern in 1837, and he served as its treasurer from 1840 to 1846. He died in 1857. Franklin Ellis, *History of Berrien and Van Buren Counties, Michigan* (Philadelphia: D. W. Ensign, 1880), 366, 467, 468, 469; O. W. Rowland, *A History of Van Buren County, Michigan* (Chicago: Lewis Pub. Co., 1912), 171, 175, 505, 506, 537.

51. Daniel O. Dodge came to Paw Paw Township in 1834 and opened a tavern on land given him by Peter Gremps, an early pioneer. Dodge's tavern, one of the two buildings on the site of Paw Paw village, became a major stopping place for stages on the Territorial Road. Originally a four-room structure, it was enlarged in 1835 and rebuilt in 1836. The meeting to organize Paw Paw Township met in Dodge's tavern in March 1837 and elected Dodge township clerk and supervisor. The owner of a sawmill in the township, Dodge also served as a justice of the peace and treasurer for Van Buren County. Ellis, *History of Berrien and Van Buren Counties*, 363, 502, 505, 507–508; Rowland, *History of Van Buren County*, 80, 398, 567, 578–579.

the back seat was a thorough specimen of a Yankee, and a Connecticut one too, who afforded some amusement. He was over fifty and had been home to get his <u>darter</u> to bring out to his new purchase, he having got near a thousand acres near here on which he had got a log cabin & was going in improving it. He was very mean & very fond of letting people know that he had money. He told how he had got passage from Albany to Buffalo in a diem boat for 1¼¢ per mile & found thought [*sic*] it very mean that they did not give dinner servings on board them. He had got completely "strained up" he said on the lake & had eaten nothing since. He took a cup of coffee at Marshall and they charged him a shilling for it, & he monopolized the conversation I don't know how long concerning "that imposition." He had paid 6¢ for a cup of coffee before and that was twice as much. But he never, no never, before paid 1 shilling for a cup of coffee, and would not again. We knew he had the most impertinent manner of [*sic*] & then thrusting out his neck "and what may your name be?" If this was answered he would follow up his queries by others & so learn every possible & <u>im</u>possible thing about one as long as they would answer. Mr. Brook, a quiet Virginian, (the one going to Niles) was proof against all his inquisitiveness, and he had to remain unsatisfied respecting his genealogy.

At Coleman's we could get no team. I got some sour milk to drink, which nearly made me sick, but which I sweetened with maple sugar at the next stopping place. So of course we went on at the Keeler's.[52] My

---

52. A native of Vermont, Wolcott H. Keeler came to Van Buren County in June 1835 and bought a substantial tract of land upon which his family settled the following year. He laid out a village around his house, which he converted into a tavern. The village remained largely a paper town, although Keeler's tavern prospered briefly as a stage stop and post office on the Territorial Road. The opening of Coleman's tavern in 1837, however, drew away business, and the post office moved to a village named Keeler, located several miles to the west. Keeler was elected associate judge of the circuit court in Van Buren County in 1837 and circuit court commissioner the following year. Keeler Township, created in 1839, was named after its prominent citizen, who also served as a township highway commissioner. Ellis, *History of Berrien and Van Buren Counties*, 360, 362, 366, 477–478, 481; Rowland, *History of Van Buren County*, 80, 171, 533–534, 587.

young lady who had the husband left us with him. They were just married and she was one of the prettiest, loveliest little things imaginable. He was a dark eyed wicked looking fellow enough, & she blue eyed and with the confiding look and appearance of a child. There was a quondam stage driver and his wife on the same stage, and I could not help smiling at the difference in manner between the two couples. At a difficult place in the road we all got out & & the new married couple went along as lovingly arm in arm as could be, while our driver left his wife to pick her way as she best could & went ahead.

As I said before at Keeler's, the newly married couple left us and the rest of us were crammed into a single stage, a narrow economy for there was much luggage and it was much too heavy a load for the poor horses to drag us 15 miles over the bad roads. We went very slow, being about 4 getting to the end of this route, our poor horses rattling with their breath so that we could plainly hear them as they panted for breath. Our driver got out and bled two of them, one of them bled profusely and an hour after when we reached the next station was still bleeding. Our Yankee left us beyond Keeler's and we had a pleasant company. Our road lay part of the way though heavily timbered woods and then again through sand & oak openings. I found all our passengers were originally from the East, though two of them were now living in Wisconsin. Nearly all the settlers I have had anything to do with seem to have come from the eastern states, principally Vermont & New Hampshire. Both these states are largely represented in Michigan and both furnish excellent settlers. Immigrants seem to go further west. They do not get satisfied till they get completely beyond the reach of civilization. Our deaf man was a perfect Hercules in stature, of most powerful build and it was pitiable to look upon a man thus deprived of one of nature's dearest gifts, for I consider it next to sight. Someone said he was a boxing teacher in Phil[adelphia]. All he said was in an affirmative or negative manner, so that we could not mistake the answer. We passed over two pretty lakes. These abound there and help out the landscape much. They look very pretty surrounded by the "openings."

It was near 6 when we reached St. Joseph. It was approached for a mile or two on a bridge, or platform, over the swamp which surrounds it. It is situated on a hill, but is very unhealthy. But little business is done here comparatively or, as one would judge, would be from its good situation. A large empty hotel on top of the hill showed lack of visitors and was fast going to decay untenanted. We were driven to a most abominable house near the steam boat landing under the hill, and I had come prepared for a fine supper of fresh fish, [but] was doomed to a grievous disappointment, and after wasting some time on a tough piece of miserable steak was forced to rise unsatisfied & disgusted as was the case with all the passengers. Mr. Brook and I determined to remain upon the road or anywhere rather than here and made immediate inquiries for a team. We finally found one owned by a fat fellow named Huff, and rightly named. For on asking him various questions concerning our road, &c. he turned round in a huff. "You are very inquisitive," said he, if "you want the team, there it is, and you may take it or not just as you please." Here was a rebuff, but there was no help for it. So we engaged his team (a two-horse lumber box waggon) for $5, and at 7 o'clock started off prepared for the worst, for Mr. Brook had armed himself with a pint bottle of brandy & water and which we never had more need of.

Oh, the horrors of that night, that jolting waggon, those log, or <u>Michigan rail roads</u> over which we went six lengthy miles, those abominable roads full of holes & water. Now we would descend into a pond of mud & water nearly to our waggon and then rise slowly out on the other side only to descend and redescend & redescend again. Add to that the dogs with hoarse throats following us for I don't know how far or long from every house we passed, snapping & snarling at us and our horses. Oh how I longed for a Colt's pistol that I had in my trunk to shoot some of the varmints. We bore up very well the first part of the jaunt with the help of the brandy, but towards the latter part drowsiness that not even our bad tasting brandy could prevent crept over us & so we nodded & jolted against each other and how we wished our journey was over. We had offered our driver an additional half dollar for himself if he would get us there by 12 and he done his best, but twas dark, the roads wretched, and he though several times he had lost his way & got out once and, wading into the swamp, felt the bark of the trees to see whether they were pine or not. A good part of the way was through heavy timbered land & very swampy & was, as may be supposed, gloomy enough. Of course we had not met a human the whole distance. Twas half past one when we slowly dragged ourselves into Niles and stopped before the hotel there. All our ringing and knocking seems to have [had] no effect, and we finally did not know but we should have to take upon quarters in the bar room floor, we having got this far. The landlord at length appeared in his trousers and going behind the bar commenced awakening the porter who[,] proof against all our racket, which I thought would disturb the whole street, had slept soundly throughout the whole. A number of kicks & cuffs had to be administered before he could open his eyes & the landlord at length dragging him to the middle of the floor succeeded, by means of well administered cuffings, in getting him awake. Then we proceeded to our rooms and very shortly were sleeping soundly.

Niles, Aug. 17th. Did not get up this morning till 8, having ordered our breakfast at that hour. Felt, as may be supposed, sore enough then. Our landlord at the *American* had provided a very good breakfast for us in spite of the villainous feather beds which he had given us & which I had by this time learned to throw off regularly, for every stopping place one is sure to have them in Michigan.[53] And we done ample justice to it. While

---

53. Nathaniel Bacon, an early resident of Niles, built the "American House" in 1835. It was the first brick building in the village and the largest structure in the city at that time. An attorney, Bacon came to Michigan from Rochester, New York. He practiced law in Niles and became probate judge of Berrien County in 1837 and later served as a county circuit judge and Michigan Supreme Court justice before his death in 1869. Ellis, *History of Berrien and Van Buren Counties*, 158, 159; Orville William Coolidge,

eating I heard a sweet voice from the adjoining room singing merrily. There seemed to be no cessation except for a clear ringing laugh now & then. And from the sound I could perceive that our singer was engaged in household occupation & this enlivened her work. So we eat and heard many old & familiar airs and, my curiosity getting aroused, I commenced questioning our waiter who was our female rejoicing in the name of Hannah. She was the daughter of our landlord, she said, an only child, just fifteen, pretty good natured and a good singer & a great pet with all who knew her. This I drew out from her by questioning to the amusement of Mr. Brook, who is not such a Yankee at questioning as I. Her name was Mary she said. Presently we heard someone whistling "Ole Dan Tucker." "That was the cook." And Mary was soon heard singing as in full chorus "Miss Lucy Long" was not forgotten and at the end of the verse "I wish I a pigeon" the door opened an[d] in came the subject of all my curiosity, the sweet singer, pretty faced Mary. I dropped knife and fork & fumbled for my spectacles. Oh, but she was pretty, a countenance, expression of movement, simplicity & complete joyousness & freedom from care, a form that many of our belles might envy, well set off by her pink dress and which had never known the pressure of stay or corset, or deep rich color to heighten a fair complexion, a pair of laughing black eyes and such a pair of lips as one does not see once in a twelve month, served to make "Mary" a "bewitching looking little creature." I thought little more of breakfast. Twas all shallowed up in "Mary," and telling Mr. Brook he might rely upon my getting acquainted with this flower of Michigan. We parted; he was going by stage to La Porte [Indiana] at noon and I took a team for Cassopolis. So we shook hands &, promising to meet at La Porte, I drove off.

Niles is a pretty little town on the St. Joseph River and for a small place does considerable business. The stores here buying the produce of the

A Twentieth Century History of Berrien County, Michigan (Chicago: Lewis Publishing Co., 1906), 653–654; Swan, *Journal of a Trip*, 103.

farmers of the surrounding country and it is shipped for St. Joseph by little steamers which ply up & down on the river. The street in which business is done is quite busy, there always being some teams in it, and the buildings aspiring to be "blocks" after the manner of cities. It publishes two papers and has two liberty poles, one hickory & one oak, and three "meeting" houses and has a population of about 1,000 I believe. Our road at first lay through lands fenced in which showed cultivation & good crops. Soon we entered openings where are no fences, passing an occasional log house with its stick chimney & log fireplace & half dozen toe headed children. About 4 miles from Niles we came to a beautiful little lake, say a mile across each way, clear as crystal and having a white sand bottom and edged around by a level beach from which sloped back green banks into the oak openings which surrounded it. Beautifully it looked, nestled in this park as it were, with green banks and fine trees around and no bush or shrub to district the view, which stretched away through the oak trees till lost among them. I have not in all Michigan seen a more lovely little spot. Nothing to note happened during my progress to Cassopolis. I had my gun in the buggy and occasionally popped away at a stray pigeon or quail but with inferior success. We arrived in the space of three hours at our destination.

Cassopolis, as the man said, was dead. It's one of those places that won't improve. A pretty lake stretches away from one side of the village and helps the appearance of it very much. Being the capital of the county, it has a court house, which is the only public building there is in it. There were many horses and vehicles fastened around and, inquiring the reason, was told there was an abolition lecture holding forth. I stopped at the best looking tavern of the two, and a miserable thing at best, and asked for my dinner for the only thing I dared eat in such a place was bread & milk. This after long waiting I got, and I was rather amused than otherwise at the curiosity of the women of the house. Not one of them, in passing through the room, would look at me even, but one going out would leave the door ajar and turning round would peep through the chink. Then, while I was eating, two of the feminine gender were apparently taking turns regarding me through the keyhole of one door, while the other one was similarly occupied by one looking through the chink of the door which was ajar.

Finishing my milk, I sought for Mr. Sherman with whom I had my business. He was at the abolition meeting, so I went in. In the first room there was a law case going on for assault & battery between brother & sister. Upstairs was our lecturer holding forth with his coat off. The room was all filled with substantial looking men and we left the courthouse together. Here was a man with ambition nearly extinguished by misfortune, honest but unfortunate. He had been ag[en]t for us and money being here very scarce, had appropriated money received for lands to his own use and had been [un]able to pay. I had now in my pocket a bond by which he had given security for the debt in everything he had. The interest was now due and he could not pay, and by that bond I could now distress him if I chose. I could not help pitying the man when I went to his house and saw his little flock of children and interesting wife, who was in bad health, and then to look upon him a man unable to do anything as it were, his hands tied, his profession relinquished, his feeling what must be the inevitable result that all he had would soon pass into our hands. I staid here till 6 and then started for Niles. The woman whose case for assault & battery was going on in court was in the bar room swinging her arms and vowing how she would thrash a lawyer somebody, who was against her in the suit "if it were not for the <u>Law</u>," and she looked fully able to do it, or to any other common sized man thereabouts.

Our ride room was pleasant, the driver well informed, the horses good and, where there was no log road, was pretty good for Michigan, though we had to go through and turn out for frequent mud holes & puddles to which those that bear the name down east are not a circumstance. The cows & other cattle were coming home in droves and near each log house were the folks engaged in milking, &c. the cattle here come home regularly & do not require much searching for. The flies & mosketoes in the woods among them do that. They seek refuge near home where in the clearing they are not so much molested. One cow of the drove usually has a bell whose tinkling may often be heard in the woods where no houses are near for miles. How the settlers collect their hogs I don't know. One sees them through the openings & woods everywhere, where they feed upon the mast & acorns from the trees in their season, upon roots &c. at other times, and get fatted sufficiently by winter to be driven into market to be slaughtered, packed & sent away. I could not help remarking the difference in the color of the soil on the "improvements." When first cleared up, the soil appears black on the surface, and on being turned once with the plow is yellow. This color gradually darkens and by the next year is as black as any.

———————————

After getting my supper I went to the parlour and there found my little singer of the morning looking still as sweetly as then. It did not take long for us to get acquainted and I was as delighted at her artlessness and naivete. There was such an innocency of look, such a simplicity of manner & countenance as was perfectly refreshing, and I congratulated myself at having found one who could help relieve the tedium of my stay in what would otherwise be a dull place. Her mother came in and gave me some account of herself. They were from Brooklyn, N.Y. originally and, meeting with misfortunes, then had gone to Michigan City [Indiana]. Here a brewery which her husband owned had burned up without insurance, & with it went nearly all they owned. They had then come to one of my last waking thoughts and were keeping the hotel in company with its former proprietor Mr. Pendle, to whom report had already given the pretty daughter.

This daughter, it seems (she did not tell me so) was not their own child, having been adopted when an infant. I went & had a dream about this pretty girl and heard her after getting to my room accompanying her sweet voice with her accordion to many old familiar tunes which brought home & home & friends and pleasant associations freshly to mind and so with "music floating in the air" did I throw off the abominable feather bed, and placing myself on the straw one underneath soon found sound

& refreshing sleep. One of my last thoughts being of a certain Mary Eliza who, with rosy cheeks & mellow voice all unconscious, was still singing away quite merrily.

<u>Sunday, Aug. 18th</u>. Welcome sweet day of rest. Twas heartily welcome because I needed a day of rest. And the skies gave token that it would be to me, so far as going out was concerned, for it was overcast & rained in showers frequently & plentifully, &c. I had my breakfast and, the rain giving no token of subsiding, mad[e] up my mind to stay at home in the forenoon, and so devoted it to reading & writing up my journal, which I got a little behind hand. Miss Mary did not go either and I soon found myself, after she came into the room, by her side at the window, and from her gained some information concerning herself and those around. She was very free in her answers and not at all inquisitive, and I soon had her whole history, all her feelings, impressions, &c. by heart. She looked very prettily, did she in her frock, her shining hair & bright morning face, & I could not help but wondering how such a sweet little thing as herself ever could have lived in Michigan, a place that had so far been to me full of bad roads, rough people, and full & disagreements of all kinds. Young ladies were very plenty here and few young gentlemen, and they not very attractive I thought. There was a young ladies boarding school here, which furnished a great number of young ladies too, but nothing to furnish young men. There were not more than half a dozen in all, but they were better looking than the young ladies. And so I drew out from her gradually all about them and all that could interest me or her in Niles.

In the afternoon I went to church, it having ceased raining for a time. The church looked forlorn. It had an organ but no player, and many a voice rang out clearly above the others chants & hymns. There she sat in the gallery, making more music than all the others and looking just as prettily as ever, for I screwed my neck around to look at her. Mr. Ingle, the clergyman, deserved to be a missionary preacher for I doubt much if many would hear him on East many times. Congregation very thin, a few women and two or three men & boys, the rainy weather having kept the majority at home. My humble self seemed to be more observed than the parson & I could not stir but every bonnet seemed turned towards me & every eye staring right at me. I made up my mind they were mostly from Down East. Went home from church in company with Miss Mary and some other girl who was half as pretty. After tea went into the parlour and found there two women who had come to call upon two lecturers who had just arrived and were about to hold forth on animal magnetism and phrenology combined. Shrewd chaps they were too, as I found on acquaintance well these women had heard tell on animal magnetism & came to find out something about it, and I was amused by their questions and our professors' answers. Presently they went away, and one of them volunteered to cure Miss Mary of a headache of which she complained by animal magnetism, and after a certain manipulation declared her cured, to which she dissented. He then took a dollar, placed it in her hands, & told her to regard it steadily while he performed certain passes. Twas worth the dollar that any look of those eyes as she rolled them quickly up at me, & making up a face, resumed her steadfast look at the dollar. She was now declared cured and assented, looking humourously at me, and our professor looked around triumphantly. Soon they cleared out and I was glad to have them, having Mary to myself to converse together, and I spent, as may be imagined, a most delightful evening. She was perfectly free in her conversation, speaking just what she thought, and I found out much concerning some of her beaux that they never dreamed of anyone else's knowing, and more concerning herself than that morning she have believed it impossible for me ever to have known. The hours passed away readily and, finally warned by Papa, a voice from the adjoining room that "twas after bed time." I left her, both promising to dream of each other.

Monday, Aug. 19. I was up and off this morning with a pair of horses for Pokagon, about 10 miles from Niles towards Cassopolis, where I had promised to meet Mr. Sherman.[54] The day was exceedingly hot and pronounced the hottest of the year, and this was the most abominable of all of the abominable roads in Michigan. I went for three or four miles through a swamp, the road full of stumps & deep holes, keeping me on the continual alert to prevent upsetting or running against logs, and my horses dodging from one side of the road to the other. It was worse than tacking at sea. I should be afraid to say how many miles I went to gained. Ahead of me was a man on foot, dodging round like myself. But he gained on me the whole way through and would have got out of sight soon had I not got out finally, & once more getting my horses on a trot, overtook & passed him. It is a wonder their vehicles do not overset more frequently, and they would were their wheels set no further apart than our own, but being very wide they do not overturn easily. Still I get constrained every time I ride out to throw my body to one side and then the other of my vehicle, thinking it certainly will upset. It is continuously up and down hill with the sides of the waggon. My road was anything but pleasant or agreeable. I twisted around now and then, enquiring my way, & meeting with defeat. I had miserable horses, one continually broke into a canter & the other was lame.

I finally arrived at Mr. Silvers. I had enquired two miles back at a house for him & was told "the second house on your right hand." I by this time knew enough not to suppose it <u>so very</u> near, if it was the second house. Here was Mr. Sherman and one or two strangers. This land was purchased of us by Mr. Silvers 5 years since and is now a beautiful farm. He said there was no finer land in all Michigan, & I should think so. It would do farmer good to look at the 80 acre lot in which his house is situated, which at

---

54. Situated on prairie land in western Cass County, Pokagon Township was home to a dispersed agricultural community of more than five hundred residents who produced grain and livestock. The Dowagiac River provided water power for one sawmill. John Farmer, *The Emigrant's Guide; or Pocket Gazetteer of the Surveyed Part of Michigan* (Albany, NY: Packard, 1830), 19; Blois, *Gazetteer*, 344.

home would fetch any time & many hundred dollars as there were acres, and yet which cost him but $5 per acre when he bought it of us. Near by several of his neighbours had lands they bought of us and all were well satisfied with their purchases and were having noble crops upon them. I spent the best part of the day with Mr. Sherman looking over the lands he owns here and those sold. He had a horse and we walked and rode by turns. I would like well that some of our Yankee farmers who are grubbing away in their impoverished lands at home might look at this land. Twas a feast for the eyes. We got back to the Silvers about 3, where was a good dinner provided for us, tea of course being prepared. I have observed it everywhere I have been as yet that either tea or coffee is provided for dinner, and I like the custom. It's better than their water, which none of the best at first grows worse from the decomposition of the wood with which their wells are logged up instead of stoned, and it certainly is better than anything spiritous. Its place will be supplied somewhat with cider I suppose when their orchards get large enough to produce it.[55]

A fat man from New Hampshire, Mr. Silver's brother, was here on a visit and was delighted with the land. He was the last one of the family left behind, all the others having moved to Michigan.[56] The father died a short

---

55. Jacob "Uncle Jake" Silver was born in 1786 in Newport, New Hampshire and migrated to Michigan in 1830. He formed a mercantile partnership with his two younger brothers, Abiel and Benjamin F., locating a store in Edwardsburg. In 1832 the partners opened a branch in Cassopolis, called the "Old Red Store." The following year they built a large distillery on the shore of Stone Lake in Cassopolis. When the partnership dissolved in 1834, Jacob Silvers retained the store, but he sold the distillery two years later. Active in public service, he was elected Cass County treasurer in 1833 and was a member of the first Michigan Constitutional Convention in 1836. Jacob Silvers died in 1872. Howard S. Rogers, *History of Cass County, Michigan from 1825 to 1875* (Dowagiac, MI: Captain Samuel Felt Chapter, the Daughters of the American Revolution, 1942), 385–387; L. H. Glover, *A Twentieth Century History of Cass County, Michigan* (Chicago: Lewis Publishing Co., 1906), 149–150; Mathews, *History of Cass County*, 157, 167, 169.

56. John Silvers Jr. was born in Hopkinton, New Hampshire, in 1788 and was an innkeeper and proprietor of a stage route in Newport for many years. He followed his parents and six siblings to Michigan and settled in Cass County in 1844. He returned to New

time since and the mother was [to] have on the next day a "barbecue," or "bee," or meeting of the whole family, when all 41 were to meet and hold festival at her house. There is scarce a family in Michigan that can do as much, and it was spoken of as something remarkable, though we at home might collect many more than that number of one's family connections in the same state. It must be recollected that all have come here from their native state within ten years.⁵⁷ Mr. Sherman and I then started for to see a lot of land which he had mortgaged to us three miles distant, and again the roads were execrable. We passed in approaching it several log cabins deserted, and they looked dreary enough. There was a log cabin too on his land, alike deserted. There was little timber and opening upon it, but principally good meadowland and would make a capital dairy with water running through it. A sand hill on which was corn was near the center of the hill, and this was poor land. The rest [was] good & would bear heavily. We now went on & soon reached the Niles road and bade him goodbye. And wishing him good luck and a payment of his interest money, soon turned my face towards Niles.

Twas very hot and I had become much fatigued with my day's jaunt. Clouds began to rise and the air grew cooler as I advanced, and presently the sky was overcast and it began to rain, but slightly however. And my oilskin cap and McIntosh were an effectual protection. I came to the lake, drove my horses in and watered them, gazed pleasantly on it[s] placid surface, and then proceeded on again. A large hawk or eagle lighted in one of the trees near me. I fastened my horses at a distance and was proceeding to shoot him when a waggon coming along disturbed him and he flew

Hampshire following the death of his wife about ten years later and died there in 1864. His son Orren remained in Michigan, briefly operating a hotel in Edwardsburg before returning to agricultural pursuits. Rogers, *History of Cass County*, 387; Mathews, *History of Cass County*, 279.

57. Born in 1763, John Silvers and his wife and Mary Buell Silvers maintained a farm in Hopkinton, New Hampshire, before joining his children in the West. He came first to Edwardsburg and to Cassopolis, but settled in Elkhart County, Indiana. John died in 1843 and Mary in 1848. Rogers, *History of Cass County*, 385.

away, and I was disappointed in my game. I arrived at Niles just after ten. My horses and myself both warm & tired.

Took my tea with Mary and thought of the pleasant ride I should have with her in the morning, for I had promised her a ride in the morrow to the pleasant lake I spoke of, but how often are hopes dissipated! Coming out from tea, while in the bar room, the owner of the livery stable, who was nearly half seas over, accosted me, accusing me of having abused his horse &, using very violent language. There were many persons in the bar room at the time and I did not want an altercation with him, but I <u>did</u> want my promised ride in the morrow. And he had told me, among other things, that I could not have his horse & buggy & should not, if I staid there 8 years. I thought proper to explain to him how I had not abused his horses, but had been longer coming 12 miles of the road that evening than his driver had the whole 16 miles the night before. I would do no good however, & so I left him using very abusive language. His brother afterward came to me and made an apology, alleging the <u>indisposition</u> of his brother as the reason and saying that he who had the horses himself knew that they were not ill treated. But I was in a <u>fix</u>. I determined however to get a horse next morning somewhere else if I could and not draw trouble.

My evening was spent of course with the pretty Mary. She wrote her name in full on one of my cards and there I shall preserve it as a memento of the prettiest little girl I had met in Michigan and promised to let me hear from her & of her welfare and to think of me and not forget me before the week was over. Twas quite interesting was this, and I felt half inclined to solemn, which but there was a touching simplicity in the way in which she said (I was speaking of her readiness at laughing) "but I can cry as easily as laugh, and I shall when you are gone." I should have thought of it as nothing in one of the flirty Down Easters, but there was a surest simplicity in the manner of saying it that spoke of truth. She soon rallied however and, giving me her little hand, told me to take one of her rings &, putting it on my finger, to wish and it would be accomplished as will whatever I wish as far as you are concerned will be accomplished. "Yes," I took the ring and wished, and whether it was fulfilled or not is no one's business. Only this I know that in my dreams that night a pair of ruby lips, and such a pair, figured very conspicuously before my sleeping vision and wishes seemed again accomplished.

Tuesday, Aug. 20. This morning I woke up thinking of my ride and started off before breakfast to look for a buggy, but was unsuccessful. Went again after breakfast and was at last compelled to relinquish all hope of my pleasant ride. I thought the more of it on Mary's account as I knew she was as delighted as a child at the prospect of a pleasant ride & to the lake too where she had never been and which I had ben describing to her. So I went upstairs slowly, she was there and looked very prettily in her neat dress ready for the ride. How sorry I was to have to disappoint her! She promised out of revenge to jilt me the next time an engagement was made between us (I mean to ride), but finally retracted and promised to ride with me the next time we met. So she went to her serving and I to my writing. I had that morning been transferred to a room opposite hers, so I left my door open while I wrote, and I was amused at her perfect ingenuousness. She never passed the door (and it was often) but she stopped to look in upon me, and if I looked up and said anything (and of course I did) she would come into the room as freely as if it were her own and stand by me or, seating herself near, would rattle away telling me of this and that thing with as much ease & freedom as if she were not in a gentleman's bedroom. Indeed she seemed perfectly ignorant that scandal could make anything out of such a thing as it certainly would "our way," but in the simplicity of her heart came in because she wanted to. And because she knew I was going away after dinner had a great deal to say. I am really afraid her mother will think she neglected her work this afternoon, and I think so myself.

At near 1 o'clock the stage drove up [and the] dinner bell was rung. This I dispatched and in spite of Mary's belonging in the house will say that twas an abominable dinner, poor bread & poor butter & when these things are poor the dinner must be. I don't know how it is, but good butter is extremely difficult to be obtained in Michigan. There are cows plenty, but not good butter making. One thing is certain. I dispatched it quickly and ran upstairs, dispatched my trunks and then, taking an <u>affectionate</u> leave of Mary, with whom a three days' acquaintance had made me feel as though acquainted as many years, made her renew her promise, and then ran downstairs again & clambered into our conveyance. After being in which I had some difficulty in doing, to get over the side and under the top I looked up, saw Mary at the window. A bow and wave of the hand and we were off, and adieu to <u>Mary</u>. Sweet girl, may you never know care or affliction! May your path through life be strewed with roses without thorns and may that merry voice & joyous laugh long be heard and still be a pleasure to all to hear. Only keep that simplicity and artlessness, which is the greatest charm ever given to women, and may it preserve to you if you remain at Niles. Once go to one of our cities, let your sight no longer be under a bushel. For it could not be where there are men to appreciate and admire and I fear some that flattery and adulation would soon replace simplicity with false airs and affectation. And then, though beauty of form & face would remain, still would you have lost your greatest charm which, God forbid! Adieu to thee, the three pleasantest days I have spent since I have left home & the pleasantest I shall have during my future progress were those spent in Niles. Foul befall the man that would injure a hair of thee or he that should cause the[e] a moment's pain, and happy will be he, he that can call thee wife, though I fear few there are here that can appreciate fully your true worth. Still you are fully competent to make any reasonable man completely happy and that you may always be as my parting wish. I shall longer remember that sweet face & lithe form, and those lips!

My companion on the stage appeared to be a bluff, hearty fellow who knew how to ask all manner of questions, and it was amusing to hear him question the driver till I wonder at his patience. We had two miserable horses and a kind lumber box covered waggon nicknamed a stage! I did not wonder at my fellow passengers squawking as we jolted over the roads. After his informing us he had traveled all the previous night & at the rate we were going had a fair chance of traveling nearly the whole of this [night], for he was bound to Michigan City. We went over much prairie land, generally cultivated, and the land and country was very good apparently, certainly looking very prettily. We change horses once the whole distance [of] 30 miles and arrived at La Porte [Indiana] about 9 in the evening, where we soon had a good supper and where I found Mr. Brook already planning an excursion.[58] My fellow passenger proved, when we parted, to be Maj. Bowes, a sup[erintendent] engineer going to take charge of the workers at Mich. City. His questioning had been the means of finding out that we had mutual acquaintances & indeed he seemed to know everybody from Maine to Georgia, having in the execution of his duties been everywhere, and he had the faculty of remembering the names of everyone he ever met. We parted cordially, he telling me to enquire for Maj. Bowes when I came to Michigan City, which was the first I knew of his name.

Chicago, Aug. 27th. I arrived here this morning at 1, having started from Michigan City at 10 yesterday. I got tired of waiting for a conveyance by water and, after being there two days, finally came to what I ought to have done at first, viz. go by land. I agreed with the stable keeper for $6 to take me through to Chicago and found, when ready to start, which was at 10 instead of 9, that he had put two other passengers in, being able to carry them at reasonable rates after my high fee. Twas a cool, pleasant morning, bracing air and just cleared away from a heavy rain, which had sufficed to make our sandy road a little more passable. I bade a good bye to Maj. Bowes, to whom I already felt as towards a friend and, leaving a pair of boots in the hands of

58. Laporte was the seat of justice for Laporte County Indiana. Settled in 1832, it grew rapidly and by the following decade contained around 350 houses and was home to about two thousand inhabitants as well as a medical school and an academy. E. Chamberlain, *Indiana Gazetteer, or Topographical Dictionary of the State of Indiana* (Indianapolis: E. Chamberlain, 1849), 286.

a shoemaker and my soiled clothes in the hands of a washerwoman to be sent on by next conveyance, I started off. The road between the two <u>cities</u> is quite sandy, laying along parallel with the lake at from one to, three miles distant. And for almost the whole way almost our road lay along one side a marsh & on the other side land banks, & th[r]ough openings with rather a thin growth of wood & no underbrush. Fever and ague were plenty here where there were houses, but these were few enough and it's singular fact that there is but one house on the road from Chicago that is not a tavern. The houses, to be sure, are not plenty, but the no. of houses compared to the no. of taverns is quite disproportionate. And so we rode at a 5 mile per hour pace through the sand, and I should think without seeing a stone so large as a hen's egg the whole way. Pigeons would more often start up from our path where they had been picking wheat fallen from the farmers' waggons, and alighting in the trees look down upon us as we passed and now and then one or two would drop down at the pop of my fowling piece, which I kept the whole distance ready for small sport. Sometimes I would fire from the buggy as I sat and again would jump out & blaze away standing, stowing away my game under the seat. Ducks too now & then rose from the marshes but at these I got no shots. A deer's horns seems to be here the emblem of a tavern as a brush is in southern Europe[.]

It was three o'clock when we stopped for our dinner at "Woodman's." I had got my feet a little damp from running through the grass after pigeons, so I went immediately into the kitchen to dry my feet and superintend o[u]r dinner preparations. A tidy, pretty woman sat near the fire and near her a cradle. There was a nice stove and a nice clean floor and everything looked clean & tidy, and I soon got to be good friends with her. She had been married but a year she said & was from New York State and here she was now the nearest neighbour 5 miles distant, the nearest doctor & church 25, and happy and contented as need be. Her husband had the ague, but he was used to it, having had turns of it for the last 7 years. So we chatted away while she got dinner, assisted by another woman, a buxom lass enough. She had not forgot how to make "flannel cakes." She said she had been seven years west and almost turned Hoosier, and she proved that fact to my complete satisfaction, for I never ate better cakes than those she stirred up while I sat talking to her. It's astonishing in how short a time the potatoes were boiled, the ham & eggs cooked & all the structures ready for a capital dinner to which a fast of 8 hours made me ample justice to.

———————————

At 4 we were off again and trotted slowly along, walking over the log & rail roads laid over the swamps & hearing near as continually the sudden roar of the surf as the waters of the lake chaffed by a north wind for four days dashed angrily against the white sand banks which line the shore. The sun set beautifully, glimmering with its last rays among the trunks of the oak trees around us, gilding its tops and then the clouds, and finally leaving alone glorious masses of clouds piled in the western horizon, towards which lay our course. Then the full moon arose, shedding upon us her soft light, and we went on silently over the sand. A star or two twinkled brightly upon us, a duck now and then rose flapping its wings from the neighbouring marsh, and that was all to break the monotonous surge of the surf rolling upon the beach. We passed a couple of Indians on horseback and, as we neared the occasional house, the cattle lying in the road would, roused from their sleep, move from our path and show that some life still remained among the almost inanimate things around us. Gradually I found myself swaying backwards & forwards under the influence of journeying & so, with occasional snatches of doze from which I would be started by our wheels hitting some stump, its black head in our path, passed the time till we reached Chicago. We stopped half an hour at a tavern 6 miles from the city and then went on. We entered the rolling prairie where was no tree or shrub, only an extended horizon. Then we passed some Hoosier waggons camped out there in a few hours, then more, and soon we were in Chicago and rolling along on streets. Stopped at City Hotel, where I soon found bed & sound sleep.[59]

———————————

59. The City Hotel was situated on the corner of Lake and State Streets in Chicago. George W. Hawes, *Illinois State Gazetteer and Business Directory for 1858 and 1859* (Chicago: George W. Hawes, 1859), 49.

Chicago, Aug. 28. Here I remain, awaiting my boots and clothes from Mich[igan] City. I know as little which route for St. Peters [Mendota, Minnesota] I should take tomorrow as I did when I started from home.[60] Noone here seems to know anything about those regions. I have been here now two days, during which time I have not stirred out of the city. I have strolled a little around the town, but there is little to interest one here. Chicago is a new, thriving and bustling town, which in '32 was a miserable hamlet of log houses, and now calls itself a city and numbers near 10,000 inhabitants.[61] Harvest is now over and the Hoosiers are flocking in here with their grain. These fellows, some of them come a long distance. The waggon is generally a long, covered one with white canvas cover, draw[n] by oxen or horses. One often sees them camping out by the wayside, for it costs money to go into a house. A kind of box, or trough, is fastened behind for his cattle to feed on. Two pails, one for water the other for grease beneath. His quarters are under cover of his waggon. And so the streets are swarming with farmers brin[g]ing in their wheat. The wharves are lined with large store houses at which the farmer leaves his wheat when sold. A kind of spout is on the outside, into which he empties his bags, and the wheat is thus carried to the different bins within. Wheat is not high at present and is of poor quality. The best wheat (winter) brings but little over 50¢ a bushel, which cannot remunerate the farmer very well after bringing it a great distance.

60. In the early nineteenth century the Minnesota River and the settlement at its mouth were known as St. Peter's. In 1852 the river was renamed the Minnesota River and the settlement became Mendota, Minnesota. "The History of St. Peter's Catholic Church, Mendota, Minnesota, 1840–1990," Church of St. Peter, www.stpetersmendota.org.

61. Chicago had fewer than 100 inhabitants prior to 1830 and only 250 at the end of the Black Hawk War in 1832; however, its population doubled the following year and began to expand exponentially. In 1837 the settlement had 5,000 residents and by 1857 Chicago was home to at least 120,000 people. William Cronon, *Nature's Metropolis: Chicago and the Great West* (New York: Norton, 1991), 28, 32; James Mason Peck, *A Gazetteer of Illinois* (Philadelphia: Grigg & Elliot, 1837), 179; Hawes, *Illinois State Gazetteer*, 36.

The streets here are wide and regular crossing at right angles. Some very pretty houses are in the outskirts. Lake Street is the principal business St. here and indeed all the business of Chicago is done here. It runs E & W and has some very good 3 story brick blocks upon it. The steamers run up the river into the city. Some go above the bridge and some remain below. The piers which form the harbour extend out, I should think, 2 or 300 yards into the lake and they are about forming a breakwater. I was looking today at old Fort Dearborn. It remains the same. Only the palisades have been taken up and picket fences substituted. These are, I should think, the oldest buildings in Chicago. This is the fort which was evacuated during the last war by Gen. Hull's order. The evacuation, or massacre by the Indians, took place within a day of the unfortunate surrender of Detroit.[62]

I saw the steamer *St. Louis* go out for Buffalo yesterday morning. She is, or rather has been, the finest boat on the lakes. But tonight the *Empire*, the finest boat on any inland water, is expected in and will make some sensation here, it being her first trip to here. The *St. Louis* will have to yield the palm, but to no other, she being the finest boat I have seen on the lakes. Quite different from the *Bunker Hill* were her cabins & accommodations. Her commodious state rooms, highly polished funnels, each decorated with a fine painting and edged with gilding. Verily I would like a trip around in such a boat from the pleasure alone of going in such a beautiful boat.

---

62. The name Fort Dearborn was given to several fortifications erected on an elevated point at the mouth of the Chicago River. The first fort was built by the US government in 1804 and occupied until 1812, when it was evacuated during the War of 1812. After the Potawatomis attacked the retreating garrison, they burned the fort. The government built a second fort on the site in 1816, but abandoned it in 1823. A war with the Winnebagos in 1828 brought a reoccupation of the fort that lasted until 1831. The Black Hawk War brought troops from 1832 to 1836, and afterward the site remained in federal hands for the use of the engineers and agents connected with the public works. Most of the fort was demolished in 1856. Hawes, *Illinois State Gazetteer*, 35–36; Encyclopedia of Chicago, "Fort Dearborn," Chicago History Museum, www.encyclopedia.chicagohistory.org.

They are having all the new boats now upper cabin and low pressure, both which are improvements upon the old plan.[63]

There is a horse market here and every morning at one of the lake shore[s] at 9 are horses offered at a[u]ction. I have been amused with the conduct of this auctioneer. Before the sale he goes riding around the streets with his horses proclaiming their merits & sells to anyone who will buy at his price. His lungs seem never to wear out. Horses certainly are cheap here, $50 will buy a good Hoosier horse, but what we call first rate horses are dearer, being brought from the East, the reason being that no really fine horses are raised here. Those that are sold being either horses which having dragged emigrants here are sold, being of no further use to the owner, or else they are horses which are brought in droves from the interior of Indiana & Illinois and are raised there in large quantities. This is a great market for horses for the West as indeed it is for everything E. of St. Louis. We call at home Buffalo the market of the West, but bless you, Buffalo is clear away down East, a thousand miles from here. Perhaps there is no one place in the U. S. where more horses are sold than here.

I am at the City Hotel. The Lake House is extinct for the present.[64] Here

---

63. The steamboat *Empire* was constructed by Capt. George W. Jones and launched at Cleveland, Ohio, on June 6, 1844, for service on the Great Lakes. At the time of its launching, the 260-foot long, 1,220-ton paddle steamer was purported to be twenty tons larger than any other freshwater steamboat. Capt. D. Howe commanded the vessel in the Great Lakes passenger trade for nearly two decades, after which its hull was converted into a sloop barge to carry lumber from Saginaw to Buffalo. "The Steamboat Empire," *Buffalo (NY) Daily Courier*, Aug. 23, 1844; "The Old Steamer Empire," *Detroit Free Press*, Apr. 12, 1862. Like the *Empire*, the steamboat *St. Louis*, commanded by Capt. G. W. Floyd, carried passengers from Buffalo and Chicago. A 192-foot long vessel of six hundred tons burden, the *St. Louis* was known for its comfortable and elegant accommodations. A traveler described it as "a splendid ship, finished in a manner that I have never seen equalled." "Description of the Steamboat St. Louis," *New York Herald*, June 12, 1845; "The Steamboat St. Louis," *Detroit Daily Advertiser*, July 16, 1844.

64. The "Lake House" open in 1836 across the Chicago River from Fort Dearborn. This elegant three-story brick building became a center for social and political activity in

are provisions, much less everything plentier [*sic*] and price of board the same as in a first rate hotel in N. Y. and living will not compare with one there. I have at every place west of Buffalo strove earnestly for fresh fish, for this is, of all places, <u>the</u> place for fine fish. And yet I have seen none but once, and then at breakfast here one morning. It's astonishing when so plentiful. I enquire always for it.

<u>Friday, Aug. 29th, 1844</u>. Was up this morning at 5 in order to be off at 6 by stage to Galena [Illinois], which route I had concluded to take. Our coach, however, did not get off till near 7. But I was glad when we had once left the city and were crossing over the long prairie which surrounds it, for I had spent the last three days there with very little pleasure or profit to myself. My day yesterday was spent in strolling through the city & feeling miserably. The *Empire*, the finest boat on the lakes, had been expected in during the day, but up to the time of my departure had not got in. I was disappointed in not seeing her. Our road for the first 12 miles lay over a level, flat & wet prairie & our road was miserable. We passed waggons occasionally loaded with wheat for Chicago or returning with lumber or merchandise from there in exchange. We passed three camped out which had come with their loads of wheat 135 miles and were now returning. These were now generally ox teams, from a distance it costs less to keep them. When night came the team is drawn up on one side of the road and the oxen turned loose over the prairie to feed till morning, when they are caught & again proceed on their journey, their feeding of course costing them nothing while their driver, getting his supper from his basket, turns in under the canvas cover of his waggon & goes to sleep on his wheat bags. At Cazenovia [Illinois] we stopped for breakfast & I fell to it as may be supposed with appetite after two or three hours ride. There were but three of us passengers in the stage, a young man from Saratoga Co., N. Y.,

---

early Chicago. Encyclopedia of Chicago, "Hotels," www.encyclopedia.chicagohistory. org.

a woman from Detroit and both going to Rockford [Illinois], half way to Galena, & both here for the first time. I was amused by the manner of the man. He had come out with a half intention of settling if he found land to suit him, but he was woefully disappointed with the first 12 miles from Chicago & seemed to think he should trace his way back home pretty soon. But from Cazenovia the country took a better aspect. We had now got onto higher ground and the long, rolling prairie stretched far away in every direction, with here and there a belt of oak opening helping to relieve the landscape. Those lands that were under cultivation too looked like gardens and showed indication of great fertility in their heavy crops. Our young adventurer now got much better & began to get in ecstacy with the land, and it certainly was beautiful. The prairie covered with flowers of every hue was spread like a garden before us, rolling off with beautiful undulations till far away on the horizon it seemed to terminate in woods, which looked blue in the distance. The openings, or "groves," which were occasionally passed were the finest I had ever seen. Stretching away, sometimes the trees seemed planted in long avenues, then in clumps and the[n] singly and with beautiful green turf & flowers beneath, and through which we rolled as smoothly as through a park, and then presently we would <u>open</u> upon that prairie again and, leaving behind us our beautiful grove, see our road for miles ahead stretching over the undulations of the ground till lost by distance. Much of the land was wild & for the first part much cultivated. The 12 miles from Chicago seemed scarcely to have been touched by the plow. Elsewhere in the road we passed some beautiful farms, as fine, I venture to say it, as can be found throughout the U.S.

We dined at Elgin [Illinois], a neat town with nothing remarkable save one or two manufactures on the stream that we saw through it. The houses are mostly brick, it being cheaper on the prairies than wood.[65] Our road

---

65. Situated on the Fox River in Kane County, the site of Elgin was settled in 1835 around a tavern and mill on the road from Chicago to Galena. The town grew rapidly in the 1840s, and a decade later, with the coming of the railroad, Elgin had become one of

still lay over prairie, much of it yet unfenced, and now and then a farm. It makes fine grazing country and the farmers are getting to understand their best interest by turning their attention to it. Sheep especially they are raising and farmers are continually going east to purchase them. A man, for example, may have a farm of say 100 acres and at the same time raise 20,000 sheep, for he has the wide prairie around him which they may feed over to any extent. Much better money do they get here than with us, where instead of flowery meadow they have only rocky hills to pick their living from and need to have their noses sharpened there to do it as an advantage. We passed numerous droves of cattle & sheep grazing. We had at night a bad creek to pass. It was a wide slew [slough], as they call it, which means a mud hole or any kind of ravine with water in it. It was a wide mud hole I say, through which ran a creek, and we had some bother to cross it. Our coach we left sticking in the mud, got a lumber box waggon & extra pair of horses, and by taking over the luggage at one load and our selves at another (we had two or three more passengers) we managed finally to get safely over. But such a mud hole I never passed through before, nor ever wish to. We were landed on the other side ('twas about midnight) and unloaded into the mud and half eaten by mosquitoes. We lighted a fire with some rails stolen from a neighbouring fence, made a smudge, and waited patiently till we were told all was ready. When we got into our waggon on top of the luggage & mails, & squeezing together after two or three miles ride got it to the next stopping place where was another coach.

We arrived at Rockford, [Illinois] about daylight next morning and waited here for breakfast at 7. I saw a fellow cleaning a gun and made some enquiries concerning game. He had been on from the East about three weeks he said, during which time he had, at odd spells from his work, shot 450 grouse! Rockford is the center of the Rock River country (the

the most important business points in the county with a population of four thousand. Peck, *A Gazetteer of Illinois*, 195; Hawes, *Illinois State Gazetteer*, 78.

river passing through it), which is the finest land in the state. Like all other towns, it looks new and thriving.[66] I got up on the box now when we left and, gun in hand, was ready for whatever game might start up. Our road lay through beautiful prairie, stretching ahead and around a great distance from some of the highest points (it was undulating). We could see the prairie far away till it was blue in the distance and we lost to view on the horizon, 20 to 30 miles we could see, the driver said. We passed occasionally farms and the occupants showed thrift and growing wealth, and it seems to me that any man with industry may make himself rich here by tilling the soil.

Dubuque [Iowa], Thursday, Sept. 5th. I little thought when I left Galena on the 2d that I should on the 5th be at Dubuque, but looked ahead to dating my journal "St. Peters, Sep 5th." Well! Noone can tell what a day may bring forth and I am waiting still [as] patiently as I can for the *Lynx*.[67] But I may has well make a retrograde movement and account for myself for the last few days, commencing with Monday, the 1st. This day I arose somewhat recovered from my fatigue and after an exceedingly long and refreshing sleep I was to have had a bath and had ordered it accordingly the night beforehand, but was disappointed and the breakfast bell ringing I proceeded to the table and so lost what I had looked forward to as a great luxury. Our breakfast table showed a different set of people than one sees

---

66. Rockford, the seat of Winnebago County, lay on the Rock River, the abundant water power of which encouraged the construction of mills following its settlement in 1836. Its placement on the principal road west of Chicago encouraged its growth, especially after the completion of the railroad from Chicago in 1850. Peck, *A Gazetteer of Illinois*, 282; Hawes, *Illinois State Gazetteer*, 186.

67. The *Lynx* was a steamboat launched in 1844 and operated in the upper Mississippi Valley. Its captain, John Atchinson, lived in Galena in 1847. The village of Haney's Landing, Wisconsin was renamed Lynxville after the steamboat In 1857. *The Galena Directory and Miner's Annual Register for 1847–8*, ILGenWeb, https://illinoisgenweb. org/; "Lynx," Riverboat Dave's Paddlewheel Site, riverboatdaves.com; "Steamboat Times, a Pictorial History of the Mississippi Steamboating Era," ILGenWeb, https:// illinoisgenweb.org.

farther east, all men and rough specimens. There was very little urbanity or politeness displayed, but much bolting of food & intentness upon the business for which they occupied their places. I saw among the regulations hung up in the bar room to the effect that noone should come to the table with his coat off. A Frenchman, one Bascette, keeps this house and makes money, but it's an uncomfortable one. I had the best room in the house and very little could be said in favor of that. Mosquitoes were in any quantity and all those animals who bite apparently.

I took a buggy with a boy to drive and show the localities after breakfast and started off on an exploring expedition, as I wished to see some of the principal "diggings" or "leads" and smelting furnaces. The roads around were disgraceful to any little hamlet of but a dozen houses and how much more so to Galena.[68] Waggons heavily loaded with "mineral" were continuously passing over it and had cut up the roads literally and noone thought of putting them in order or repairing them. A mile or two from Galena and we crossed a little stream whose waters were of a turbid red color, discolored by the washing of the "mineral" looking up for the cause. I saw a little shed built over the stream where was a man with a shovel engaged in throwing in the ore, or "mineral" as they call it, and turning it over and over till all extraneous substances were washed off (generally a

---

68. As the seat of justice of Jo Daviess County, Galena was the principal town of the lead-mining region. Far from a small settlement, Galena had 1,000 to 1,200 inhabitants in 1837 and 5,500 at the time of Henry Sanford's visit seven years later. It was situated in the center of the lead-mining industry on the upper Mississippi, a district that occupied the northwestern portion of Illinois and the southwestern corner of Wisconsin, together with a strip a few miles in width on the opposite side of the Mississippi in Iowa. Galena became the region's leading port during the 1840s, and its harbor shipped 93 percent of the lead produced in the upper valley. Galena's business expanded during that decade, but later dropped as lead production declined and the railroads syphoned away trade. Gary Henry, "Galena, Illinois during the Lead Mine Era" (MA thesis, Eastern Illinois University, 1976), 42, 48–52; Peck, *A Gazetteer of Illinois*, 208; *Fanning's Illustrated Gazetteer of the United States* (New York: Ensign, Bridgman, & Fanning, 1855), 133.

reddish clay), would then throw it out as clean, which would then be taken off to the smelting furnaces. Thither we proceeded. We stopped at one of the principal furnaces. Part of the same stream of water that turned their wheel came tumbling down from a trough in front of the furnace and here a man was engaged in rewashing the "mineral." The large pieces at first washed were here broken up into pieces of about the size of walnuts and again washed and were then ready for smelting. I was astounded at the purity of the ore. Here were heaps of it glittering like silver and seeming to me to be pure metal. The yield they told me was from 75 to 85 percent! This fine mineral was thrown into what they called a "hearth," a kind of open furnace to which a blast was applied, and onto this hearth charcoal pieces of wood and the mineral were being continually thrown on and blazing up with a greenish flame and white vapour. The gasses were carried off by a flue which was carried underground along the hillside till it reached the top. This gas or smoke is very poisonous & will set one coughing quickly should he inhale any of it. The lead was running slowly down, red hot, into a pot below which, as soon as filled, it was baled out into cast iron moulds which formed the pig. These are triangular in shape and about 18 in. long, weighing about 70 lbs. They make here about 140 pigs per day. They pay $17½ per 1,000 lbs. of mineral and get $2.80 per 100 lbs. when smelted. The mineral is as much cash as flour.

A miner discovers a "lead" and works on it, and he finds plenty of buyers for his mineral at market prices and cash. I obtained here some very good specimens of mineral and then went to visit one of the principal diggings. This was found about 2 years since by Mr. [blank], a miner who was lucky enough to find a good "prospect" and is now making money very fast. He was then worth nothing and is now rich. A gambling business is this mining. An[y] man has a right to come and dig on sands not already occupied. These being mineral lands are not sold by the government, only leased &c. it is cut up into 10-acre lots, which anyone that chooses can take up and must pay ⅟₁₅ of the mineral he finds to government. So many men have dug here for years and found nothing; another man may strike on his first attempt on a "fissure" and find a rich vein. This is called a prospect, and he will then set his stakes to make his 10-acre lot and offer his prospect for sale, and it will sell according to the <u>prospect</u> at from 5 to 500 $, or very often it is the case that a miner will at the gambling table (they are great gamblers here) put up his prospect at so many dollars and in the morning find that he has gambled away "prospect" and everything else. When all he has to do will be to take his spade and try his luck again. Of course it is all chance and it leads to their trusting very much to fortune and to gaining. Most all the groceries or liquor stores have gaming rooms attached and if one chooses to enter them he may see these fellows sitting around tables, each with his pile of money and a pair of pistols in front of him, staking perhaps their all. And daylight will find them still gaming and with haggard faces you may see them go down the street, gainers & losers, only to change places, perhaps at their next meeting.

This man has been wiser than most of the miners. He has held on to his prospect and it has proved to be one of the richest in Galena. There was not much to show the riches within from the outside. There was a sort of shed, or shanty, erected over a hole in the ground, very much like a well, and over this hole was a windlass. Or crank, on which ran a rope, and two men were turning at this and hoisting up tubs full of what appeared to be yellow earth & clay. Yet this sand, when washed, produced say 500 lbs. in 2,000 of earth. To go into the mine I must descend this hole I found by letting myself down part way a ladder, and on this I descended. There was no curb, nothing to prevent the earth's caving in upon one but its own adhesiveness, and I felt somewhat afraid lest it might at this particular time tumble down upon me as I gradually felt my way along the dirty ladder down this jagged hole there were several ladders spliced together and the last one seemed to me very much like breaking; however, I at last found myself after a descent of 90 feet at the bottom, standing face to face with a grim, smartly looking fellow who was holding up a swirling tallow candle in my face. This was a miner! And this a mine! And such a mine! Instead of long vaults or chambers supported upon pillars, I found myself in a little hole as it were hardly large enough to allow two persons to pass each other or to permit me all the time to stand upright. I took a candle, having a quantity of clay around its base to serve for a handle and followed my conductor. The candle light showed the ore glistening here and there, over our heads, in the sides or under our feet. Presently we came to another miner at work shovelling in the tub I had carried up and was full of glistening pieces of mineral. He gave me an excellent specimen of the mineral in block and then took me in another direction to show where they got out the "big mineral" in that layer masses, and after going some 300 or 400 feet, part of the time on my hands and knees, I came upon a miner with his pick axe pulling out from its clay bed larger masses of the pure, glittering ore and it was glistening on all sides. Some of the time he had to blast, he said, and he showed me an obstinate rock which he should have to break to pieces with powder. So I left him pecking away at the mineral and soon found myself at the shaft and looking up 90 feet and so getting my eyes full of dirt from a descending bucket. Then I commenced climbing, having compensated our miner for his trouble, when I reached the top, returned to the miner his greasy fur cap which he had lent me to protect my head, gave him his bonus and then departed. This mine has several shafts, as when the "<u>drifts</u>" get extended very far from one it is difficult to transport the mineral very far to be hoisted. So they sink a new shaft into the "drift" below.

We now turned our faces homewards. The ground is rough and uneven and on all sides piles of stones and earth show where unsuccessful diggers have worked. We stopped at another furnace on our way, where the slag is melted over and more metal extracted, a more powerful heat and blast being used. We passed again our red stream. These waters are poisonous and cattle are often poisoned by drinking them. Again we went over the miserable roads which mark the entrance to Galena, and by the miserable huts and houses which so abound here and drove up to the "Americana" in time for dinner.[69] After our dinner, where everything was roast, I proceeded down to the levee. Saw three or four steamboats in looking very singularly compared with our eastern boasts, resembling a two story house with large chimneys placed upon a little boat that looked ready to sink under the load above or turn over from being so top heavy. I found her[e] the steamboats "*Otter*" and "*Lynx*," both from St. Peters and both going up there the next day. And here was the commencement of my very ill luck. A steamer came in shortly after (the *Uncle Toby*) and she giving her freight to the *Otter*, this latter boat determined to go on that night.[70] I made particular enquiries of the captain of the *Lynx* as to when his boat would start (her handbills said at 10 next morning). He would be off by night certainly of next day. I concluded, as the *Lynx* was a new and very superior boat, to wait a day for her in preference to going in the *Otter*, which was anything but capable of making a man comfortable, and go up in her to Dubuque and then remain till the *Lynx* came. So receiving the captain's word that he would be off in half an hour (it was then 3), I hurried back to my hotel, settled my bill and putting my luggage on a porter's back, went on board the *Lynx*, engaged a stateroom, received the assurance of the captain that he would be there (Dubuque) by sunset next day, and taking nothing but my gun and macintosh, hurried on board the *Otter*, expecting to hear the last bell strike every moment. And here I waited for

---

69. In the 1840s Galena was beginning its transformation from a rough frontier settlement catering to those engaged in lead mining to a more settled community characterized by increasing divisions of wealth. Despite the development of churches, schools, newspapers, and other social institutions and the expansion of services and retail trade, the town's appearance remained shabby, characterized largely by the shabby log buildings arranged along its unpaved main street. Henry, "Galena, Illinois," 68–71.

70. The *Uncle Toby* was a side-wheel packet steamboat launched in 1844 in Pittsburgh, Pennsylvania. In that year it plied between St. Louis and St. Peters, Minnesota, under the command of Capt. George B. Cole. It later ranged as far north as St. Paul, Minnesota. *Uncle Toby*, riverboatdaves.com. The steamboat *Otter* was launched in the 1830s or early 1840s and operated on the upper Mississippi valley as far north as St. Paul during the period of 1843–1845. "*Otter*," Riverboat Dave's Paddlewheel Site, riverboatdaves.com.

it to strike. It tolled three times in the in the course of the next two hours and finally about six I had the gratification of finding ourselves moving, but only to stop, after we had got almost out of sight of Galena, to wait for a passenger who had got left behind, sending the small boat after him. To my great astonishment, for he was a deck passenger & I had thought the captain too crabbed to do such a thing. But time does not seem to be very precious on the Mississippi.

———————

However we were soon underway again and, following the tortuous windings of the Fever River to its junction with the Mississippi.[71] The scenery down was not very remarkable. The bluffs, or head lands, were the most so, presenting some singular shapes with their projecting rocks. The river was nothing but a stagnant inlet from the Mississippi, which rejoiced in the name Fever River and ran up a mile or so above Galena, which is 6 miles from its mouth and thus serves very conveniently for access by st[eam] boats. Of course there is no current in it. We went puffing along all points of the compass apparently, occasionally passing a flat, laboriously impelled along by setting with poles, & loaded with wood or sand and occasionally one of those long, narrow dugouts, impelled swiftly along by a single paddle, till finally with a turn a little more abrupt than the many we had made since leaving Galena, we came to the bosom of the broad Mississippi! Why! It did not seem so very broad. I was very sure the Connecticut River at Hartford was full as broad. The banks were all wooded and up and down all was dark green forest. The waters were smooth & transparent & reflected the green banks faithfully. And we went thus puffing along, we alone disturbing the universal stillness, and I looked around admiringly upon the green forests and into, as far as I could, the deep recesses from

---

71. The Fever River passed through Galena in a southwesterly direction and entered the Mississippi seven miles beyond the town. It was navigable as far up as Galena and two miles above it in high water. Although the stream ran with a swift current above Galena, its course in the deep water below was sluggish. Peck, *A Gazetteer of Illinois*, 200.

which flocks of startled pigeons would fly at the sound of our steamer and, going rapidly by us, would be lost to view among the trees on the other side, from whose dark shade too some solitary duck, alarmed like the pigeons, would squatter away and with outstretched necks fly away ahead of us only to be again roused as we again neared them.

It was just after sunset and I felt just in the mood to admire and wonder. Soon we came out into what was indeed the Mississippi, as here it was as wide as two Connecticut Rivers! What I had supposed to be the shore or bank was but an island, and now I saw the river in its whole width, but just ahead ready again to divide itself among the islands and be like so many smaller rivers, and so large if there were no Mississippi. And so we went slowly on, now emerging from among the islands into the open river and then again diving into the dark recesses of the woods, and by some passage before unseen pursue our course through the narrower channel, again among the islands and again among the broader channel. And so we went on, now and then passing a solitary log house with its pile of wood before it, and these were few and very far between. And presently the darkness came on and still I remained on deck, listening to the hollow sounds emitted from our steam pipe and looking up at the dark shadow beneath. Some French voyageurs were on the lower deck rollicking forth their boat songs by no means unmelodically, and thus we alone seemed to break upon the universal stillness which surrounded us, almost profanely as it seemed to me.

But presently are lights seen ahead. We enter a narrow channel, our engine ceases its huffings and we stop directly against the shore, to which our boat is fastened. This is Dubuque. A plank is run over the side and I, McIntosh and gun in hand, descend, and here I am in Iowa. I enquire my way to the Washington Hotel, how large that sounds for Iowa, a country that has always been considered the jumping off place almost, and assailed by yelping, barking dogs, wading through sand and stumbling into gullies in the darkness, I presently find myself at the Washington House. I enter a neat, carpeted room, neatness itself, find a young man who had just come like myself only in the *Uncle Toby*. Presently the proprietor appears, conducts us to neat rooms where, I speak for my room, are tempting beds with snow white coverings & sheets & pillows, inviting refreshing sleep. T'was delightful the sensation of throwing our weary limbs upon such comfortable beds where refreshing sleep could not fail but visit.[72]

<u>Tuesday, 2d</u>. The jingling bell in the yard awoke me from a most refreshing sleep. I dressed and soon found myself seated at a most excellent breakfast where everything was nice, and particularly the coffee. A fine looking old gentleman soon came in and hoped we had all slept well &c., with so much heartiness that I could not help loving him. In conversation with him after breakfast he proved to be father to Plumbe, the daguerreotype <u>man</u> of N.Y. and was a very intelligent person, father of the proprietor of the house.[73] He had graduated at the University of Leyden & with some honor too if I could judge from what he said of it, spoke & wrote Latin with great fluency, besides Greek & French, and altogether was a very superior man. From him I got directions concerning Booth's diggings, which are very famous here, and which he said were only a pleasant walk's distance from the house. So the young gentleman before spoken of, Mr. Fox & myself started for the mine. Our pleasant walk turned out to be one of over two miles and was not so pleasant, over the hill with a hot sun down upon us and not a tree in sight to refresh one with by looking at even. Our coats were soon off and

---

72. Thomas Graffort operated the Washington Hotel, located on Oak and Locust Streets as early as 1836. Weston Arthur Goodspeed, *History of Dubuque County, Iowa* (Chicago: Goodspeed Historical Association, [1911]), 53.

73. Richard Plumbe succeeded Thomas Graffort as proprietor of the Washington House in 1837. The elder Plumbe may have been John Plumbe Jr., who became a prominent citizen of Dubuque in the late 1830s. He served as secretary of the Temperance Society as well as the Dubuque Lyceum and was a member of citizens' committee to improve mail service to the town and a frequent contributor to the local newspaper. Goodspeed, *History of Dubuque County*, 59, 60–61, 62.

after some enquiry and a long walk we found ourselves at the diggings, which are the most productive ones in Dubuque.

Booth's diggings were discovered but a few months since and will and indeed have made the discoverer a wealthy man.[74] I don't know if I have before said it, but this is the fact that if in sinking a shaft it strikes upon a fissure or crevice, here will always be found mineral. Now and then, to be sure, is found in a barren crevice, but seldom. This is one of the <u>biggest kind</u> of crevices. In sinking the shaft it pierced into a large crevice, or cave, extending east & west (all of them do almost) 900 feet or thereabouts, being forty feet in width and from 10 to 30 in height, and full of rich mineral. By a shaft similar to the one of the day before I descended, only this time I put my foot in a loop in the rope and so was let down. One of the miners showed me around and was very intelligent & polite. This shaft we descended was about 30 feet. In the cave was a kind of railroad along which the mineral was transported to the shaft. Here and there too were other shafts sunk below the cave, from which buckets full of glistening mineral were being continually drawn up and piles of it were sparkling here and there as we passed onwards. Water was dripping from the top of the cave and this formed spur which was hanging like pendants all over the top. I descended another of the shafts and found myself in a perfect bed of mineral. Twas above, below and all around me. They had just commenced a drift along the vein and it looked very much like tumbling down upon one did the earth just supported upon wooden props as they undermined it and ladened with this heavy mineral. I felt better when once again in the comparatively secure place above and we wended our way back to the other shaft, knocking off a few pieces of spur as we proceeded. They average here near 50,000 here a week in mineral and might get out much more if they

---

74. Another notable citizen of Dubuque, C. H. Booth was elected its first mayor upon the adoption of a charter and the establishment of a city government on April 5, 1841. Ibid., 71.

would, and this is almost clear profit to the owner, about half a dozen men being employed I should think in the mine. Twas refreshing this being once again on top of ground again and seeing the clear sky and breathing fresh air! Having washed our soiled hands and faces we proceeded back again to Dubuque, much gratified with our visit to the cave.

As we reached the hill behind Dubuque I could not help regard with a kind of wonder. Here was a city with corporation mayor and common council. Here were fine brick stores & blocks, more of them being built. Here were on opposite corners two rival newspapers breathing thunder upon each other's principles and politics. Here was Dubuque, where ten years ago was a wilderness and where now were steamboats coming and going and all the attributes of a thriving business place.[75] Back of Dubuque was a high bluff and here I went to look upon the view displayed around. Twas of up and down the river a long distance and was a very fine one. The Mississippi was seen for many, many miles, here and there glistening among the trees in which it hid itself. The high bluffs have a very picturesque appearance.

75. American settlers began to arrive in eastern Iowa following the opening of the land held by the Sacs and Foxes to settlement in 1833. Attracted by the lead deposits, miners poured into the region, and by the following year at least three hundred people inhabited a village of log buildings on the bank of the Mississippi. Dubuque was surveyed in 1836 and within the next few years grew rapidly to include the Dubuque County courthouse, Catholic and Protestant churches, four hotels, fifty stores and shops, grist- and sawmills, a market house, a theater, lyceum, and fifty-five dwellings, many made of brick. The Iowa legislature incorporated Dubuque as a city in 1840. Ibid., 51, 53, 55–56, 58, 60, 73. Congressional appropriations brought improvements to Dubuque's harbor in 1843–1844, greatly enhancing trade, and within a decade Dubuque's population grew to an estimated ten thousand. N. Howe Parker, *Iowa as It Is in 1855: A Gazetteer for Citizens* (Chicago: Keen & Lee, 1855), 127; Dubuque County, Iowa, "County History," eReference Desk, ereferencedesk.com/resources/counties/iowa/dubuque.html. The two warring Dubuque newspapers were the *Visitor* of 1836, which became *Iowa News* in 1837, and the *Miner's Express*, which began publishing four years later. Residents often referred to the latter as "The Thunderer" as a result of its editorial style. Goodspeed, *History of Dubuque County*, 52, 67, 70–71, 73.

In looking around the horizon it seemed as if the tops of the hills had been cut off in an even line, all along so straight and regular were they. There was only one deviation and that was directly across the river where arose a conical mound, or peak, and which might be distinctly seen a long distance. When seen nearer, these bluffs present still more singular phenomena. Turrets of rocks and rocks of all shapes, but primarily resembling huge arms of capital of immense columns will start out from the sides and seem to hang there as by some invisible agency and making a singular appearance as seen from the distance. I went in the afternoon to visit Dubuque's grave, which is two or three miles down the river. I took my gun and promised to meet a Mr. Fanning, the owner of a digging near, and where I took to it, then when I returned and so have some sport shooting. The ground as usual displayed on every side tokens of unsuccessful digging for ore. I found myself in due course of time at the smelting furnace, where leaving my horse I proceeded on foot of the bluff where Dubuque is raised.

The bluff terminates in a high ridge extending out towards the river, from which is a beautiful prospect at the extremity of this ridge, which here slopes down very abruptly to the river, is Dubuque's grave. A low stone building covers it, and this he had lined with lead as also the door. The door has been carried off, the lead stripped from the sides, and the grave even robbed. I looked in. All that remained of Dubuque seemed to be a thigh bone, which was a little too large for relick hunters to pocket. On the back side of the tomb was a wooden cross and on this his name, Julien Dubuque, age 45 years & time of death, 1810, March 2d, and all around and on the roof of the building were cut the names of aspirants for immortality who had visited the place. Nearby was a rough shanty over the grave (also robbed) of an Indian chief. Several chiefs have been buried here and only chiefs were esteemed worthy the honor of being buried near Julien Dubuque.[76]

---

76. Born in Trois Rivieres, Quebec, in 1765, Julien Dubuque clerked in the Indian trade at Michilimackinac and in 1788 joined his brother Augustin at Prairie du Chien on the Mississippi. There he made an agreement with the Meskwakies to mine lead on their lands and set up a trading post and smelter to produce lead for export and

The view here extends many miles up and down the river. Just opposite and for a mile or two up and down, the river was comparatively narrower & free from islands. Then again it widened out into a large basin almost on either side and, cut up into many smaller channels, was seen winding through the many wooded islands which choked up its channel almost. And then the high bluffs which lined its banks all very beautiful. I turned from this prominence with regret and we made the best of our way to Fanning's diggings.[77] When here he asked me to descend a new shaft where they had just struck the mineral. I did so[. T]his shaft was surrounded by a fine crib and I felt very safe in descending. At the bottom was the mineral. They had struck upon a large mass of heavy ore and this was some 300 yards from his other shaft, and so the vein bid fair to be very productive. When I arrived at the top I learned that the crib had very nearly given way that

---

later acquired official title to the land from the governor general of Spain, the nation then claiming sovereignty over lands west of the Mississippi. Dubuque is believed to have married Potosa, daughter of the Meskwakie leader Peosta and remained at his post until his death on May 24, 1810. He was buried by his Indian associates on a high bluff above Catfish Creek overlooking the Mississippi River. Dubuque's grave was originally covered with a wooden and stone shelter with a gable roof. George Catlin observed this structure in 1835 and reported that Dubuque's bones were visible inside. The tomb was the one observed by Henry Sanford during his 1844 visit and remained intact at least as late as 1845. The building had been removed and relic hunters had reportedly vandalized the grave by the 1860s; however, excavations at the site by a group of Dubuque citizens in 1895 revealed the intact remains of five individuals, including Dubuque, Potosa, Peosta, and two other Indians. In 1897 Dubuque's remains were reburied beneath the circular stone monument erected on the site of his grave. George Catlin, *Letters and Notes on the Manners, Customs, and Conditions of the North American Indians*, 2 vols. (New York: Dover Publications, 1973), 2:130; "Julien Dubuque," Encyclopedia Dubuque, www.encyclopediadubuque. org.

77. The Mr. Fanning mentioned was likely either Timothy or James Fanning, both of whom were well-known citizens of Dubuque. The former was elected one of five trustees of the town in 1837 and served on a committee to improve the harbor. He served as an alderman in 1841 and 1843–1845 and held ferry privileges on the river from 1847 to 1848. Citizens elected James Fanning an alderman of Dubuque in 1842 and mayor in 1843. Goodspeed, *History of Dubuque County*, 57, 71, 72, 74, 75, 82.

day, the timbers that line lined it having cracked like pipe stems under the weight of some mineral around it. Had I known this I should not have descended with so much security. Fanning whistled to his dogs, jumped into the waggon & we were soon off for shooting. But why tell of what we got or saw? Suffice it to say that I found it quite fatiguing enough, this tramping over the fields and quite disappointed in only getting 2 grouse, which however sufficed to make an excellent breakfast next morning. We got home by dark.

I was very much afraid the steamer might have come and gone while I was away, but I had not the least cause for fear, it had not come. And what is more, it did not come and at ten o'clock, tired and fatigued with waiting & shooting, I went to bed.

And here, Sept 6th I am, waiting for that infernal *Lynx*. I had brought no change of clothes, having left all on board of her. Oh, put not your faith in steamboats as well as princes! Did I not receive the assurance of the captain that he would certainly be here by sunset of Tuesday, and is it not now Friday and no sign yet of steamboat? It certainly is decidedly annoying. Mr. Fox went down Tuesday. Col. Ross, Register of land office for the southern part of Iowa, a fine, gentlemanly and intelligent man, who has seen near 60 years, has been here till yesterday when he departed and now I am—not quite disconsolate, but confoundedly vexed. The col. was very agreeable and gave me much and valuable information that I think will more than repay me for the time I lost. He has told me of the payment of the Sacs & Foxes, which is to take place week after next, and every day puts the possibility of my being able to attend it very far in the background, if I go to St. Peters. It is one of the most interesting payments I could anywhere see & I should be sorry to miss it, though I should have much fatigue in getting to the payment, which is on Raccoon Fork, 120 miles inland from Burlington [Iowa].[78]

I have spent my time quietly enough, taking a walk two or three times a day down to the landing to see that the st[eam] b[oa]ts don't leave me and the rest of the day in reading or talking. Now Col. Ross is gone, old Mr. Plumbe has taken his place and does his best to make my stay amenable. He is a fine old man of much intelligence and everybody around respects & likes him apparently. It's rare to find a man as old as himself so far west. The majority of persons one sees west of the lakes, & I might say west of Ohio, are all apparently men of middle age or in the prime of life. Mr. Plumbe is a man of nearly 80, I should think, with a shining bald head and a few white hairs, & but few men of 50 are more hearty or vigorous than himself. As straight as an arrow with a fine voice and quick perception, few would take him for his bearing to have seen the age of two score and ten.

———————

Dubuque seems to be made up entirely of taverns, stores & groggeries. There hardly seems room for any dwelling houses. Its business street has some good stores opening and more putting up. A man told me that 3,000,000 of brick (how many houses that will make I don't know) were already contracted to be put up for next season. The hope is somewhere between 12 & 1,500.[79] But much business is done here. The country back (thinly settled to be sure) for 60 miles comes to Dubuque to trade & it bids fair to be a thriving place. It will have difficulty, however, with its landing

———————

78. The payments were a result of the treaty between the United States and the Sacs and Foxes signed October 11, 1842, in which the tribes ceded to the federal government all of their lands west of the Mississippi River in exchange for $800,000 to be paid annually and other considerations. The place of payment is likely to have been near present-day Des Moines, Iowa, where the Raccoon River joins the Des Moines River. "The Sac and Fox Treaty of 1842," *Annals of Iowa* 12 (1920): 375–381; K. E. Schilling and C. F. Wolter, *Water Quality Improvement Plan for Raccoon River, Iowa* (Iowa City: Iowa Department of Natural Resources, Geological Survey, 2008), 21–23.

79. Two brickyards operated in Dubuque as early as 1837, and the first brick house was erected there that year. Goodspeed, *History of Dubuque County*, 51, 58.

for steam boats. At present the water is high and they come directly up to the town, but when the water is lower they have to land at one of the islands opposite, from where goods and passengers have to be transported to the town in boats. Government has given several appropriations and they may be able to remedy the evil in some way, but the current or chief channel of the river at present is among the islands farther out in the stream.[80]

---

80. Subsequent to his visit, work on Dubuque's notorious harbor confirmed Henry Sanford's observation that low water presented difficulties to boats attempting to land there. Congress had appropriated funds to improve Dubuque's harbor, and in 1845, pursuant to an act of Congress passed the previous December, the US Topographical Corps. undertook a survey of the harbor. That work produced several plans to resolve the problem, yet it would be many years before the difficulties were finally resolved. Ibid., 73, 76–80, 89, 103, 106–107.

CHAPTER 3

Henry S. Sanford Journal, Buffalo Hunt Journal, June 25 to October 9, 1846

enry Sanford's second sojourn to the West differed from his previous journey in that he traveled strictly for pleasure rather than business. Conceived from the start as a grand tour and hunting trip, it became the most ambitious of his western ventures. Following a different route that took him down the Eastern Seaboard and Ohio Valley, the young traveler took a leisurely journey that allowed him to tour New York City, Philadelphia, and Baltimore, after which traveled overland to Pittsburgh and on the Ohio River to Cincinnati, and then across Ohio to the Great Lakes, skipping rapidly over southern Michigan and following lakes Michigan and Superior to Wisconsin. From there he proceeded westward to Minnesota, and into the Dakotas, enduring sickness as well as the challenges of an overland journey through the wilderness. In the course of his travels Sanford passed through the developed regions of the

All of the journal entries in this chapter come from Henry Sanford, "Journal: Buffalo Hunt, July–September, 1846," HSSP, Box 3, Folder 5.

Eastern Seaboard, the newly settled country of the Middle Border, and the contested western lands only nominally controlled by the United States. Here encountered he a cross-section of antebellum America, from urban residents of the great cities and immigrant farmers in the hinterlands to the traders, missionaries, government agents, miners, lumbermen, hunters, and Native Americans who ranged across the forests and prairies of the territories beyond. Through his eyes we meet boatmen, celebrities, and entrepreneurs, as well as soldiers headed south to fight in Mexico. On his return through Kentucky and Virginia Sanford toured the scenic attractions of the middle South and experienced its plantation society. Henry Sanford's 1846 sojourn proved to be the longest of his recorded western trips and covered the widest territory. His journal constitutes perhaps the most complete account of his travels in America, and the addition of the letters to his fiancée Janey Howe fill out the narrative with the impressions of a young man seeking to record his feelings as well as his observations.

Journal

<u>Thursday, 25th [June]</u>. Left Derby for NY per Naugatuck [Connecticut]. At Stratford met with Mr. Booth of NY & so concluded to return with him to Derby. Called on Miss Priscilla Par. Met there Miss Dowdel, or Dougal, a fine girl. The latter is a thinking girl, the other rather ____. Priscilla went on to NY, taking my luggage & a bargain & a bag having $900 specie in it. Called on Mr. Rice after walking home with Miss D., intending to spend the night here. Mr. & Mrs. L. were out. They came home soon & were very cordial.

――――――――――

<u>Friday, 26th</u>. Took a horse & waggon in comp[any] with Mr. Booth. Forwarded to Derby. People not a little astonished to see Mr. Booth. Spent the morning of the day showing Mr. Booth around. Called on Miss Jordan

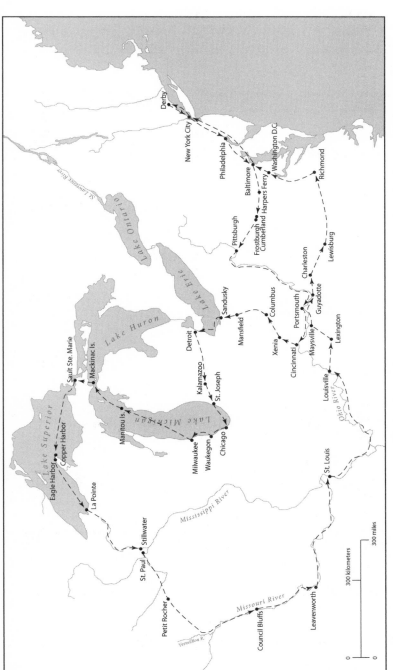

In 1846 Henry Sanford set out on his most ambitious trip to the West. Departing from his earlier itinerary, he traveled to major urban centers along the Eastern Seaboard before heading inland. He again crossed southern Michigan on his way to hunting buffalo on the distant Great Plains. Traveling via the Great Lakes to northern Wisconsin, he again visited St. Paul on his way to the Vermillion River in present-day South Dakota. His return trip to the East followed a new route across the upper South.

MAP BY E. WHITE.

and let Miss Worth meet the new neighbours. Good head & off tomorrow to take the next boat Arrived at 8½ and turned in immediately.

———————

Saturday, 27th. New York. Went to Bond St. House.[1] Spent the morning in making purchases & afternoon making calls. Met Miss Lewis in Broadway & walked up with her to Union Park.[2] All the girls manifest polite interest in my trip. Called on Mr. Russell & took tea there.[3] Called in the eve[ning] on Mrs. Lansdale, Miss Douglas, &c.

Letter

Henry Sanford to Janey Howe,
June 27, 1846, New York[4]

We sail today dearest Janey, but this morning has brought with it an old fashioned northeaster, and while awaiting a notice from the captain as

———————

1. A well-known hotel at 23 Bond Street, the Bond Street House was a three-storied brick structure. Managed by a Mrs. Cowing at the time of Henry's visit, the building was valued at $30,000 in 1849. It later became a private residence and was closed about 1870. Deserted except for a caretaker, the decaying building still stood at the turn of the nineteenth century. *Charleston (SC) Courier*, Apr. 18, 1847; *Opinion Cabinet* (Schenectady, NY), Dec. 18, 1849; *St. Albans (VT) Daily Messenger*, Nov. 10, 1898.
2. The Lewis family of New York were cousins related to Henry through his maternal grandmother, Charity Lewis. Harriet Chapell Owsley, *Register: Henry Shelton Sanford Papers* (Nashville: Tennessee State Library and Archives, 1960). Union Square Park appeared on an 1811 plan for the city of New York. Called Union Place, it was located in Manhattan where Broadway and the Bowery Road came together and extended from Tenth to Seventeenth Streets. It was landscaped and reduced in size in 1832 and renamed Union Square. "Parks for the New Metropolis (1811–1870)," NYC Parks, https://nycgovparks.org.
3. C. H. Russell was a friend and business associate of Henry S. Sanford. Owsley, *Register*, 70. Fanny Russell, referred to later, was his daughter.
4. HSSP, Box 93, Folder 15, Letter 3.

to whether he will go down as far as the Hook or not today. I sit down to say a word or two to you. I have just had a mishap which I look upon as an unfavorable omen. Last evening in coming home I found a note for me, which was signed Mary L. S., and a few lines of poetry wishing me god-speed, assuring me of her daily prayers for my welfare & wishes for a safe return, to my mother &c. this was written by Mrs. Stone & I prize it very highly & this morning I have lost it, how I know not & for a trifling thing has made me very nervous.

Yesterday was occupied in good byes & farewell calls, which are anything but agreeable & make one pull a very long face. The ladies of the Bond Street House say I shall receive a "round robin" from them. The Stagg's, Lewis's & Douglas's are all to write me a company letter to go out by Mr. Fairman on the 1st April. So I am in for enough lady correspondents you will say. You enquire about my parting with Mary Stagg. We didn't either of us shed tears or look sentimental, but there has scarcely anyone else in the city that I felt more sorrow in parting with. She's a noble, whole souled girl for whom I feel a very warm friendship. Twould be a joke wouldn't it if she as <u>Mrs.</u> Fairman should be the bearer of my joint letter! I called on your grandfather yesterday PM also to say good bye, made a short stay.

Now then for my bit of romance I promised you yesterday. I remembered I told you I had seen Mary Boynton & how I felt for her alone in the city with few friends who could advise her & surrounded by very many snares & temptations which an artless girl like herself knows not how to guard against. Agreeable to promise I called then the other day & felt much commiseration when I learnt all her story. She is quite pretty & has attracted the attention of a number of young men who, though of high families, are without principle & more than one endeavor had been made to enlist her affections when to object could have been anything but honorable. And there the girl is, alone almost, with a weak, fond mother, no society or friends among her own sex scarcely & little to occupy her mind but thoughts of the pleasant home she left in Michigan & her own sense of loneliness. I told her before that she ought to go to school, but her father is reduced & unable to send her. I have therefore made arrangements that she be sent to me. The enclosed papers show my correspondence on the subject. The girl & her parents were by no means willing at first, but the whole thing is settled now & she is to commence in a week or two. And I do feel that I have been doing a good action & one which my conscience approves. Mrs. Vaught of whom I speak, the copy of my letter enclosed has called upon her & is to accompany her & Miss Haines & place her under her charge & feels much interest in her already, and a year's close application will do much for her both in occupying her & keeping off young men & in giving her much improvement. Had I thought it necessary I would have told the girl that I was another's, but it was not. I told her I owed to her associations of the then pleasantest days I had spent in many years, & that I wished to repay the obligation in some way, that I never expected to see her again, and wanted her to distinctly to understand that I had no idea of getting in love with her or wished her to be. Neither did I want to correspond with her. I told her it was dangerous business for her &c. & I was not disposed to. To her father & mother I gave my reasons in full for what I had done & proposed & they seem to be very grateful, told them I should be glad to hear of Mary's marrying well &c., &c. [A]ll this sounds very singularly perhaps, but I have not time to go into particulars as I had wished.

Journal

<u>Sunday, 28th</u>. Rainy. Went to Grace Church in the morning.[5] Saw there Miss Lewis & walked up town with them. Called on the Healeys. Did not

---

5. Grace Episcopal Church of New York was founded in 1808, an outgrowth of Trinity Church. Its first house of worship was situated on the corner of Broadway and Rector Streets in Manhattan, but the church later moved to a larger Gothic structure on Broadway between Tenth and Eleventh streets. The new church was consecrated

get to church in afternoon or evening. Dined with Mr. Russell & spent afternoon there. Was engaged to take tea with Gil Smith. Was raining & did not go. I deposited Saturday $925 in Gil's hands to purchase 10 shares D[elaware] & Hudson scrip.[6]

<u>Monday, 29th</u>. Raining. Making purchases & getting ready to be off. On Aunt Helen [Sheldon] & the Douglases.[7] Missed the cars at 4½ o-clock. Stopped at Justice Hotel & then went to table and saw a number of ladies I knew. Walked home with the Lewis' &c.

<u>Tuesday, 30th</u>. Raining. Up at 4½ & off at 5½ per Camden & Amboy R.R. to Phila[delphia].[8] German immigrant musicians. Gentleman from Springfield. Bordentown. Stopped at Healey's then went around on business. Very poor success. —— anticipated this fall on acct. of low price of produce.

March 7, 1846, within several months of Henry's visit. "History," Grace Church in New York, gracechurchnyc.org.

6. The Delaware & Hudson Railway grew out of the Delaware & Hudson Canal Company in 1823 and was engaged in the lucrative conveyance of anthracite coal from Lackawanna Valley in eastern Pennsylvania to growing markets in New York City. The railroad began operating with steam power between Carbondale and Honesdale, Pennsylvania, in 1829. Jim Shaughnessy, *Delaware & Hudson: The History of an Important Railroad Whose Antecedent Was a Canal Network to Transport Coal* (Berkeley, CA: Howell-North Books, 1967), 2; "The Delaware & Hudson Railway: The Bridge Line," American-Rails.com, american-rails.com.

7. Helen King Shelton was the wife of Henry Shelton, the brother of Henry's mother Nancy Shelton Sanford. Owsley, *Register*.

8. The Camden & Amboy Railroad was chartered in 1830 to connect Philadelphia and New York City. By 1841 all segments of the line had been completed, offering through-traffic between Camden, New Jersey, opposite the former city, and Jersey City, New Jersey, across from the downtown Manhattan. "The Camden & Amboy Railroad," American-Rails.com, american-rails.com.

Letter

Henry Sanford to Janey Howe,
July 1, Philadelphia[9]

... The last hold on home is now severed, for I look upon New York almost the same as home and do not consider myself beyond the borders till away from the city ... Monday was spent by me in New York making purchases & good byes. Everybody is engaged in preparations for departure to the country before the 4th and the first questions after the usual "How do you do's" are where are you going this summer. But how the girls are scattering! North, east & west! Broadway already begins to look deserted and I missed some familiar faces who had "gone to the country." My adieus to some of them that did remain & I called upon were of course very affecting. Mr. Mays, he sure to be back for Mr. Polk's parties next winter. Another makes me promise to bring her such a dear little pair of moccasins. To speak of small moccasins leaves a very nice opening to thrust in a compliment concerning tiny feet, talk of <u>antlers</u> young ladies!! Another has given me a pretty bouquet arranged especially for me, which I am to hold fast to under all circumstances (it's at this moment snugly enveloped in paper, packed up for the journey), and in return to send her from the far West a bunch of prairie flowers. And another is to have a full account of all my adventures through the "Spirit of the Times," which she is hereafter to read constantly.[10] And so we go. I have not yet called on a single young lady here

---

9. HSSP, Box 93, Folder 15, Letter 4.
10. *The Spirit of the Times: A Chronicle of the Turf, Agriculture, Field Sports, Literature and the Stage* was an American weekly newspaper published in New York. Founded by William T. Porter in 1831, the publication was aimed at an upper-class readership composed largely of sportsmen and relied heavily on the contribution of amateur correspondents who covered sporting events, but also submitted fiction related to horse racing and to hunting and contributed humor writing. Norris W. Yates, *William T. Porter and the "Spirit of the Times": A Study of the Big Bear School of Humor* (Baton Rouge: University of Louisiana Press, 1957).

[Philadelphia] and doubt whether I shall, for I am tired of repeating over the same story about sun down, Indians &c.

But I have not told how I left New York[.] Monday afternoon at 4¼ saw me in a carriage proceeding down Broadway on my way to the Phila. boat, a gun in a black case beside the two carpet bags and a trunk surmounted by a Spanish saddle, shooting jacket & tent cover strapped upon it, made up my equipage, all which were rather conspicuous and gave rather a suspicious look. A black bag containing bullets and ammunition has passed, I suspect very generally among the porters as being full of specie, and this causes some suspicious glances. I should not wonder some day to find the bag missing, some thief expecting to make a fine haul. Won't he be disappointed! I feel half ashamed to tell you of my untraveler-like commencement of my journey. I trusted to the hotel keeper as to the hour of starting & consequently found when I got to the boat that he had mistaken the time and it had gone half an hour before. Here was a bad omen and quandary, go back to the Bond Street House I could not or a wait till next morning in the city. So I went to the Mount Hotel, and being too lazy to dress and call upon anyone, strolled up to Niblo's to see the Ravels & if you had reason in your admiration of them hoping to meet noone I knew, but ill luck was against me. A full half dozen young ladies I knew were discovered after I could not back out and, being recognized, explanations & reasons why & wherefor had to follow, all of which is especially <u>agreeable</u>. The Ravels are all the rage. Niblo's is packed nightly. I need hardly say that I am pleased. Gabriel has by no means deteriorated since you saw him. A tumbler, or rather a succession of them, called the "Italian Brigands" was excellent.[11]

---

11. Niblo's Garden was a New York theater on Broadway built by William B. Niblo in 1834. It occupied a block and grew from an outdoor restaurant venue serving food that also hosted concerts. In 1843 Niblo opened a three-thousand-seat theater that hosted plays and other fine entertainment. It burned and was rebuilt in 1846 and was demolished in 1895. The Ravel family performed as acrobats. They were also tightrope walkers, and Gabriel Ravel performed as a pantomimist. The "Italian Brigands" were also acrobats who performed with the Ravels at Niblo's on June 29,

Today is rainy, so was yesterday and the day before, & so on back almost to April. Do you get the blues ever! If so you cannot have a more appropriate season. Fine weather this for traveling or seeing sights. I have had it in anticipation that it would have finished raining by the time my journey commenced, but it's hopeless. They will have to take up those telegraph wires which are drawing all the rain & electricity from the clouds and threaten to cause another deluge! . . . Mr. Russell comes tonight & we commence our travels together next morning.

Journal

<u>Wednesday, 1st [July]</u>. Raining part of the morn[ing], heavy showers at night. Dr. Harrison As well. Called in the evening at Mr. ____. Mr. Russell came at 9.

———————

<u>Thursday, 2d</u>. Off for Baltimore via York & Lancaster. At Broad Street ran over a man, which will hereafter have to walk on one leg. Mr. R's. book purchase of the boys. Beautiful country through Lancaster & Chester Co[untie]s. Men & women harvesting. High land. Lancaster busy town, pop. 9,000. Columbia, pop. 5,000. Bridge across the Susquehanna 1¼ miles long, cost $132,000. R. R. crosses it. <u>Wilder</u> scenery from here to Balti[more]. York a large shuffling town. Patapsco River. Manufacturies. Baltimore a[t] 6½. Stopped at P. O., no letter. Stopped at Barnum's.[12] Went to IOOF Hall installation.

———————

1846. *Commercial Advertiser* (New York), June 29, 1846; Katy Matheson, "Niblo's Garden and Its 'Concert Saloon,' 1828–1846: The Evolution of a Performance Space (MA thesis, New York University, 1991); "Niblo's Garden," SoHo Memory Project, https://sohomemory.com; "Niblo's Garden," Internet Broadway Database, ibdb. com; "Ravel Family," WorldCat, worldcat.org.

12. Following the success of his American Museum in New York City in the 1840s, P. T. Barnum began acquiring additional attractions, including established museums. Among these was Peale's Museum at Seventh and Chestnut Streets in Philadelphia,

Letter

Henry Sanford to Janey Howe,
[July 3, 1846], Baltimore[13]

Philadelphia looks much the same as usual. They are making some improvements, which consist in building a few more brick blocks of houses just alike, making it impossible for a man, unless he starts at the he corner & counts doors as he goes along, to find his new house. The Quakers have just as broad brims & straight cut coats as ever, and pretty girls and demure looking Quakeresses are just as plenty as ever of a pleasant afternoon on the shady side of Chestnut Street. The "pleasant afternoons" are however are diminished in number and have been rarely seen of late.

Any city has some peculiarities which strike a stranger on entering it, something which distinguishes it from its neighbours. The differences are in persons as much as through customs. Philadelphia strikes a stranger very forcibly by some of its peculiarities. Exactitude to the extreme is a marking characteristic. The streets seem universally of such a size, laid out with as much propriety and exactitude as a backgammon board. No, I mean <u>chess</u> board, and the houses have all the same similar brick front so resembling each other that a man can't think of his home unless he joins forces with a dozen and thinks of the whole block. Neatness reigns and the water from the Schuylkill is used full as plentifully as in New York is the Groton, only they are exact about their manner of using it and persons desirous of avoiding deluging have only to stay at home till after 7 AM. The markets are patterns in the way of neatness and stretch along the center

the nation's first major museum, founded in 1786. Barnum's Museum attracted more than four hundred thousand visitors in 1846. In 1851 it was destroyed by fire. "Philadelphia History," Independence Hall Association, ushistory.org; "Phineas Taylor Barnum (1810–1891)," Geni, https://www.geni.com.

13. HSSP, Box 93, Folder 15, Letter 6.

of Market Street for I should think a full mile, and the neat white covered market waggons, ranged along the streets by hundreds, specimens in their way, each of them containing a woman in her clean white cap & apron who deals out the fresh butter, eggs &c. of her own raising. The Quakers give the city a hard and respectable appearance. One can go nowhere, but he sees either the broad brim with the straight cut coat covering some respectable looking gentleman or the plain, drab bonnet & cloak which seldom adorn ought else but a benevolent looking continence. A Quaker always inspires me with respect and confidence and they are noted here for their benevolence, upright dealing & conscientiousness. No Quaker is found who is a pauper, and the finest benevolent institutions here are founded & are under the supervision of Quakers. Some pretty faces peep out demurely from beneath the drab bonnet and a pretty face is set off to great advantage by one so much as that it looks to me rather coquettish than otherwise.

The style of architecture here is peculiarly conspicuous. Everything is Grecian and they have some of the best specimens of that order, and some of the best models of various buildings of ancient Greece to be found in this county. I have not seen a Gothic building in the city. They exceed in the liberality and benevolence displayed in their public institutions any city in this country that I am acquainted with and the Quakers are to be thanked. A week could be well spent by a stranger in walking through their public buildings & would well repay the trouble. Most of them and, as far as I have been I may say, <u>all</u> are models in their way. And yet how many [of] them [there] are that go to Philadelphia stay one day, walk through Chestnut Street, & say they have seen Philadelphia! Chestnut Street, by the way, is the Broadway of Phila., but is narrower & has much less business & bustle upon it. Here is where ladies go shopping & strolling.

Philadelphia was left yesterday morning and Mr. Russell and I concluded to go to Baltimore via Lancaster & York. It takes the whole day, but we were amply repaid by the gratification afforded at seeing a most beautiful

& highly cultivated country. Chester & Lancaster counties are the <u>crack</u> ones in Penn. as far as regards agriculture. There is some beautiful rural scenery and the road to York was like one continued garden. The German inhabitants display most pride in their farms, flocks & huge granaries or barns. The houses they live in are comparatively mean. Everyone was harvesting & it was a cheerful sight to see every wheat field nearly having men & <u>women</u> merrily at work gathering in the ripe grain. The latter part of the route had some wild scenery which was an agreeable contrast. The road followed a stream whose valley was filled with rocks & trees, with occasionally a log house. At 6½ arrived in Baltimore after a travel of one hundred & sixty miles.

And here I am in Baltimore, famous for its monuments, short towers, & intellectual & pretty young ladies! The rain is pelting down unmercifully and I am sitting in my room writing to you . . .

Journal

<u>Friday. [July 3]</u>. Rainy as usual & this day raining. Mr. R. went to Cumberland [Maryland][14] & I am to meet them there tomorrow. Went around part of the day on business & then wrote letters. Evening went to theater. Burton played.[15]

---

14. The seat of Alleghany County, Maryland, Cumberland was a center of mining and ironworking, as well as a major hub of western travel and transportation. It was the eastern terminus of the National Road, and the Chesapeake & Ohio Canal and Baltimore & Ohio passed through it. With a population of 6,067 in 1851, Cumberland was the second largest settlement in Maryland. R. S. Fisher, *Gazetteer of the State of Maryland* (New York: R. S. Colton, 1852), 66–67.
15. William Evans Burton (1804–1860) was a popular British dramatic actor who left his career in England to emigrate to the United States in 1832. He occupied a prominent place as an actor and manager in Philadelphia, Baltimore, and New York City, where he operated Burton's Theater. In 1837 he established the *Gentlemen's Magazine*, devoted to poetry, fiction, and the sporting life. After selling the magazine in 1840, Burton went on to edit other magazines and wrote several books. James Grant Wilson

Saturday, July 4th. Wet & rainy. Bad day for a national jubilee. Started at 7½ for Cumberland per R.R.[16] Met Foster of Washington on the steps bound the same way. Fine scenery along Patapsco River. Ellicott's mills.[17] Land slip. Harper's Ferry.[18] Survivors of wreck of *Sutty*. Gen. Taylor's daughter. Mrs. Davis' husband just appointed colonel.[19] Arrived at Cumberland late,

---

and John Fiske, eds., "Burton, William Evans," *Appleton's Cyclopedia of American Biography* (New York: D. Appleton, 1900).

16. Henry traveled westward on the Baltimore & Ohio Railroad. The first common-carrier rail line in the United States, the B & O was incorporated in 1828 and began construction from its namesake city the following year. The line was extended to Cumberland, Maryland, in November 1842. "Baltimore and Ohio Timeline," Baltimore and Ohio Railroad Network, borail.net.

17. Ellicott's Mills, founded by John, Andrew, and Joseph Ellicott on the Patapsco River in 1772, became a center of saw and grain milling and other industry by the early nineteenth century. In 1830 it became the first terminus of the Baltimore & Ohio Railroad outside Baltimore. R. S. Fisher, *Gazetteer of the State of Maryland* (New York: J. H. Colton, 1851), 70; "Historic Ellicott City's History," Ellicott City, ellicottcity.net.

18. Situated at the confluence of the Shenandoah and Potomac Rivers in present-day West Virginia, Harper's Ferry, Virginia, marked the passage of the latter river through the Blue Ridge mountains. The town contained several factories and mills, and was the home of the US Armory. A focus of transportation routes, Harper's Ferry was located on the Baltimore & Ohio Railroad line, and the Chesapeake & Ohio Canal passed along the opposite bank of the Potomac. The railroad crossed the river here on a single-track line on a bridge designed by Benjamin Latrobe and opened in 1837. Richard Edwards, *Statistical Gazetteer of the State of Virginia* (Richmond, VA: By the author, 1855), 263; Herbert Harwood Jr., *Impossible Challenge II: Baltimore to Washington and Harpers Ferry from 1828 to 1994* (Baltimore: Barnard Roberts & Co., 1994), 65.

19. Mary Elizabeth Taylor (1824–1909) was the youngest of five daughters of Gen. Zachary Taylor, then in command of the American army in Mexico and later president of the United States. She married Capt. William Wallace Smith Bliss in 1848. Following his death three years later, Mary Taylor Bliss married Philip Pendleton Dandridge in 1858. "Mary Elizabeth Bliss," Geni, https://www.geni.com. Mrs. Davis's husband Col. Jefferson Davis (1808–1889) served as an officer in the US Army from 1828 to 1835, but resigned his commission to marry his first wife, Sarah Knox Taylor, another daughter of Gen. Zachary Taylor, who opposed the match. From 1835 until 1846 Davis was a cotton planter and served in the US Congress. Sarah Taylor Davis died

12 PM. Damage by rains & flood considerable. Crops hurt, bridges & RR endangered, had to cross bridge very cautiously, me on foot. Pd. for the baggage $3.75.

Letter

Henry Sanford to Janey Howe, July 4, 1846, "Point of Rocks"
[on train from Baltimore to Cumberland, MD][20]

I shall add this to my part-finished letter commenced at Baltimore. There has been a "land slip" at this point and we have been waiting here three hours and shall have to wait two more while the track is being cleared off. We are 109 miles from Cumberland & 69 from Baltimore. Some two hundred passengers content to remain quiet in the cars and sleep if possible. I have found a sheet paper and some ink at a miserable house here and not being inclined to sleep, I shall write you a few lines . . .

What a power steam has! Surely as the current phrase is, it does "annihilate time & space." The transition from Derby to Cumberland is by no means difficult. Steam all the way. Take your map and follow me, in imagination at least. Would you were here in person & reality, I think you might enjoy it. Imagine me whisking over the sand plains of New Jersey, through neat villages & luxuriant gardens of peach trees & strawberry vines, & passing away time by watching the actions & persons of a <u>lot</u> of German immigrants

---

in 1835 and ten years later he married Varina Howell, whom Henry encountered. Jefferson Davis returned to the army in 1846, and his heroic behavior in battle at Monterrey and Buena Vista earned him national acclaim and the respect of Gen. Taylor. During the following decade he served as a US senator from Mississippi and secretary of war, resigning in 1861 when Mississippi seceded from the Union. He was named president of the Confederacy in 1861, an office he held until the Civil War's end four years later. "Jefferson Davis," Biography, http://www.biography.com.

20. HSSP, Box 93, Folder 15, Letter 8.

just imported. Among them a family of four, & good musicians play and sing many familiar airs not unskillfully.

Imagine me then walking up Walnut Street followed by a black porter, there are no white ones here, & finally "bringing up" at "Head's," that prince of good-livers.[21] You should see his dinner table. At the head, Head himself sits with rubicund face, immense form & gouty feet, just such a man as Hogarth would have painted did he wish to delineate an English gentleman fond of turtle & roast beef. Around his table in cushioned arm chairs are principally portly gentlemen who are capable of judging of the merits & capacity of the <u>artiste</u> who presides over the <u>cuisine</u>. The waiters speak scarce above a whisper and seem shod in velvet. And here is the best cook, the best table, the best landlord and the most <u>homely</u> (<u>to be</u> sure) place to be found in the country. It is devoted almost exclusively to bachelors, but you take no interest in this.

Would you [be] in Chestnut Street, the Broadway of Philadelphia? Here is the place of a pleasant afternoon to see the beauty and fashion of the city. The most fashionable bonnet however does not cover the prettiest face. Did you ever see a Quakeress? If so, you remember the oddly shaped drab hat they wear. Well some of these very hats set off to admirable advantage some of the prettiest faces in the town. It gives the most demurely coquettish look in the world. Here is the capital of Quakerdom, and one cannot walk out without meeting either a drab bonnet or a broad brimmed hat. They have great influence in giving the city a staid & respectable look in all respects.

---

21. A well-known resident of Philadelphia, Joseph Head reopened the Munson House as Head's Hotel on South Third Street in 1843. A contemporary account described it as "the model for a hotel, for the use of those who would live quietly and luxuriously. Better breakfasts and better dinner no man could desire, and the wines were superlatively fine. Mr. Head himself presided—a landlord who is by birth and association a gentleman—and he saw to it, like the host of a private house, that every guest received all possible attention." *Daily Picayune* (New Orleans), June 29, 1843.

Journal

<u>Sunday, 5th</u>. At 2 AM picked up Mr. Russell at Frostburgh [Maryland].[22] Passage of the Alleghenies by stage coach. 9 in my coach—hard sleeping. Scenery good, looking its wilderness, for they are <u>girdling</u> the forest trees for cultivation. Arrived at <u>Brownsville</u> [Pennsylvania], the first stop, at 3½.[23] The last of the others did not reach until 6. Started for city at 1½ & to Pittsburgh at 6. Slack water navigation. 3 hours heavy toll. Coach passengers 25¢. Fright of all kinds high. Arrived at Pittsburgh qt 12.[24] St. Charles Hotel almost full. Some of our passengers had to go elsewhere.

<u>Monday, 6th</u>. Spent day looking at factories. Iron working & steamers. Gas works & glass do. State House. Evidence of the great fire almost gone. Money contributions there for divided as follows: 50% among all losses under $300, 25% for all losses under $3,000, & the remainder about 20% among the others. The market men ar[e] those who owned that land around which has risen. Population of Allegheny cities & Birmingham, Manchester, &c. is 60,000. Heaviest iron works are Sligo works.[25] Principal

---

22. Frostburg, Maryland, was situated on the National Road and was the center of an extensive mining industry. Fisher, *Gazetteer of the State of Maryland* (1851), 73.
23. Brownsville, Pennsylvania, was a largely Quaker community located at the point the National Road bridged the Monongahela River. Its industries included a steam engine factory, a steamboat yard, and a glassworks. Thomas F. Gordon, *Gazetteer of the State of Pennsylvania* (Philadelphia: T. Belknap, 1832), 67.
24. The industrial center of western Pennsylvania, Pittsburgh lay at the confluence of the Alleghany and Monongahela Rivers. Founded in 1785 and linked by water to central Pennsylvania west of the Appalachians, southward to Maryland and Virginia, as well as westward to the Ohio and Mississippi drainages, and by rail to the Susquehanna Valley, Pittsburgh industries carried on an extensive trade. Using the vast reserves of coal from the surrounding area, its forges, rolling mills, and foundries turned out a vast array of machines and iron goods. Glass factories and cotton, wool, and paper mills also flourished here, as did grist- and sawmills, distilleries, and other industries. The Western University of Pennsylvania, now the University of Pittsburgh, was incorporated there in 1819. Gordon, *Gazetteer of the State of Pennsylvania*, 377–380.
25. The Sligo Furnace was a cold-blast steam furnace located on Licking Creek at Sligo,

manufacturers are manufacturers of iron. There are 8 or 10 cotton mills. PM visited the arsenal & U. S. Armory. Shipping off arms &c. to Mexico now.[26] Cemetery. An old mansion. Pretty situation. Allegheny & Monongahela Rivers. Wire suspension bridge. Monongahela House.[27] Miss Ward from Arkansas Trace at evening. Maj. Beard, Col. White, Mr. Hopkins. Walk at evening through the city. Small auction stores. The Point. Rafts & timber. The Point is of no importance, though very similar to the Battery, NY. All business is done up near the bridge.

Tuesday, 7th. Up early & packed. Took a horse & wagon about in morning to see tack factory. Stopped coming back to see the Sligo works. They make iron from the ore & own mines for coal & iron. Coal in all the hills around Pittsburgh & here coal is shipped down from the mines to the foundries. They make nails & do heavy ironware. Left at 10 on steamboat *Hibernia*, Maj B., Col. W., Mr. Ferry, Mr. Russell.[28] Mr. R. Determined to land at

---

Pennsylvania, near Pittsburgh in 1845. In 1845 and 1847 it produced fifteen hundred tons of iron, which was shipped by water via several nearby wharves on Licking Creek. "Sligo Furnace, Piney Twp., Clarion County, Pennsylvania," Ancestry, https://www.ancestry.com.

26. After much debate in Congress regarding the cause and goals of a war with Mexico, the United States declared war on its southern neighbor on May 13, 1846. The Mexican-American War, concluded by treaty nearly two years later, resulted in the acquisition by the United States of lands claimed by Texas north of the Rio Grande River as well as the Mexican provinces of New Mexico and Upper California, a total of 525,000 square miles. Amy S. Greenberg, *A Wicked War: Polk, Clay, Lincoln, and the 1846 U. S. Invasion of Mexico* (New York: Alfred A. Knopf, 2012), 259–260.

27. Managed by James Crossan, the Monongahela House was a principal hotel in Pittsburgh. Opened in the spring of 1841, it was situated on the bank of the Monongahela River at the corner of Smithfield and Front Streets. *Daily Picayune* (New Orleans), Apr. 16, 1841, May 3, 1842.

28. Under the command of Capt. John Simpson, the steamboat *Hibernia* made runs between Pittsburgh and Cincinnati in the 1830s and 1840s, making thirty-seven landings between the two ports. In 1844 it completed the trip down river in thirty-three hours and the return trip to Pittsburgh in forty-nine hours. *The Bee* (New Orleans), Jan. 1, 1831; *Richmond (VA) Whig*, Dec. 21, 1847; "Riverboat Captains," Riverboat Dave's

Beaver [Pennsylvania] & proceed to Cleveland direct.[29] Changed his mind, however, when there & proceeded with us. Stopped at Wheeling [Virginia] at 6 PM.[30] Saw Dixon, Mrs. Com. Stewart. Castor oil.

<u>Wednesday, 8th</u>. Blennerhassett Island.[31] Coal banks. Portsmouth [Ohio].[32] Speech offering by drunken doctor.

<u>Thursday, 9t[h]</u>. Arrived [at Cincinnati] at 6 am. Stopped at Broadway House, Mr. Longworth's place. Mr. Auburn. Pretty residences. Pork packers. Camp Washington. Volunteers, embarkation of. The business of Cincinnati, pop estimated at fr. 90,000 to 100,000. Buildings increase. Built last 2 years, 1,500 per year. Steamships. Manufacturing of screws, nails, latches, &c axes &c.[33]

Paddlewheel Site, riverboatdaves.com; "Steamboating on the Rivers," Steamboats. org, steamboats.org.

29. Bedford, Pennsylvania, was the seat of Bedford County, situated on the great road leading from Philadelphia to Pittsburgh. The town was famous for its mineral springs, believed to have curative powers, that drew visitors during the warm months. Gordon, *Gazetteer of the State of Pennsylvania*, 38–41.

30. Wheeling, the seat of Ohio County, Virginia (now West Virginia), was situated at the confluence of Wheeling Creek and the Ohio River. A center of river trade and the manufacture of ironware, glass and paper, flour, and woolen goods, the city would become the western terminus of the Baltimore & Ohio Railroad in 1853. Edwards, *Gazetteer of the State of Virginia*, 411–415.

31. Blennerhassett Island is an island in the Ohio River below the mouth of the Little Kanawha River. In 1798 Harman Blennerhassett purchased the island and built his mansion there. It was here that he and Aaron Burr allegedly plotted treason by attempting to establish an independent empire in the Southwest. The mansion accidentally burned in 1811. "Blennerhassett Island State Historical Park," West Virginia State Parks, blennerhassettislandstatepark.com.

32. Portsmouth's location on the Ohio River at the terminus of the Ohio Canal provided access to the interior as well as to Lake Erie. The seat of Scioto County, Ohio, Portsmouth was a major port of call for steamboats on the Ohio River and contained flour mills and sawmills as well as factories producing iron and brass products. Warren Jenkins, *The Ohio Gazetteer and Traveler's Guide* (Columbus: Isaac N. Whiting, 1839), 370.

33. Known as the "Queen City," Cincinnati was the seat of Trumbull County, Ohio, and

COURTESY OF THE SANFORD MUSEUM, CITY OF SANFORD, FLORIDA.

Cincinnati, Ohio, from the Kentucky side of the Ohio River at the time of Henry Sanford's visit. The lithographed image appears on a letter he sent to his fiancée Janey Howe after his arrival at the western metropolis June 9, 1846.

Letter

Henry Sanford to Janey Howe,
July 9, 1846, Cincinnati, OH[34]

I write anticipating a letter from you at Detroit dear Janey and hope it will tell me of your welfare & those around you. The heading above tells

---

the largest and one of the oldest commercial cities in the West. First laid out in 1789, it grew rapidly in the early nineteenth century and was home to an estimated forty thousand inhabitants by 1840. Situated on the Ohio River, the city offered access by water to the lakes via the Ohio Canal and by railroad as far as Xenia, Ohio. A major manufacturing center, Cincinnati produced steam engines, cotton gins, sugar mills, steamboats, and other finished goods, and was the principal center of pork packing in the West. The state's medical college was located here, as well as a teacher's' college, athenaeum, mechanics' institute, museums, a commercial bank, and the lunatic asylum. Ibid., 110–118.

34. HSSP, Box 93, Folder 15, Letter 9.

you where I am, but it is a very poor view of a very fine city & I rather regret sending it for it takes up too much valuable room. Do you see in the center of the picture a house surrounded with trees? I have just been over the grounds of it, which is one of the finest residences in this country. Here are grounds with an area of six acres laid out in grove & garden. One forgets that here he is in the center of a city of 90,000 inhabitants. Hot houses full of plants & flowers abound & fruits & flowers without are all in great abundance. I was given some ripe apples from the trees there. The owner, Mr. Longworth, is an old resident who commenced here in a log house, has seen the city grow up and increase around him but still keeps his grounds which would sell for vast sums as building lots having the true philosophy of the thing that he can enjoy his land better so than if the sale of it yields him millions. He has many pictures &c., many of them poor ones too, and showed me the first bust Powers cut. It is head of a female of exquisite beauty.[35]

---

35. The estate Henry Sanford visited was that of Nicholas Longworth. Born in Newark, New Jersey in 1783, he moved to Cincinnati in 1803 and was a lawyer, banker, and horticultural expert. Longworth was a successful winemaker, having cultivated Catawba grapes on the Ohio River as early as 1813. Entering commercial production in 1820, by the 1840s he distributed his wine throughout the United States and Europe and became one of the wealthiest men in America. "Nicholas Longworth," Ohio History Central, ohiohistorycentral.org. In 1846 a contemporary account described Longworth as "an extensive and wealthy horticulturist, near Cincinnati, [who] has about 100 acres in grapes, strawberries, raspberries, peaches, &c. Fifty acres are devoted exclusively to grapes and strawberries. He is engaged in making wine, the quality of which is said to be very little, if at all inferior to the foreign." *Richmond (VA) Whig*, Sept. 15, 1846.

The bust was by Hiram Powers (1805–1873), an American sculptor who grew up in Cincinnati, where he began his artistic career modeling wax figures for Joseph Dorfeuille's Western Museum there. With the support of poet Francis Trollope, he moved to Washington, DC, in 1834 to produce plaster busts of celebrities. He later moved to Florence, Italy, where he gained international fame as a sculptor in marble. "Hiram Powers," Encyclopedia.com, http://www.encyclopedia.com/topic/Hiram_Powers.aspx; Francis Trollope, "The American Sculptor Powers," *Daily National Intelligencer* (Washington, DC), Mar. 15, 1844.

Two days ago & we left Pittsburgh & now we are five hundred miles distant. You see in the "frontispiece" the kinds of boats that transported us. We are approaching military scenes. Cols., captains & majors are plenty as blackberries & Gen. Taylor of "Halls of Montezuma" are watchwords in everybody's mouth. I came down in company with a major of the Army belonging to Gen. Gaines' staff & who is but lately from Mexico.[36] He goes around "on the large figure" & is rather a lion. He has been quizzing some of the passengers at my expense. "Who is that young gentleman in spectacles," said one of them to him yesterday. "What, don't you know who he is?" It's Lieut. Sanford of Flank Co., Infantry, &c, &c., who distinguished himself so much at Matamoros.[37] Don't you recognize his name? Twas in all the papers?" "Oh, yes, I think I do." So presently someone comes up confidently & insinuatingly, "well lieutenant" &c, &c. As Cincinnati has been the rendezvous for the Ohio troops, three regiments, and the streets have rather a gay appearance, presenting continually the uniforms & trappings of soldiery. A regiment is now embarking at the levee, many of the soldiers are mere boys, & will soon repent their volunteering for Mexico. A steamer with a company of dragoons has just landed at the arsenal, they too being on their way to Mexico. All this infuses quite a martial spirit & gives quite a martial air to the place. Don't you think I will do much better shooting Mexicans than buffaloes and had better try & see how much glory "Lieutenant" Sanford can win?

36. A native of Virginia born in 1777, Brevet Major General Edmund P. Gaines was commissioned in the US Army in 1806 and served as a colonel in the War of 1812. As commander of the Western Division of the army he participated in the Black Hawk and Seminole Wars and continued in this position during the Mexican-American War. *The Mexican War and Its Heroes: Being a Complete History of the Mexican War* (Philadelphia: Lippincott, Grambo & Co., 1848), 268–270.
37. On May 8, 1846, prior to a declaration of war, US Army units under Gen. Zachary Taylor defeated Mexican forces who attacked in response to an American military advance into Mexican territory south of the Rio Grande River. The victory at the Battle of Matamoros and the subsequent Mexican retreat opened the way for an American military invasion of the country. Greenberg, *A Wicked War*, 121–122.

I think one of the river steamboats would make quite a sensation in the North River. You see what they are, a superstructure two stories high on a canoe-shaped boat which looks ready to sink under the weight heaped upon it, which with cough & groan as though each turn of her engine was great labour & with each groan throwing out a cloud of white steam, goes paddling along on the western waters. One of an army of one thousand of them which navigate the Mississippi & her tributaries.

Journal

<u>Friday, 10th</u>. Took Little Maumee R.R. for Xenia [Ohio]. Pretty girl on RR. Berman Leonard. Pretty scenery along the river. Distance to Xenia 68 miles.[38] Dined there. Made acquaintance with the pretty girl. 29 of us were packed on 2 coaches for Columbus [Ohio]. I on top. Very hot & dusty. One of the volunteers on top, who had been sick. Treatment by the garrison of the soldiers shameful—almost nothing. Reached Columbus at 10½ PM.[39] "Neil House," conduct of agt. no help.[40] Started for Mansfield [Ohio], 12

---

38. The Little Miami Railroad was the second railway built in Ohio. Construction began at Cincinnati in 1837 and by the summer of 1845 was completed as far as Xenia, Ohio. "Little Miami Railroad," Abandoned, abandonedonline.net; "Railroads," Ohio History Central, ohiohistorycentral.org. Xenia, was the seat of Green County, Ohio. Situated on Shawnee Creek three miles from the Little Miami River, it had a population of about one thousand. Jenkins, *Ohio Gazetteer*, 485–486.

39. The seat of Franklin County and capital of the State of Ohio, Columbus was linked to the east and west by the National Road and by the Sandusky Turnpike to Lake Erie. A feeder canal tied Columbus to the Ohio Canal, which connected the lake with the Ohio River. Home to about six thousand residents, Columbus housed the state government offices, as well as the state penitentiary, the Ohio Asylum for the Deaf and Dumb, a lunatic asylum, a theological seminary, and a commercial bank. Jenkins, *Ohio Gazetteer*, 137–143.

40. The Neil House was a popular hotel situated across the street from the statehouse in Columbus, Ohio. Under the proprietorship of K. Wynne, the hotel was described as "the most extensive in the city" and was the site of conventions and meetings. "Neil House," *Daily Sanduskian* (Sandusky, OH), Dec. 6 and 12, 1849.

on a stage, I on top. Beautiful morn, beautiful country & pretty fine farms & farm houses. Jolly fellows on top.

Saturday, 11th. Hot & dusty. Horrible. One horse dropped dead. Very fatiguing traveling. Have never suffered more in traveling. Miss Allen, Mr. & Mrs. [blank], don't remember the lively little fellow & pretty wife. Wells & Co agent. Neil Moore & Co have 1,300 teams of horses & drivers, 900 stages, 60 agents & 8,000 miles of wire. Arrived at Mansfield at 3½ after a hard day's work.[41] Brown with shrubs & trees dry & burnt up. Took cars for Sandusky [Ohio] &c. cows on the track, all the while rattle along.[42] The land & the marshy low country. Arrived at 6½. Lake Erie, again stopped at the verandah kept by porter. Bath in the lake. Most sick & to bed early.

Letter

Henry Sanford to Fanny Russell,
July 12, 1846, Huron, OH[43]

You must then ask [your father] to tell you of our ride over the rail road along the Little Miami River to Xenia and of our being packed with twenty-seven other passengers in two stage coaches, on the top of one of which myself and four others had the necessity imposed upon us of riding under the hot sun & over the dusty roads, with the thermometer at 98° to Columbus, the capital of the state. He must then tell you of the

---

41. Situated on the National Road, Mansfield was the seat of Richland County, Ohio, and home to two thousand residents. Jenkins, *Ohio Gazetteer*, 280.
42. Sandusky was a port town and port of entry on Lake Erie. The seat of Huron County, Ohio, Sandusky's success was tied to trade, and it was a busy Lake Erie port for travelers between New York and the Mississippi country. Its shipyards constructed steamboats, and its quarries supplied building stone for export. The city was linked to Columbus by turnpike. Ibid., 395–396.
43. HSSP, Box 93, Folder 15, Letter 10.

"Neil House" where we stopped for supper at half past ten at night, of his strenuous endeavors, get packed a little less closely in another coach, he having with one more been squeezed into a seat with a very large man who could not fail accommodating himself with one half of it, the effects of which seemed already apparent in the diminished size of your father. Be particular to ask him concerning his fat companion & how much he enjoyed the ride from Xenia to Columbus. All his eloquence availed not, however, & having only the satisfaction of giving the agent a lecture he deserved, & which was the only relief he got. Was forced to bear repacking with eight others inside the coach while three more of us mounted on top, & at almost 12 at night started for Mansfield where we were to take the rail road to Sandusky City. He will doubtless tell you of the agreeable night he passed inside the coach now drowsing on the shoulder of his neighbour, then having his neighbour with no gentle pressure reposing on him at one time & the passenger opposite bowing & and nodding at each other with much gravity & apparent politeness till bumping each other's heads both woke up rubbing their foreheads & wondering at the uncivil behaviour of their vi-a-vis. At another time nodding backwards a lady behind wakes up with a scream & complains bitterly of a smashed bonnet of all this. Of his pleasant dreams & quiet slumbers please enquire about, for being on top I can give you no information concerning them.

Henry Sanford to Janey Howe,
July 13, 1846, Detroit, MI[44]

I have your letter and thank you heartily for it. It carries me back home & you are talking to me again . . . You would like to know how I got here. It makes me groan in spirit to think of it & by the way I wrote yesterday a letter to Mr. Russell's daughter, a school girl, and as it's rather more lengthy than I had intended, [I send] it to you & attempt to send her a more pithy one.

---

44. HSSP, Box 93, Folder 15, Letter 9.

It will serve to show you the route I have followed. The country through Ohio has certainly appeared to me very beautiful. A few years' since a wilderness, & now the third state in the Union in point of population & power. Its resources are infinite & it would seem as though it would soon yield the palm to no state. It is scarcely to be realized & one thinks of fairy land at passing by its beautiful country seats, fine farms & pretty villages. It is now harvest & every wheat field presented a busy scene, and crops were being gathered in of an amount to astonish a New England farmer. At the lowest calculation they estimate the wheat crop at 50,000,000 of bushels! & some of the counties will raise double the amount they were put at.

We arrived here last night, making the second Sunday of travel since my departure. There is no hearing the organ for me. I thought of you playing away bravely at church yesterday (by the way I saw Mr. Autry this morning who has improved somewhat in health) and a week ago Sunday, while I was on my way to Pittsburgh, you were writing to me! I commend you for having a better occupation than I had & I hope yesterday found you writing another letter to me at Mackinaw . . .

Journal

Sunday, 12th. Took carriage to Huron 10 miles. Remained there until 2 & then st[eam] b[oa]t *New Orleans* came all aboard for Detroit. Arrived at 9. Stopped at National [Hotel].[45]

———————————

Monday, 13th. Charley Rice called, same Mr. Chandler. Drove around with gentlemen to see the town, the fort. Lt. Meigs, Ryan, & Mr. Trout got lost in the woods. River road, Gen. Cass house, his operations in real estate.

———————————

45. The steamboat *New Orleans* operated on lake Erie in the 1840s, calling on Ohio ports between Buffalo and Detroit under the command of Capt. Nicholson. *Daily Sanduskian* (Sandusky, OH), July 14, 1848, May 3, 1849. Both Henry and his parents had previously made the National Hotel their home in Detroit.

Saw Mr. Ashley. Took tea with Mr. Chandler, pretty wife, Mrs. Moore.[46] Rode out with them after tea. Pretty carriage & horses. Fort Nonsense, the pleasant "Wales House," where Gen. Hull surrendered, the Saratoga corner.[47] At 10 PM Mr. Fox, who was present, suddenly concluded to leave for Buffalo, & has so, much to the chagrin of his son.

Tuesday, 14th. Left this morn[ing] at 8 in cars for Kalamazoo with Mr. Russell. This was his desire, not mine, for I have been over this route too often. Reached K. At 6½ PM.[48] Took stage at 7 for St. Joseph, 55 miles distant. Seven passengers, very dirty. Heat for last fortnight at K. Has averaged 98°, lowest this month 94°, highest 104°.[49] Quite a change came

---

46. Mr. Chandler was likely Zachariah Chandler. Born in New Hampshire, he settled in Detroit in the early 1830s and became a wealthy wholesale merchant. He was active in assisting the afflicted during the cholera epidemic of 1834 and was involved in public service as a member of the Merchant's Exchange Board and the Young Men's Benevolent Society. One of the most influential politicians in Michigan from 1835 to 1860, Chandler became the boss of the state's Republican Party during the first twenty-five years of its existence. Chandler served as mayor of Detroit in 1852 and 1853, a US senator from 1862 to 1871, and secretary of the interior under President U. S. Grant. During the Civil War, Chandler was among the Radical Republicans in Congress. He was active in the administration of the Michigan State Bank and various plank road companies. Chandler Street in Detroit was named for him in 1881. Silas Farmer, *History of Detroit and Wayne County and Early Michigan* (Detroit: Gale Research, 1969), 49, 102, 140, 372, 650, 785–786, 864, 939; Willis F. Dunbar and George S. May, *Michigan: A History of the Wolverine State* (Grand Rapids, MI: William B. Eerdmans, 1980), 364–365.
47. Fort Nonsense, also known as Fort Croghan, was erected in 1806 at what became the corner of Park and High Streets in Detroit. This circular fort consisted of an earthen embankment surrounded by a ditch. Farmer, *History of Detroit*, 226.
48. The Central Railroad of Michigan, which had only been completed as far as Marshall at the time of Henry's 1844 visit, continued to extend its tracks westward. On February 6, 1846, Kalamazoo became its western terminus. Graydon M. Meints, "Michigan Railroad Construction, 1835–1875" (Ann Arbor: Transportation Library, University of Michigan, 1981, typewritten), 6.
49. The high temperatures that Henry described represented a period of hot and dry weather that affected Michigan and Wisconsin that year. One observer reported temperatures as high as "103° and 105° in the shade" and added, "In some sections

on, very cool, making overcoats necessary. The Phrenology Lecture, this evening, &c., DeWitt Clinton.

———————————

Wednesday, 15th. Breakfast at 12 miles from St. Joe after a miserable night, very dirty & very cold. Found clover leaves frozen stiff. Thermometer could not be much shot of 40°, so much change from 98°! Reached St. Joseph at 9½ o'clock, almost 15 hours for 55 miles. Horrible roads, corduroy, &c. Took steamer *Champion* for Chicago overnight.[50] All hands seasick. I had good dinner & went to sleep. Stopped at Mich[igan] City. Trouble, then on a/c [on account] of the wind detained half an hour. Went to sleep again & kept so till we reached Chicago at 8 o'clock. Stopped at Lake House, kept by Richards, good.[51] Gave woodcock &c for supper. Saw Pinckney, an old school mate. Went to hear Chrysty's Minstrels, good, & then went to bed.[52]

———————————

of the country the drought had been very excessive." *Augusta (GA) Chronicle*, Aug. 25, 1846.

50. The steamboat *Champion* was built in Newport, Ohio, by Messrs. Ward and launched July 4, 1843. With a keel of 140 feet, a deck 144 feet, and a beam of 20 feet, the boat was intended to sail between St. Joseph and Chicago under the command of Capt. E. B. Ward. The extension of the Central Railroad between Detroit and New Buffalo opened a new western mail route, and the *Champion* became the important link between western Michigan ports and Chicago. "Steamboat Launch," *Detroit Daily Advertiser*, July 20, Aug. 21, 1843; Joel Stone, *Floating Palaces of the Great Lakes: A History of Passenger Steamships on the Inland Seas* (Ann Arbor: University of Michigan Press, 2015), 70.

51. The "Lake House," which was closed at the time of Henry Sanford's 1844 visit, had been refurbished and reopened two years later. It was described as being "in a convenient situation on the north side, near the river and steamboat landings, and is provided with a large dining saloon and parlors, and airy and commodious apartments completely furnished throughout, with a large yard and stable attached. The bar will at all times be supplied with the choicest liquors, and the table with all the delicacies of the market and season." William Richards, its proprietor, had until recently managed the American Hotel in Buffalo. *Daily Picayune* (New Orleans), Apr. 21, 1846.

52. Christy's Minstrels were a blackface group formed in New York by Edwin P. Christy in 1842. They performed in various cities during the next two decades and were known for performances of "various Southern airs and burlesques." *Evening Post*

Thursday, 16. Took a walk before breakfast. Had a capital one at 7 & then went aboard st[eam] b[oa]t *Superior* for Milwaukee.⁵³ Fare viz to Milwaukee $3, to Mackinaw $10, from Mackinaw to Buffalo $10, from Chicago to Buffalo $12. Chicago looks busy & is improving. Old man who wanted to sell his property, &c there, an amusing specimen. Arrived at Little Port [Waukegan, Illinois] about noon. Took a wagon (Mr. R. & I) to see if we could find any grouse. Had to content ourselves shooting woodpeckers, &c. Little Port is quite nice & thriving.⁵⁴

Arrived at Southport [Kenosha, Wisconsin] about 4. Pop. 2,600, is increasing rapidly.⁵⁵ Minister had been to St. Peters [Mendota, Minnesota]. Pretty woman in house. This blue water of the lake brown along the shore. Mosquitoes abound. Have been looking over my expenses. They are up to today $152 for 22 days! Conversation with the pretty woman is from

(New York), Feb. 8, 1847; "Law Intelligence: Minstrels in Court," *New York Daily Times*, Sept. 14, 1855.

53. Launched at Perrysburg, Ohio, on July 17, 1845, the steamboat *Superior* had a length of keel 184 feet, a deck of 195 feet, and a beam of 27 feet, 8 inches. Commanded by Capt. Samuel Hubbell, it initially operated out of Maumee, Ohio. Nine years later the *Superior* was hauled over the portage to Lake Superior, and despite the efforts of its experienced master, Capt. Hiram J. Jones, it sank near Pictured Rocks in a storm on Oct. 30, 1856 with the loss of fifty lives. *National Daily Pilot* (Buffalo, NY), July 23, 1845; "Navigation on Lake Superior," *Buffalo Daily Courier*, July 26, 1854; Karl Bohnak, "Tragedy on Lake Superior: October 30, 1856," Upper Michigan's Source, uppermichiganssource.com.

54. The seat of Lake County, Illinois, Littleport, later called Waukegan, was situated on a high bluff above Lake Michigan about forty miles north of Chicago. A trading center, the village was a regular stop for steamboats on the lake. James Mason Peck, *A Gazetteer of Illinois* (Philadelphia: Grigg & Elliot, 1837), 223.

55. Situated on the western shore of Lake Michigan, Southport was settled by a western New York company in 1835. Later, as part of the city of Kenosha, it became the seat of Kenosha County. Its harbor, formed by a small bay, was the southernmost port in Wisconsin. John Warren Hunt, *Wisconsin Gazetteer, Containing the Names, Locations, and Advantages of Counties, Cities, Towns Villages, Post Offices, and Settlements . . . in the State of Wisconsin* (Madison, WI: Beriah Brown, 1853), 117–118.

Norwich, has her little girl with her, name is, I think, Fuller. The minister (as I thought) will be hunting from the same place.

Racine [Wisconsin] is a pretty town, prettily situated on a bluff, pop. 2,700. Has a large hotel.[56] Arrived at Milwaukee a 8½ PM. Stopped at U. S. Hotel. Considerable difficulty finding which one was best house. There are 4 that call themselves "crack." This is the newest & best & is a very large house.

<u>Friday, 17th</u>. Woke in Milwaukee. Threatens of rain. We arrived with Mr. Russell. Pop. 9,000, 5,000 increase in 2 years! The brick is a light yellow color, preferable, I think, to red. A great deal of business done here. Much competition, it is said, among the dry goods men. Almost ruinous—6 large hardware stores sell everything. List of hardware [stores]: Fraser & King, W. H. Bryan, J. C. Creamer & Co., H. W. Beebe, L. J. Farwell, Knoeeland & Fay, Shoefinster, Allen & Allis. A great deal of grading is needed & being done. There is a creek, the Menominee, running through the town, with a dam 2 miles up, has several mills & factories upon it, & is navigable to the dam. Rode up there. Like all other places here, all the trees are cut down. Improvements going on rapidly. Everybody says they are doing well. There are 4 churches: Catholic, Epis[copal], Presby[terian], & Baptist. Believe there is a Methodist also.[57]

Saw S. P. Grant of Hartford, the forger at tables. He looked rather

---

56. The city of Racine was the seat of Racine County, Wisconsin, and a major lake port with an improved harbor. A city of three thousand inhabitants in 1847, Racine was the second most populous in the state. Its industries included mills, furnaces, mechanic shops, and shipyards. Ibid., 183–185.

57. The seat of Milwaukee County, Wisconsin, Milwaukee was the territory's largest city and was home to more than fourteen thousand residents in 1847. It was situated on a bay at the mouth of the Milwaukee River, which provided abundant water power for the city's numerous mills, factories and other industries. Milwaukee boasted several institutions of higher learning, including the Milwaukee University Institute, and the US district court met there. In addition to its role as a port, the city had become the hub of a network of overland routes into the interior of the state. Ibid., 146–150.

weary & knew I knew him. Attended an auction for things for an outfit for California & bought several things useful for my purpose. Lands along the river low & swampy. Bluffs back & around, making pretty situation for houses. Saw Mr. Garrett of Chicago. He says he will go with me on the prairies. His stories concerning land sales, &c. [B]een around town making up my out-fit, rather a curious one. Left at 9 o'clock per st[eam] b[oa]t *Great Western*.[58] She got in at 9½ & remained 4½ hours. Took passage in her for Mackinaw.

Saturday, 18th. Continued cloudy & promises rain. Stopped early in the morn at Sheboygan and left just as I got up—is a flourishing place.[59] Passengers on board very ordinary. Two would-be young ladies in curls who play in the band are most conspicuous. The chamber maid would pass for more of a lady than any of them. Ill-kept & ill-arranged boat, large cargo of wheat, wool for the eastern states, maybe sent on here, & hay up. Stopped at Manitou Island to wood at 6 o'clock PM. Took gun & went out after pigeons. Shot a dozen or so. Great quantities of them. Rail roads for transportation of wood. These islands are leased by Reed. All the boats stop here to wood. Sandy with pine woods. Game supper in the pantry. Capt. Walker & new boat, <u>polite</u> steward, mate &c.

---

58. The *Great Western*, on which Henry Sanford's parents had traveled in 1839, had been rebuilt after the fire at Buffalo that year and returned to service under the command of its builder, Capt. Augustus Walker. Walker had the hull towed to Detroit in the fall of 1839, and the vessel was back in service on the lakes by the following summer and continued under Walker's command in 1846. It operated at least as late as 1849, by which time Capt. Whittaker was its master. "Destruction of the Steamboat 'Great Western,'" *Western Herald* (Sandwich, Ontario), Sept. 18, 1839; *Alexandria (VA) Gazette*, Sept. 16, 1839; *Albany (NY) Argus*, June 16, 1840; "Capt. Walker, Buffalo," *Spectator* (New York), Oct. 21, 1846; *Daily Sanduskian* (Sandusky, OH), June 18, 1849.
59. The seat of Sheboygan County, the village of Sheboygan lay at the mouth of the Sheboygan River on the shore of Lake Michigan. In 1846 it was home to about four hundred souls. Hunt, *Wisconsin Gazetteer*, 204–205.

<u>Sunday, 19th</u>. Arrived at Mackinaw at 4. Went to Harrick's mission house. Currently shops, "Injun curiosities." Went to church in the garrison, having first taken a ride with Mr. R. around the island. Good roads made by Capt. Scott. Young growth of trees, limestone foundation. The fort is [a] stockade, blockhouse, garrison small & <u>green</u>. Capt. Casey & lady, Rev. Mr. O'Brian. Fine view of harbour from Capt. Casey's quarters.[60] St[eam]m b[oa]t *Boston* came in.[61] Miss Howard & Mrs. Whitney. Mrs. Cornwell—widow in black. Rev. Dr. Shelton of Buffalo preached in the afternoon. Catholic service. Chanting priest. Walked to Fort Holmes. Arched rock & Sugar Island.[62] Raspberries, currants & cherries ripening. Trout & white fish caught in gill nets. St[eam]m b[oa]t *St. Louis* came in in the even[in]g, bro[ugh]t many passengers, a number for the house, bound for the Sault.[63] Gentlemen from Buffalo & Detroit. Dr. Shelton, wife & sister, charming as cousins.

---

60. This was likely Henry's uncle Philo S. Shelton and his wife, Georgiana Homer Shelton, and daughter Georgiana Albertina or daughter Helen. Owsley, *Register*.
61. The steamboat *Boston* was a new vessel, costing $50,000, operating on the Great Lakes in 1846. It was lost without loss of life off Milwaukee, Wisconsin, on November 14 of that year. *Rondout Freeman* (Kingston, NY), Dec. 19, 1846.
62. Although still an important focus of trade, by 1845 Mackinac Island had become a center for commercial fishing and packing of lake trout and whitefish. This industry was largely in the hands of French, métis, and Indian fishermen who went out in the lake in Mackinac boats fitted with seine nets and hooks. Lake steamers between Buffalo and Chicago called at the island's commodious harbor twice daily. The United States maintained a garrison at Fort Mackinac, and a federal Indian agent was stationed on the island. Fort Holmes was abandoned after the War of 1812 and had fallen into decay. Both Catholics and Protestants continued to have a presence in the town of Mackinac, but the large mission house built by the United Foreign Missionary Society had been abandoned when the organization moved its mission to the shore of Lake Superior. A Mr. Harrick of Detroit acquired the building and converted it into a tavern to house the increasing number of visitors. "Mackinac County, Michigan, from Our Regular Correspondent," *Daily Union* (Washington, DC), July 8, 1845; Francis Paul Prucha, *A Guide to the Military Posts of the United States, 1789–1895* (Madison, State Historical Society of Wisconsin, 1964), 89; "Fort Holmes," Mackinac State Historic Parks, mackinacparks.com.
63. The *St. Louis*, under the command of Capt. G. W. Floyd, was owned by Charles

Monday, 20th. Up at 6. B'fast at 6½. Large party bound to the Sault. Took st[eam] b[oa]t *Gen. Scott* at 7½.[64] Left my place some pleasant company, Dr. Shelton, Miss Howard, Mr. Green. Rain, cleared off & very hot. After getting among the islands, very pretty scenery, shoals & swift water. Forest trees white birch, cedars & pines. Arrive at Sault at 6 PM. Has a number of new buildings since last year & has altered rapids. Don't seem so large.[65]

Manning Reed, whose organization owned a number of Great Lakes steamboats. It was constructed before 1841 and regularly sailed between Chicago and Mackinac Island. The vessel was in service as late as 1847. Stone, *Floating Palaces*, 72, 112–113; *Daily Picayune* (New Orleans), Aug. 27, 1846.

64. Built in 1839, the steamboat *General Scott* was a high-pressure steamer of 240 tons. In 1845 it traveled regularly between Green Bay, Wisconsin, and Sault Ste. Marie, Michigan, from which travelers could debark for destinations on Lake Superior. "Early Navigation on the Lakes," *Commercial Advertiser* (New York), Apr. 7, 1846.

65. Situated on Saint Mary's River between Lakes Superior and Huron, Sault Ste. Marie was home to a Chippewa community and focus of trade in the Great Lakes region at the time of European contact in the seventeenth century. It became the site of a French mission and an important focus of the fur trade that extended from Montreal to the country above Lake Superior. Although the French fortified the site in 1751, it passed into British hands at the close of the French and Indian War in 1763. The region south of the Saint Mary's River was ceded to the United States in 1783, but remained contested until after the War of 1812. The British Northwest Company, formed in 1783, controlled the bulk of the trade south of Hudson Bay and the upper Great Lakes and maintained a presence on the Canadian side at Sault Ste. Marie. By the 1820 Treaty of Sault Ste. Marie, the Chippewas turned control of a portion of land to the United States for the construction of Fort Brady. Subsequently the American Fur Company established a presence at Sault Ste. Marie. The settlement remained a center of trade and commercial fishing, and, following the Treaty of 1836, which ceded northern Michigan lands to the United States, it became the seat of Chippewa County and by 1856 had a population of about sixteen hundred French Canadians, métis, and Americans. Paul Chrisler Phillips, *The Fur Trade*, 2 vols. (Norman: University of Oklahoma Press, 1961), 1:548, 584, 634, 2:124, 128; "Treaty of Sault Ste. Marie, 1820," Chippewa Ottawa Resource Authority, 1836cora.org; "Treaty with the Ottawa and Chippewa, 1836," Michigan Family History Network, mifamilyhistory. org; H. Huntington Lee & Co. and James Sutherland, *State of Michigan Gazetteer and Business Directory for 1856–57* (Detroit: By the authors, 1856), 191–192; Prucha, *Guide to Military Posts*, 61–62.

Stopped at Carson's. Agree to have a dance with the girls at the Vanander House, whatever pretty squaws or half breeds. Dr. Shelton starts off over the rapids in a canoe. The girls go up to the head of the rapids in a wagon. Mr. R. & I go on foot. The st[eam] b[oa]t *Julia Palmer* is most over-drawn by windlass walked by horses on ground ways, 3 lengths this day. Will be launched Saturday.[66] Copper specimens. Large quantity of ore for Boston. 5 sail vessels above & below. Supper of white fish & trout. Missed my dinner. No music. Young men singing "Mary Blain.["][67]

<u>Tuesday, 21st.</u> Up early & up for a bath in the rapids. Water cold & refreshing. Indian boy recognized me as being here last year. Engaged a brother of the man I had last year, Augustin Le Comer, to take us fishing, &c. st[eam] boat goes, takes Dr. Shelton & Miss Howard, &c. Start fishing. Go up along the side of the rapids, not much work. Indians don't want to go back of the island. Go there & catch some fish. Our dinner, roasting trout & wild pigeons. Descend the rapids at 4. Get home with 54 trout. The largest weighs 1¼ lbs. Saw one caught by an Indian boy 4½ lbs. Bowling alley. Soldiers for Texas. View from hill back of town. Fort Brady. The fur

---

66. The *Julia Palmer* was a low-pressure steamboat of 280 tons. Built at Buffalo in 1836, it carried passengers on the lakes under the command of Capt. Robert Wagstaff. In 1846 the *Julia Palmer* was hauled overland to Lake Superior at Sault Ste. Marie, Michigan, and became the first steamer to sail on Lake Superior, under Capt. Moody. The ship was broken up prior to 1857. Lewis Marvill, "First Trip by Steam on Lake Superior," *Michigan Historical Collections* 4 (1883): 69; John Disturnell, *A Trip through the Lakes of North America* (New York: J. Disturnell, 1857), 16; "The Fleet on Lake Superior," *Cleveland Weekly Herald*, July 21, 1847; "The Storm on Lake Superior," *New York Daily Tribune*, Dec. 10, 1847.

67. "Mary Blane" is an American song that was popularized in blackface minstrel shows during the mid-1840s. Several different versions are known, all featuring an enslaved male protagonist whose lover, Mary Blane, is abducted variously by Indians, blacks, or abolitionists, or is sold by her owner and subsequently dies. G. L. Kittredge, "Note on the Song of 'Mary Blane,'" *Journal of American Folklore* 99 (1926): 200–207; William J. Mahar, *Behind the Burnt Cork Mask: Early Blackface Minstrelsy and Antebellum American Popular Culture* (Urbana: University of Illinois Press, 1999), 293.

co. Hudson's Bay Co. Missionary. Slatiers. Squatters. Tame crows. Capt. Tyler. Maj. Forsyth. Farnum, [who] writes about hunting &c., gave me an information respecting buffalo shooting, etc. party returned from Pointe aux Pins & Gros Cap.[68] Preparations to go tomorrow by Mr. R.

Wednesday, 22d. Mr. R. Up at 5 & off to the Gros Cap to see Lake Superior. I went off trout fishing at 8½, taking 2 Indian boys & a canoe. Poor luck. Mr. King, our pompous, fat friend, & family relations go too in two canoes. At noon I make a fire roast some trout & a pigeon I shot. Knocked down 3 pigeons at one shot, but lost them in the bushes. Woods on fire. Effect on taking a single tree, furious flame, rapid ignition, pyramid of fire. Caught but five trout & returned early. A party of the other house got about 200 from [the lake] in 12 hours almost. Mr. R. returned soon after I did. Had a pleasant trip. We took a walk. Fine view from hill back of the village missionary station. Am[erican] Fur Co. fort, stockade & blockhouses in the village. Bark mat & log & frame.[69] People of all tinges from copper color to white. Specimens of copper ore at the storehouses.[70] Arrival of st[eam] b[oa]t *Gen. Scott.* Did not bring my plaid. Mr. Russell talks concerning himself & family of the first time. He had a wife & 10 children & has now has but two daughters. Our discussion concerning ambition & the object to be gained in life.

Thursday, 23. My gun loses two screws. While taking it to the gunsmith's

68. Gros Cap and Pointe aux Pins were situated on the Canadian shore of Lake Superior north of Sault Ste. Marie.
69. The mat buildings were presumably the traditional wigwams commonly erected by the Chippewas. They were round or oval structures with a dome-shaped top, constructed using a framework of intersecting poles covered with bulrush mats. Frances Densmore, *Chippewa Customs* (Washington, DC: Smithsonian Institution, Bureau of American Ethnology, Bulletin 86, 1929), 22–24.
70. Specimens of pure copper and silver, as well as barrels of ore from mines on Lake Superior, began to be shipped through Sault Ste. Marie on a regular basis in the summer of 1846. *Evening Post* (New York), July 20, 1846.

to be repaired the st[eam] b[oa]t went away with Mr. Russell & I did not see him. He returns home. The *Detroit* came in from Detroit with passengers &c.[71] Mr. Livingston of Amer[ican] Fur Co., introduced by Mr. Russell, gives me some information respecting my route & offers a letter of introduction to the ag[ent]t at LaPointe [Wisconsin]—will be very useful. Bought my blankets, frying pan, &c. & 1 gal. of brandy! Have spent the day in reading & writing, expecting all the while the schooner *Algonquin* to start for Copper Harbour.[72] Capt. said he would start by noon, then 4 PM & now it seems will tomorrow noon. Wrote a long letter to James, enclosed my pin for him to keep for me till I return, if I don't, to keep as a souvenir. Wrote to Peter King & Gil Smith & told latter to hold on to the $925 I gave him to purchase Del[aware] & Hudson stock for me till he heard from me, as I thought I might purchase some copper stock.[73] Everybody talking of "show of mineral grey ore." Location, &c., &c. sent carpet bag home by express & st[eam] b[oa]t *Detroit*.

---

71. The steamer *Detroit*, a low-pressure steamboat of three hundred tons, was built in the Pittsburgh area and launched in 1837 and operated on the Great Lakes. "Alleghany Country's Boat Building," Riverboat Dave's Paddlewheel Site, riverboatdaves.com; "Early Navigation of the Lakes," *Commercial Advertiser* (New York), Apr. 7, 1846.

72. Launched in 1839, the seventy-ton schooner *Algonquin* was built by George Washington Jones at Black River (now Lorraine), Ohio. It was purchased by the Cleveland North Western Lake Company later that year and taken to Sault Ste. Marie, where it was the first schooner hauled over the falls of the St. Mary's River. In 1840 the *Algonquin* began to operate on Lake Superior between fur-trading posts at the Sault and La Pointe, on Madeline Island in Wisconsin. By 1845 the boat began hauling flour and freight to Superior, Wisconsin, and later copper ore from Copper Harbor on the Keweenaw Peninsula. The *Algonquin* sank at Superior about 1866. "New Enterprise—Fishing Expedition to Lake Superior," *Oswego (NY) Palladium*, Nov. 20, 1839; *Daily National Pilot* (Buffalo, NY), June 13, 1845; *Marine Review* (Cleveland, OH), June 25, 1891; "Birth of Algonquin and Portage around St. Mary's Rapids, 1839," Old Algonquin, oldalgonquin.net.

73. Peter V. King was a business associate of Henry Sanford as well as a relative through his mother's brother Henry Shelton's wife, Helen King. Owsley, *Register*, 67.

Letter

Henry Sanford to Janey Howe,
ca. July 23, 1846[74]

I have discarded boots and am at this present with my feet encased in a pair of moccasins completely at my care as regards corns and pinched toes. Calico shirt, loose trousers & shooting jacket and there you have me. But I must tell you that our sail from Mackinaw sure was a dyspeptic one. This morning in & out, many islands of every size, from that of the table you write on & the respectable one containing a whole Indian village. Many span acres, & the trees and the stones & look of the water! It reminded me though on a grander scale of the Bay of Islands in the St. Clair Islands. Very pleasant was the trip and one's eyes were kept employed constantly and pleasantly. The first view of this place was beautiful, a sunset and a glorious one too, and the first object lighted up by last rays was the stars & stripes waving over Fort Brady. Soon we saw the white palisades & block houses of the garrison, then the missionary Indians, presently the rapids, where waters were foaming & tumbling over the rocks, & presently at their very foot we stopped in front of the village, or settlement of Sault Ste. Marie, composed of all kinds of tenements that Indians can lodge in. And across on the other side was Canada & the white buildings & wall of the Hudson Bay Co. opening as it were &, as the two are in rivalry of [page torn] American Fur Co. on [page torn]

Journal

Friday, 24th. Went this morn a fishing, Capt., saying he would sail by 10. Came back at 10 & have waited all day. Wind is not fair. Caught fine fish

---

74. HSSP, Box 93, Folder 15, Letter 1.

today & staid 2 hours. Have mounted a pair of moccasins. We are daily expecting the propeller from Copper Harbour with soldiers from Fort Wilkins who will join those from Fort Brady & go to Texas.[75] The st[ea]m b[oa]t *Detroit* is waiting for them. The *Julia Palmer* will be launched probably tomorrow & will go to Copper Harbour next with a new crew in navigation of Lake Superior. Have done little today, the weather very warm. [John] Tanner, the murderer of [James] Schoolcraft still at large, all feared him. He is probably crazy. He shot the brother of the one intended according to the Indian rule, as he could not shoot H[enr]y. R. Schoolcraft. James, the one he shot, he liked![76] The propeller & st[eam] b[oa]t both

75. The federal government established Fort Wilkins in 1844 near Copper Harbor to keep the peace between the resident Chippewas and the large influx of miners attracted by the mineral deposits in the Keweenaw Peninsula. It was abandoned in 1846 when its garrison was sent to Mexico. It was not reoccupied until 1867. Company C, of the Second Infantry, under the command of Capt. Byrne, remained at Fort Brady. Later that year the post was vacated by the army and garrisoned by Michigan volunteers for the next two nears. The post was again occupied by regular troops in 1849. Prucha, *Guide to Military Posts*, 61–62, 116; Charles S. Hamilton, "Memoirs of the Mexican War," *Wisconsin Magazine of History* 14 (1930): 63–65; *Daily National Intelligencer* (Washington, DC), July 17, 1846; "The Present Condition of the Army," *Daily National Intelligencer* (Washington, DC), Dec. 28, 1846.

76. John Tanner, in his fifties when this incident occurred, lived in Kentucky as a child and was purportedly abducted by Chippewas from the Saginaw area. He was raised by the Indians and later worked as a government interpreter at Sault Ste. Marie. Despite his background, Tanner did not associate with Indians and remained a strange, mysterious, and unsocial character. Having borne a grudge against the Schoolcraft family, he was suspected in the murder of James Schoolcraft at the falls of St. Mary's River on July 5, 1846. Tanner burned his house and escaped, never to be found. Joseph H. Steere, "Sketch of John Tanner, Known as the 'White Indian,'" *Michigan Historical Collections* 22 (1899): 246–250; John Tanner, *A Narrative of the Captivity and Adventures of John Tanner, (U. S. Interpreter at the Sault Ste. Marie), during Thirty Years' Residence among the Indians in the Interior of North America* (Minneapolis: Ross and Haines, 1956). James's more famous brother, Henry Rowe Schoolcraft, was an explorer and first US Indian agent at Sault Ste. Marie and was instrumental in negotiating the 1836 Treaty of Washington that ceded Chippewa and Ottawa lands in Michigan to the federal government. He was appointed superintendent of Indian affairs in the Northern Department in 1839. Schoolcraft was a

came in this PM & both brot. passengers—tanned, or rather browned ones from the lake & curious white-faced ones to the lake. The propeller agrees to leave on Sunday morn., so there is hope of getting off at last. Wrote to Uncle Philo [Shelton], telling him to get the refusal of some Boston & Pittsburgh Co's. stock to the amt. of not over $1,000 for a fortnight & I would write from the ground to him, & if pleased take it.[77] Wrote a letter to *Spirit of the Times*. Quantity of moths in the room while writing, air filled with them, paper covered &c.

<u>Saturday, July 25th</u>. Both st[eam] b[oa]ts leave this morning, one for Detroit, the other for Mackimaw. The *Gen. Scott* brought up my shawl which I though[t] had been lost. Mr. Livingston went to Mackinaw this morning & a great many pass[en]gers went to Detroit—a number of young ladies, &c. "Balloon" & post & grit houses. The first must be sheathed when so stronger than any other. Each board of the sheathing becomes a brace, fastened with 10 nails. Arrival of a cruiser from up the lake with doz[en] rafts, long beams, &c. Steamer *Detroit* in the rapids—firing at marks. The Pittsburgh company of gentlemen loafers. The excited Dutchman with his ducking gun. Wrote a letter to Greeley of the *Tribune* today. Aurora Borealis at evening, or northern lights, very beautiful. Bud in the north & went with pale light radiating from it. Saw Mr. Barbeau relative to my proposed route. Is an old trader. Lake of the Woods. Fires all around. Great fire west of the village. Danger apprehended to the buildings. Fire spreads along the ground & consumes to the depth of 1 or 2 ft., is like a punk. Fire

---

prolific author, publishing numerous works detailing his explorations and studies of Native Americans.

77. Investors from these two cities formed the Pittsburgh and Boston Mining Company in 1844 as an association to exploit the copper resources of the Keweenaw Peninsula. Later incorporated, it operated the rich Cliff Mine near Copper Harbor. Richter, "The Copper Mining Industry in the United States, 1845–1925," *Quarterly Journal of Economics* 41 (1927): 243–244.

runs saplings to the top of a tree covered with hanging moss.[78] Sch[oone]r *Algonquin* sailed this eve[ning].

Sunday, 26th. Took my bath as usual & got ready to start. Propeller was to sail at 8. Ordered yesterday a pair of moccasins, very beautiful of caribou skin. Left $3 to pay for them. Paid my bill $11 50/100 & started for the portage with Capt. Tyler & Mr. Coe.[79] Found both were from Connecticut. Mr. Dwight of Boston.[80] Waited till near 11 before getting on board at Tinker's store house. Sounds of the *Julia Palmer*, the first st[eam] b[oa]t in Lake Superior. Pretty half-breeds going whortleberrying to Pointe aux Pins. Fire in the woods near burning a house. Fire dreaded by many of our passengers & others. Grand & beautiful appearance—woods like tinder. Went off in last boat & got underway. Very descent accommodations. Took

---

78. The forest fires that accompanied the drought in the summer of 1846 were said to extend as far as Fond du Lac on Lake Superior, located in the present state of Minnesota, and perhaps as far as the Mississippi. *Spectator* (New York), Sept. 16, 1846; "Tribes: Fond du Lac," Indian Affairs Council, State of Minnesota, http:// mn.gov/indianaffairs/tribes_fonddulac.html.

79. This was likely the Reverend Alvin Coe, an itinerant Presbyterin minister who preached in the pioneer settlements of Ohio and the surrounding region. Born in Granville, Massachusetts, in 1783, he moved west following the War of 1812. He also interacted with Native peoples of the Great Lakes region and served as an interpreter at treaty negotiations. Although based in Ohio, where he operated a mission school for Native American boys, Coe frequently traveled, visiting northern Michigan and Mackinac Island, where he was active among the Chippewas and Ottawas and esteemed as a "great friend." Alvin Coe married Sarah Smith in 1811, and she accompanied him in his missionary labors. He died April 5, 1854, and Sarah passed away March 16, 1883, at age ninety-two. "Running Barefoot—the Mary Ann Coe Story (Part 3)," American Pomeroy Historic Genealogical Association, americanpomeroys. blogspot.com; Andrew J. Blackbird, *History of the Ottawa and Chippewa Indians of Michigan* (Ypsilanti, MI: Ypsilanti Job Printing House, 1887), 37–38.

80. Although it is not possible to identify Mr. Dwight precisely, he presumably was a member of the prominent New England family descended from John Dwight and his wife Hannah, who immigrated to America and settled in Dedham, Massachusetts. Benjamin W. Dwight, *The History of the Descendants of John Dwight of Dedham, Mass.*, 2 vols. (New York: John W. Trow, 1874).

a stateroom with Mr. Dwight & his friend, Mr. [blank]. They are going to La Pointe & thence to the Mississippi by St. Croix. Stopped at Pointe aux Pins for wood. Fire broke out in the forest & spread rapidly, probably would burn up the piles of st[eam] b[oa]t wood. Beautifully grand fire darting up the trees & smoke rolling upwards. Got away near 3 PM. "Gros Cap." Great fire on west side. Western horizon filled with heavy masses of smoke. Our cabins & the air filled most unpleasantly with it till we left the wharf. Air very smoky.[81] Fair wind. White Fish Point & <u>Lake Superior</u>![82] Go on finely at 8 miles per hour. Mr. Greene & odd fellow has introduced me to his friends Doct[or] Burch, Mr. Bates of Detroit & others. Had my moccasins stolen while I left them on deck today. Fine trout caught by an Indian.

Conversation with everybody on <u>copper</u> mines, &c. Williams of Boston.[83] Took on Gen'l. Nelson in Eagle River P. & Rosto Co. have 1,000 tons ore out that they estimate will yield subs[stantial] profit $60 per ton. Getting out now 10 tons per day, will work to more advantage presently. Can get out—they say 100 tons per day. Stock sells about $100 at the present rate of getting out they will have $120,000 at the end of the year. Div[idends] of $30 per share. Long conversation with Mr. Bates during the eve[nin]g on this stock, &c.

Miss Platt of Detroit, formerly of Kalamazoo or Marshall, supposedly seduced by a young Blackwell in Detroit—could say—artful. Affair with

---

81. Contemporary newspapers reported that "a large tract of country on both sides of the St. Mary's River, and on the upper part of the lower peninsula in the neighborhood of the Straits of Mackinac, has been on fire for several weeks." *Spectator* (New York), Sept. 16, 1846.

82. Whitefish Point is situated at the extreme southeastern end of Lake Superior and is a critical turning point for ships sailing into or out of Sault Ste. Marie. It marks the eastern end of a treacherous stretch of the lake's southern shoreline where many shipwrecks have occurred. "Whitefish Point Light Station," Great Lakes Shipwreck Museum, shipwreckmuseum.com.

83. Lemuel Williams of Boston was one of the trustees of the Lake Superior Copper Company, the first organized mining company on Lake Superior. Richter, "Copper Mining Industry," 243.

Cass, Jr. Out with him later. Seen coming from her office at 11 at night. Affair with Strong in an unfinished building. Her broken leg—& party same eve[nin]g. Her leaving Detroit. Cass, Jr's conduct after. His servant carried her baggage to the boat—$400 in gold—when she came back. Cass was attentive. Night fixed for wedding. They heard he had sailed for Harve. She is granddaughter of Judge Platt. Father has some $40 or $50,000 got by attorneyship of business to bankruptcy.[84]

Capt. Tyler & Charter Oak Co., Clinton co. & boat.[85] This party camped out at the portage. Fresh oysters & brandy. Punch in Bates, Greene & co. state room. Called before I left & sent to see if Mr. Livingston had left a letter for me to Mr. Burch. His clerk promised to bring one up to La Pointe in the propeller.

Ill managed & unregulated vessel. Captain has no force & has a hard

---

84. The son of Lewis Cass Sr., brigadier general and governor of Michigan, and Elizabeth Selden Cass, Lewis Cass Jr. was born about 1814 in Ohio. In May 1845 he was selected as US chargé d'affaires to Portugal. On January 18, 1846, he departed for Le Havre, Manche, Besse-Normandie, France. Three years later Cass Jr. was appointed chargé d'affaires to the Holy See and served as minister resident to the Holy See from 1854 to 1858, after which he returned to Detroit, where he lived for at least the following decade. During the Civil War he was active in raising enlistment bounties for Michigan units. He died in Paris on February 28, 1878. "Lewis Cass, Jr.," US Department of State, Office of the Historian, http://history.state.gov; "Lewis Cass, Jr.," Ancestry Library, ancestrylibrary.com; *Charleston (SC) Courier*, May 8, 1845.

Mornelia Platt was the daughter of Zephaniah Platt, the attorney general of Michigan from 1841 to 1843. She was described in 1845 as a woman "in all the bloom of belle-hood, and the acknowledged belle of the city [Detroit]. She is beautiful and fascinating in her manners, and of a highly cultivated mind." She is reported to have "eloped" from Detroit for reasons that are unclear, with the intent of placing herself in a nunnery purportedly at the instigation of the Catholic bishop Le Févré. Under the care of James A. Hicks, she was traveling on the Hudson River on the steamboat *Swallow* when it struck a rock near Athens, New York. She and Hicks were later rescued. Farmer, *History of Detroit*, 92, 311; *Daily National Intelligencer* (Washington, DC), Apr. 18, 1845; "The Swallow," *Massachusetts Spy* (Worcester), Apr. 23, 1845.

85. The Charter Oak Mining Company was organized in 1846. "Charter Oak Mining Company Articles of Association" Charter Oak Mining Company Collection, MS-680, Van Pelt and Opie Library, Michigan Technological University, Houghton, Michigan.

set of hands. Thinks to get back in time for the excursion advertised—to come off the 31st. To bed at 10.

<u>Monday, 27th</u>. Have had a fine wind all night & has brought us within 30 or 40 miles of this Point at 8 o'cl[oc]k. Hope to get in by 2 PM. Weather cool & chilly. Water cool & good. Out of sight of land. Trolling for trout. Fish are [said] to give diarrhea. Have not been troubled. Many outbound are. A little swell like the oceans, but shorter. Smoky air. Has been no rain in near 6 weeks & the woods are like tinder & burning & smoking in all directions, when we see them. Have a hard set of rowdys on board, Pittsburgh party especially. Clinton & co., Messrs Garrison, Wade & co. & 6 men. Stopped at the Bay de Gris [Bete Grise] to put them off at a location they had bought for about $5,000 without seeing. A single log cabin & 2 men, woody, rocky &c.[86] Clinton co., rather homesick, went on shore. Log cabin made without a board or nail. Door & roof of bark. Locations along shore. Kewarwana [*sic*] Point (portage).[87] Pine woods, wild enough.

Met schooner *Algonquin* rolling & pitching, passengers on deck. Dutchman with the ague, purser had 2 calomel pills, & if they did not operate, two more, & after 1 quinine pill every three hours. Gave four pills of each kind. Enquired in the course of PM how he got on & found he had given them all to him. T'would kill a Yankee. Told Doct[or] Leland. He told story of a would be Yankee doctor here who said ham & eggs, "good for Dutchman, bad for Yankee."

---

86. Bete Grise (French for "Gray Beast) is situated on a sheltering bay of the same name, southwest of Copper Harbor on the south shore of the Keweenaw Peninsula. "Bete Grise," Pure Michigan, www.michigan.org/city/bete-grise/.
87. Projecting into Lake Superior, the Keweenaw Peninsula is the northernmost part of Michigan's Upper Peninsula. The peninsula is bounded on the east by Keweenaw Bay and the isthmus formed by Portage Lake. Prior to the copper boom, Indian and European traders employed the isthmus as a portage to the western lake. John T. Blois, *1838 Gazetteer of the State of Michigan* (Knightstown, IN: Bookmark, 1979), 308.

Agreed with Capt. Tyler, or rather told I thought I would, to take 150 shares of Charter Oak Co., which he represents as follows. 75¢ assessment has been paid. I pay that & any more assessments for 2 yrs., at the end of which time he binds himself to take ½, paying all I paid on it, & I keep the other half, 3,000 shares, 2,000 to be sold for the benefit of the co.

Reached Cass Harbor at near 10. Did not go on shore. Sent for my letters & asked Capt. Tyler to bring on any that came before he left, as he intended staying on till the *Algonquin* came in, & go on in her. Messrs. Greene & Bates went on shore in the PM, would not open the letter box twas so late & I missed my letters. A rowdy came off & had a time with the Pittsburgh co. rowdies. Made a great noise. Have got a stick for a captain, knows nothing & can do nothing, has no force, sense or energy—rowdy crew.

———————————

Tuesday, 28th. Started at 2 AM for Copper Harbour. Regret not seeing it—said to be pretty. Fort Wilkins is here. Little mining done, comparatively. Arrived at 5 at Copper Harbour.[88] Came near being carried by Mr. Coe & wife. Messrs. Dwight & Wheelwright & self landed & some duck passengers. Pretty bay. A few houses, say 4 or 5, constitute the place Jay's House, capital log house, neat wife too. Himself a fine fellow. Walked before b[reak]fast to see the mine. Lumps of pure copper, 10 tons is broken. 2 men cutting one lump, 3 or 4 tons in two with a cold chisel to transport. Copper veins in rock running into the water. Shafts not deep. Mr. French agt. Specimens of pure copper & silver. Bath in the lake. Mining co. is a little

———————————

88. Situated at the northerly tip of the Keweenaw Peninsula, Copper Harbor was the site of the federal Mineral Agency established in the summer of 1843 by Walter Cunningham, the special agent for the mines of Lake Superior. During the Copper Rush the agency issued nearly six hundred mining permits by the end of 1845. Largely a tent city in 1846, Copper Harbor's buildings included the land commissioner's house and D. D. Brockway's hotel, a newspaper, and several "intemperance establishments." A post office was established there in 1846. Charles Lanman, *Adventures in the Wilds of the United States and British American Provinces*, vol. 1 (Philadelphia: John W. Moore, 1856), 121; George W. Hawes, *Michigan State Gazetteer and Business Directory for 1860* (Detroit: F. Raymond & Co., 1859), 159; "Villages of Copper Harbor and Eagle Harbor," Michigan Family History Network, mfhn.com.

beyond. Doing little. Pine woods. Pleasant provenance. Wild appearance. Capital breakfast, best since leaving Chicago. Trout fishing in the brook.

Start after b[reak]fast for Copper Falls. Miles, 2½ long miles. A trail called a road. Shoot at some ducks & pigeons. Copper—blueberries. Quite a village at Cop[per] Falls, where we arrived in 1½ hours.[89] Mr. [blank] agt. from Utica. Cabinet of specimens. His mustachoes. Some copper & silver. 3 shafts 100 & 200 fett apart. Drifts run in straight lines, seem all to run toward the center of the lake. So far as yet descended on Lake Superior. Descend 1 shaft near 100 feet. A copper rock almost, pure, blocks up the shaft. Almost 12 feet long, 9 wide, 6 in. thick. Sent to a Boston foundry to cut it out. One got out not very pure. Got out some native copper. All the ore seems to contain is principally in a pure state. The silver is not mixed, but seems welded with the copper, a thing that chemists now cannot do. This is owned by Henshaw, Ward, &c. [of] Boston.[90] Have 6 or 8 log houses. Bring hay from Detroit for horses, &c.

Start there for Eagle River Co., about 7 miles on a very crooked trail. Hard walking, stumps, roots, fallen trees, bushes, bogs &c. &c. Made it about 1. Lake Superior Mining Co. Most of a village here have seen yet, a dozen or more log & frame houses. Large frame stamping mill. Water power saw mill. "H. Johnson's Hotel." Got a good dinner there. Post office, A. T. Hale agt. of U. S. Mr. Col. [blank] agt. 1,200 shares, $80 paid in for shares—a great deal squandered. Mr. Hale shows us the works. Old stamping machine (costing 10¢ per lb.), new eccentric motion. Descend

---

89. The village of Copper Falls was situated near the mine, operated by the Copper Falls Company. Established in 1846, the mines comprised a series of shafts excavated in the vicinity of Copper Falls on Owl Creek, lying south of Eagle Harbor. Walter Romig, *Michigan Place Names* (Detroit: Wayne State University Press, 1986), 133; Lanman, *Adventures in the Wilds*, 120.

90. The Copper Falls Company regularly consigned cargos of copper and silver ore to Henshaw, Ward & Co. *Evening Post* (New York), July 20, 1846. David Henshaw of Boston was US secretary of war and a trustee of the Lake Superior Copper Company. Richter, "Copper Mining Industry," 243.

shaft 130 ft. Drift at 100 for copper lead. Copper boulders. Evidently a stream [has] been here once. Vein between 2 walls, well defined. Col. Stephens, formerly a prof. at West Point, left in a huff with Gen. Scott & now is pecking away as head miner, is a fine-looking fellow. Boulders [of] pure copper, 800 lbs. since yesterday morning. Copper is broken into fine pieces, washed & the copper dust sent on. Specimens of copper in weighing room. Mine is rather damp under Eagle River. Stock worth $100. Hale thinks the Cliffs rather fancy. Shows me return of all the co[mpanie]s. He receives 6% of all mineral. Speaks favorably of Montreal River Co.[91] Dixon, Ward &c. started there.

———————

Started for Cliff Mines, 3 _very_, _very_ long miles west.[92] Got there at 5½ o'clock. A perpendicular cliff in which drifts run into the rock, one [on] top of the other clear to the top. Quite a settlement here, 70 hands at work. Quite busy. Jennings agt. Mr. Henry of Pittsburgh. Mr. Hubbard the geologist in ticking blouse, &c.[93] German workmen. Coopering. Blacksmith

91. The Montreal River Company operated on the river of the same name in the Keweenaw Peninsula about ten miles south of Copper Harbor. "Circular 25, Mining Records," Archives of Michigan, www.michigan.gov/documents/mhc_sa_circular25_49722_7.pdf.

92. The Cliff Mine was owned by the Pittsburgh and Boston Mining Company, whose systematic exploitation made it the earliest profitable copper mine in the United States, paying its first dividends as early as 1849. Richter, "Copper Mining Industry," 244.

93. A Renaissance man in nineteenth century Michigan, Bela Hubbard was a naturalist, geologist, writer, historian, surveyor, explorer, lawyer, real estate speculator, lumberman, and civic leader in Detroit. When the state created a Geological Survey under the direction of Douglass Houghton, Hubbard was appointed his assistant. During the next four years he participated in the extensive fieldwork conducted by the Survey in lower Michigan as well as a survey of the copper region along the Keweenaw Peninsula in 1840. Following Houghton's death in 1845, Hubbard continued his surveys in the Upper Peninsula's Baraga and Marquette Counties as well as adjacent areas. Presumably Henry Sanford encountered him at the Cliff Mine while he was engaged in these activities. "Bela Hubbard Biography," Bela Hubbard Papers, Michigan Historical Collections, University of Michigan, Ann Arbor; Bela Hubbard, _Memorials of a Half Century_ (New York: G. P. Putnam's Sons, 1887), 21–90.

shop. Weighing platform. Breaking & barreling. Ore wheeled directly from the mine to the platform. Bates & Green gone to the Albion Co. Waited for them till near 8 & took tea three. They did not come. Statistics from Mr. Jennings. 70 men, paid an average of $25 per month & board, green hands $18, some old ones $30. Board $2 per week. Are getting out 60 or 70 tons per week, ½ has 35 or 40%, remainder say 10. The 35 & 40% is packed in bbls., 300 lbs. each. Cost 50¢ & made on the ground. Cost to get out per ton 2 o[r] 3¢, cartage to mouth of river $2, freight to Boston $15. 60 tons of the first copper out yielded 20¾% & $70 per ton. Will get out soon a greater proportion of ore when they work to better advantage. Says he will get out 2,000 tons this winter & make 12,000 bbls. Some silver & pure copper. Most of the silver rings, &c come from here. Got out last week in one day 10,000 lbs mineral, so rich in silver. Thought it worth $1 per pound. Mr. Hubbard thought different. $4 per share has been paid on the stock. Is worth now about $100, has sold for 200 or 300. Will pay a dividend next spring.

Walked 3 more <u>long</u>, long miles to the mouth of Eagle River. Fires in the woods. Got there at 11 o'clock. Tents pitched here & there. Mr. Johnson's tavern. Fat man. Card playing & a rough bed on the floor on a blanket. 1s[hilling (12¢)] a drink for brandy. Pittsburgh co. camped out across the river from the house.

<u>Wednesday, 29th</u>. Up at 4¼ with sore limbs & joints, blistered feet, & sore groins. Took my gun, which seemed very heavy once more. Have shot out one pigeon. Took a cracker, hominy & a little brandy water & started for Eagle Harbour. Rough pebbly beach. Tents & deserted appearance of the place. After a mile came upon sandy beach. Better walking for 4 miles or so. Then struck off into the woods, winding, twisting around following blind trails & blazed trees 3 or 4 miles to Eagle Harbour.[94] Arrived at 9. Bath &

---

94. Situated sixteen miles west of Copper Harbor, the village of Eagle Harbor was established by the Eagle River Mining Company in 1845. The following year the village had a boardinghouse, a sawmill, and a store, "where drinking is the principal

breakfast compensated for fatigue & mosquitoes. Have lain still the rest of the day. Looks stormy. Boat came with the bag. Mr. Mercer & son, Phelps. Mr. Handscome, the rowdy who came on board at Cop[per] Harbour, was formerly Speaker of the House of Repres[entatives] of Michigan, 2 yrs. since, badly drunk.[95] Started off, though the wind rather dangerous. *Algonquin* has got into Copper Harbour. Fears of being left. Been writing letters this PM. Told Uncle Philo to get $800 worth of Boston & Pittsburgh & if he can get any Montreal River for about $5, get 25 shares. Mr. Coe got back from the mouth with comp[any] in fine spirits. Fine location, fine specimens—North Amer. Co. Lots of native copper by Gen. Phelps, John Kensie on north side. Discovered a vein 14 ft. with grey sulphur at 4½ ft. with silver with quartz. Mr. Morrell, his travels in NW, Yucatan, &c. Douglas one of Fremont's men. Our quarters, 4 beds in one room, all double beds but mine. Merry time. Gen. Phelps snoring. Mr. Coe & his wife in next room.

Thursday, 30th. Gen. Phelps & Co. Are off. Messrs. Dwight & Wheelwright go with them to Eagle River, [I] think to meet the sch[oone]r. I think to

---

business transacted." Lanman, *Adventures in the Wild*, 121, estimated the combined population of Eagle Harbor and Copper Harbor was about fifty. "Villages of Copper Harbor and Eagle Harbor," Michigan Family History Network, mfhn.com.

95. Alfred H. Hanscom came to Michigan from his native Rochester, New York and was admitted to the bar in Oakland County in 1838. He was elected to the Michigan House of Representatives in 1842 and 1845 and became Speaker of the House during his second term. During the Mexican-American War he served as a captain in the regiment of Michigan Volunteers under Col. A. S. Williams. The unit served only briefly at the close of the war, being deployed in December 1847 and returning the following July. In 1850 Hanscom was a delegate to the Michigan state constitutional convention. He formed a brief law partnership with Jay A. Hubbell in 1853 at Ontonagon in the Upper Peninsula, after which he served as US consul to Rio Grande do Sul from 1853 to 1857. Farmer, *History of Detroit*, 303–304; Samuel W. Durant, *History of Oakland County, Michigan* (Philadelphia: L. H. Everts, 1877), 46; *Memorial Record of the Northern Peninsula of Michigan* (Chicago: Lewis Pub. Co., 1895) 381; "Michigan: State House of Representatives, 1840s," The Political Graveyard, politicalgraveyard.com.

do my waiting here in good quarters. Has rained & blowed hard all night. Lake rough. White caps & surf. Mouth of the brook blocked with sand. Nearly all the rivers on this lake have blind mouths & changeable, moveable sand carried by the waves here, true of each one on the sand. Bath before breakfast. Sloping shore. Had all the morning. Sketches of the fair sex & language of nature or attractions of language. This last very able & shews much knowledge of the natural sciences & great observation. Mrs. Coe with chills. Sent a note to P.M. at Copper Harbour to have my letters sent to La Pointe. PM at the dinner, which was only with Mr. & Mrs. Joyner & Mrs. Coe. Went after trout. Walked half a mile around the bay to a little brook. Caught 30 or more in about as many minutes. Filled my pockets & came home. Fish small. After tea went in a boat to see them take in their trot lines, 350 ft. long, 25 hooks. Caught 6 fish, largest a trout weighing 27 lbs., 3 other trout 4 or 5 lbs. each, & 2 cir—something like the trout, but fatter. Great luck, saw house of the two mackinaws. Dressing fish, blowing bladders. Beautiful sunset, calm lake, pretty bay, moon & trees, &c., &c., cow bells. Still air. Contemplation, musing, dreaming.

Letter

Henry Sanford to Janey Howe, [July 28, 1846], Sch[ooner] Algonquin, *Lake Superior, off Eagle River*[96]

Lake Superior! Dear Janey! Doesn't it cause a thrill of excitement, the idea of bounding along over the waves of this vast inland sea, till lately almost unknown save for the tales of some venturesome persons who, sent on some important mission, crossed its tempestuous waters & coasted along its wild deserted shores. Lake Superior! Father of lakes! A very patriarch & chief among all bodies of fresh water ! All hail to thee! A change has come

96. HSSP, Box 93, Folder 15, Letter 12.

over thee. While the waters of other lakes dependent on thee have been swarming with steamers & vessels of all kinds, filled with thousands of bust, eager speculative mortals, thine have bourne but the occasional canoe of the wild Indian or the bateau of furs bound for the settlements. Thou hast kept aloof from the noise & clamour which characterize the busy shores of thy sister lakes. No passing steamer has dared to profane the silence rippling along the thy desolate borders. Naught but the whoop of the Indian or the cry of wild beasts & birds have echoed along the fifteen hundred miles of wilderness which form thy boundaries. No improvements in the form of mushroom cities & towns have been here. For centuries all has remained in silence & quietness away from the busy world & scarce spoke or thought of but as being far away, beyond anything that was desirable.

———————————

How changed now within a short year! Steamers already commence paddling & snorting along thy whole extent. The white sails of vessels are now seen dotted along on thy broad surface. Cabins & settlements have, as if by magic, sprung up on every bay & indentation of thy shores. The noise of hammers & axes, of powder tearing up rocks, of men talking & disputing of "conglomerate," trap & sand stone, grey sulphur &c., green oxide, "native metal" is heard continually. A population of near 15,000 are now scattered through the vast wilderness bounding thy southern border, all seeking to rifle thy shores of some of the treasures so profusely scattered there, all gathered from all parts of the country for one object, more dollars, more gain. A few years more shall have passed by & Lake Superior known only as reigning supreme over desolateness, shall fill the world with its fame & riches, shall enrich nations with its precious ore, shall see populous towns & villages where now are dense forests & thickets, wild, barren rocks. The changes that have been wrought already are wonderful; those that will be are to astonish the world. Those now made are but the commencement of the beginning.

All placid & calm now is the lake. There is not a breeze to ruffle the surface, which stretches along until it meets the horizon on three sides of us. On the other side, dense forests of pine rising from rocky shores meet the eye. A little schooner with flapping sails rests on the quiet surface. Some children playing on the deck watch with curious eyes, the sticks they have thrown over to see whether we really move or not. One time they shout in glee that we are leaving them behind & presently with astonishment declare that <u>they</u> (the chips) are beating & leaving us. The skipper paces the narrow deck, looking by turns at his sails & the horizon & whistles for wind. The man at the wheel lolling easily against it with occasionally a creaking turn, holds up his hand to know if a breath of air is stirring & then with hat slouched over his eyes seems to meditate profundity or slow dozes. The passengers (some of them are missionaries) are lounging around as well as the circumscribed place will admit. One has his Bible, another has got onto the subject of abolitionism, while an old newspaper is being read with intense interest by a third and I am stretched at length on the hatchway occupied as you are. But hark! A strain of music comes sweetly upon the ear from a little cabin below me! Tis from a missionary & his wife who are singing one of their Indian hymns, & solemnly does it break upon the stillness and leads the mind into a more sober & reflective mood. A dark haze is seen on the eastern horizon behind us fraught with unfavorable noises, perhaps with storm & tempest. In return for calm & stillness, a little ripple in the water is already seen. The sails are squared, bright bubbles go floating by slowly then glance along now rapidly & now we see the rocks & trees on shore continually changing & giving place to others seemingly as we glide quietly & noiselessly along.

There Janey! If you got through with all this preamble you must have a very lively sense of where I am. Eagle River I think is not upon any map you will probably have. You will find "Keewanna [*sic*] Point," about half way from the Sault. The first river beyond that is about where this letter is being written. I have been in the Copper Region two or three days, have had my ears stunned with all sorts of learned & scientific names appertaining to geology, mineralogy, &c., & appertaining to copper especially, have been astonished at the vast resources in mineral wealth of this heretofore unproductive country. Why, the every rock & stone we tread upon here is charged with one of the rich metals. Copper is not alone on Indian faces. It's stamped in every rock. And now thousands are engaged in mining and all are successful, or say they are.

I am now bound for La Pointe direct, save stopping at Ontonagon River, which is about half way. This vessel is taking up goods for the Indian payment, which comes off on the 10th or 15th, and if I stop to it shall let you know something of it, and at any rate shall send this from La Pointe.

Journal

Friday, 31st. Up as usual & around the beach to take a bath before breakfast. Water cool & bracing, lower strata cold & freezing. Coming back [I] saw a sail standing in apparently. Mr. Jay, after breakfast, rowed out to it, while Mr. Hunt & I went to the diggings to see the copper. Pretty town. He came back, said it was the *Algonquin*. Would wait ½ hour. Hurried off & rowed as hard as we could to her. Twas calm & still. Got on board. Found Capt. Tyler was not there, had started to coast it in a canoe. So I sent a draft on to N. Y. to Mr. Coe, payable to his order (Phelps, D[odge] & Co.), telling him to get the stock &c. [F]ound I had left my sole reliever in the shape of trousers behind. Told Mr. Jay to send them on by the propeller. They then left, but we remained becalmed nearly all day. Did not stir for several hours. Little schooner of 60 tons. Living horrid, sleeping d[itt]o. Same Mrs. Mercer. Messrs. Ely & Wright with their families & Mr. Elton bound for La Pointe.[97] Frank, the youngster, singing songs. Got opposite to Eagle River

97. Appointed by the American Board of Commissioners for Foreign Missions, Edmund F. Ely continued missionary work begun at La Pointe in the early 1830s. Like his predecessors, he lived among the Chippewas rather than attempting to draw them to an outside mission. He was a claimant for debts incurred in the ceded district. Disagreements in 1845 concerning the management of the Pokegama mission

later in the PM with a slight fair breeze. Fired a gun & lay to. Saw noone coming & started off. After a short time looked back with spyglass. Saw Dwight & Wheelwright getting into a boat, so we hove to again. They came off. Jas. Paul (of Copper Rock memory). Biddle, Downy, & c. sent a letter to the PM [at] Copper Harbour to se [*sic*] send my letters to La Pointe. Saw Mr. Hale, the U. S. Agt. Agreed to take 100 shares NY & Lake Superior Co. stock at $18, deliverable in NY Nov. 1 & payable there to draw on Phelps, Dodge & Co. Have seen a canoe with a sail apparently chasing us. Thought it might be Capt. Tyler. Has not overtaken us, however. Night, very little wind, half moon, very pleasant eve[nin]g, haze in the east[war]d. Hopes of fine breeze. Sleep in blankets spread on cabin floor. Most sleep in the hold on the planks & blankets. Sick & squalling children. Get my head kicked by the strange children.

<u>Saturday, Aug. 1st.</u> Have done very little last night, gone perhaps 18 miles. Sand bluffs, some very bold & beautiful. Water falls over them into the lake. Find Mr. Ely, the missionary, a very sensible man & get many ideas from him respecting Indians, &c. also from Mr. Mendenhall [a] description of Indian battle between Sioux & Chippewa in May '43 or '41.[98] Plan of route. Recommends by Sandy Lake & St. Louis River, said Selkirk's settlement & Red Lake.[99] Rev. Mr. Wright & wife from Red Lake, his difficulties, much

---

among the Chippewas led to his reassignment to LaPointe the following year. Upon returning from a visit to his family in the East, Ely and his family journeyed to the mission in the late summer of 1846. Keith R. Widder, "Founding La Pointe Mission, 1825–1833," *Wisconsin Magazine of History* 64 (1981): 201; Theresa M. Schenck, *The Ojibwe Journals of Edmund F. Ely, 1832–1849* (Lincoln: University of Nebraska Press, 2012), 397–404; "Treaty of La Pointe 1842," The Bad River Band of Lake Superior Chippewa Tribe, badriver-nsn.gov.

98. Cyrus Mendenhall entered three sections on the west side of the Ontonagon River for the Isle Royale Mining Company. It became known as the Mendenhall location. George N. Fuller, ed., *Historic Michigan: Land of the Great Lakes*, vol. 3 (Dayton, OH: National Historical Association, [1924]), 52.

99. This proposed route would have taken Henry northwestward from Lake Superior along the St. Louis River across Minnesota. The river was a vital link between the

to mortification of new married wife. Mr. Ely has a half breed wife & 3 squalling children.[100] Mr. Mendenhall is an old settler of La Pointe, made some of the first locations. That for Mr. Williams. How lost through Mr. Drury. Taken for H___ of Hartford. Locations commenced immediately after the sale by the Indians. 1st location made in Ontonagon River acct. of farmers, blacksmiths, &c. employed by government for the Indians. Gen. Harrison has made, or suggested, the present plan for surveying our wild lands. Geological survey also included marsh. Stopped some 20 miles from Eagle River to get some of Mr. Mendenhall's men who were on a location there. I went ashore with him, hard walk of 5 miles. Vessel becalmed. Meet a stiff breeze going in. These men were Cornish miners. Little brook near the tents. Capt. Teague. Fish for trouts. Baking bread. Water & wild berries. Go off at 1, the vessel then having a good breeze, having left at 9. Had dinner as usual. Fresh breeze in afternoon. Sandy bluffs, forest, forest. Make the point at dark & are towed into the river. Two log houses & a half dozen tents & boats. Quite a settlement. Spread our blankets on shore. Mr. M. & J. Brandy punch. Songs by Dwight & Wheelwright, both pretty tight. So came to bed. Biddle & delirium tremens. Operation for Mr. Wright not successful.

Great Lakes and the upper Mississippi drainage. Travelers portaged from the St. Louis to Lake Vermillion and the Rainy River, on the US-Canada border, to the Red River of the North, which offered further access to the west. Thomas Douglas, the Fifth Earl of Selkirk, located the Red River Colony, also known as the Selkirk Settlement, on the river in 1811. Situated on an enormous tract granted by the Hudson's Bay Company, Selkirk's colonization effort fared poorly during its early years, plagued by poor harvests and conflict with the rival Northwest Company. By the 1840s the agricultural colony had stabilized and also become a center for missionary activity in the region. George E. Carter, "Lord Selkirk and the Red River Colony," *Montana: The Magazine of Western History* 18 (1968): 60–69.

100. The Reverend Edmund F. Ely married Catherine (Golais) Bissell, a part-Chippewa métis on August 8, 1835. Having made a lifelong commitment to spread the evangelical gospel, she accompanied her husband in his missionary work among the Chippewas until 1854. Catherine Ely died in 1880. Keith R. Widder, *Battle for the Soul: Métis Children encounter Evangelical Protestants at Mackinaw Mission, 1823–1837* (East Lansing: Michigan State University Press, 1999), 129, 141.

Sunday, Aug. 2d. Got up at 6½ after a fine sleep out doors. Bath in the lake. Disch[argin]g cargo all the afternoon. Taking up ballast all the PM. Paul's cabin & grocery. U. S. Agt. Row up the river for stripping elm bark for Mr. Wright. Good sized river, wooded shores, cupberries, &c. Sail down with ashen sails, <u>an ashen hush</u>. Little dog. Attempted to buy of a Frenchman. Made a bargain & found he did not own it. [T]ried to get fish of an Indian. Indian comfort, squaw & lodge. Salmon, trout. Mr. Hurd, surveyor of Charter Oak Co., showed me new specimens of rich silver ore, though stock worth at least $10. Wrote to Capt. Tyler for more. Hands come here again, & drunk. Take a sail with Dwight & Wheelwright & co. [S]and cherries. Pitchers of brandy. Fight between two half breeds. Looks like a storm. Not quite like a Sunday in Derby. Write part of a letter to Janey [Howe]. Sketched on my camping ground. Not getting away tonight. Mr. Eleason the U. S. agt., Connecticut bred. Mustachoes & whiskers is surveying a crooked river in the Ontonagon. Says he crossed the west branch 29 times in 2 days in running lines for 6 miles. Whiskey has been introduced here but lately. Now ships are at every point & plenty of drunkenness. Mr. E. has been here 14 months. Horrid state of society & morals among the half breeds & miners. Fish for tea, which the Indians had caught. A Mackinaw trout, not so good as white fish.[101] Camp out as the night before. Captain saying he should be away by daylight. Fair breeze & strong, threatens storm.

---

101. Fishing had always been important in the economy of the Lake Superior and Lake Huron Chippewas, who fished extensively for subsistence and trade. W. Vernon Kinietz, *Indians of the Western Great Lakes, 1615–1770* (Ann Arbor: University of Michigan Press, 1965), 323–324.

Letter

Henry Sanford to Janey Howe,
August 2, 1846, Ontonagon River[102]

I cannot forbear saying a word or two because it is Sunday, and on Sundays you are especially brought to my remembrance. Not that you are not often thought of, but it's on this day alone that I can follow you as it were through the day, imagining what you in particular as well as the family at home are about. Rev. Mr. Somebody has preached, I suppose, perhaps Mr. Ashley. You have done your share towards inclining the mind of the congregation to solemn things. Your accustomed fingers no longer tremble, but pipe it never so loudly. There fair owner is not startled by the noise they produce. You are in a capital position up there in the organ loft to discover any new dress, bonnet or ribbon, but I <u>fear</u> are not half so much <u>edified</u> by any discoveries made in that <u>line</u> as some of your neighbours who think more seriously on such <u>important</u> subjects. You would completely <u>overlook</u> me were I were in my old seat (don't do so I beg you) & by the way, how does my seat look as I am on Lake Superior). And by the way how does my seat look, deserted? Or were the Misses Hulls finally contented to put a row of bonneted heads, then which heads belong to their little charges, the Wheelers? I wish I could just look in upon you for a minute, could see that you were all there and well. I find it not so difficult at any rate to look twenty-five hundred miles in imagination. And that must content now. "The sound of the church gong bell' is no longer to be heard by me in some time. Had I known it sooner, I would have got out a small bell which I have just heard is on board for the Missouri at Red Lake and <u>would</u> have heard it. It's just sunset, calm & beautiful, & were I in Birmingham with such an evening we should, your consent being obtained, be taking a stroll up the Embankment I think.

---

102. HSSP, Box 93, Folder 15, Letter 12.

Not very able to do this, please take a stroll of 2,500 miles and take a peep at my quarters on Ontonagon River, where I arrived here last night . . . I am stretched at length on some blankets covering the ground where I slept last night (camping out you see) and with paper on a corner of my tent cloth I am scratching away. Close by me in the river, whose wooded banks here join the shores of Lake Superior, lies the schooner. Across the stream are some Indian lodges from which the thin, blue smoke rises lazily into the still air. The broad surface of the river is mirror-like save where disturbed by a mackinaw boat, which rowed by some French voyageurs "with chorus song & measured stroke" glides swiftly over it, leaving the water broken by a thousand sparkling ripples. Sweetly sounds their boat song coming across the waters, and as it grows fainter & fainter in the distance, the ear is trained to catch the sound once more of the song, and clear away at the bend of the river is heard its last notes as all voices joined in the chorus. Tis all the music I have heard this day and even that I am grateful for & of course delighted with. Nearby are two or three log shanties and a half dozen tents and as many boats drawn up to the shore, and in and around them are six times that number of drunken, swearing vagabonds who have come a mining & to seek their fortunes in this land where law and order are unknown. The solemn forest, La vierge foret [*sic*], is all around, save on the side towards the lake. As water is necessary to complete a beautiful landscape, so is a forest to make a grand one. As one adds to the beauty so does the other to the grandeur of a scene. I wish you could see one of these (I should say this, for it's one forest from the Sault to Fon du Lac) wild forests, just as nature made them, just as time has left them.[103] Huge

---

103. Fond du Lac, located on the Fond du Lac River at the head of Lake Winnebago, was one of the earliest frontier settlements in Wisconsin. The river afforded access by steamboat and water power for a number of mills for the manufacture of lumber and flour. The seat of justice for the county of the same name, Fond du Lac was incorporated as a village in 1847 and a city five years later. It had a population of four thousand in 1853. Hunt, *Wisconsin Gazetteer*, 91, 246–248.

trunks, like columns supporting a leafy canopy high overhead, making nature a fitting temple where the sun never comes but with a subdued light, no gleaming beams to penetrate the somber masses of green verdure. No man with death-dealing axe (here it's changing now alas) to lay at the root of these living pillars, but standing erect for centuries ne'er pulled down save by the hand of time, and then with mouldering trunks stretched along the ground giving new life & sustenance by their decay to those around them. Oh! But I do love the forests! And this is such a grand one! Sorry shall I be to see the day when vulgar corn & potatoes shall sprout over where now stand these monarchs of the wild, our forest trees! When cabins, houses, palaces, cities shall rise over their ruin & calculating, busy, dollar-seeking men shall rest his hands in delight at the improvements he has wrought! I have coasted along now over 300 miles along one grand, unbroken forest. How many years will elapse and all shall have been swept away!

This day has passed very little like Sunday to me and indeed few of my Sundays have since leaving. I am sorry to say the schooner has been discharging freight, taking on ballast, men around are talking & laughing, swearing & drinking, and I have done little [but] loll under a tree on the banks of the lake with thoughts turned homeward. Sunday last we left the Sault for Copper Harbour and that brings to my mind, have you ever seen a forest on fire?

Journal

Monday, 3d. Did not get away till after 8. Had fine & fair breeze. Mr. Mendenhall left us. Went but a few miles & fell calm. Yankee trading. Flute & coronet. Familiar airs. Reading Bible in French & Locke & Bacon. Nothing of importance transpires. Conversation with missionaries respecting the two routes to Mississippi River. Half determined to take that by Sandy Lake. Lord Selkirk's settlement 15 days by way of Sandy Lake, 7 days by way of St. Croix & the Brule.[104] Dr. Jones pd. Dr. Mowat last year $70 to be sent away by St. Croix. Lord Selkirk's settlement has 5,000 or 6,000 inhabitants, dependent on noone. Raise their own flour & productions & cloth. Mr. Wright is from Red Lake & goes there. [I] think of going from Fort Snelling to the "settlement" via "Lac qui Paile" [Lac qui Parle, "Lake That Speaks"][105] PM more wind, but ahead blows hard & makes passengers sea sick. All made preparations to spend the night on Deck. Cabin small, dirty & bad smell up. Mr. Ely's half breed wife & children come likewise. Got my blankets under head of the "house on deck" & turn in.

Tuesday, 4th. Less sea, pleasant weather though hazy. Wind not quite fair though, little of it. Have made little ground during the night. Apostle Islands came up, with the outward one wooded with sand bluffs worn by water. Arches & caves. Fruit trees, all kinds. Norway pine. More islands. Fair wind. Bays & inlets. Green forests & sand bluffs, pretty. Beautiful bay

---

104. The Brule River empties into Lake Superior just inside the Michigan border. Its headwaters extend westward into Wisconsin. A tributary of the Mississippi, the St. Croix River drainage extends across eastern Wisconsin, where travelers could reach Lake Superior by a portage to the Brule River. James Taylor Dunn, *The St. Croix: Midwest Border River* (New York: Holt, Rinehart and Winston, 1965), 32–35.

105. Lac qui Parle, situated in Lac qui Parle County in western Minnesota, is a French translation of the Dakota name meaning "Lake That Speaks." "Lac qui Parle State Park," Minnesota Department of Natural Resources, dnr.state.mn.us.

The US Army established a post to protect settlements in the northwestern frontier at the confluence of the Minnesota and Mississippi Rivers in August 1819. Initially named Cantonment Hope, and later Fort St. Anthony, it became Fort Snelling in 1825. The fort established a military presence to protect American interests in the fur trade at this important junction, and the associated Indian agency helped keep the peace between the Chippewas and Dakotas who inhabited the area. Fort Snelling became the key federal installation in the upper Mississippi valley. It was named for its first commander, Col. Josiah Snelling, under whose direction troops began the construction of a stone fort on a high bluff overlooking the river in the fall of 1820. Prucha, *Guide to Military Posts*, 108; William Duffield Neill, *The History of Minnesota from the Earliest French Explorations to the Present Time* (Philadelphia: J. B. Lippincott & Co., 1858), 337; "Historic Fort Snelling," Historic Fort Snelling, Minnesota Historical Society, historicfortsnelling.org.

of islands. Oak island. Arches in the rocks through which water flows & canoe can pass through. First view of La Pointe. Presque Isle a low, sandy point, dotted with Indians like blackbirds.[106] White lodges. Madeline Island 12 miles by calm & a long while going to. Boat came & took off missionaries & children. Canoes coming in with Indians all the while. Counted 20 in sight. Commenced towing presently, a slight breeze which carried us in. At the other end of the island some Indians came off on board a canoe. Gave them bread & meat. They said the fire had burnt up everything. Woods on fire. A canoe with 2 young Indians pursued us 3 or 4 miles coming up. Had a little fish to sell. Did not want them. Dodged at a spy glass. La Pointe is two points stretching out & forming a large bay 2 miles wide, I should think, & 1 deep, almost landlocked by islands & mainland. A few houses

---

106. Oak Island, Presque Isle, and Madeline Island are part of a group of twenty-two islands in Lake Superior off the northern Wisconsin shore. Called the Apostle Islands, they are characterized by boreal forest vegetation, deep bays, enclosed lagoons, and sea caves. Long occupied by Native people, the Apostle Islands were inhabited by Chippewa bands at the time of French contact in the late seventeenth century. Fur traders established a trading post near the large Chippewa village on Madeline Island in 1718 and maintained it until 1762. Following the French and Indian War the British assumed control of the trade in the Great Lakes, and in 1816 the American Fur Company took over the post on Madeline Island. In 1827 a portion of the island was ceded to the American Board of Commissioners for Foreign Missions, and three years later missionary Jedediah D. Stevens visited La Pointe in the winter, and Frederick Ayer established a mission school there in the summer of 1830. In 1835 the American Fur Company moved the post to La Pointe on Sandy Bay and Father Frederic Baraga established a Catholic mission there. Widder, "Founding of La Pointe Mission," 191–193; Janet Busch, *People and Places: A Human History of the Apostle Islands; Historic Study of the Apostle Islands National Seashore* (Omaha, NE: Midwest Regional Office, National Park Service, United States Department of the Interior, 2008), 42–44, 93–100; Bela Hubbard described La Pointe in 1840.

What is called the company's "fort" consisted of two large stores painted red, a fish storehouse at the wharf, and a row of neat frame buildings painted white. The latter were occupied by the half dozen families in the company's employ. These dwellings, with the two stores, formed opposite sides of a broad street, in the centre square of which was planted a large flag pole. Upon this street also clustered sundry smaller and unpainted log tenements of the French and half-breeds. Half a mile from the fort were the Protestant and Catholic missions. Hubbard, *Memorials*, 59–60.

La Pointe, Wisconsin in 1842. This contemporary view, purportedly sketched by a Native American youth, shows the settlement much as it looked at the time of Henry Sanford's visit four years later. Visible are the buildings of the American Fur Company as well as the mission churches.

COURTESY OF THE WISCONSIN HISTORICAL SOCIETY, IMAGE ID 42457.

& red storehouses of the Fur Co. & a great many Indian lodges.[107] Tall Indians in gay colors standing on the bluffs. Plenty squatted down, think enough everywhere. Came to anchor at the east end of the bay near the mission house, a large building 3 stories. Some Indians & ½ breeds came off. I went ashore with them, leaving D. & W. aboard.

Mr. D. has seemed to feel rather cold towards me, though when he speaks [is] exceedingly polite. [He] is a young man with many things to learn, green, thinks <u>he knows</u> & feels too big to ask. [I] have showed on

---

107. Commercial fishing had become a substantial part of the American Fur Company's business on the Great Lakes, and Bela Hubbard observed the long storehouse at La Pointe in 1840. Busch, *People and Places*, 98; Hubbard, *Memorials*, 60.

some few subjects he was in error & suspect he notes me for it. Small minds could not be more annoyed than by wounds to their vanity like these. Mr. W. is silent rather but disposed to be friendly. D., though a boy, seems to have everything his own way & pushes forward in little matters of any kind as if <u>he</u> was lead & us followers.

Landed on the beach, which stretches toward the village. Fine sand, plenty of lodges & Indians. Saw canoe making, Indians making mats &c. Dirty & filthy &c. Naked boy swimming & squatted on the beach. Store houses of the Am[erican] Fur Co., two large red buildings with some smaller ones on a square called the fort. Saw the sign "boarding house." Went into a little house called Mich. Found some Indians squatted on the floor of a room where were more benches & a rough board table. No one could speak English. Started off & a man overtook me, the proprietor. He kept a boarding not a <u>lodging</u> house. Saw Dr. Borup, the agt., a stout, burley, vindictive, selfish man. Told him I wanted a place to lodge & showed him my letter for Chatham &c. and that I wanted to go to Fort Snelling. Couldn't help me. Passage? There would cost me $90 to go through. Didn't know where I could lodge. The man is a dunce & is the nabob of the place where all stand in awe of & hate him.[108] Walked around seeing the Indians, &c. Lodges everywhere, women putting them up. Gay colors & paint of

---

108. Dr. Charles W. W. Borup was the agent for the American Fur Company at La Pointe. He represented the company as a signatory of the 1842 La Pointe Treaty. Described as "a Swede, a social good natured man, who had quite high notions of his own importance," he had recently returned from Detroit with his métis wife and two children in July 1846. Upon reaching La Pointe, he was informed of his youngest child's death, an event that deeply disturbed his wife and raised fears for her recovery. This tragedy occurred less than three weeks before Henry's arrival and may well account for Borup's behavior toward him, which stood in sharp contrast with that experienced by Charles H. Titus, who had accompanied the Borup family on their recent western trip. George P. Clark, ed., *Into the Old Northwest: Journeys with Charles H. Titus, 1841–1846* (East Lansing: Michigan State University Press, 1994), 104–108; "Treaty of La Pointe 1842," The Bad River Band of Lake Superior Chippewa Tribe, badriver-nsn.gov.

Indians coming in continually. Counted 20 canoes coming in. Went back to the vessel to sleep. Traders here. Little flags & designs. Jews speaking all languages. Frolic of D. & W. on board, drinking.

Wednesday, 5th. Went on shore to breakfast on fish at the boarding house. Found a young man (E. Egarton) just came over from St. Croix. Walked 80 miles across the portage. Took a stroll & a bath together after b[reak]fast. (I had taken a dive from the vessel when I rose.) Pretty squaws making a lodge. The baker, Mr. Parks, whom I did not know, introduced me to the Indian agt., Mr. Hays. Says 400 Indians around yesterday. Got acquainted with some of the traders, &c., Mr. Samuels, Mr. Arnold. Heard a talk at the agency. Indians seated around. One gets up, shakes hands with the agt, &c. & speaks, then shakes hands & sits down. Pipe giving.[109] "I give you the hearts & arms of my people." Indians are without provisions & hungry. Supplied sparingly by the agt. Thinks there will be 3,000 here, 5,000 in all. Took notes of speeches in part in back of this book. D. & W. engaged two men to go to St. Croix. I understand not a word said to me. Unkind as free men can be perceived. Pay $1 per day, ea[ch] man going & coming. Went to gov't. blacksmith to get my gun fixed. Charged ½$, for nothing is pd. by gov't. Chiefs wear medals given by gov't., the only distinguishing mark was eagle feathers they wear. The traders charge $1 for trinkets of all kinds, beads & bells, silver are preferred, scarlet cloth, paint, vermillion. Some [Indians] with bodies painted black in sign of mourning.[110] Saw a squaw with her papoose cradle, which they carry from the forehead suspended by a strap, empty, having only some feathers & trinkets attached. Sign of

---

109. Among the Chippewas tobacco was perceived to have "magic power," and its use made an obligation or agreement binding between the parties. The smoking of tobacco was an essential part of making a treaty. Densmore, *Chippewa Customs*, 145.
110. The use of black paint as a sign of mourning was common among the Chippewas. A man in deep mourning painted his face black, but a black circle covering each eye indicated a lesser degree of bereavement. Women were said to cover their faces entirely black or with black steaks. Ibid., 77.

death of child & mourning of mother. Few women have many trinkets or fine dresses. Young dandies [have] chains in their long braids of hair. Painted faces, &c. Medicine bags. Pipes of red, black & whitish stone, all in almost one shape. The Chippaways have a red pipe stone quarry 120 miles from here on Chippaway where they get their stone. Catlin is mistaken about it.[111] Kinnekinik Indians here from Red Lake. Even a great extent of country is represented, 5,000 souls, 3,000 will come here. 400 came yesterday, 1,663 here now in all.[112] Have spent the day in looking around & at Indian agency office.

---

111. Henry was probably correct regarding the source of the Chippewas' Catlinite pipes. The pipestone is likely to have come from a quarry situated in Barron County, Wisconsin, which lies about 120 miles from La Pointe. J. N. Gunderson, "Wisconsin Pipestone: A Preliminary Mineralogical Examination," *Wisconsin Archaeologist* 68 (2003): 1–21. George Catlin, the noted artist, traveler, and ethnographer, had erroneously attributed the Chippewa pipes to the well-known but more distant quarry on the Côteau des Prairies in southwestern Minnesota. L. J. P. Gaskin, "Centenary of the Opening of George Catlin's North American Indian Museum and Gallery in the Egyptian Hall, Piccadilly, with a Memoir of Catlin," *Man* 40 (1940): 18; Densmore, *Chippewa Customs*, 144.

   Archaeologists have found Catlinite pipes inlaid with lead at the sites of eighteenth- and nineteenth-century villages throughout the Mississippi and Missouri river drainages. See Donald G. Lehmer, *Introduction to Middle Missouri Archeology* (Washington, DC: US Department of the Interior, National Park Service, 1971), 150; Mary Elizabeth Good, *Guebert Site: An 18th Century, Historic Kaskaskia Indian Village in Randolph County, Illinois* (Wood River, IL: Central States Archaeological Societies, 1972), 74. These pipes were produced employing the following process. First, the maker prepared a sand mold of the bowl. The pipe was then removed and designs engraved in it. After being returned to the mold, hot metal was poured in and, when it cooled, the pipe was removed from the mold, the excess metal cut away, and the pipe then smoothed and polished. G. Hubert Smith, *Like-A-Fishhook Village and Fort Berthold, Garrison Reservoir, North Dakota* (Washington, DC: US Department of the Interior, National Park Service, 1972), 64–65.

112. The Indians gathering at La Pointe came there to receive goods, provisions, and tobacco under the provisions of the Treaty of La Pointe of 1842. In exchange for their ceding large portions of Michigan's Upper Peninsula and Wisconsin to the United States, forty-one Chippewa bands were compensated with money, supplies, schools, agricultural assistance, and blacksmith services. "Treaty of La Pointe 1842," The Bad River Band of Lake Superior Chippewa Tribe, badriver-nsn.gov.

Thursday, 6th. Spent the day as before. Our boarding house has a number of traders, &c. get some new information from them, all the while living here. Saw where to get fish, which are rather scarce here. So many hungry Indians are here. They are white fish, lake trout & siskewit, these being very fat & a cross with the trout. No potatoes or vegetables. Put my blanket in the council room of the agency & slept last night & do hereafter. Edgerton & I joined forces, he furnishing buffalo robe & I blankets. Slept very well. Took a bath as usual in the lake before b[reak]fast near the lodges at the point. *Algonquin* sailed this PM with Mr. Edgerton. D. & W. left with their men for St. Croix. The portage is 80 miles on foot before striking the river. German dr., a geologist, came in with his men. Sick man. Dr. Borup refused to tell him what to do, is hated by everybody, didn't seem to have a friend among white or Indian. Sent to the mission for assistance. Mr. Wright is improving. Catholic church threatened by fire from the woods, great hubub. Indians sat around the church smoking, their squaws working hard extinguishing. Acct. by Gen. Phelps when in Eagle Harbour of fire at Copper Harbour very near caused loss of life. Begging dance, hard work for muscles.[113] Fine forms of Indian copper statuary.[114] They come in with heavy packs strung from the forehead. Indian gambling. Cards like "marriage," "the shoe game," "chawed bullet" & "turn up" with red & white bones. Gamble for trinkets. Singing very monotonous.

To report his band, the chief brings a bundle of sticks containing same numbers of his band & counts off by each family. Count is taken in a book by b&, ea[ch] name entered with number of persons, sexes &c. with regard to giving the goods, as payment put in h&s according to the

---

113. The "begging dance" was a Chippewa social dance in which the participants went from house to house, or tent to tent, begging food for a feast. Densmore, *Chippewa Customs*, 107.

114. Presumably these objects were made of native copper, which had been mined on Lake Superior long before contact with Europeans, and may have been charms, which the Chippewas used for various purposes. Ibid., 113–114; Kinietz, *Indians*, 374–375.

wants of the families & numbered & ea[ch] number corresponds to a name which, when called, is given. Ea[ch] chief signing receipts before goods are delivered. After that the money is divided in the same manner. The payment takes 1 day, getting in bundles, &c. beforehand, 3 or 4 days. Indians were called on the 10th & it can't come off before the 20th or 30th. Great injustice because it is the season for collecting rice. 3 days' rations allowed them for subsistence. Many traders here to get their dues of the Indians as soon as they are paid off. Whole amt. about $14 per person in goods, &c., $4 of which is money $22,000. Goods $29,500, $4,500 in provisions & tobacco, $4,000 for blacksmiths, $2,000 for farmers, 4 of the $5,000 agricultural fund for buying instruments & use about $350 per year. $2,000 for schools, divided among all the schools, $800 for carpenter, $750 for sub agent, $300 for interpreter. The blacksmiths make their tools, &c. & the carpenters frame houses, repairs, &c. [T]he farmer has [to] keep ground house & must cultivate so much ground, have a model farm & furnish the Indians with seed & instruction. All, however, like all the rest, are great rascals & line themselves without much care for the Indian, save taking their money.

There are 5 schools belonging to as many missions in the territory, which the fund is divided among. They have to make reports to the gov't., &c. the mission school has about 70 scholars. Little good have they done it is said. The men they have educated, making use of their knowledge for sociality, went to the mission to call on Mr. Ely. He gave them an Ojibwa spelling book which I shall use as a vocabulary. Half breeds here generally rascals, remind me of Maltese. Are very hardy & like water rats or ducks. Exercise much influence among the Indians. Whiskey is forbidden here & any liquors found are destroyed. The traders elsewhere sell it freely, but this good rule here is strictly observed. Wrote a letter to Janey & Mother today, waiting to mail it after the propeller gets in with my letters.

Friday [7th]. Propeller got in at midnight, Indians made a great hubub as this is the first steam vessel here. Got a letter from Capt. Tyler & my trousers from Mr. Jay. Brought no mail from Copper Harbour, so I have no letter. Disappointed. Capt. T. promises to get me some more stock. Wrote to him if he could get 100 or 500 shares. If over $2 or as high, to get no more than 100, & enclosed a letter from Mr. Coe authorizing him to draw for $150 in Philadelphia to pay investments, to Capt. Tyler towards stock he might purchase, he taking the papers as an overage. Wrote to Phelps, D. & Co., advising them of this & to honor his drafts or mine. Wrote to Uncle E. [Edward N. Shelton] also about money, to Mr. Russell concerning copper, &c. & to his daughter Fanny about the Indians, &c.

Has rained tremendously during the night. D. & W. must have got a soaking, have 2 blankets apiece. Has rained during the day. Propeller has but few pass[en]gers & has brought the Indian goods & provisions, much to their joy. No money has yet been appropriated by gov't. for the payment! They adjourn the 10th, & if not done before that time no money can be given, & it would cause some trouble. Have been writing all day & making preparations to go off. Difficulty in getting men. Finally engaged 2 for $30 & their provisions with ways to go, but when I talked of starting tomorrow morn[ing], one said he could not go till Monday. Engaged another, a boy of 19 & an Indian & bought 16 lbs. hard bread, 6 lbs. sugar, 13½ lbs. ham for provisions 7 days. Looks like rain & if so should not go. Have a heavy load for 2 men to take full 150 lbs. Sold my shot for 16¢ full in exchange for hard bread at 12½¢. Lost my umbrella. Hole in the Day (*Bugus no gesich*) arrived this PM.[115] A large boat filled with warriors in

---

115. Hole-in-the-Day, the Younger, or Hole-in-the-Sky, who was also known as Bugo-naghezhisk, Bagone-giizhig, or Bug-o-nay-ki-shig, was a chief, or *ogama*, of one of the bands of the Mississippi Chippewas. Born in 1825, he was still a young man when he succeeded his father, Hole-in-the-Day the Elder in 1846. Because Chippewa society at large possessed weak institutions of social integration and central political authority, such status was based on charisma and demonstrated ability. Hole-in-the-Day the Elder attained a position of influence for his bravery in war against the Sioux and had been recognized as a chief by the federal government for his loyalty

full costume, whooping & drumming. Had a fine appearance as all stood up, but the women. Indians covering the propeller, examining machinery, &c. Have stirred out very little. Indians have kept quiet on acct. of the rain. Barbeau & others from the Sault have come up that I know. Beautiful pipes are presented by the Indians at their talks. One brought in today a fine sturgeon as a present to the agt. Gave some young Indians some beads—whoop! They said!

---

to the United States during the War of 1812. His son assumed leadership of most of the Chippewa bands through his ability to ameliorate changes brought about by American expansion through his ability to negotiate with the US government. Recognition as "first chief" by federal officials placed Hole-in-the-Day the Younger in a powerful position, and he played a key role in the treaties between the western Chippewas and the United States. He was a signer of the 1842 Treaty of La Pointe that ceded lands west of Lake Superior to the federal government and would met with federal officials to negotiate land sales in exchange for annual annuities and other benefits. His use of his special position to gain additional compensation himself and his family made him wealthy but earned him the enmity of some of the bands. A prosperous official and owner of several farms, the younger Hole-in-the-Day adapted to American culture, learned English, dressed in fashionable European-style clothes, and became a frequent visitor to St. Paul as well as the national capital. In 1862 his efforts to secure regular acquisition of the promised payments—he threatened to join the Dakota uprising—failed to tarnish the US government's perception of him as the voice of his people, but resentment of his actions during the US-Dakota War incensed his enemies among the Chippewas, and he was assassinated by members of the Leech Lake band on June 27, 1868. Mark Diedrich, *The Chiefs Hole-in-the-Day of the Mississippi Chippewa* (Minneapolis: Coyote Books, 1986); Anton Treuer, *The Assassination of Hole in the Day* (St. Paul: Minnesota Historical Society Press, 2011); Victor Barnouw, "Chippewa Social Atomism," *American Anthropologist*, n.s., 13 (1961): 1006–1013; Theodore C. Blegen, "Armistice and War on the Minnesota Frontier," *Minnesota History* 24 (1943): 15–16; "Bagone-giizhig (Hole-in-the-Day the Younger), 1825–1868," Mnopedia, mnopedia.org; "Indigenous People's Literature, Hole-in-the-Day as Remembered by Ohiyesa (Charles A. Eastman)," Indians.org, indians.org/welker/holenday.htm.

Letter

Henry Sanford to Janey Howe,
August 7, 1846, [La Pointe][116]

The propeller came in today, but she brought no mail from Copper Harbour, and so I have no letter & am much disappointed. But as I have written, I have written supposing your letters are on the way. I shall send this to you keeping Dr. & Cr. in mind. You owe me now four letters, two of which I feel certain are on the way now. Please direct to me at Council Bluffs, Missouri River, which is, I believe, the highest point where is weekly mail communication.[117] I shall take huge delight when I do get hold of some of your letters there, for I have directed those which I expected here to be sent on there, & ought to receive some time next September or October quite a <u>lot</u>, to use a mercantile word.

I shall now start off for the Mississippi and it's a rather arduous

---

116. HSSP, Box 93, Folder 15, Letter 14.

117. Situated on the east bank of the Missouri River ten miles north of the present city of Omaha, Nebraska, Council Bluffs was named for the site where the Lewis and Clark expedition camped and held meetings with the Missouri and Otoe Indians in 1804. At the time of Henry's visit, the site of Council Bluffs was occupied by Potawatomi Indians removed from Illinois and Wisconsin in 1837 as a consequence of the 1833 Treaty of Chicago. A group at least 1,450 Potawatomis under the leadership of Billy Caldwell, a métis fur trader, established villages at Council Bluffs where an agency was established that year. Called Caldwell's Village, it became the site of a blockhouse erected at the present site of Council Bluffs to protect the resident Potawatomis in 1837. The following year the St. Mary/St. Joseph Catholic Mission, which included a fort, church, school and other buildings, occupied this location. The government closed the agency in 1846, and most of the Potawatomis subsequently relocated to Kansas in 1848. About seven miles north, the American Fur Company operated a post at Traders' Point, which by 1846 consisted of about forty structures. David R. Edmunds, *The Potawatomis: Keepers of the Fire* (Norman: University of Oklahoma Press, 1978), 249–253, 274–275; William G. Hartley, "Council Bluffs/Kanesville, Iowa: A Hub for Mormon Settlements, Operations, and Emigration, 1846–1852," *John Whitmer Historical Association Journal* 26 (2006): 18–19.

undertaking. I take a canoe from this point to the foot of the bay on the mainland 15 miles then go on foot along a trail through the wilderness 80 miles, accompanied by my Indians, for voyageurs & <u>packers</u> or carriers of my effects. These fellows will go through with a load of from 75 to 150 lbs. in two days! At the end of the portage is the St. Croix River on which I go in a canoe to Lake St. Croix & then across to Fort Snelling, I have got very well accustomed to sleeping without a bed. My sleeping quarters here are a corner of the council room of the Indian agent. I spread my blanket & sleep famously. Last night I was awakened from confused dreams of fighting Indians or by the arrival of the propeller about 10 AM & found my dreams were not altogether without foundation, for the puffing exhaust of the first vessel propelled by steam that ever came here had put the Indians in a ferment & they were making all sorts of whooping & yelping.

Two men from Boston, who proposed going on with me to the St. Croix started off yesterday without saying a word to me, having engaged the only two men to be procured that would go across before the payment. They have been well paid, however, for their bad faith. It came as to rain tremendously last night and has rained all this forenoon. Probably they are by this time repenting, with drenched clothes & baggage, their haste in getting away. They had only two blankets apiece & nothing to protect them from the weather.

––––––––––––

The propeller has brought news of the postponement for a fortnight or so, & I shall find no difficulty in getting through. The time is somewhere from eight to ten days required for the passage. Many a painted face & gaily dressed head have looked into the window beside which I write, looking at the characters on the paper, have seemed to consider them good medicine if one can judge by their frequent "how-how." I am living on fish almost entirely, vegetables seeming to be almost [remainder of letter missing]

Journal

<u>Saturday, 8th</u>. Fine thick mist & rain. Concluded not to go. Hole in the Day took up his quarter in the council room. Heard him <u>talk</u> yesterday. Is a fine looking man <u>in his way</u>. Shows calmness & intelligence with savageness. Is their <u>greatest</u> orator. The last time he was here, while speaking, an Indian interrupted him. He went on & after struck him at the head with his hatchet, which cut off one of his braids of hair. Has been a bloody mess. Slept in next room to them last night. This morning before getting up heard him harangue his band.

Shall probably now wait till Monday before starting. Indians are feasting now, provisions in abundance. The amt. of provisions, apart from the 3 days' rations allowed by gov't., amts. to $4,500, is enough for 40 days. All is squandered, burned up before they leave.

Whole number of Indians: 5,296.

Whole number of families: 580.

Amt. for each in money: $4.15.

Amt. for each in goods about $7.00.

That in money, provisions & goods about ornaments.

Mr. Covel & the Indians' medicine man. His cures—6 days fasting to become a brave—his cure.

Attempt to get off this PM as it has become clear. Half breeds will not go. Jean Battiste. Dearness of things here, rice 12¢, shot 25¢ per lb. &c. sell my bag at 16¢. Sell my knives & hat to the Jews. Dances of the Indians at the propeller & Hole in the Day's band. He keeps quiet in his tent, has not ornaments or paint. Tall, dark features, low forehead. Has had a tent today got for him. He slept last night in <u>my</u> quarters. Liquor smuggled in here, sold at $1 per bottle. Trick on the black barber & others are of the st[eam] boat who were looking for squaws.

Nag-awn-ab [Nagan'ab] (Sitting Ahead) came to the agency to have a talk this eve[ning].[118] Stayed till 11½. Twas about some murders committed by a neighbouring band. Says he tries to keep back his people from taking the matter in their hands & comes to him (the agt.) To talk about the best course, &c. I grew sleepy & did not hear all the agt. says. He stops their payment for punishment. Mr. Samuels says there will be some difficulty. The bands of Indians at variance, who have murdered each other are yet to come. Thinks they will get liquor & may have a fight. Also that a fracas may ensue by the Indians refusing to allow the ½ breeds any money from the payment this year instead of being equal as before. It is optional of the Indians to give or not. Jew traders speaking al languages are here, have been everywheres. Just the same here.

Sunday, 9th. Day of rest for once. Went to the Moravian church. Rev. Mr. Hall preached for a congregation.[119] Indian looking in curiously. Sermon on the condition of Israelites with the fiery serpents contrasting us with sin, &c. considerable discourse in PM on the young sick man & Jesus, the need for religion over everything, vanity of riches, &c. Tried to get off this evening so as to camp the other end of the bay & be ready for an early start. Found it difficult to get my two men started. Have tried since Friday. They are the only ones I can get. Got the sullens like all half breeds. Can hardly get an answer from any. Could not get a boat. Dr. Borup predicts I shall not reach them, the men (George LeGros & Geo. Dayton) not strong

---

118. Nagan'ab was the leader of the Chippewas at Fond du Lac, Minnesota. He rose to this position because of his extraordinary success as a trapper. His use of hepatica as a lure to trap fur-bearing animals led him to become wealthy, and he is reported to have had credit at all traders' stores. Densmore, *Chippewa Customs*, 110.

119. The Reverend Sherman Hall was the superintendent of the La Pointe mission, where he resided with his family about thirteen years. In 1853 he moved to Crow Wing, on the Mississippi. With the help of Native interpreters he translated the New Testament into the Chippewa language. Madeline Island History, Ashland County, Wisconsin, "The Old Home Mission, and Its Missionaries to the Ojibwa Indians on Madeline Island, Lake Superior, Wisconsin, by Rev. Stanley Edwards Lathrop," Wisconsin Genealogy Trails, http://genealogytrails.com/wis/ashland/history/madelineislandhistory.htm, 26, 28.

enough &c. Rather frightened me. He is a selfish man & a mean one, has offered me no civility since I have been here. Mr. Hays, the Ind[ian] agt., is different. I sleep in his room now. Last night he gave me his mattress, a fine one which has <u>just</u> come. So I slept until 7½, too late almost for breakfast & for my bath took one after. An Indian followed me down. His modesty. Crowsfoot's son, well educated. Manner of courting. Lodge front of Mr. Park's bakery, squaws, &c. Hole in the Day speaks to the young men, quite warm apparently. Very rapid interjectional one. Has been a very hot day. Potatoes not yet larger than walnuts, peas & cucumbers just come on. Haven't a vegetable, beans, fresh fish & maple sugar.

Sent by Mr. Coe letters to Capt. Tyler, Mr. Coe, Mr. Jay, P.M. Mackinaw, Dr. Howe (Janey), my mother & Uncle E., *Spirit of Times*, & Phelps, Dodge & Co. to have P.O. at Mackinaw give letters to P. D. & Co. to Mr. Arnold who took them to Cop[per] Harbour P.M., telling to send my letters to Council Bluffs. The propeller left very early this morn[ing]. Quite foggy.

<u>Monday, 10th</u>. My men were to be off at 3. I got up at 4½. Found them happy to wear a portage collar than with furs packing, &c, &c. Twas after 5½ when we started. Took a canoe & two Indians & cross over to the foot of the bay, saw pheasants, & bid fair to be cool rather than get off. Met a canoe full of Indians. PM portage. Fishing nets & buoys. Bluffs of sandstone strata, arches, boulders, &c. Very beautiful black river, &c. Reached them at 10½. A narrow foot path, half hid in bushes. Way of packing, heavy <u>overcoming</u> loads. Hard going. Rest every 11 minutes, full half the time. Traces of young D. & W. Camping grounds dif[ferent] between Indian & white do. Make first day but about 10 miles. I think men complain a great deal of heavy packs. Build a fire, cook coffee, soft hominy. Roll up in blankets. Wolves, &c. See nothing to shoot. Keep gun along all day.

<u>Tuesday, 11th</u>. Up at 4½, off at 5. Take breakfast near a little lake, 4 miles. Shot 1 pigeon. Passing <u>pines</u>. Very hot. No rain though wind overheard. Sandy hills. Movement of tall pines by the wind, bent often. Largest stamp

25 min. pass little lakes. No ducks. Trace of D. & W. Old frame. Is Dayton obliging, is LeGros? Drink often. Find a hat band of Dwight's. Dine off crackers, sugar & gingerbread. Stop all the while. At 5 came to a stream from a lake. Try to fish. Camp here. Fresh clams & small fish. Soft turning threatens rain. Way of fishing for it. Break a loon's wing. Don't get him. Have made about 25 miles I judge. Try essence of coffee, capital. Get boughs for a bed & hope to sleep a little easier. Wolves & bears, porcupines, squirrel.

———————

Wednesday [12th]. Made preparations for rain last night. Put up sticks to rest our luggage on & covered with India rubber cloth. Put poles & my tent cloth over my bed. Very long thunderstorm, lightning, rain, thunder. Put my cloth down on me almost. Another shower at daylight. Make LeGros get up & fix a good lodge over me as I keep very dry. Comfortable feelings. Breakfast & got away at 9½. Got clear ahead of my party. Find camping ground of D. & W. Small lake & ducks. Chase around it after some. Wait 2 hours, noone comes. Whoop. No answer. Walked ahead a mile, find no traces & come back. Finally a whoop & they come on slowly. Traces of D. & W. LeGros kills a partridge. Came to prairie, or barren. Like moors of Scotland. Kill two grouse. 4 miles across. Walk past several pretty lakes. Pick one out for camp, make fire, &c. capital supper. I attempt to go fishing.

———————

Thursday, 13th. Wake up cold & damp. Heavy dew. Pack up & march. Plenty of pretty lakes. Cedar barrens. Small growth of woods burnt & dead. Fresh traces of D. & W. Stop at 9 to breakfast by a pretty lake. Attempt at duck shooting. Dive as soon as I shoot. Killed a chicken hawk. Cook 1 prairie hen for breakfast. Gun foul & fine shot can't kill ducks. See at next lake ducks & 1 otter. Shoot ball at him. Don't hit. Get 1 pigeon. At noon meet a sick man with large pack. Had pleurisy & fever. Got out of provisions & had sent his companion on to La Pointe for some 4 days since. Had eat[en] nothing for 2 days, started from the river 4 days since. 2 days ago D. & W. passed him. They were much crippled. That they would not get there that day. Gave him _ of our bread & sugar, wished him good luck & went on. Lost my knife there. Buffalo River, a small, cold brook. Plenty of fine trout. Catch some with grasshoppers. 4 miles farther came to B. Lake & cross B. River again, which is its outlet 4 miles more. St. Croix River.[120] Steep hills. Bushy roads. Height of ground. See long, white river in a low valley, still & full of wild rice. Relics of previous voyageurs. Clothes, bags &c. Canoes. Make fire. Little wood. Hunt for hidden things. Find paddles, &c. all who came here hid canoes, &c. sick man gave us his canoe, camp kettle, &c., but D. & W. had taken it. Cook supper while men get canoe & fix it. Find a gig, good luck. Go a fishing by torchlight. No luck. Make bed of boughs & fix the tent to keep off dews. Very cool. Plenty of mosquitoes.

Friday, 14th. Sleep very cold, heavy dew. Got away late, 8 o'clock. Wild rice. Manner of tying it. See Indians gathering, beating it with sticks into a canoe. Stopped at lodge to get some meat. No one there. Fish, potatoes, dog, &c., that's all. Go on little way, find old woman. Came back & made a trade for potatoes & wild rice. For some bread, fresh venison. Shoot a duck, don't get him. Plenty of ducks along the rice fields. Great extent of rice. Shot at a great many ducks. Got only one. Pass another lodge & getting rice. Hear from D. & W. Have been along 4 days since. They say

---

120. The St. Croix River rises from St. Croix Lake in Douglas County in the northeastern corner of Wisconsin about twenty miles from Lake Superior. It then flows south and southwest to form the border between Wisconsin and Minnesota for 130 miles until its confluence with the Mississippi below St. Paul. The river contains stretches of interesting geological formations, including the tall, perpendicular cliffs, those of the Dalles, rising several hundred feet above the river. Occupied by the Chippewas, the St. Croix Valley had been an important source of furs, but much of this land was ceded to the United States by the Treaty of St. Peters in 1837. By the time of Henry's visit in the 1840s, the region had been opened to logging, and sawmills had been erected on the St. Croix as well as other major rivers. Dunn, *The St. Croix*, 66–72; *History of Northern Wisconsin, Containing an Account of Its Settlement. . . .* (Chicago: Western Historical Co., 1881), 721–722; Eileen McMahon and Theodore J. Karamanski, *North Woods River: The St. Croix River in Upper Midwest History* (Madison: University of Wisconsin Press, 2009), 73–75.

were out of provisions, &c., only 1 meal left. Very low grounds, & water at first after rapids but all very low, skirted with pines, & great care necessary with canoe. Proves strong. Meet 4 copper explorers in PM who have been around Fon du Lac & this river since May, in a "dugout" made yesterday. Had to carry it half way. Bound to the brook. Gave them some tobacco. One of them, Mr. Wilde, gave an order on a man who keeps his camp 15 miles down for some flour, as we were most out. Hard looking men, beards, red shirts, &c. spoke like gentlemen. Said D. & W. came to their camp 35 miles above sunrise on Tuesday. That they were to the Miss[issippi] by today, were out of provisions & came to beg some flour. Indian fish-ware [weir].[121] Camping nomads. Battlefield of 6 years since. Canoe leaks. Medicine man has grown in 20 years tobacco & paint upon it in offering to the Manitou. Hope to get to the Mokagon R[iver] by night, but very bad rapids & low water.[122] George LeGros has difficulties in <u>running</u> them. Finally frees our canoe & have to haul up on shore & as it was dark made preparations to camp. Plenty of mosquitoes & long grass. <u>Bouillon</u> for supper, wild rice, &c. bread about gone.

<u>Saturday, 15th</u>. Off at 6, canoe mended. Little pitch, very difficult to make it tight. At 9 o'clock came to Wildes & co's. camp. Find his man who gives us a little flour & we cook breakfast & mend canoe again. Dayton sulks. The man Bouchard is a Frenchman from Montreal. He has been with the

---

121. Known today as the St. Croix Trail Fish Dam, the weir was used by Native people, presumably the Chippewas, to corral fish, an important component of their diet. This feature consists of a submerged V-shaped stone structure with its widest portion facing upstream. It has a narrower opening at the narrower downstream end. It is situated in Burnett County just below the St. Croix Trail bridge. See also Herbert Kuhm, "Wisconsin Indian Fishing," *Wisconsin Archaeologist* 7, no. 2 (1927–1928): 61–114.

122. Henry was probably referring to the Namekagon River, which arises in Lake Namekagon and flows southwesterly as the principal tributary of the St. Croix River, which it joins in northern Burnett County, Minnesota. "St. Croix River, Minnesota, Wisconsin," National Wild and Scenic Rivers System, www.rivers.gov/rivers/st-croix.php.

company exploring since May. The American M. & M. Co. from Detroit &c. Eat a hearty breakfast. Manner of making bread. Capital potatoes. Bad rapids after leaving at 10½ till we reach Mokagon R. At 12½. Large, swift stream. Plenty of water & good current after. Headwind & looks like a storm. Indian burial ground. Covers over their graves. Chief's grave at mouth of Mokagon R.[123] Have left wild rice. Pine barrens. Concentration of those we passed at the portage. LeGros & Dayton have traded among the Indians. The power of whiskey to get any of them selling either <u>daughters,</u> wives &c. Attempts to get by force. 1 pint ½ water. Whiskey sells for 50¢ or exchanged for sugar at that rate at 3¢ per lb. George tells of an Indian giving him everything he had on for whiskey. Whiskey always diluted with ½ water. Get to Yellow R. About 5.[124] Beautiful grounds around. Fine situation on bluff at the junction. Hunt for potatoes. Fear of getting out of provisions. Old Indian lodges. All gone to payment now. Yellow color of Y. River. Yankee names in comparison with Indian names of rivers. Those with English names emptying into St. Croix River (or some of them). Rice, Rattlesnake, Hay, Rum, Rush, Willow &c., &c. rivers![125] Encamp about 14 miles below Yellow River. Have made good day's work. <u>Bouillon</u> for supper, a hearty one. Plenty of mosquitoes. Cloudy again.

---

123. Chippewa burial customs involved wrapping the body in heavy birch bark along with implements necessary to accompany the deceased on the four-day journey to the hereafter. After being placed in a shallow grave, the body was covered by birch bark or reed mats over which a low grave house was erected. Densmore, *Chippewa Customs*, 74–75.

124. The Yellow River of northwestern Wisconsin, more commonly known as the Red Cedar River, is a tributary of the Chippewa River, into which it flows in Dunn County. The latter joins the St. Croix River, and Henry may have been referring to this confluence here. "Wisconsin Water Search," Wisconsin Department of Natural Resources, dnr.wi.gov; Neill, *History of Minnesota*, 376.

125. The Hay River is a tributary of the Red Cedar River, which it joins in Dunn County. A tributary of the Mississippi, the Rush River has its confluence at Lake Pepin in Pierce County. The Willow River is a tributary of the St. Croix, which it joins in St. Croix County. Neill, *History of Minnesota*, 376.

<u>Sunday, 16th</u>. No day of rest for us. George got a pocket full of little potatoes only yesterday & we have enough food in all for one more meal. Finding a little rice. Up at 4½ & off. Very cool. Thick coat comfortable. Dew heavy. Mosquitoes have been ferocious <u>all night</u>. Mosquito net no protection. Swift current & go down rapidly. No shallows, wide river. Pretty islands, pretty shores, well <u>wooded</u> without forest bottomlands. Stop to b[reak] fast at 8 till 9½. Just before we met an Indian who had shot a deer. Got a quarter for 50¢. Young & tender. Capital breakfast & no fear of hunger. Manner of shooting deer with light. He shot buck last night, gave us some jerked venison. Very good. Have seen deer tracks several times. Saw a crane. Logging shanty. Men came in winter to cut logs for mills below & draw onto the river to flow down when it breaks up. Hay stacks for their cattle in winter. Change in character of rock strata on the river. First part more boulders. Sandstone formation peculiar to upper Miss[issippi] or "on the mouth" & other arched rocks worn by the weather. Passed several rapids, a long one between Rice & Snake R. Wood River. Pretty shores. Higher water. Go rapidly. Started this noon for Sun Rise R., where is the first [trading] house—going down.[126] Have spent the day sitting still (hard work). Read liturgy & services for the day. Prayer book. Read Lord Bacon & eulogy. Studied my map, read over some letters, & shot at ducks. No luck, canoe unsteady. Pass a great many logs cut last winter. 15 teams, 6 oxen in ea., & 12 men per team employed. Wages from $16 to 26 per month conferred. Logs cut at 12 & 16 feet. Men cut from 3 to 6 logs. Low water & great quantities of logs left her, all marked. Duck shooting. Creep along the banks for nothing. Dayton very surely. Give him a blowing up. Reach

---

126. Both the Snake River and the Wood River are tributaries of the St. Croix River, emptying into the larger steam in Pine County, Minnesota, and Burnett County, Wisconsin. Farther downstream, the Sunrise River joins the St. Croix in Chicago County, Minnesota. Neill, *History of Minnesota*, 376. The St. Croix River becomes wider and shallower and dives into several channels at the "Head of the Rapids," a point about seven miles above the mouth of the Snake River. "Canoeing the Saint Croix River, Wisconsin," Hunt Fish Camp Wisconsin, http://huntfishcampwisconsin.com/StCroix.html.

Sun Rise at 7. Long day's walk over 5 miles. Mr. Ladden, the clerk, three Frenchmen, &c. Trading post. Whiskey. Whiskey. Eat supper. Baked bread once more. One–legged fellow for cook. Smashed his ankle. Left so for 2 months. Mortified & cut off at knee, bunglingly done. Mr. Ladden tells of Egerton, a mean scamp. Left without paying, sponged all along. (He has given me 2 letters. Shan't present them.)

<u>Monday, 17th</u>. Left word to get off at 4½. George up early & fixed the canoe. Work 1½ hrs. Dayton sleeps. Lazy day. Get off at 7 after a good breakfast. Pay $1 for supper, b[reak]fast & lodging (on the floor for 3). 4 hours' distance to the falls. D. & W. passed Thursday PM. Had nothing to eat since Wednesday afternoon. I enquired (these men) had just shot 2 deer, lost one & not eat half the other <u>there</u>, very largely. George's stories of deer shooting & elk & wolf &c. manner with ea. by light. Beautiful river, still & pleasant. Shot at mallard ducks. "Big Rock" & "Turtle" rapids, hard ones & dangerous. Take in some water. Hold my life preserver. Have a passenger. Everybody rough men. Arrive at the falls at 11½. Boom for logs made with piers. Dam & sluice. Getting over logs in the water. Falls have 1 saw & grist mill (for corn). Trees sawn. Buzz & lath mills. 30 M [thousand] per day, 40 M lath per d[itt]o. 60 hands. Wages from 16 to 26$ per mo. Mr. Hungerford the owner.[127] When I stopped in from C[onnecticu]t & spent the day with me talking & showing around. First place a co. started here &

---

127. William S. Hungerford was a member of a consortium that formed the St. Louis Co. to carry on a general lumbering, manufacturing, and trading business in 1838. The company built a dam, sawmill, several stores and shops, and about twenty dwellings. Hungerford was prominent among those who settled in St. Croix County, Wisconsin, from 1845 to 1848. Lumbermen exploited the forests along the St. Croix River, employing steamboats to deliver sawmill machinery, men, and supplies. The first mill was erected at St. Croix Falls in 1842, and within several years large rafts of lumber were being floated down the St. Croix and Mississippi Rivers to St. Louis. By 1855 seventeen mills in the St. Croix Valley were producing 28 million board feet of lumber annually. "History of Inland Water Transportation in Minnesota," Minnesota Historical Society, mnhs.org; Dunn, *The St. Croix*, 72; *History of Northern Wisconsin*, 722.

failed partly & he bought out. The lath pays for the whole mill's expenses. Sells here at $10, at St. Louis at from 13 to $20. Logs cost to get sawn $2.38 per M. Lumber to get to St. Louis $2.50 per M. Manner of getting location by Chippeway Treaty contract. Copper is found all around. Loss of dam 2 years since $60,000. Seems to be making money now. Wants some on next. Beautiful scenery. Convulsions of nature very evident. Cliffs 300 to 400 feet high. Eddy for fixing rafts & cribs. Fine land, good crops, corn, potatoes & oats. Corn ground at mill for 12½¢ per bush[el]. Lumber sawed on shares for [blank]. 20 to 30 teams of oxen kept idle here in the summer to be used in winter. River narrow & very deep. Fall at the "Falls" 20 feet. Wheels used are small flutter wheel, has a kind of turbine also. Great power of water & facilities for improving. Paid George & Dayton $15 each & gave them provisions to go back on foot. Tried to go down to still water 30 miles this PM. Offered George $2. Could get no boat. Have lost nothing by staying. Mrs. H[ungerford] & daughter, Sarah & Adelaide. Mrs. H's complaints &c. show of agents &c. have commenced this PM immediately at landing with sneezing & catarrh. Fears of asthma. If continues will break up all my plans. Must go to N[ew] Orleans. Looks like storm. Sound of the water here very pleasant. Good bed once more. Mosquito bars, &c. Hurra for a good night's sleep!

Tuesday, 18th. No chance to get down. Rained last night & this morning. Sat still during the forenoon. Wrote to Mother & Peter King, expecting the mail, which turns every fortnight, hourly. PM cleared a little & went down the river shooting. Saw little, ducks, hawks &c. [illegible]—a man from the mill went out & has traded with the Indians. Says he took out once 10 gals. alcohol which he kept diluting with water & sold at 50 ¢ a cup. Got $80 in cash & $60 in furs &c. for it of a tribe of Indians. Got them drunk at first with the rum alcohol & kept adding water. After always fight when drunk. Squaws hide guns, knives &c. Profits at store near 100%. Clothing, provisions & a great item. Flour at cost of $3.35 sells at 6 to 6.50, pork at 18¢. Lumber is sold to lumbermen in St. Louis & Galena. Have orders ahead for the whole season. Would make 40% more with a lumberyard to send it to St. Louis. Sells there for $13 & 20. In yard sells at $18 & $30, always cash. Lath sells at $2 per M. Makes 20 M per day. Work up slabs &c.

<u>Wednesday, 19th</u>. No boat nor opportunity to go down & have <u>loafed</u> all day. Cornelians a hunting in th[e] PM, got nothing. Blackberries plenty. Has looked like rain all day. "Scaling logs" served as evidence of native copper found around the mill. Indications strong d[itt]o. of iron. Water power immense, whole river can be used. Flutter wheels. To be used in sinking shafts for mines. Quick motion of saws. ¼ in. thick. Got lost in the woods. Rocks 7 crags in abundance. Pretty lake. Flat boat building. Mr. H's farm. Good soil, beans well. Agates & cornelians numerous. Mrs. H's collection. ___. Her daughters. Character of meals & equipage. No excuses. Feel asthmatic as I have from the moment I put foot on shore. Surveying, &c. am studying maps for a trip in the Gulf of Mexico, Central America.

<u>Thursday, 20th</u>. Cloudy & light rain as usual. Wild geese. Mrs. H. has some domesticated. Breakfast like all other meals, pork, potatoes, good coffee, bread & butter. Manage to get off. Take a skiff for "Marine" mills in company with a Mr. Clark & Northrop.[128] Stop at "Osceola" to dinner.[129] Small stream runs this mill with a great fall. Beautiful scenery. Trap [dark-colored,

---

128. Anson Northrup was one of the early settlers of Stillwater, Minnesota, where he established a hotel in 1846. "History of the Town of Osceola," Town of Osceola, townofosceola.com; *History of Northern Wisconsin*, 722.

129. One of the first sawmills to open on the St. Croix River, the Marine Lumber Company began operation in the summer of 1839. By 1840 the mill floated eighty thousand feet of lumber per year. It was located nine miles below the falls. The Marine Mill remained in operation until 1895. Dunn, *The St. Croix*, 72; Hunt, *Wisconsin Gazetteer*, 140; Historic Sites, "Marine Mill," Minnesota Historical Society, mnhs.org. Osceola Mills, established by the Kent brothers, was situated on the St. Croix River in Wisconsin in 1845. A settlement here became the village of Osceola in 1859 and the seat of Polk County. *Wisconsin and Minnesota State Gazetteer, Shippers' Guide and Business Directory for 1865–66* (Indianapolis: Geo. W. Hawes, 1865), 35; "History of the Town of Osceola."

fine-grained igneous rock] & conglomerate rocks. Wild geese, turkey, buzzards, bald head eagle. The river narrows & very deep, crooked like a succession of pretty lakes. Wrote yesterday a little to *Palladian* respecting Indians, &c. No mail yet. Heard that D. & W. had gone from Stillwater to the Falls [of] St. Anthony by land, the canoe waiting to take them down to Lake Pepin. Should have overtaken them, could I have got away Monday.[130]

Lumber is sawed in halves at the Falls Mills, at times not so profitable he says. Mr. H. wants some money with a partner. Has got $12,000 mortgaged on ½ now at 10%. It is worth nothing for he has no claim but preemption title to it. Think I might do over by such abundance. Could stash the St. Louis part. Twill pay $30,000 per year. There has been a great lack of good management at the Falls, so much so that the Marine Mills with but 2 saws have cut more lumber than Falls with 5. They (Falls) have lost their dam twice. Can't command the water. Hungerford sold to [blank] for $40,000 & had to take back again. Is now doing well they say. Northrop has Osceola Mills. Dined there. Saw 2 saws on a small stream running to river with great fall. Diameter of wheel (overshot) 30 ft., same as Marine. The Marine, 11 miles from Osceola & 18 from Falls, has 2 saws well managed. Mr. Buffalo &c. cuts as much lath as the Falls with single instead of double saws. Got a man for a dollar to help me paddle to Stillwater, 11 miles farther.[131] Left at 4½. River all the way very pretty. End of trap & beginning of sand &

---

130. Lake Pepin is situated on the Mississippi River below its confluence with the St. Croix and is formed by the backup of water behind the sedimentary deposits of the Chippewa River's delta. With a surface area of forty square miles, it is the largest lake on the river and was a hindrance to moving log rafts by hand before steamboats became available to tow them. "Lake Pepin," Minnesota Department of Natural Resources, dnr.state.mn.us/areas/fisheries/lakecity/pepin.html; "History of Inland Water Transportation in Minnesota," Minnesota Historical Society, mnhs.org.
131. John McKusick formed the Stillwater Lumber Company and in the spring of 1844 established a sawmill on the St. Croix River. By 1846 Stillwater's population consisted of about ten families and twenty single men. Two years later it later became the seat of St. Croix County, Minnesota. Washington County Historical Society, "History of Stillwater, MN," wchsmn.org; Dunn, *The St. Croix*, 72; *Wisconsin and Minnesota*

limestone conglomerates. Wild game. Pretty scenery. Had to paddle till after dark. Arrived at 7½. Stillwater is about 1½ miles from head of the lake, which is 25 & 1 to 2½ miles. Fish jumping. 2 kinds of sturgeon. Swan. Many people at tavern (Kennedy's). Hear of D. & W., their troubles with horse flesh. Met Teague. They had paid for his canoe $8 & $39 beside. Found they have left this morn[in]g on skiff for Galena. D. foundered a horse going to the Falls. Had to pay $25. W. lost his & saddle. Had to pay $10. Sleep as usual in a room with half a dozen beds & dirty sheets. Protest always against comp[an]y.

―――――――――

<u>Friday, 21st</u>. Rainy morning. Has rained hard during night. Had to hire a pair of horses & lumber box wagon for $8 to take me to St. Pauls. Stillwater has about 15 to 20 houses. County seat. Tardy movements setting off, catching & harnessing horses &c. leave at 11½. Prairie with trees here there & groves of very beautiful mounds. Mr. Bissell's place. Mound & beautiful view from it. Park scenery. Different formation of soil of <u>mounds</u>.[132] Beautiful farming country. Houses all outdoors. No trees. Prairie hens. Got one. Pretty lakes & streams. Saw mill. Reach St. Pauls about 6. Pretty situation on the river. Peculiar bluffs.[133] River low. No mail in 3 weeks. Tidy hostess.

―――――――――

State Gazetter, Shippers' Guide and Business Directory for 1865–66 (Indianapolis: Geo. W. Hawes, 1865), 23.

132. Although the site of Mr. Bissell's house is uncertain, a review of archaeological literature reveals that mounds were constructed by Native people in Middle to Late Woodland times (AD 600–1600) in the St. Croix Valley north of Stillwater, Minnesota. The Archaeological Site Files at the Minnesota Office of the State Archaeologist identified one mound site just north of the city as well as twenty-four recorded mound sites in surrounding Washington County, Minnesota. Caven P. Clark, *An Archaeological Survey of the Lower District of St. Croix National Scenic Riverway*, Technical Report 126 (Lincoln, NE: US Department of the Interior, National Park Service, Midwest Archaeological Center, 2010), 10–12, 81; Minnesota Office of the State Archaeologist, Fort Snelling History Center, St. Paul, MN.

133. The site of St. Paul, on the east bank of the Mississippi River, was occupied by French and French Canadian traders in 1840, when pioneer settlers from the failed Red River colony in Manitoba and the eastern United States began to arrive in the area. Called L'Oei du Cochon (Pig's Eye), its name changed the following year to

Capital supper. Mr. Stapleton & his fox. Wild, tame geese. Sioux. Bows & arrows. Difference in language with Chippewas &c.

Saturday, 22d. Up at 5½ after excellent b[reak]fast off for the falls. Beautiful prairie & grove country. First view of the falls. U. S. Mills. Masses of rock, 24 ft. perpendicular, 47 the fall. Whole length of island. Something like Niagara, 2 shoots.[134] Cross over in wagon above the falls to Iowa side, walk down to the foot of the falls.[135] Fine place for fishing. Walk then across the prairie 9 miles to the fort. Open ground & hot. Little falls from 40 to 60 ft. got to the fort [Snelling] at 12½. Letter to Maj. Clarke. Situation of his house, of the fort, fine, new. Mrs. Clarke & sister, Mrs. Emerson, very hospitable. Dine there. Soup & silver forks. Once more go afterwards to Mr. Sibley's. [C]hild dying. He sends for a man & 3 horses below St. Pauls.

St. Paul, the favorite saint of Father Lucien Galtier, who erected a chapel on a bluff overlooking the river to serve the French Canadian community. St. Paul grew slowly at first. At the time of Henry's visit only thirty families lived there, but when it was named the capital of the newly organized Minnesota Territory in 1849, the city had nine hundred residents who occupied the bluffs as well as the older lower town on the river. J. Fletcher Williams, *A History of the City of St. Paul, and of the County of Ramsey, Minnesota* (St. Paul: Minnesota Historical Society, 1876), 109–112, 149.

134. This was undoubtedly St. Anthony Falls, the only significant waterfall on the upper Mississippi River. Following the establishment of Fort Snelling in 1820, the falls became an attraction for tourists, artists, and writers, and in 1848 the settlement of St. Anthony was established on the east bank of the river. The town of Minneapolis grew on the west bank, a dam and mill were erected, and by 1856 the area's population had grown from three hundred to more than fifteen hundred. "St. Anthony Falls Historic District," City of Minneapolis, minneapolismn.gov.

135. Originally part of Michigan Territory and later Wisconsin Territory, Iowa Territory became a separate entity in 1838. At that time its eastern boundary included all lands west of the Mississippi River and north of the Missouri River, including those within the present state of Minnesota. Controversy over the territory's size arose in 1844 when Iowa applied for statehood and delayed its admission to the Union for two years, at which time the state's present boundaries were established. Continuing disputes over Wisconsin's western border continued for another two years, and in 1849 the Territory of Minnesota assumed its present size. "Steps to Statehood," *Annals of Iowa* 27 (1946): 217–219; William E. Lass, "How Minnesota Got Its Boundaries," MinnPost, minnpost.com/mnopedia/2014/06/how-minnesota-got-its-boundaries.

Walk them to St. Pauls, a hard one. Meet Indians on prairie, their first appearance on coming to the fort. Wade partly across the river & hallou for a canoe & cross to St. Pauls at 6½. Capital supper. Eat a great deal. Take a little whiskey & feel better. Found a mail carrier has come & gone to the fort. Write a letter in the eve[ning] to send by him in the morn, and I can't get my letters till after he has gone. The silver grey fox.

Sunday, 23d. Bellaud, the man Mr. Sibley engaged, came here this morn[in]g with one horse, which I mounted with my saddlebags &c. rode up to the fort on east side of the river. Mr. Fenbault. Beautiful prairie. Man gives letter for me to take to the Green Stone. Bellaud says he would like to go with me. Is a capital man. Go across in a canoe & swim our horse. Services in chapel. Rev. Mr. Gear.[136] Mrs. Baker's singing. Soldiers all attend. Some Catholics go the other side & their church. Go over there to see Mr. Sibley.[137] Catholic priest recognizes me. Mr. Sibley makes arrangements

---

136. Born in Middletown, Connecticut, in 1793, the Reverend Ezekiel Gear was an Episcopal minister and became post chaplain at Fort Snelling in 1837. In 1860 he was transferred to Fort Ripley, Minnesota, and retired in 1867. Gear died at age eighty in 1873. Williams, *A History of the City of St. Paul, and the County of Ramsey, Minnesota* ([St. Paul]: Minnesota Historical Society, 1876), 179.

137. Henry Hastings Sibley, one of the most prominent figures in early Minnesota history, was born in Detroit in 1811, the son of Judge Solomon Sibley, a prominent public official in the Northwest Territory and later Michigan. The lure of the West drew him to Sault Ste. Marie, where he entered the service of the American Fur Company as a clerk. By 1834 he was a partner in the company and extended its operations to the Dakotas (Sioux) on the upper Mississippi. He established a post at St. Peters (Mendota) on the west bank of the Mississippi River just east of Fort Snelling and was active in developing the trade in present-day Minnesota. Having learned the Dakota language, Sibley was a key figure in the 1837 negotiations with the federal government for the cession of Dakota and Chippewa lands east of the Mississippi. With the decline of the fur trade, the payment of annuities to the Indians, and the arrival of colonists, the company's business shifted to retail sales and banking, firmly establishing Sibley at the center of the regional frontier economy. His political career began in 1838 when he was named justice of the peace for Iowa Territory, which included substantial lands west of the Mississippi. Sibley married Sarah J. Steele in 1843. He was a delegate to Congress from the Territory of Wisconsin in 1848, where

with Bellaud to take me to La Framboise with 3 horses for \$35, & to have his horses at \$50 apiece after I get there if I want. La Framboise is going to the Missouri & it will be a fine chance.[138] Feel asthmatic & eyes bad. Shall

---

his efforts helped secure the creation of Minnesota Territory the following year. As a member of a treaty commission, he helped negotiate the cession of Dakota lands in 1851. From 1849 to 1853 he served as a territorial delegate to Congress and a member of the territorial legislature in 1855. He was a member of Minnesota's constitutional convention in 1857 and in 1858 was elected the state's first governor. As a colonel and later brigadier general of volunteers, Sibley led state forces against the Indians during the Sioux Uprising of 1862 and the following years commanded an expedition against the Sioux on the Missouri River. He retired as head of the district of Minnesota, which included present-day Minnesota, Iowa, and Wisconsin as well as the Dakota Territory. He retired as a major general in 1866, after which he became involved with banking, railroads, and other business corporations as well as serving in public capacities as a member of the University of Minnesota's board of regents and president of the Minnesota Historical Society and a federal Indian commissioner. Ibid., 50–54; Wilson P. Shortbridge, "Henry Hastings Sibley and the Minnesota Frontier," *Minnesota History Bulletin* 3 (1919): 115–125; "Sibley, Henry Hastings, 1811–1891," Biographical Directory of the United States Congress, bioguide. congress.gov; "Henry Sibley Biography," Minnesota Historical Society, mnhs.org; William J. Peterson, "Steamboating in the Upper Mississippi Fur Trade," *Minnesota History* 13 (1943): 224, 233.

138. This is likely to have been Joseph P. La Framboise, the son of Louis Joseph La Framboise and Marguerite Magdelaine Marcot, both important fur traders and residents of Mackinac Island. Following her husband's murder in 1809, Magdelaine La Framboise expanded their business to include posts throughout northern and western Michigan's Lower Peninsula before selling out to the American Fur Company in 1818. Her son, Joseph P. La Framboise, was born in 1805 and became a trader in Minnesota in 1834, managing posts on the Cottonwood River and the mouth of Petite Rocher (Little Rock) Creek in Nicollet County, Minnesota. He also served as an interpreter at treaties signed between the United States and the Dakotas. His death occurred in 1854.

Although he appears to have been older, a Joseph La Framboise was also a fur trader who worked for the American Fur Company at Prairie du Chien, Wisconsin. He was sent by the company to open a store on the upper Missouri River in 1817 and established Fort Teton at the mouth of the Teton River in present South Dakota. Nearby La Framboise Island in the Missouri River was named for him. La Framboise operated the post until at least 1819 and afterward returned to Prairie du Chien. He later operated posts on the Sioux River near present Flandreaux, South Dakota, and the headwaters of the Du Moines River.

try to go on, however. Beloit is to come tomorrow at 2 & we are to start the next morn[in]g early. Get back to Maj. Clarke's later for dinner. Eat a cold one. Mrs. C. said [she] has watched with Mrs. S's. child. Complaint water in the head, been dying 10 days. Mrs. C's. boy, Sanford Clarke, Mrs. E's. girl. Pretty children. Building at the fort a barrack building of stone. Attend service at 5. Nobody there but 4 or 5 women & 1 man & some children. Sermon short. Pleasant society at Maj. Clarke's. very comfortable.

<u>Monday, 24th</u>. Warm as usual, but considerable air. Feel considerably asthmatic. Wheezed a little last night. Eyes were very bad. Began to think it will be folly to go on to the prairies. Think about it some time & finally go across the ferry (with Frenchman) to Mr. Sibley's. [T]ell his clerk to send down immediately to Bellaud, tell him to leave his horses & come upriver in a canoe with another man to take me down to Galena. Hard work to say so, but think it best. Doct[or] Turner surgeon of the fort. Ideas respecting asthma &c. thinks my eyes will suffer. Sore eyes prevalent on the prairie. Indian name for March (Sore Eyes Month). All their names are in a corresponding manner descriptive. Mr. S's. child dies. Indians from interior "Sleepy Eyes." Canvas back ducks and redheads. Great variety of stuffed ones. Great pike, 11 feet long. Pike in abundance. Black bass. Rev. Mr. Gear fishing. Grouse shooting great. Mr. Sibley's dogs. Feel miserable

---

Julia La Framboise, the daughter of Joseph P. La Framboise and a Dakota mother, was educated in the mission school at Hazelwood and W. F. Seminary and other schools in Ohio before returning to Minnesota as a missionary teacher. "Madeline La Framboise," Grand Rapids Historical Commission, historygrandrapids.org; "Louis Joseph La Framboise and Marguerite Magdelaine Marcot" and "Joseph P. La Framboise & Daughter of Sleepy Eye," The Thelen and Margraf Family Tree, michellesfamilytree.com; "Joseph Laframboise, 1805–1856," Find a Grave, findagrave.com; Stephen R. Riggs, *Mary and I: Forty Years with the Sioux* (Boston: Congregational Sunday School and Publishing Society, 1883), 406–407; Doane Robinson, "Joseph LaFramboise, First Settler," *Monthly South Dakotan* 11 (1901): 353–358; G. Hubert Smith, "Fort Pierre II (39ST217): A Historic Trading Post in the Oahe Dam Area, South Dakota," in *River Basin Survey Papers, No. 18*, ed. Frank H. H. Roberts Jr., (Washington, DC: Government Printing Office, 1960), 90.

all day. Bellaud comes at 4. Get off at 5½, paddled by a couple of squaws in a dugout. Pleasant time. Come down in 1 hour, 20 min. stop at Jackson's. [H]is tidy wife.[139] Bellaud came by horse, is looking for a canoe to start tomorrow. Eyes very bad, much inflamed. Letter from the young ladies at Derby, the only one rec[eive]d by the mail. Left word at PO to send my letters to 41 South St., New York.

Tuesday, 25th. Has rained tremendously during the night. Feel this morn[in]g so-so, cough & raise somewhat. Bellaud was to start at 10, but it has rained too hard. Whiskey drinking in the store. 5 or 6 store men supported mainly by whiskey selling. Two of them told me the proportion of whiskey sold was in this wise 2 bbls. whiskey to 1 ea. pork & flour! Great many Indians around. Bow & arrows common. Fight McLeod & Battiste.[140] Revolvers & bowie knife & gun. Threatened murder. Wrote letters to Janey, Peter & Mother to put in PO at Galena. Should I go on to St. Louis instead of

---

139. A native of Virginia, Henry Jackson came to St. Paul in 1842 following an erratic early life that saw him participate in the Texas war for independence in 1836–1837 and unsuccessfully attempt to operate at business in Buffalo, New York, Green Bay, Wisconsin, and Galena, Illinois. He opened a small log store in St. Paul, a prosperous store that became a favorite stopping place for Canadian voyageurs and Sioux Indians. Jackson became a leading citizen of St. Paul. Politically ambitious, he was appointed the city's first justice of the peace in 1843 and postmaster in 1846. In 1847 Jackson was later elected to a two-year term in the Wisconsin State Assembly. When Wisconsin became a state the following year, a meeting was held at Jackson's store to discuss the territorial status claims of its western territories that later became part of the newly organized Territory of Minnesota. He later served in the Minnesota Territorial Legislature. He moved to Mankato, Minnesota, in 1853 where he died four years later. Williams, *History of the City of St. Paul*, 117–118; Neill, *History of Minnesota*, 490–491; Edward D. Neill, *Occurrences in the Vicinity of St. Paul, Minn. before Its Incorporation as a City* ([St. Paul]: D. Mason & Co., 1890), 37–38.

140. This may have been Alexander Roderic McLeod, the son of a Scots-Canadian trader who came to St. Paul in 1843. He worked in the area fur trade, married a métis woman, and built a large log hotel in St. Paul. A man of extremely powerful physique, he was known for feats of endurance and once beat a man to death in a fight. He enlisted in the Union Army in 1862 and died two years later of disease. Williams, *History of St. the City of Paul*, 135–136.

N.Y. This rain will probably raise the water sufficiently. Mr. Stapleton's ideas of New York's cleanliness & police regulation. Mr. Jackson, the candidate, goes stumping, drinks whiskey with everyone. Mrs. J, small, sharp-featured, most precise, tidy &c, &c. Flowers, plants, & gardens in the lady's home.

Letter

Henry Sanford to Janey Howe,
August 25, 1846, St. Pauls[141]

Dear Janey,

How often I receive letters from my fair correspondent! Have you an idea? The last one was at Detroit and I have hopes there are four more on their way and I shall get them, if so, sometime, though they would be very gratefully received just at this present. I am now with my face turned "downstream" and am in anything but good spirits. I was to have started from Fort Snelling this morning, I had three horses and a guide and tonight, said I, I will sleep on the prairie and each day will increase the distance between myself and everything "common or unclean." Two months had been passed in getting to the point where my journey was to commence. My foot is on the threshold, but like Lot's wife I'm turned back & now I am on my way south, feeling ill bodily & mentally, most grievously disappointed I can assure you. I have sent back my horses; & my guide for the prairie is to steer a canoe for me down the Mississippi. The 22d has come with it my asthma & here like a rat in a trap I'm caught, and & have got to go wheezing & panting onwards till I reach New Orleans, where I hope to get a ship bound for somewheres, Yucatan if possible. The river is unusually low. Steamboats cannot get up here and the only way to get down

---

141. HSSP, Box 93, Folder 15, Letter 15.

is by canoe for me over 300 miles, where I hope to get steam conveyance down. I have been so confident, have made all my preparations, taken all the advice how to travel, how to camp, to avoid hostile tribes, or robbing Indians, and just as launching forth in the unknown I am checked in my course and turned into the stagnant mill where all is dead & listless. Well, "Allah Karim" [God is most generous] as the Turks say. Of course all's for the best.

The only letter I rec'd. at Fort Snelling was the quadruple one and I was glad to hear from you even this way, but why, you naughty girl, did you cut me off with a half page? You had no need to display such delicacy in regard to writing to a young man, and so few dashes with pen and ink, you shall make amends for it by a confidential communication of as many pages as the whole letter, won't you? I had intended to have written to the quartet but shall wait till I feel in better spirits. "I shall write no more to Janey," said I to myself, "till I get a letter from her," but as I find I have from you two letters to but one from home, I shall send you one more precious bit of dullness to let you know of my whereabouts.

———————————

I wrote to you from La Pointe & sent by a private conveyance to Mackinaw to be mailed there. From thence I came through to this point with some fatigue but more novelty. Walked 80 miles across the portage, my men carrying my baggage of provisions on their shoulders, when arrived at the St. Croix River, took a canoe & paddled & waded down to Stillwater. I enjoyed this trip much. We were four days getting from La Pointe to St. Croix, and the route was most of the way through the wilderness, a narrow trail leading through swamps & fallen trees. Night would come on, our camp was made our simple supper cooked & relished more than many a daintier meal. And then rolled up in my blankets, my tent pitched if it looked like rain, if not, making the "broad canopy" my cover. I would sleep sweetly, the coughing of the wind among the treetops, or the far-off wailing of the wolves sneaking around but fearful to come too near our campfire, passing for lullaby. And when in the canoe, paddling among beautiful islands & rice fields, along shores lined with somber forest, passing and occasional wigwam & saluted by the whoop of the Indians. At night running up to some pretty landing place for a camp, hauling up our canoe, sleeping away in spite of ferocious mosquitoes, and at daybreak up & off. Twas all delightful I can assure you. There are some rapids in this river which require no small degree of skill & dexterity to "shoot" or "jump," the water boiling & tossing among the rocks & descending with great rapidity, our boat, the frailest thing in the world, twisting, swimming like a duck & <u>jumping</u> over the waves like a horse, partaking of the nature of both. My voyageurs with whoop-up rocks, giving chorus as we darted down. A slight touch against a stone suffices to make a rupture in the birch bark which forms our canoe and many a time we had to carry on shore, empty it, patch up, & repair and on again.

Our stock of provisions (fat bacon & hard bread) got exhausted and, by way of variety, we had the prospect of suffering a little from hunger. But my gun and some Indians preserved us from absolute starvation, between game & wild rice & venison we got on very well. A frying pan, tin cup plate were my cooking apparatus, so you can imagine our simplicity. My men each had a jackknife and I a case with knife, fork & spoon. And we got on famously. When arrived at the falls of St. Croix, for the first time in about three weeks I slept in a bona fide bed and to so an unusual a circumstance may be ascribed the fact that for the first time I think in that period I slept till after 6 in the morning. I was well rec'd. at Fort Snelling. Major Clarke, the commander, & his wife were very hospitable and I took up my quarters with them. Soup & silver forks once more! What luxuries!

I had been shivering & feeling symptoms for several days. This should not have deterred me, but my eyes commencing as usual to be inflamed, one of the symptoms of asthma, found that I should risk the loss of them by traveling over those wide prairies where the sun pours down with such force, and so having put my "hand to the plow," turned back. I shall yet reconcile presently, I suppose, the trip by canoe at any other time down the river. I should feel like enjoying, for the scenery is unsurpassed, and

I have often longed to loiter along the shores of Lake Pepin. Well, I may see the mines in Central America and the Pacific, perhaps Matamoros & our army of occupation.[142]

When will this wandering cease? I've had enough of it and would be glad to look forward to a few years uninterrupted quiet. It is a great mistake to suppose that much traveling is of use to a young man "giving," as the phrase is, "a knowledge of the world." This latter it may do in a measure, but it is at the expense of a great many more opportunities of advancement, at the risk off [*sic*] losing many other useful acquirements, giving a distaste for quiet, rational enjoyment, and a desire for change, a restlessness & dissatisfaction with present things highly pernicious. I find this in my own case, and wish to avoid the rock I may split on.

To travel well one needs to be a kind of walking encyclopedia with a knowledge of history, men, and of the natural sciences enough to occupy him almost till middle life in acquiring. Then, and not till then, can a person travel to the most advantage. Every tree & stone then speaks to him eloquently in the language of nature to which he has the key. Things which we in our ignorance pass by unheeded, are to him subjects of deep interest. Oh! The field I have just been over, and the one I was about going over, would have given great pleasure to the naturalist, while to me it is almost a sealed book. I could enjoy it with one sense as it were, while I ought to have the capability of enjoying it in four or five years more.

How I have wished to catch up with the time I have lost, thus frittered away as it were between scampering all over the world and then as breathlessly chasing after dollars. Everything seems to have gone wrong since six years ago I left college, not in the eye of the world perhaps, who measure right & wrong by dollars, but I know that little advancement has

---

142. Following its victory at Matamoros in May 1846 the US Army continued to advance into Mexico's interior and captured Mexico City in the fall of 1847. The American occupation of the country lasted until the signing of the Treaty of Hidalgo the following year. Greenberg, *A Wicked War*, 223–224, 238–240.

been made since then on the path I would like to go upon. I despise the nobility which wealth gives and if at life's close I have no other to boast of, it will indeed have been misspent. "Resolve and re-resolve and die the same." I have heard you in common with myself assent to that. I have an idea that this famous line of Pope may be proved a libel. What think you Janey? We have both complained of good resolutions too easily broke in upon by lesser duties. Ah! Well. Time goes on rapidly, 23 and so little done yet! But what am I about! Pressing in this lugubrious manner to you Janey! You'll scarce thank me for it I would have been little more, and I would have gone off in some humdrum, lacking a classical discourse that would have given you also the <u>blues</u>.

I shall send this I think without envelope. Have you not written to me at Fort Snelling?

Journal

<u>Wednesday, 26th</u>. Commences cloudy & looks much like rain, & a settled one. Asthma not annoying. Do not breathe quite close, but should think nothing of it, or were it not for catarrh in my head & eyes. Latter much inflamed. Unwell this morn[in]g. Suspect the water does not agree with me. Shall watch the effect upon my eyes. Have heard physic recommended for inflamation of the eyes. Why shouldn't diarrhea have a good effect! Bellaud comes this forenoon. Told him to get ready for a start tomorrow. By noon feel worn, can eat no dinner. Severe headache, pains in back. Weak from diarrhea. Feverish at times with slight chills. Fear fever & ague. Take in the PM 2 of the calomel pills given by Dr. Delefiels. Send for Bellaud. Tell him not to come for me till I send (if I feel better day after tomorrow), and if my asthma seems gone now & eyes better, that I <u>may</u> start for the prairies. Feel miserable in head & body.

<u>Thursday, 27th</u>. Feel somewhat better. Went up to the cave with Mr.

Stapleton, walk of 2 miles. Curious sand cave, lake inside & cold stream running from it. In the PM went down with Mr. S. in a canoe to see Bellaud. Go by Little Crow village. Young Little Crow, both arms broke. The boy that shot his two brothers.[143] Domestic tragedy. Bluff. Pig's eye. Hard paddling back. Beautiful bottom & fine trees. Disturbance of my sleep by an Indian last night wanting whiskey. Told Bellaud to get ready to be off early tomorrow morn[in]g. Determine to start.

Letter

Henry Sanford to Janey Howe,
August 27, 1846, St. Pauls[144]

"Another change, and such a change! Oh! night," &c., &c., don't be surprised dear Janey, I intend tomorrow morning, when mounted on my horse and while six miles on my way towards a point midway between the Mississippi rivers, to have this at the post office at Fort Snelling. My asthma & symptoms are gone. Yesterday I had symptoms however of fever and ague. Prompt medicine checked it and I am now well and tomorrow morning I have directed my guide and horses to be at the door, and I am congratulating myself that two days of rain have stopped my farther course downstream. I feel pretty relieved, and now a la bonheur (the happiness)!

---

143. Little Crow, also known as Ohiyesa, was the eldest son of Cetanwakuwa (Charging Hawk), the leader of the Kaposia, a Sioux band. Following his father's accidental death in 1840, leadership passed to his eldest son. But Charging Hawk had three wives, all of whom came from different bands, and two of Little Crow's half brothers planned to seize power by murdering him. In the ensuing attempt Little Crow received a broken right arm, which remained crooked the rest of his life. Later a council of the Kaposias condemned the two half brothers, who were subsequently executed. A year after the Sioux defeat in the Dakota War of 1862, Little Crow was assassinated. "Little Crow," Indians.org, indians.org.
144. HSSP, Box 93, Folder 15, Letter 15.

Wish me good luck and a safe trip Janey and let me hear from you at St. Louis. You cannot write too soon. My letters to come to Fort Snelling I shall direct to be forwarded there. So I hope to have quite a feast in letter devouring when I reach there.

Good night, pleasant dreams and, by the way, I hope no interruptions as I had last night. Twas somewheres upon the small hours that I was awakened by somebody seizing hold of my foot as I lay in bed and commencing a most outrageous jabbering in Sioux. I sprang up in bed somewhat startled and could discern the outline of a tall Indian standing by my bed who was talking to me most earnestly and apparently determined to pull me out of bed. Reflecting a moment I thought he could have no evil intentions or he would not make so much noise. It turned out he was drunk and wanted some more whiskey & so had come into my room, which is on a ground floor & next door to the store where it is sold in the same building. There are several villages of them around and they make hideous at times with their yelling during their drunken frolics. There are many splendid Looking young men among them. The old ones are besotted with whiskey.

Journal

<u>Friday</u>, 28th. Very hot. Eyes bad. Commences a little like asthma. Keep indoors all day. Finish a letter to *Spirit of Times*, written horribly. Also to Janey. Get hers & a letter to Mother ready to put in the PO at Fort Snelling. At noon Bellaud comes. Have been reading *Wandering Jew*. Good dinner, beef & black bass &c. start at 1½, 3 horses, Bellaud on Indian pony, my saddle & fixings. Locksmith's imposition, 3¢ for cleaning my gun lock. Hot ride to St. Peters. Reach the river about 3. Ferried across. Soldiers with a fine fish, sheepshead. Arrived at Mr. Sibley's. [H]e had gone to the chase after grouse & plumbs. Must wait for him. So, as he does not come by 5, concluded to wait over. Had hoped to have slept 30

miles ahead tonight. Went over to the fort on one of the horses. A good heart, Maj. Clarke tho[ugh]t him cool. Commissary changed a $100 for me. Rev. Mr. Gear, Dr. Turner & Trent Delmar. Take a glass of wine with them & take tea with Dr. Turner, Mrs. Baker & Mrs. Stewart. The later has asthma. Mail comes in on st[eam] b[oa]t to St. Croix. Get 9 letters, 3 from Janey, 2 from Mother, 1 from Aunt Lizzie, 1 ea. Uncles E[dward Shelton], P[hilo Shelton] & Peter King. Very glad. Put a letter ea. for Janey & Mother in th[e] PO. No time to write as mail departs immediately. Take over Mr. Sibley's letters. He has not come. Get 2 or 3 of his *Spirit of Times* &c. to read & go into his office & read them & my letters. His clerk & the little Frenchman, also a clerk. Mr. Sibley comes in at past 9, eats his supper & comes down. Says I had better stay to breakfast instead of departing at daylight. Agree as it's late for him to write letters for me tonight. Take his wife's sister's bedroom. I suspect my neat manners & such. A delicious bed. Dr. Turner gave me some medicine, hydro patteas, for my asthma. Commenced taking 15 drops 3 times per day. Before leaving the fort, called on Mrs. Clarke & Emerson. Very cordial. Such a hearty shake as she gives.

Saturday, 29th. Up at 6½. Splendid bed, hair mattress & pillows & linen sheets. Slept famously. Capital breakfast, grain cakes, & maple syrup, agreeable ladies &c. Mr. Sibley's hunting stories. Has been out 4 or 5 months, a whole winter & move ala Indian. Corresponds with *Spirit of Times* "Hal Dacotah." Give letter to La Framboise & other traders. Get provisions. Get off at 8¾. Fine men for the hill. Prairies beautiful, parks, scenery, groves. Trees high, grain, mounds, hillocks, knolls &c. table lands. Indian villages. Houses made. Taught by the farmer, a good one. His home is a Canadian summer & winter lodge. Indians & horses. Squaws working. Indians smoking & riding. Stop at noon by a creek to feed ourselves & horses. Are overtaken by a half breed & an Indian. Read my letters over again. See no grouse. Village of Sixes. Mr. Fenibault's. Stop on the night. Fresh eggs, milk &c. plenty of dogs. Good bed. Indian lodges. Manner of drying corn. Continual wonderment at my gain. Indian tombs. Two lay up in red blankets. One lay on one platform. Medicine poles.[145]

Letter

Henry Sanford to Janey Howe, August 29, 1846,
Prairies!, 30 miles for St. Peters[146]

Need I say how much justified I was dear Janey over three letters from you last night? How I thanked my stars that all this sort of ill-luck as I thought it then had happened! Strange are the tissue of the circumstances which here detained me late. In the first place, I was to have started Tuesday for the prairie expedition as asthma came on, and I kept on my guide for a canoe to go down the river with me, he came, I went down to St. Pauls & he was to come next morning with a canoe. The next morn[ing] it rained. The next his wife was sick and the next I was. Then, finding symptoms of asthma gone, I sent word to him to come on Friday morning with his horses & I would go to the prairies. The horses had strayed away and consequently were not found till later and it was in the afternoon that we got off. When arrived at St. Peters Mr. Sibley, on whom I retained letters to traders on the Missouri, was off shooting, so I had to give up the idea of getting to this far to sleep last night, and staid there. In the eve[nin]g Mr. Sibley came & obtained a mail and I was happy nine letters.

---

145. The Dakotas practiced open burial in which the deceased was placed on a platform or scaffold outside the village. The body was wrapped tightly in a robe with his or her personal pipes, medicines, and weapons or tools, and other offerings were placed beneath the scaffold. H. C. Yarrow, *Introduction to the Study of Mortuary Customs among the North American Indians* (Washington, DC: Government Printing Office, 1880); J. R. Walker, "The Sun Dance and Other Ceremonies of the Oglala Division of the Teton Dakota," *American Museum of Natural History, Anthropological Papers* 16 (1917): 51–221.
146. HSSP, Box 93, Folder 15, Letter 16.

We departed this morning with a light heart, myself on a lean long-limbed but powerful roan mare, having finally found a use for my Spanish saddle frame, over which is strapped a red blanket and hanging from the peak is my gun, while I in blue shirt with coat & hat dangling behind me, take the lead on the trail. Of my guide who is a large, wiry made Frenchman with both good nature & courage, one of those sort of men who are only found in the frontier, are inured to every sort of hardship, capable of going through anything. He has some provision bags strapped to his saddle, and lastly on an Indian pony comes my equipment, camping <u>materiel</u> &c., & on top of the saddle bags is perched a young Indian of 14 or 15 years with shaggy hair, some little of it, after their manner of plaiting in braids. There! You have us as we have gone on the march today, over, it seems to me, as beautiful a country as was ever seen, a beautiful, undulating prairie with scattered oak trees here and there upon it, and occasionally a pretty grove. We have been on a rising table land & following the course of the St. Peters [Minnesota] River.[147] Several Indian villages have been passed and many Indians. It's a wild sight to see these fellows who are famous riders.

Journal

<u>Sunday</u>, 30th. Up & off at 5½. Drink some warm milk. Continue on till we reach the Bois Franc 25 miles at 11½. Stop till 2. Eat & rest. The rest came as yesterday. Get in a mud hole. Meet 2 Indians. Shake hands &c. one riding on a mule. They catch them wild Bellaud says. Saw 2 covey of grouse. Shot twice at one covey. No use. Bois Franc is 16 miles along & we camp on Prairie des fleches, at the extremity of it. It is mostly maple trees. Much sugar is made here. Great deal of honey found here, discovered in winter

---

147. As Henry proceeded westward he encountered a vast prairie landscape dotted with lakes, marshes, and patches of deciduous forest that would increasingly give way to mixed grass steppe. Waldo Wedel, *Prehistoric Man on the Great Plains* (Norman: University of Oklahoma Press, 1964), 210.

by the dead bees outside the trees or by the fishers who like honey. Shoot at a number of pigeons, get feathers, nothing more because its Sunday. While resting wrote a few lines to Janey. Commenced letters home last eve[ning] to send back by Bellaud. Plenty of mosquitoes at our camping ground, covered with them.

<u>Monday</u>, 31st. Up & off at 5½. No rain yet. Have slept badly, mosquitoes plenty, some of them large. At times rubbed my eyes & made them irritable. Took some coffee & biscuit & off. Reach Frannoids de Sioux in 2 hours, 16 miles across the prairie. Mr. LeBlanc. Mr. Riggs missionary station.[148] Stop here & see him & his wife. Pleasant place. School house. That not a lodge around. All off gathering rice at Rice Lake &c. got some milk & a <u>piece of pie</u>. 45 miles from there to Petite Rocher where La Framboise lives. Commence assault of the Great Prairie. No trees save near the rivers & on the lakes. Undulating prairie like the sea in a color after a storm. Moraines dry. In ordinary times very difficult to pass. Was mired yesterday in crossing a stream. It takes 5 or 6 days to go to Francis de Frome to Petite Rocher by water & but one by land. Meet occasionally an Indian. Sleepy Eyes. Give us some plums. Went 20 miles to Swan Lake, the borders all mud. Bellaud goes to find water & I get under a tree to finish my letters. Here in a wood an Indian comes up & sits down beside me. Takes dinner with us after Bellaud comes. We eat first, the custom. Hot day, long trotting. Reach Petite Rocher at 7. St. Peters River 7 woods again. Le Fr[ramboise], his salutations. Wife back (In the morn[in]g we had met Dr. Williams,

---

148. The Reverend Stephen Return Riggs was a Christian missionary and linguist born in Steubenville, Ohio, in 1812 and educated at Jefferson College in Pennsylvania. He married Mary Longley of Massachusetts in 1837, and together they lived and worked among the Dakota people in present Minnesota. He began his missionary work as a teacher at the Presbyterian mission at Lake Harriet and later took charge of the mission school at Lac qui Parle. He died in Beloit, Wisconsin, in 1883. Riggs served as interpreter at the trials of the Sioux Uprising in 1862. Neill, *History of Minnesota*, 447; Riggs, *Mary and I*, 23–25, 29, 123–124.

the missionary, at Laque Pales [Lac qui Parle] who said so).[149] Pretty half breed she is. Fever & ague. Give them some quinine. Le Fr. would go up with me but for that. Sends out for one of his Indians. It is soon arranged. The Indian comes, a son waits. He (the second born) a fine looking fellow, wore eagle feathers in his head. He agrees to go. Le Fr., Stephan Francis will go as interpreter. Supper of dried buffalo meat. They had finished supper at 8. That killed at one shot by Le Fr. Le Fr. seems very glad to take me.

Friday, 1st Sept. Bellaud departs. Send letters by him to put in PO at St. Peters for Mother & Aunt Lizzie & Janey. Write also to Mr. Sibley. LeFr's. pretty wife & sick children. Palisades around his house &. Sort of small village. Indians bring on him corn about meal time. Drove of[f] horses & mules & 11 cows that he don't milk. Very careless. Go near a spring to fish. Get one bass. St. Peters very low. Good shining water around. Plan to go fishing with his son Joseph a mile off. Go on horseback. Shoot at ducks. Catch 4 bass. Pretty fishing. Get some plums & come back. Louis LaCrosse, good packer from Missouri R., packs my effects. Get ready for a start in the morn[in]g. Have had asthma all day. Toward night breathe bad. Wrote out the letter to Mother to send by LeFr. to St. Peters. Have eat nothing but game since I have been here, fish, ducks, dried buffalo meat &c. LaFr. is to have $50 for 4 horses & his nephew for the journey. I pay the Indian $20. I paid Bellaud $35 & his provisions, bread, pork, dried meat, sugar &c. instructions, cautions &c. go to bed feeling bad with asthma. Give LeFr. my coat, powder flask & 100 pins. He gives me an Indian shot pouch. Indians mourning for their father. Have wounded themselves in legs & arms with knives & arrows, blackened faces, bad dress.[150] Give away all their good

149. The Reverend Thomas Smith Williamson, considered the father of the Dakota Mission, served at a number of posts, but occupied the Lac qui Parle station at the time of Henry's visit in 1846. He remained there until the fall of that year, when he was transferred to the mission station at Kamposia. He died at St. Peter, Minnesota, in 1879. Neill, *History of Minnesota*, 480; Riggs, *Mary and I*, 28, 135.

150. These mourning ritual customs were typical of those practiced by the Dakota upon

dresses. They mourn one year, women 2 years. Traders always conceal their goods. Have none of LeFrambois'! Last winter he bought 60,000 muskrat skins. They spear & trap them.

Letter

Henry Sanford to Janey Howe, September 1, 1846,
Petite Rocher, Monday eve[ning][151]

After near sixty miles riding today behold me at last at La Frambois's, 150 miles from St. Peters! Not badly done, is it in 58 hours from there! (How strange I am constantly <u>translating</u> from <u>French</u>. I have spoken not a word scarcely a word beside in three days.) At 7 o'cl[oc]k we rode up to La F's, a collection of log houses surrounded by palisades. "How are you here," says he & then coming forward lastly, Ah c'est vous mon cher [it is you my dear] Sanford," and I was made heartily welcome. I have just come from a supper off from buffalo meat. I have just finished making arrangements for a start the day after tomorrow. An Indian is to take me across with his family & La F. sends one of his nephews, a half breed to interpret, furnishing me with baggage, horses & one "<u>bon </u>cheval pour le chasse aux buffalo" [good horse for hunting buffalo] and now I seem like being on the prairies, and this I send back with other letters by Bellaud, who returns tomorrow morning to St. Peters. Here comes Francois La F's nephew with a bow and a bundle of arrows. He is going to show me, when we come to the hunting grounds, how to shoot an arrow completely <u>through</u> a buffalo while riding at full tilt.

You are having yonder news directly from the interior. And now a few words concerning the <u>dangers</u> Miss Augusta and some of my kind friends talk of. There is a danger of having horses stolen, but as I only hire them,

---

the death of an individual. Yarrow, *Introduction to the Study of Mortuary Customs.*
151. HSSP, Box 93, Folder 15, Letter 17.

it concerns me little. If we meet a war party we may be robbed, nothing more, and I can assure I have to[o] high an estimation of the value of my life and scalp to thrust either in the way of being taken without occasion. So have no fears, the route with the guardianship I have is as safe as from Derby to New Haven. I go by the pipestone quarry and strike the Missouri at the Vermillion River and in turn going from there to the Great Bend and shall probably descend on a canoe to Independence [Missouri] or Fort Leavenworth [Kansas].[152] Let your next letter be mailed for Detroit.

---

152. The pipestone quarry, located in southwestern Minnesota just north of present Pipestone, Minnesota, is a complex geologic feature in which an underlying layer of metamorphosed sandstone, known as Sioux quartzite, forms a structure within which are found beds of sandstone, from which the cementing agent has been leached, and beds of compact siltstone, or "pipestone," of reddish-brown color. The pipestone was named catlinite, after George Catlin, who visited the quarry in 1836, though Catlin was not the first white man to visit the quarry. Joseph Nicholas Nicollet's expeditions of 1838 and 1839 brought the quarry to the attention of the American public, and the site was well known at the time of Henry Sanford's visit to the area in 1846. Pipestone became so closely identified with Minnesota that three years later territorial congressional delegate Henry H. Sibley recommend that the legislature contribute a sample of catlinite as the territory's contribution to the new Washington Monument. He argued, however, against naming pipestone catlinite. Instead Sibley advocated its Sioux name, Eyanskah. The pipestone quarry had long been a source of catlinite for many aboriginal groups. Material obtained there was highly valued and widely traded in native North America and continued in use into historic times. The Sioux controlled the pipestone quarry in 1846 and retained access to the site by treaty in 1858, but the land passed into the hands of the federal government in 1893. Congress declared the quarry site, which consists of a series of pits, mounds, and workshop areas, a national monument in 1937. National Registry of Historic Places, "Canomok'e—Pipestone National Monument," National Park Service, npgallery.nps.gov; Wedel, *Prehistoric Man*, 106, 176, 156, 210; Henry H. Sibley to M. McLeod, Sept. 11, 1849, quoted in Neill, *History of Minnesota*, 513–514.

A tributary of the Missouri, the Vermillion River rises in eastern South Dakota. Its eastern branch rises in Kingsbury County on the Coteau des Prairies and its western branch originates in Miner County. Both streams flow southward to their confluence near Parker, South Dakota, and join the Missouri River south of the present city of Vermillion, South Dakota. Elmer Ward and Patty Sexton, *Vermillion River Basin Watershed Implementation Project Segment 1* (Pierre: South Dakota Department of Environment and Natural Resources and the US Environmental Protection Agency, Region 8, 2013), 1–2, denr.sd.gov.

I have read through your letters today as I have jogged along on horseback and they have afforded me much companionship. May I receive yet two more at least before I reach home! And may the latter event take place some time in October. I was comparing dates when we have written letters and find that several of our letters have been written at the same time. Your last example was written on the Sunday that I was writing to you on Ontonagon River. I hope you were writing to me yesterday & dispatched one today for Council Bluffs. In answer to that you might have rec[eive]d it about Saturday. I feel rather stiff from horseback riding. It's one thing to be taking a pleasure ride with Janey Howe or even a gallop against time and a thundershower, & quite a different thing to ride near 60 miles in one day & under a burning sun. the prairie today had the appearance in a calm of a storm, uneven & irregular, the green however mottled with flowers. One sees the horizon bounded by some eminence. The eye strains after it for hours. It is finally reached, ascended and the view beyond is of another exactly similar one in the distance.

Adieu Janey,

Henry

Journal

Wednesday, 2d. Got off at 9½. 3 mules & a horse which I am on. New clothes of the Indian quite smart leather. Paid Mr. LeFr., for him ¢20 & also gave LeFr.¢40 & aim to send ¢10 back by his boy. LeFr. came down to the river. Good bye & off. A mile or two through wood. Grapes & p____ &c. Then am on the great prairie. Shot a grouse & shoot at some ducks. Meet noone. Stop at 2 to water horses & get some plums. Camp near a little lake where the Indian shot a duck. Game supper. My tent. Francois "Our Marsienne." Wheeze badly, mosquitoes buzz around. Fiery appearance of sun at setting, like globe of hot iron. Have unpacked as before. Has threatened rain for 2 weeks.

<u>Thursday</u>, 3rd. Foggy morn[in]g. Small mule got away in the night. Indian off at daylight after him. Have still asthma. Wheezed a good deal. Dream of becoming worse. Better towards morning. Have a comfortable bed, 3 blankets, plaid, life preserver & saddle, shooting jacket for pillow, weapons besides &c. horses were picketed close to us. Cry of wolves. Indian gets back at 8. Has had a long chore to find the mule. Francois kills a duck (mallard) & we make a good breakfast. Get off about 10. Quite a job to pack our animals & get ready. Straight course. Our Indian makes S or SW I should judge. No trail. See a flock of cranes. First signs of buffalo, a horned skull & bones bleaching in the sun. [S]tones on the prairie. Boulders along the ridges. Stop at a little river called "Oyet." Plums & grapes along the shores. Shot a duck & eat plenty of plums, some bread & dried meat. Off at 2¼. Go on till 6. Camp near a small lake. See some white cranes. Shoot a grouse. That & the duck serve in part for supper. Very rainy looking. Have breathed very well during the day. Commenced wheezing towards night. Eyes irritable, stick together, have matter in &c. camp arrangements. Looks like a shower. Very black & lightning. Hasten to making a cover. Slight sticks. Wind blows them over & changes from N to W. Blows violently. Heap our baggage up, put tent cloth under & leave a place to camp under. Eat our supper in the dark.

<u>Friday</u>, 4th. Up & off by 6. Have slept badly. India rubber tent cloth too worn. Francois under it too. Has not rained, is very cold. Wind from NW. Keep my shooting jacket & plaid on. Eyes run badly, breath free. Signs of elk, a camp where they have eaten one. A badger chase, shoot him. Pretty lakes, plenty of plums. Stop at 11 near a very pretty lake with sandy bottom. Swarms of plover, ducks &c. myself & Indian chase after some cranes. I shot one. He furnishes me with some quills. Dinner off from badge[r], very good. Indian sick, don't eat. Dog has a feast. Crane about 5 ft. high, wings 6 feet across. Abundance of them. Off at 2. Pass a lake full of ducks & pelican. Francois shoots pelican. We are on the Couteau, a sort of table land, one

of pretty lakes, many of them [with] sandy bottoms.[153] Signs of elk. Lake Shilok [Shetek] just north of us.[154] We cross a stream running from it, which the Indian says runs into the Missouri. Here are the reservoirs for the tributaries of both rivers. No buffalo today. Stopped at 5½ near a large, clear lake supplied with cranes, ducks & plover. Crane excellent. Indian still ill. We are near the center of the prairies. Indian fears we may meet a war party of Sioux, who come up here every summer. Says we must take a long march tomorrow. Find grapes. Full moon, clear & beautiful. Wind NE. Our course SW. Wheeze a little & cough.

Saturday, 6th [5th]. Off at 6. Wind SE blows strong & fresh. Cool nights & mornings. Coughed continually last night. Did not breathe so good. Eyes very bad, water & matter coming from them. Wind bad for them. See traces of buffalo & elk where they slept last night. Many tracks of buffalo, their course about NW. Indian smells them, he says. Level prairie grass not so much dried. Indian very watchful, looking for buffalo & Indians. I suppose he looks like an Arab in manner of wearing his blanket, gun &c. Fear I lost two letters from my coat pocket yesterday, one from Mother & Aunt L., the other from Janey. Put back to look for them. Comfort in

---

153. One of the most remarkable landforms in North America, the Coteau des Prairies is a wedge-shaped plateau bordered on the west by the prairie flatlands of eastern North and South Dakota, northwestern Iowa, and southwestern Minnesota. Its eastern boundary rises from the Minnesota prairies in a distinct region known as Buffalo Ridge. The Coteau is approximately two hundred miles in length, and its widest portion is about one hundred miles and is composed largely of glacial sediments overlying bedrock. "Inner Couteau Subsection," Minnesota Department of Natural Resources, dnr.state.mn.us; "Digital Shaded Map of the Coteau des Prairies, North Dakota/South Dakota," North Dakota State University, ndsu.edu/nd_geology/nd_maps/nd_map4.htm; "Feature Detail Report for Buffalo Ridge," US Geological Survey, geonames.usgs.gov; Wedel, *Prehistoric Man*, 210.

154. Lake Shetek lies in Murray County in southwestern Minnesota and is the source of the Des Moines River. Beth A. Spieles, "Lake Shetek," in *Draining the Great Oasis: An Environmental History of Murray County, Minnesota*, ed. Anthony J. Amato, Janet Timmerman, and Joseph A. Amato (Marshall, MN: Crossings Press, 2001), 113–123.

reading them while riding. My letters from home. See traces of buffalo, fresh. Indian thinks he smells them after a rain or so at 10. He cries out, "saton-ka, saton-ka," buffalo, buffalo. Could pass by last night. 3 specks in the prairie at the south. We go towards them making a detour. He & Francois leave & tie their horses to creep toward them. I pull off my coat, hat &c. & get ready to run after them. I hear the fire, wait some time, go around, see one buffalo running, make after him. Horse timid & don't go fast. Do not overtake him. Came back & found that each had killed a bull & are cutting out tongues & best pieces. Horrid-looking heads & shoulders, no hair from the shoulders to the tail. Am vexed I didn't get a shot. Got off at 12. Indian has a fit of pleurisy. Leave him on prairie & go to a high peak. Pile of stones on it. See another similar [at] end of Couteau. Descent towards the Missouri. See 4 herds of buffalo to in sight N & South, the edge of the horizon black with them. See a small herd of 50 a mile off. Gallup after them. Horse too fatigued. Had to shoot at a distance, killed none. They kick up a dust, vultures &c. flying over them. Cows & calves &c. bulls turn & look to act like fighting, run however. Come back. See 3 bulls coming slowly towards us from the N, the advance guard of a herd we see on the edge of the horizon. In an hour or two they are within a mile. Francois & I creep towards them. Run & creep till I get out of breath gain a ground to shoot them from as they pass. They discover us when within gun shot & run. Both fire but kill nothing. Indian comes at 3 o'cl[oc]k, very ill with no water or wood in sight. Start on to camp when we find either. See another small herd of buffalo, 50. Head them off & shoot as they run by us. I hit one. Go on, find a place where there is somehow water & willows & camp at 5. Supper of buffalo meat, tough, tongue & all marrow bones. Give Indian calomel & after quinine. We are in a bad fix. Do not even fire my gun off to clean it on acct. of Indians. Fear war parties &c.

Sunday, 6th. Hope to have rested today, but though the Indian would be glad to, being sick, is afraid & we go on at 7. Have had little asthma & some coughing. Getting well. Cloudy, windy & threatening rain. Heavy & black

Conclusion of a buffalo hunt on the Plains, a nineteenth-century portrayal.

clouds. Ride on till 11 at a good trot. See 4 bulls, but they run from us. At 11 found good water & plums. Start to go further to camp near the river of which we see the trees in the distance. In ½ hour see a herd of buffalo on the other side of the river. Go around to cut them off. Francois & the Indian prepare to do as yesterday, creep & shoot, but said no & galloped off towards them. Could not make my horse go into the herd & had to <u>fire</u> at the <u>rear</u>, & when they wheeled passed a couple of calves, not <u>noble</u> game enough. Francois said, "don't shoot but <u>one</u> & shoot a cow." So I shot a fine cow, hit several besides. Could have got more. I jumped off & cut her throat as she lay kicking, jointed a leg & took out marrow bone &c. in <u>approved style</u>. Francois & the Indian came up & commenced cutting out the best pieces. This fat & tender. Took the tail as a trophy. Go & camp at about 3½ near the river. Are descending all the time. Prairie void of water or trees, only grass on the hills. See wolves, brown & white. Flock of antelopes. Passed buffalo bones bleaching on the ground. Has rained & thundered a little. Strong breeze all the while since I started. Foggy towards night. Clear evening, however, over a feast of buffalo meat bouillon & "sole" with marrow bones. Delicious. Eat [blank] lbs. Eat. Eat. Camp is little hollow well-protected from observation. Indian fears the Sioux all the time. Quantities of plums, some grapes. Read the psalms for the day to make amends for my buffalo hunt. Feel little like Arthur. Indian has bad headache.

Monday, 8th. Up at 5 & off at 7 after another meal on bouillon & sole without bread. Beautiful morning. Fire at the prairies. See the smoke all along the northern horizon. See 2 bulls. They run. Come up with them in the course of the forenoon in a ravine unexpectedly. Fire but don't kill. Antelopes. Fire at them. See the course of the river defined by trees, cottonwood. Pretty sight, trees winding through the prairie. Each little ravine full of flowers, yellow, & joining each other finally reaching the river. Very pretty. Antelopes bound out occasionally. Camp near the river at noon. Quite a stream. Out of one of the bottoms a deer was startled. Shot at it. Could have killed it with buckshot. So near. Aspect of the country, brown grass, dry & like tinder. Blazed when we made our fire. Green in the ravines & along the river, whose course we are following. Very rank growth of vegetation in these places. Grass short in the hills. Camp under some cottonwood trees at 12. Indian says we shall presently see a great many Indians. Start at 2½ after eating buffalo meat, roasted, & tongue. Like the meat better, & without bread, pepper, or salt. Are most out & hope to see more buffalo. Go along about ½ mile from the river. Indian is sick, same as forenoon. Just as we were going to camp saw a herd of buffalo the other side of the river. Went across, stopped our horses in high grass & go after them on foot. A long chase of 2 miles. Go around with Francois to head them off while the Indian fires. They come straight out towards us. We both fire. One runs ¼ mile & falls, a fine cow. Francois thinks he killed it, I that I did. Expertise. Cutting up some time after dark when we reach camp. Loss of 1 mule. Indian & Francois start after him. Dry, high grass, like tinder. Manner of making a fire in it. Most as high as our heads, weeds higher. They return with the mule, which brayed. Recovered it safe or it would have been lost, wolves. Feast on buffalo meat. Fine <u>moon rise</u>. Strange noises. Indian seems apprehensive & extinguishes fire immediately. Have had to have it late tonight for cooking enormous quantity of meat. I eat. We consume in 1½ to 2 days as much meat as F. & the Indian can lug. What we got from the cow may last till tomorrow night, though both brought heavy loads.

Letter

Henry Sanford to Janey Howe, September 11, 1846, On Board Steamer Cleremont [sic], Missouri River near Council Bluffs[155]

Don't this look like "homeward bound," dear Janey? Don't you wonder how that when my last letter of Sept. 1st was on the prairies, you so soon see me <u>heading down</u> the Illinois River! I do and can scarce account for it how I am here. But a chilling northwester closed doors and a rousing fire assure me that I am on the best course. Where shall I <u>bring</u> you? I don't know yet, probably the Gulph of Mexico. And now for a little retrospect, the cause, why & wherefore, the <u>how</u> &c.

I left Petite Rocher on the morn[in]g of Sept. 2d, with an Indian, a half breed Frenchman, three mules and a horse, and struck across the prairies towards Vermillion River, and have had a delightful trip, have seen the most beautiful prairie the world can boast of, have passed the Couteau, where the tributaries of the Missouri & Mississippi take their rise, and have been seven days crossing a country that is owned as home by no living things. Indians, wild beasts & birds and buffalo roam or migrate over it, but it is scarce the abiding place of any. And I have passed the time delightedly

---

155. HSSP, Box 93, Folder 15, Letter 20.

sometimes a whole day crossing a parched desert as it were and then among lakes beautifully set in flowery borders, one time creeping stealthily along to get a shot at swan or pelican or crane (I am writing with a quill I plucked from one of these last), at another galloping after or among a herd of buffalo, shooting always my meat for supper. At night, when by my campfire with horses picketed around, with one or two camp kettles filled, one with hot coffee, the other with "wild meat," while certain sticks around the fire supported nice pieces & choice cuts that were browning & seething, preparing to be eaten, then falling to with an appetite ought but prairie life can give. Need I say how much I enjoyed it & lest too there was in its being an adventure in there being a spice of danger with all. Carefully would my Indian at night full scan the horizon for signs of foe in the shape of some war party of Sacs, carefully extinguish the fire that it might at evening give no clue of our whereabouts. Our guns too were the last things looked to, placed by our sides ready for instant use.

On daybreak up, the remains of the last night's coffee & supper dispatched and to horse till noon. In spite of the predictions &c., &c., I have neither been scalped or robbed and turned adrift on the prairies, nor had my horses stolen. I am here safe, without any accident save one. Prepare yourself. I have lost one of your letters. I had one day taken all the letters I had received at Fort Snelling & put into my pocket for leisurely reading as I jogged along. I had reread them all and, as it was warm towards the middle of the day, threw off my coat, having in the pocket my letters, and placed it over my saddle, & when next examining my budget your first letter to Mackinaw and one from mother and Aunt Lizzie were missing. The loss is great and I hope you will forgive my carelessness and write me another. It's probably ere this, tramped to pieces by some herd of buffalo, also my letter!

Wednesday, the eighth day after leaving Petite Rochers, saw me in a most soaking northeaster, which it seemed impossible for the macintosh or India rubbers to keep out, endeavoring to get our jaded beasts into a trot as we approached the Vermillion River after a twenty five miles ride through the rain without any thing to eat since the night before. Lucky it was that I had eaten a hearty supper the night before. I can hardly say how much, only five buffalo ribs and a steak roasted before the fire (remember if you please that I had traveled the whole day however over a dry prairie without anything to eat since morning. We were approaching the Vermillion River today & [saw] something white ahead of us the Indian said were lodges and that there was a terminus a little nearer. And the indistinct white proved to be the steam escaping from the *Cleremont*, which was aground there.[156] We passed some lodges swarming with dogs, Indian squaws & children, the first humans I had seen since leaving, who told us that the boat was from up the river and moreover that the Omahas, a hostile tribe of Indians, were hovering round and committing depredations nightly.[157] Pressing on, I hailed the boat and twas a comfort to hear English again & found they

---

156. By the mid-1830s steamboats regularly delivered goods to support the trading posts along the Missouri River as far north as Fort Union, at its confluence with the Yellowstone in present North Dakota. Annie Helouise Abel, ed., *Chardon's Journal at Fort Clark, 1834–1839* (Pierre: Department of History, State of South Dakota, 1932), 69, 118. The steamboat Sanford encountered was likely the *Clermont*, a sternwheeler constructed in Cincinnati, Ohio, in 1845. Used in the Missouri River trade, the vessel made a round-trip voyage from St. Louis, Missouri to the mouth of the Yellowstone River in July 1846. It took forty-seven days going up river, dispatching traders to the Sioux and Blackfeet. The *Clermont* completed the voyage in September despite low water on the upper Missouri River that detained the steamboat for two weeks at Antelope Island, and hostilities among the Indians of the region. The steamboat was lost in 1852. *Evening Post* (New York), Sept. 28, 1846; "A Comprehensive List of American Paddlewheel Riverboats by Boat's Name," Riverboat Dave's Paddlewheel Site, riverboatdaves.com; Daniel G. Taylor, "Journal of Steamer *Clermont* from St. Louis to the Mouth of the Yellowstone River of the Missouri, July 7–28, 1846," Steamboats and River History Collection, 1802–1986, Box 1, Folder 9, Missouri Historical Society Archives, St. Louis.

157. The Omahas were a village-dwelling people native to the Upper Mississippi who migrated westward from southeastern Minnesota and northwestern Iowa at the beginning of the eighteenth century to occupy lands in present-day eastern South Dakota. Hostilities with the Sioux and other Plains groups forced them south along the Missouri River into present-day eastern Nebraska, where a smallpox epidemic decimated the Omahas in 1800. Further conflict with the Sioux continued during the 1840s and by the time of Henry's visit they had fled to the safety of the Indian agency

were going down immediately, had just come from the Yellowstone.[158] Proceeding on to the fort so called, a collection of log houses standing in a huge mud puddle so suspicious-looking my horse dared not venture in, and surrounded by stockades. Proceeding in the first building I found it filled with Indians. I had come on ahead of Francois and there was nobody there but Indians. I sat down by a fire, pulled off my dripping macintosh and that laid down my gun and sat down. Suddenly an old Indian sprang up. One hand held his hatchet and blanket to his breast, the other was outstretched. A commanding appearance. He had made me a speech as to what I know not. The others all responded by a "how" "how," then shook my hand and then several more came up and we all shook hands. The pipe was passed round. I commenced puffing and was soon comfortable, wondering all the time where was the agent of the Fur Co., whose station this was. Presently he and Francois & some of the st[eam] b[oa]t men came and so many difficulties were thrown in my way as to going any further. It had already snowed at Fort Pierre,[159] there was no guides, no horses, no anything, that,

at Bellevue, Nebraska. Judith A. Boughter, *Betraying the Omaha Nation, 1790–1916* (Lincoln: University of Nebraska Press, 1998), 11–13.

158. The Yellowstone River rises in northwestern Wyoming and traverses southern and eastern Montana and northeastern North Dakota, joining the Missouri River near the present town of Buford in the latter state. In 1828 the American Fur Company established the trading post of Fort Union at the confluence of these two rivers. Smith, "Fort Pierre II," 97.

159. Fort Pierre was built on the Missouri River by the American Fur Company in 1832 to replace and earlier trading post inundated by the river. Situated on high ground on the west bank of the Missouri across from the mouth of the Teton River, it was named for Pierre Chouteau Jr., whose St. Louis trading firm operated the store. Francis A. Chardon, a trader on the upper Missouri, mentioned traveling there from the Vermillion River in the mid-1830s. Abel, *Chardon's Journal*, 379–380. The post consisted of a four-sided timber stockade enclosure about 235 feet square within which several buildings were situated. Fort Pierre served as the entrepôt of the upper Missouri country until 1855, when the company sold it to the federal government for use as a military post. It was abandoned when replaced by a newer fort two years later. Reuben Thwaites, ed., *Travels in the Interior of North America by Maximilian, Prince of Wied*, trans. Hannibal Evans Lloyd (Cleveland, OH: Arthur H. Clark Co., 1905), 314–315; Smith, "Fort Pierre II," 91, 118.

turning to the captain of the boat, who came in just then, I said I'm going down with you and in two hours after my arrival I was puffing down the Missouri in a most unexpected manner. Everybody talks about my being lucky, for there is but one st[eam]boat a year comes up here. But I didn't come up here to go a steamboating.

———————

Henry Sanford to Janey Howe, September 13, 1846, St. Boat Belmont [Clermont], 25 miles below Council Bluffs, Missouri River[160]

Sunday, my dear Janey, seems to be a day partly consecrated to thoughts of home and letters to you, and though in all probability another will lapse before I shall be able to send this, yet I will hold a "talk" with you on that very interesting subject, myself, and afterwards turn to some of your letters for answers. That must satisfy me for the present. It seems that when I started I was not fated to hear one church service or an organ very frequently. I have been here today looking over where I have been during my twelve Sundays' absence, and find that on three Sundays have attended public worship since leaving, viz. at New York, Mackinaw & La Pointe. I get out my prayer book, read the whole service and the Psalm of the day perhaps, look at the chants and think of you, at the Commandments and think of Aunt Lizzie. Last Sunday I was shooting and eating part of a buffalo on the prairies without a thought of having my face turned homeward for near a month to come and today I am on board a steamboat bound for St. Louis.

You would like to know the how of all this? Well, we'll look back a little. I wrote you a queer sort of letter, "penciling by the way" literally, which I concluded and sent back by my guide from Petite Rochers 150 miles from St. Peters, and which you will have rec[eive]d probably a week in advance of this. From thence across to the Missouri River I have had a most delightful trip, getting to the Vermillion River on the eighth day. We

---

160. HSSP, Box 93, Folder 15, Letter 18.

took provisions for three days for myself, Indian & Francois which, with the exception of the bread, we brought all along with us, for the lakes and prairies furnished us with enough to eat and game suppers were common. There was very much that was novel to me in this trip. The wide & desolate prairies, with here a lake or a stream bordered by green trees or bushes and surrounded by rank flowers & herbage, then a desert as it were, where rising each mound served to show but another bounding the horizon & so traveling all day, the high places brown & parched with a short growth of grass ready to kindle at a spark, the ravines bright with flowers & herbage. The Coteau des Prairies was very interesting, beautiful. Here the tributaries of the two great rivers find their source. A high tableland, level, covered with verdure & filled with beautiful clear lakes, whose borders of green were fitting frames for statues. Looking glasses.

––––––––––––––

I need say nothing of my enjoyment of camping at night, halting by some little pond whose willow-lined banks would furnish us wood for a fire, cooking and eating the game we had shot during the day, with our appetite and relish. There's no need discoursing about [horses] picketed near by and the ground serving us, guide, horses and all, with one common bed. A little rest was derived from the fact that my Indian feared meeting a war party of the Sacs, in which case my valued scalp might probably have figured in quite a different place than nature intended or I cared it should. At sunset he would look carefully around for signs of anything approaching. Then the fire would be extinguished and, looking to our arms the last thing, would, placing them beside us, betake ourselves to our rest. Let an unusual noise be heard and the Indian was on the alert, getting up in the night & looking carefully around, or with a bow and arrows creeping stealthily out to reconnoiter, were by no means unusual events. No war whoop, however, disturbed at any time our slumbers, and save wild birds and beasts, we encountered no living thing till we reached our destination.

When we came among buffalo there was plenty of sport, and as I was speaking of last Sunday's doings, you ought to have a full confession. I had hoped to have made it a day of rest and remained quiet, but my Indian feared to, & so we took up our march as usual, finishing in the morning the remainder of the nice bits taken from a buffalo shot the evening before, and trusting to luck to get something for supper. In the afternoon we came in sight of a herd of buffalo, and nothing but a stout appetite would have induced me to have given chase. But appetite appeals fully as strongly on Sunday as any day[. M]y coat and all my superfluities in the shape of hat, water flask, saddle cloth &c. were on the ground in short order, and I was dashing into the herd in search of a fat cow with my horse at full speed. She was soon found and shot down and I on the ground beside, seizing the horns of the struggling animal and giving the coup de grace with my knife. And there, with some of the choice bits cut out & strung over my horse, was soon galloping back to find a place for camp and a supper. I have never eaten such delicious suppers as I have on the prairies with naught but buffalo meat. Sans salt, pepper or bread. Cutting it off the stick it was roasting on before the fire & devouring with <u>such</u> a relish! But what care you for hunting buffaloes or eating them.

Wednesday morning I awoke in a rain storm and little only did it rain during the day, as I can testify who rode near thirty miles to the Vermillion River through it without eating anything since the night before. Something white ahead, and which was mistaken for Indian lodges at our destination, proved to be a steamboat aground, a welcome sight to me. A few miles further and we come to the C's station, a collection of three or four log houses surrounded by stockades, & standing in a mud hole of such an unknown depth that my horse would not venture, though he had before forded streams & plunged through bogs with me. Without difficulty. I jumped off & proceeded in. There were about one hundred lodges of Indians around, and Indian squaws, dogs and children were in crowds. I could see no white man, and Francois I had left a mile behind.[161]

---

161. Henry Sanford visited a trading post of the Columbia Fur Company established at

Proceeding into the first building I found that too full of Indians but noone else, all looking at me and not a word said, the windows and doors too were crowded with faces, & getting a chair I threw my dripping McIntosh & hat, laid down my gun & sat down by the fire. An old Indian sprang up, one hand outstretched the other grasping his hatchet, held his blanket to his heart and made a short speech to me & ending by extending his hand, which of course I shook. And then there was a general shake with the principal looking men, a pipe lighted & passed around and I was by the time Francois, the agt., & some of the st[eam] b[oa]t men came, puffing & drying myself. I found many difficulties in getting to Fort Pierre, no Indians, no guides, no horses, cold weather. It snows there by the 7th Sept. Had lastly touches of my asthma, and by the time the st[eam] boat had come down, I had made up my mind to go in her, and in two hours from my arrival was on my way most unexpectedly, I found myself, to St. Louis. People here call me Mr. Lucky, and perhaps I am. But I feel somewhat disappointed though I had already begun to receive warnings of cold weather. A week since I woke up in the morning with my blankets covered with sleet and ice in the water flask and today I am trying every expedient to keep cool & avoid mosquitoes.

There, let me breathe a little! First asking you what you think of the weather having an influence over our reasoning powers. Had I arrived at the Vermillion on such a day as this, I should probably bear this present on my way to Fort Pierre in company with about 500 Indians who were to

---

the mouth of the Vermillion River in 1843. In May of that year the famed naturalist John James Audubon visited the post and left the following description.

> We came to the establishment called that of the Vermillion River, and met Mr. Cerré, called usually Pascal, the agent of the Company at this post, a handsome French gentleman of good manners . . . the fort, if the place may so be called, for we found it only a square, strongly picketed, without post holes. It stands on the immediate bank of the river, opposite a long and narrow island, and is backed by a vast prairie, all of which was inundated by the spring freshet. Maria R. Audubon, *Audubon and His Travels*, with Zoological and Other Notes by Elliott Coues, vol. 1 (New York: Charles Scribner's Sons, 1897), 494–495.

start forth on a hunting expedition of 30 or 40 days the day after we left, and the chances would probably have been against my getting back this winter, for I have since learned more of the difficulties of a return than I had anticipated. A month's hunt with the Indians would have satisfied all romantic ideas concerning them (nearly wished out already), I doubt not. When I tell you that but one steamer comes up there a year you may wonder at the chance of my meeting the Belmont which is, however, an extraordinary boat sent up to the Yellowstone by a new company.

And this is the far famed Missouri. Its beauties are all humbug, a dirty, muddy stream running between clay banks lined with cottonwood, and continually caving in to form still muddier water & more snags, which we go crooked along, getting a snag or aground continually, making from 10 to 100 miles per day. The scenery around Council Bluffs is bolder & more pleasing. Here are Mormons in any quantity—2,500 waggons (a waggon normally constituting a family) being encamped here and around. How I pity these persecuted people.[162] There is no p[ost] office within many miles of Council Bluffs, so I shall not get your letter very quickly, as that P. O. is off the river. I hope, however, to get it in New York, having left a line to that effect. Our arriving at "the Settlements" was celebrated by firing our gun, and all hands, commencing with the captain, commencing clipping their unshaven faces, unconscious for the part of two months of razors, in order to appear at last civilized. "The Settlements," however, do not <u>properly</u> commence until we get near 200 miles below. This idle life, though now after so much exercise as I have had. I am getting used to sleep under covers and through the first two nights a roaring fire in the stove did not keep the cabin warm. But all the passengers were crouching over it. I

---

162. In the 1850s Council Bluffs became a destination for Mormon refugees fleeing from Nauvoo, Illinois, in the wake of the Mormon colony's expulsion following the murder of its leader, Joseph Smith. Alice Felt Tyler, *Freedom's Ferment: Phases of American Social History from the Colonial Period to the Outbreak of the Civil War* (New York: Harper & Row, 1944), 104–107.

could not endure the air of closeness, and my stateroom door opening as is usual with all western boats. Outside has been kept wide open. Today there is a high wind, in spite of which we are all sweltering with heat. It is sufficient, however, to prevent our boat going down, and she is moored to the shore while the hands are engaged getting a store of wood which is furnished by the floods leaving heaps of drift wood "all along the shore," and prepared with their (the men's) axes. There are for passengers an Indian agent, two adventurers like myself fresh from prairie life & Fort Pierre, and a lady who got on board this morning & who is a missionary among the Pawnees.[163]

Henry Sanford to Janey Howe,
September 18, 1846[164]

I have finally got among the "settlements" and have been able to get some ruled paper. Fort Leavenworth, where was a regiment of volunteers just about starting for California was passed on Wednesday and we are now passing continually towns, villages, log houses & improved lands, and with my good luck may reach St. Louis Saturday night, where I hope to get late dates from you.[165] Have a half mind to go from thence to New Orleans, if

---

163. The female passenger most likely served at the Pawnee Mission on the Missouri River at Bellevue, Nebraska. Established at the Indian agency there in 1834 by the American Board of Commissioners for Foreign Missions, the missionaries conducted their work among the Pawnee villages along the Loup and Platte Rivers; however, increasing attacks by the Lakotas resulted in the abandonment of their activities in the interior and a retreat to Bellevue in the summer of 1846. Richard E. Jensen, "The Pawnee Mission, 1834–1846," *Nebraska History* 75 (1994): 301–310.

164. HSSP, Box 93, Folder 15, Letter 19.

165. Cantonment Leavenworth was established in 1827 on the west bank of the Missouri River in present-day Kansas. The post was renamed Fort Leavenworth in 1832 and served as a starting point for military expeditions to the West. Following the American declaration of war against Mexico in May 1846, the United States moved to acquire Mexican territories in the West. Col. Stephen Watts Kearny was directed to march the Army of the West, composed of regulars, mounted volunteers, and

for nothing but to lengthen our correspondence a little. Already I begin to see the approaching finale of this to me pleasant correspondence. It has been to me, I frankly confess, another bond to home. A pleasure as great as any I have experienced during my absence has been given when receiving one of your letters and each place where I am expecting letters from home derives additional interest from the fact I am to get one there from you. We have never, either of us I suspect, carried on a similar correspondence, and it derives an additional <u>piquancy</u> from the partly clandestine manner of carrying it on. I will own myself, a fact too outrageously apparent, a most careless correspondent. My letters have been rather a hurried detail of my doings & goings than anything else. But nevertheless the idea is by no means to be relished that although this correspondence as originally proposed is near its end, that further letters between us should be concluded <u>in toto</u>. Please put me on your list as a perpetual correspondent and say we shall correspond whenever either leaves home, won't you? The ice is already broken. Your father is by this time, I doubt not, accustomed to receive letters of no small bulk enclosed to him for his daughter and cannot object to a continuance.

Well, it's now three months since leaving and I suppose you are all about the same, a few more houses, a few marriages and deaths, an autumn in the place of spring, a great clarity in place of the unsightly rocks in front of you, when, I suppose a perpetual series of salutes has served to keep me in mind & to wish rocks and workmen were anywheres but in Birmingham, which place, by the way, I fear from what news I gathered from the newspapers

---

Mormon refugees, from Fort Leavenworth along the Santa Fe Trail to occupy Santa Fe and capture the Mexican provinces of New Mexico and California. Prucha, *Guide to Military Posts*, 85; Greenberg, *A Wicked War*, 121–122; Winston Groom, *Kearny's March: The Epic Creation of the American West, 1846–1847* (New York: Alfred A. Knopf, 2011), 123; Robert W. Merry, *A Country of Vast Designs: James K. Polk, the Mexican War, and the Conquest of the American Continent* (New York: Simon & Schuster, 2009), 296–298.

I am now within reach of is once more is destined to be, if not already, more quiet in its manufactures than heretofore. Being away so much I have almost got over wondering as to changes that may take place during an absence, but take them all as a matter of course. But I am indulging this time a little. You will have got home from your <u>trip</u> I suppose by the time this reaches you, delighted of course. "Boston was a beautiful city with <u>such</u> a common, <u>such</u> suburbs," "Springfield charming" &c, &c. you shall tell me all about it. I truly wish we could take such a trip in company. I don't care a fig for a young man for a companion, and hence in all my voyaging have carefully avoided being transmitted by one as I <u>do</u> of the other sex. It doubles the enjoyment. The pleasantest portions of any journeyings are when I have joined some company where the other sex were prominent. Just before leaving you home, I took a trip to Portland, but there was as much that was beautiful in scenery & the many pretty villages & towns that we passed through, that to enjoy it properly I wanted someone that could enjoy it with best likewise. Don't you often have that feeling? That a pleasant sight to be properly enjoyed must be in company with one who thinks & feels similarly! I have felt the want of such a companion keenly when looking upon something beautiful in act or nature, whether gliding in a caique along the Bosporus with its fairy like shores, or in a *traineau* [sled] crossing the rugged Alps surrounded by all that was good & sublime in nature almost, or in the galleries of Italy where Rafael or Titian had given colors life on their canvases, or when Praxiteles or other of those Italian sculptors whose names are lost in the lapse of ages have left their works <u>breathing</u> in cold marble. On the wild & desolate prairies & in the crowded city the feeling is still the same, the yearning for sympathy, for congeniality, and how little satisfied! Not certainly in the gay life of a city. It checks chills or ague, whichever you will, can't satisfy. Excitement supplies the place of everything else, pleasant at the time but unsatisfying in the retrospect. Put a truce to this sentimentalizing that I have commenced marching into at such a rate. I must leave some space for answering your letter when I get it at St. Louis & just telling you that I have other honors beside <u>lieutenant</u>. Col. Moon, the Indian agent & formerly our minister to Columbia, has been telling me that he has embalmed & immortalized me in his report to Gov[ernmen]t by an account of meeting "Mr. Sanford of Conn., <u>the traveller</u>." As honors are the thing, you see.

———————————

[Henry Sanford to Janey Howe, September 20],
Sunday eve., [St. Louis][166]

I have finally reached St. Louis, but must wait till tomorrow for my letters. Another Sunday passed without hearing again one church service! I have been wandering around this evening in spite of my odd dress & moccasined feet, to find an Episcopal church open, for I had a feeling of thankfulness such as I have when coming from a sea voyage, and longed to hear and participate in the solemn service of our church, but finding none went into a Methodist [church] where I heard an eloquent discourse and by a very young man. Just before reaching the church a young man of my acquaintance met me & taking my arm offered to show me the church & a seat, & to my no small mortification marched up to one of the side pews near the pulpit . . .

———————————

Henry Sanford to Janey Howe,
October 1, 1846, Maysville, KY [167]

Hurry straight to your map, dear Janey, in wonder to learn by what way I have got here, "on horseback & through Michigan," and how it is that I am waiting here for a steam boat to Guyandotte from whence I propose going to Richmond, when my last spoke of Detroit, Buffalo and the lakes.[168] A

---

166. HSSP, Box 93, Folder 15, Letter 19.
167. HSSP, Box 93, Folder 15, Letter 21.
168. Founded in 1796, Guyandotte is the oldest town in Cabell County, Virginia. It is presently a neighborhood in Huntington, West Virginia. Joe Geiger Jr., "The Tragic Fate of Guyandotte," *West Virginia History* 54 (1995): 28–41.

steamboat brought me to Louisville, and thence to Frankfort, Lexington & Maysville.[169] Stage coaches and railroads done the rest. I had my passage engaged to Peoria, having found that over crowded stages, hot weather & horrible dusty roads wouldn't be pleasant for a trip of 300 miles by land. On my way to the boat someone endeavored to discourage me & talked of low water, uncertain time in getting up the Illinois River, and just then passing a steamboat on the point of starting for Louisville, went on board, met an acquaintance in Mr. Conner, the magician and an actor of some note, and this decided me.[170] And in a few minutes we were steaming down the Mississippi in the new steamboat *"76."*[171] I rather like this impulsive manner of progressing, for then one cannot anticipate very far ahead and we always lose, I think, by anticipating. So I concluded to go to Louisville and thence, as you see, to Maysville, Guyandotte and through Virginia, see

---

169. Situated at the falls of the Ohio River, Louisville was a natural barrier to river navigation and became an early transshipment point. Settlers from Virginia came as early as 1780, and the city grew rapidly as a shipping port. By the time of Henry's visit it had a population of thirty thousand. George H. Yater, *Two Hundred Years at the Falls of the Ohio: A History of Louisville and Jefferson County* (Louisville, KY: Filson Club, 1987), 9–10, 48–49. Following Kentucky's admission to the Union in 1792, Frankfort was established as its capital. Lexington was founded in 1781, by 1820 was one of the largest cities west of the Appalachians, and by 1840 had become a major manufacturing and commercial center with a population of more than seven thousand. Thomas D. Clark, *A History of Kentucky* (Ashland, KY: Jesse Stuart Foundation, 1992), 112–114, 172. Maysville, on the Ohio River, attracted settlers as early as 1775 and became one of Kentucky's principal river ports. The seat of Mason County, it had a population of three thousand in in the 1830s. "Old Washington Historic District," Maysville, Kentucky, cityofmaysville.com.

170. Edmon S. Conner (1809–1891) was a distinguished nineteenth-century American stage actor. He began his career at the Walnut Street Theater in Philadelphia in 1829 and became a regular member of the theater company. His success led him to become the leading man at the Chestnut Street Theater. He later went to Cincinnati and joined the stock company of the Columbia Street Theater and traveled extensively throughout the eastern United States. *New York Times*, Jan. 5, 1891.

171. The fast-running, light-draft steamboat *Seventy-Six* sailed on the Mississippi and Ohio Rivers, calling at New Orleans, Cincinnati, Louisville, and various intermediate ports. *Daily Picayune* (New Orleans), Dec. 4, 1846.

the Kanawha Salines, the White Sulphur Springs, Natural Bridge &c., &c. <u>See something new</u> from this route from Louisville I have never been over.

And so you would not send me a letter to St. Louis <u>in time</u>? I was outrageously disappointed. A hurried line from Uncle Ed, saying that business went so & so, prices so & so, so & so had failed, and that some men had got 45 in a well they are digging for me, was all the tidings I had from Birmingham. It's too bad this writing a letter <u>so far off</u>, for so it seems. If I get one from you it seems as if we were together almost and I can sit down & chatter away to you like a magpie and never say half I thought I should in commencing. Well, I shall have a packet of good things when I get to New York, I doubt not, for your letters sent to Council Bluffs, St. Louis & Detroit will I hope all reach me there, besides one sent there direct, which I hope to get.

I anticipate seeing Birmingham in about a fortnight, perhaps not so soon as I shall probably stop a short while at Richmond, Washington, Baltimore, Philadelphia & of course New York. I want to see how Washington looks in the dull season, when bright faces have departed & fashion & gaiety have their heads diminished "<u>a few</u>." You have never been there, I believe. There is no city gayer during the gay season and I presume none duller the rest of the time. In the winter there seems to be here a reunion of all the honor, learning wealth & beauty of the land. There is no place I would take a foreigner sooner in order to give him an idea of the <u>beauty</u> of our country, though at the same time I should be loth to give him a sample of the new legislators, the body comprising the House of Representatives. I suspect Saratoga in the winter has something the aspect of Washington in summer. Apropos of Saratoga and our watering places, I am continually meeting scores of summer pleasure seekers returning from their tour of the eastern watering places. All the steamboats & public conveyances coming west are crowded while, so far, coming east I have fallen in with no pleasant company worth speaking of. It's too bad, and besides only think of it! I have not had a waltz or a polka since last spring and it seems a tremendous long while. This and encountering none of your sex to talk to makes me feel stupid enough. Apropos of waltzing, I am in hopes your father's idea concerning it will undergo a change before cold weather. I believe in fact you are as fond of it as myself. Can't we, by one joint argument, convert him from his <u>dis</u>-belief and have an occasional waltz this winter?

It is a week today since I left St. Louis, the passage repetitious, the river being extremely low, and we were from four and a half days' coming, and then passed scores of boats aground, some of which had started before we did. There is one place, in descending the Mississippi to the mouth of the Ohio, that deserves notice. It is called "the Graves," and many a boat and many lives have here had in truth their graves. There were, when we passed, the wrecks of eighteen boats lying on either side of the channel. There is scarce a week during bad water but some boat strikes here. I have passed, in coming from Council Bluffs to Louisville, a great many wrecks of steamboats which had either exploded or been snagged. I should fear to say precisely how many, but should not wonder if the number reached 50. We passed two in the Ohio, the wreck of the *Lucy Walker*, the terrible explosion of whose boiler and loss of 60 lives you may remember last September.[172] Life on a steamboat on these waters is not very delightful, consisting of preparing to eat and eating and the rest of the time lounging & sleeping. Some few gamble and much money changes hands on these boats and some read cheap novels. What I <u>should</u> have done, had it not been for Conner, I know not, but we kept by each other thru all the while and as he is a man of talent, speaks & converses well, I found much pleasure in his society. He had just been <u>starring</u> it in St. Louis and was quite the

---

172. The *Lucy Walker* was a side-wheel packet steamboat of 182 tons, launched in Cincinnati, Ohio, in 1843 for David Vann, a Cherokee entrepreneur of Webber Falls on the Upper Arkansas River. The boat was named after a famed racehorse owned by Vann. David Vann was captain of the *Lucy Walker* on its second trip and was killed along with seventeen others in a boiler explosion that destroyed the boat at New Albany, Indiana, on Oct. 25, 1844. "*Lucy Walker*," Riverboat Dave's Paddlewheel Site, riverboatdaves.com; "Terrible Steamboat Disaster," *Commercial Advertiser* (New York), Oct. 30, 1844.

rage. Louisville, like all other western towns, shows strongly the march of improvement, numbering near 40,000 and increasing rapidly. I was to have had letters to some of the Louisville belles, but as they did not reach me according to promise of the lady who offered them, of course I did not present them.

I met, however, soon after getting to town young Throckmorton who made some noise you may remember last winter by running away from a boarding school in Phila[delphia] with a Miss Ward of Louisville, a girl of but 15 years who had been sent there by her parents to get her out of the way of him. Her sister is the belle there now and indeed I believe of all Kentucky. Now for the moral of runaway matches. A short time since the loving pair had some hard words about nothing which ended in her cutting off in a pique her ringlets, which were her greatest ornament & concerning the arrangement of which I think the difficulty began. If she looked like a girl before, she certainly did look now like one and with her hair cropped, and Throckmorton gave her a whipping and got one afterwards from his own brother in return. The father & mother of Miss Ward made a runaway match themselves and must see the curse in the fruit of it. I stopped at the Galt House where Throckmorton was staying, but felt too great a contempt for him to accept his invitation to visit them. This is a warning to belles to take heed of good looking mustached beaux.[173]

The route from Louisville to Maysville is through a most beautiful country, unsurpassed in the states almost.[174] The rendezvous of the better classes

---

173. The scandal to which Henry referred involved a Miss Ward, of Louisville, Kentucky, who became engaged to C. S. Throckmorton, described as a medical student and late of the US Navy, in the spring of 1846. Her parents refused to consent to the marriage and placed her in the care of Mrs. Segoine, who operated a boarding school. Failing in his attempts to meet with her there, Throckmorton carried her off while she was taking a walk with her governess. They were married that night and moved into the Galt House, one of Louisville's most stylish hotels. *Spectator* (New York), May 9, 1846; *Daily Picayune* (New Orleans), Jan. 13, 1847.

174. The roads Henry traveled were constructed by private stock companies that extended

are all situated in large grounds shaded by forest trees and some of the situations particularly around Lexington are like some of the country seats in England. The upper classes through Kentucky are such in more points than wealth alone. They are born & brought up gentlemen and are such. The frank, hearty & open manners which characterize them. I admire the line of demarcation here between the upper & lower classes is very striking. It's the aristocracy and the canaille, which the seats of the country gentlemen show taste & refinement, the country villages show filth & carelessness. Slavery is a blight on this fair land & puts it behind the age in improvement &c. [S]eeing early in the morning a camp with tents, waggons &c. crowds of black people around them, I enquired if it was a camp meeting. "No, it's a drove of niggers." The slaves, so far as I saw anything of them, seem to be a fat & lazy set of fellows who don't work hard enough to hurt themselves. Ashland, where Mr. Clay lives and one mile from Lexington I did not have time to visit or I might have called & paid my respects.[175] We passed the Blue Lick Springs, the water of which is as famous in the West as Congress water in in the East, and a great place of resort, in summer now about deserted.[176]

---

westward from Maysville to Lexington and from there to Louisville. Boatmen returning from New Orleans took this overland route to Maysville, from which they travel to Pittsburgh and other river towns. Maysville was further connected by national highways connecting Cumberland, Maryland, with New Orleans via the Zanesville and Natchez Traces. Clark, *A History of Kentucky*, 181–182.

175. Famed Kentucky statesman Henry Clay built his mansion home, Ashland, on a six-hundred-acre estate outside Lexington in 1812. A US congressman and senator, Clay made three unsuccessful bids for the presidency. A supporter of the Union, he worked to prevent secession until his death in 1852. "Ashland, Henry Clay Estate," National Park Service, nps.gov/nr//travel/lexington/ahc.htm.

176. The Blue Lick Springs are mineral springs lying on the Licking River in Nicholas County, Kentucky. Drawn by the saline springs, explorers entered the area in the late eighteenth century, but the availability of high-brine deposits elsewhere led to the decline of the salt industry there. By the early 1800s residents began marketing the water for medicinal purposes, and by the 1840s the Blue Lick Springs had become a spa with large hotels. Clark, *A History of Kentucky*, 11.

[Henry Sanford to Janey Howe], October 3, 1846,
Guyandotte, [Huntington], VA

I arrived here last eve[nin]g; leave on stage this morning for White Sulphur Springs, three days' journey from here & then for Richmond via Char-lottesburgh & Staunton or Lynchburgh. And is this truly the last letter I can write to you? The correspondence has not closed so far as you seemed to anticipate in letters to Fort Snelling and I hope it is even now very far from its end. Alas paper & time are limited. I must end this. I hope at New York to get the latest advices now home to you.

Adieu, Janey,

Henry

Henry Sanford to Janey Howe,
October 4, 1846, Charleston, VA[177]

This is our day of writing letters to each other. I shall improve the opportu-nity" and add on a little to what ___ fair to be another "penciling" yesterday. I wrote six but not at the PO as I was hurried into the coach yesterday, so I shall carry with me to White Sulphur Springs then mail it. And here am I spending my Sunday in a country town in "Old Virginy!" Have just now come from the Methodist church. Here were the galleries full of blacks and the church itself crowded with whites divided off according to sex on either side. Nothing remarkable there, unless it were my joining in the prayers of a congregation once more after so long I know how the Methodists &c. h___ prayers, at each petition that seems to ___ of its members' cases, they groan out an assent. During all ___one's mind, unaccustomed to such performances, d ___ ready composed. Imagine the change when at the ___ [The rest of the page is torn.]

---

177. HSSP, Box 93, Folder 15, Letter 2.

Henry Sanford to Janey Howe, [October 8, 1846],
[Kanawha River at Charleston, VA][178]

There are many familiar faces among the crowds here. Mary, whom I would be glad to see, with myself not visionary eyes and exchange greetings with. Let us notice particularly some of them there holding open the gate.

This valley of the Kanawha has reminded me of home, a beautiful tract of land under cultivation with occasional tall forest trees scattered over it and winding through the center of the river, broader & deeper than the Naugatuck, its banks lined with the cotton & buttonwood trees, while, bounding the borders of the valley rise on either side high, wooded & rocky hills that, as we go on, grow higher and higher and are now almost mountains. I had begun to be disappointed in the scenery, but I am now beginning to get delighted.[179] Charleston is prettily situated on a bluff of the Kanawha, but I must leave now to say a word at the White Sulphur.[180] Good bye till then.

----

178. HSSP, Box 93, Folder 15, Letter 21b.

179. The Kanawha River is the largest inland waterway in West Virginia, finding its source in the New River and traversing the state in a northwestward direction, joining the Ohio River near Gallipolis, Ohio. From there the river was navigable by steamboat beyond Charleston. In addition to agriculture, the Kanawha Valley was exploited for coal and stone, as well as the salt derived from saline springs above Charleston. Edwards, *Gazetteer of the State of Virginia*, 281; "Kanawha Salines," West Virginia Cyclopedia, wvexp.com/index.php/Kanawha_Salines; "Geographic Names Phase I Data Compilation (1976–1981)," US Geological Survey, geonames.usgs.gov.

180. Charleston, now the seat of Kanawha County and capital of West Virginia, was an important river port in antebellum Virginia. Home to flour mills and transportation-related industries, Charleston had a population of about two thousand in the 1850s. Situated in a valley in the Alleghany Mountains, White Sulphur Springs was the most celebrated resort in antebellum Virginia. It was known as the "Queen of the Watering Places," and its mineral waters drew elites from the southern states to its cottages and hotels, which could accommodate as many as 1,550 guests. Edwards, *Gazetteer of the State of Virginia*, 203, 457.

[Henry Sanford to Janey Howe],
October 9, 1846, Lewisburgh, VA[181]

Have but time to say one word. Have just arrived & leave tomorrow morn[ing] at 2 AM. The scenery is very wild & beautiful, some portions of it, particularly the New River cliffs & the Hawks Nest.[182] Have had very pleasant company too, a couple of young ladies who leave us here, one very intelligent & agreeable. We pass some tall mountains tomorrow. I go to Fincastle and then to Natural Bridge, Staunton &c.[183] [F]ear I shall not see home before Sunday morn[ing].

    Truly yours,

    Henry

---

181. Lewisburg, the seat of Greenbrier County, Virginia, is situated nine miles west of White Sulphur Springs. It was described as a place of active business. Ibid., 289–291.
182. This ancient river flows from its origins near the North Carolina–Tennessee border through Virginia and West Virginia before joining the Gauley River to form the Kanawha. In West Virginia it cuts through the Appalachian Plateau, and steep cliffs line the river here, forming the New River Gorge. "New River," Giles County, Virginia, gilescounty.org. Hawks Nest is a peak on Gauley Mountain in Fayette County, West Virginia. Here the cliffs rise 585 feet above the New River. Its name derives from the numerous ospreys (fish hawks) that once nested there. Hawks Nest State Park, "Official Site of Hawks Nest State Park," West Virginia State Parks, hawksnestsp.com/.
183. Lying in a valley in the Blue Ridge Mountains, the village of Fincastle is the seat of Botetourt County, Virginia. Staunton, the seat of Augusta County, Virginia is situated on a branch of the Shenandoah River. Well known and extensive caves could be found in the nearby limestone formations. Natural Bridge, located in Rockbridge County, Virginia, is a geological formation that occurred when Cedar Creek carved a gorge through limestone deposits to produce a cave, of which the bridge is a remnant. Edwards, *Gazetteer of the State of Virginia*, 237, 387; Edgar W. Spencer, *Geology of the Natural Bridge, Sugarloaf Mountain, Buchanan, and Arnold Valley Quadrangles, Virginia* (Charlottesville: Virginia Division of Mineral Resources1968), 3–6. Natural Bridge was known to European settlers by the early eighteenth century. Purportedly surveyed by George Washington and later owned by Thomas Jefferson, the Natural Bridge lay on the Valley Turnpike, a principal north-south route from Pennsylvania to the Carolinas. It became a popular destination for visitors traveling by stage in the

Henry Sanford to Janey Howe, [n.d.],
Steamboat Knickerbocker [184]

Haven't I a right to say "Dear Janey" <u>now</u> mine own on? I have always had a
sort of sneaking feeling about using it before, for I supposed you considered
it as meaningless and yet could not altogether persuade myself <u>twas</u> so. Ah!
Our "first series" was a singular correspondence, each checking & cooling
down to ordinary temperature warm feelings & heartfelt expressions. We
are not now of our false positions, and our "second series" commences.
How different from the first! Our feelings are now defined and cannot we
now express these feelings to each other? Each is certain in the other's
love, need there be doubt longer? We write, feeling confident that each
thought feeling, as expressed by one tenet or cord of sympathy in that
the other, which thrill in union in that the Rubicon is passed, henceforth
we go together & in love. Our "third series" is yet to be, may we hope,
and may its termination be far distant? I had thought to write you a long
letter to say so much & so many things. I have commenced & am dumb.
I cannot give my thoughts expression. I must avoid giving you the blues
if they are contagious, for a sort of joy of low spirits has hung over me
today & I have been conscious of my suspicions. Nearly everyone I meet
had something to say concerning my proposed absence, and my thoughts
today so continually directed to it, have set me brooding over the future

---

nineteenth century. Dianne Pierce and Joseph Pierce, "National Register Inventory/
Nomination: Rockbridge Inn," dhr.virginia.gov.

184. HSSP, Box 93, Folder 15, Letter 23. Constructed in 1843, the steamboat *Knickerbocker*, of the Merchant's Line of Albany, traveled on the Hudson River between New
York City and Albany. In the fall of 1846 the vessel sailed daily except Sundays. Early
on the morning of September 1, 1856, the *Knickerbocker* struck the mast of a sunken
vessel near Fort Montgomery, New York, near West Point, and sank; however,
all passengers were rescued. *Evening Post* (New York), Aug. 2, 1843; *Commercial
Advertiser* (New York), Oct. 14, 1846; "Accident to the Steamer Knickerbocker,"
Connecticut Courier (Hartford), Sept. 6, 1856.

till I have seen nothing but uncertainty, doubt & ill luck in store for me, have reproached myself for enlisting the affections of a sweet girl who may have to hope on for years amid apprehension & anxiety, or who may perhaps be a prey to chilling doubts. But writing or taking to you must put me in spirits dear one.

Oh, you went to Humphreysville through sleet & rain to make amends for your stay over the evening before? Hope you enjoyed yourself, but I'll warrant Miss Wooster had cause to wonder what made you <u>so absent</u> some of the time, for if I can judge you by myself, we have both been thinking <u>considerable</u> within the last few days. I left on Thursday PM and in the forenoon had a talk with your father on the important subject in which you are so closely concerned, his daughter & her happiness (don't you imagine I shall tell you one half the flattering things he said about you) expressed his approbation and sincere willingness &c. rather to my surprise, I confess, for I anticipated some demur on his part to (to use a business phrase) "contract in time." And we had a long conversation during which I expressed myself frankly concerning my feelings, situation, doubts, prospects &c. I am thinking that he is about as willing things should remain as they are if not more so than if there was a prospect of a more speedy termination as we could wish it for, and he has a perfect right to be selfish in this respect, he will feel confident of keeping you a few years longer and no more suspicions or uneasiness concerning the attentions of every single man that calls upon you.

I was amused at his reply to my opening remark in our conversation that I supposed Janey had told him of our present position. Oh yes, she had told him everything from the beginning, the idea of your having a <u>feeling</u> that he was not cognizant was impossible to him. I don't doubt of your telling him much and the intimacy between parent & child where they have similar feelings ought to be cherished, but I doubt of your opening your heart to him as each feeling sprang to life in it. Nature rather teaches concealment. These tender feeling seem sacred, no[t] to be spoken, only to be reflected on in solitude. And I don't care what degree of intimacy a young lady may have with another, no sooner does she feel the first germ of love then there is an intuitive feeling for concealment of it. He expressed a desire to know how my own family were disposed in order that he might know the position in which the two families stand to each other. I satisfied him on that head, but I see he has not the care for concealment that either you or I have, but thinks that in a place like ours "murder will out" (with myself it makes little difference, but with you publicity concerning our position to each other would be material one. And four years or more is a long while to be looked upon as affiance by the world & will necessarily, I mean consequently through you under such circumstances are in a false position which there is no avoiding. The single girls will scarce own you as one of them. You are without the pale. The married ones, d[itt]o., d[itt]o. You are not in the pale young men & others of my own sex, feeling a delicacy to making visits that would cause more unpleasant remark than if you were in either of the classes named above, would though a feeling of friendly desire for your society keep away. And I assure you, you would by the expiration of the first year find the situation you were placed in an unpleasant one. Were I to be here it would be different. We could have each other's society & care less for that of others. But that I fear may not be.

I stopped in N. York as usual at the Bond St. House and have been busied all day in running around on various errands. I stopped in to a sale of paintings at Coleman's for five minutes and bid on one, a sea sketch which is not a bad picture.[185] I ordered it sent up by Saturday's boat. And when you get perfect in landscapes you may be disposed to try your fortune for the waves (that's a very poor double entendre, but I was thinking of your promise to go to Europe).

---

185. William A. Coleman operated a store at 203 Broadway offering artwork for the public as well as supplies for artists, cabinetmakers, and upholsterers. *Commercial Advertiser* (New York), Nov. 17, 1847.

Here's a spot almost finished and I have scarce said a word of what I intended to. Have hardly commenced. This journey saddens me for when I return my decision will have been made and upon it hinge in all likelihood all the future events of my life. One certainly has been terminated, one important step made. I mean as regards yourself, and now comes the rest. Had I only my own family to leave together with the petty prospects of ambition which had been formed, I should have cared less. But a new tie is now formed, a closer bond, binding me to home & you and now absence seems hard indeed . . .

Notes Appearing on the Last Page of the 1846 Journal

TRIP EXPENSES

Lands at Auction	[$] 2.70
Powder & shot	3.25
Shrouds	2.70
Hat	3.38

Hat	[$] 1.00
Blanket	4.00
Gunlock	3.00
Sugar & salt	1.25
Shirt	1.50
Board & meals	2.00

DISTANCES	MILES
Derby to NY	75
NY to Phila.	90
Phila. To York	96

York to Balto.	57
Balto. to Pittsburgh	291
Pittsburgh to Cincinnati	496
Cincinn. to Sandusky	250
Detroit to Chicago	275
Chicago to Mackinaw	350
Mackinaw to Sault	90
Sault to Copper Harbour	200
LaPointe to St. Croix	100
St. Croix to Stillwater	150
Stillwater to t. pauls	25
St. Pauls to Fort Snelling	8
Fort Snelling to St. Peters	8
St. Peters to LaFrambois	150
Petite R. to Missouri	300
to St. Louis	1,000

Speech of Chief Hole-In-The-Day to Government Agent [at LaPointe, Wisconsin]

I come of the same ground as one of your children who just spoke. I never give trouble. I know I am foolish, but I can speak as my brothers speak. Father, I come from inland. Always nothing to eat. If we go by as you prefer, the ½ breeds will have the provisions through the year & we shall be starving. There is plenty of flour &c. with the traders. Our father can give us flour of that till our provisions come from over the lake. Our flour you gave us as for our brothers. Inland was stolen & for ourselves we gave to our stranger brothers who came. I have done.

Answer from the Agent [Charles W. W. Borup]

I am glad to hear my children talk. Unless we talk nothing can be done & I want everyone to expect his reward clearly. Whatever our great father has promised, he will perform. Every passing month he has acted up to. You shall have <u>yours</u>, every bit. But there is a greater father who rules the winds &c. It is for that reason they have not come. Goods & provisions will come together. They can't take their goods till they get their provisions. Last year you got all that belonged to them.

    Go-be-ni-ge-shick

    "Hole-in the Day" (sky)

EPILOGUE

Although Henry Sanford's return in the fall of 1846 marked the close of his western adventures, it was not the end of an active life, one that involved the enterprising young man in travel, politics, diplomacy, and a number of business ventures that took him far from New England and the West and enmeshed Sanford in the affairs of Europe, Latin America, and Africa, as well as the postbellum American South. He served the United States officially in posts in Russia, Germany, France, and Belgium and represented American interests in Mexico and Central and South America. He also became embroiled in African colonization and Belgian efforts to penetrate the upper reaches of the Congo Basin. At home he initiated bold but unsound agricultural projects in the South. With varying success Sanford pursued diverse activities that reflected the determination and cleverness that successfully took him to the far reaches of the West, as well as the arrogance and naïveté that had habitually clouded his business dealings and financial investments. Sanford's efforts sometimes fell short, but his life was never dull.

Returning home to Derby, Connecticut, Henry again joined his uncle Edward N. Shelton at the tack factory, but disagreements regarding the conduct of the business led him to separate from the venture and sell his share in the factory to his elder relative the following year. His interest now turned to public service, and in 1847 he began a career that would focus his attention largely outside the United States. Anxious to enter the world of international diplomacy, he again sailed for Europe to study languages. That year Sanford accompanied Ralph Ingersoll, a fellow Connecticut resident who had recently been appointed minister to Russia, to St. Petersburg as a temporary attaché. This experience led to connections that brought a series of diplomatic appointments in subsequent years, as acting secretary to the American Legation at Frankfurt in 1848 and secretary to the American Legation in Paris the following year, a post he held until 1854. To promote his career Henry attended Heidelberg University, graduating with a doctor of laws degree cum laude in the spring of 1849. Experience gained in these positions and the personal ties he made helped the ambitious young man enhance his diplomatic credentials in the American foreign service.[1]

■   ■   ■

Concurrent with his rise as a diplomat, Henry Sanford began a parallel career as an agent of American political and commercial expansion in Latin America, a move in keeping with increasing American imperialism directed toward its neighbors to the south. Upon returning to the United States from his post in Paris in 1854, he became involved in a claim made by his uncle Philo Shelton against the Venezuelan government. The controversy arose from a conflict over rights to extract guano, a substance increasingly popular as fertilizer in the United States, from Aves Island, perceived by Americans to be unclaimed land. When a new arrangement between a rival guano company and Venezuela established that nation's sovereignty

---

1. Joseph A. Fry, Henry S. Sanford: Diplomacy and Business in Nineteenth Century America (Reno: University of Nevada Press, 1982), 7–15.

over the island and threatened the extraction rights of Shelton and his associates, they sent Sanford to prosecute their claim to the territory. Henry's aggressive nature led him to pursue the case with a zealousness that turned a minor altercation into a major diplomatic confrontation. His domineering attitude and forceful in demands for payment of indemnity soon entangled the US State Department in the negotiations that reached a final settlement decades later.[2]

Additional Latin American ventures involved railroads, and Sanford represented American companies on least two occasions. One grew out of a failed plan by the Transoceanic Railway Company to construct a railroad across the isthmus of Panama. Within two years of its organization in 1855, managerial incompetence and difficulties working in the tropical environment threatened the project and prompted its chief promoter, Ephraim G. Squier, to call upon his former diplomatic colleague to take charge of affairs in Honduras. As Squier's special agent, Sanford reorganized the company and successfully negotiated arrangements with the Honduran government; however, his efforts were ultimately in vain and the venture collapsed following his departure.[3] An attempt to protect the Panama Railway's monopoly in Colombia in 1860 met a similar fate. Henry's renewed diplomatic career abruptly reduced his role as a corporate agent after 1860 but did not mark the close of his involvement in the region.

■　■　■

The tumultuous decade that followed civil war threatened the United States, and Henry Sanford's role as a foreign diplomat expanded markedly. Following the election of Abraham Lincoln in 1860, many of the southern states seceded to form a Confederacy whose government immediately sought foreign recognition and support in their struggle for independence. An ardent supporter of the Union, Sanford sought to demonstrate his

---

2. Ibid., 20–26.
3. Ibid., 26–30.

loyalty to the new administration in a capacity with which he had already proven his capability. He drew on his previous experience as well as his connections to acquire a diplomatic posting in Europe. With the support of influential Republicans, and particularly through his close friendship with publisher Thurlow Weed and William H. Seward, Lincoln's secretary of state, Sanford was appointed by the president as minister resident to Belgium in the spring of 1861. This position gave a man of Sanford's unique abilities a role much broader than his title indicated and one central to promoting American interests in Europe. As representative to a small nation, his limited duties at the Belgian court allowed the lively and energetic diplomat to undertake much broader European assignments intended to thwart the varied activities of rebel agents already active on the continent.[4]

During the next five years Henry Sanford conducted extensive espionage and surveillance, directing his early efforts at counteracting Confederate attempts to obtain arms, vessels, and supplies. Working through American diplomats, he dispatched detectives and other agents to identify, investigate Southern operatives, and disrupt their activities in England; however, dissatisfaction with his methods led him to confine his efforts to the continent.[5] He shifted his operations to France, where he concentrated on disrupting Confederate purchases of clothing and weapons. His widespread surveillance brought to light Southern activities in several countries, including France, Prussia, Belgium, Italy, and Spain, and his efforts severely limited the acquisition of a wide variety of war materiel, including ironclad warships under construction at Bordeaux.[6] Sanford also played a central role in European purchasing operations, by

---

4. Walter Starr, Seward: Lincoln's Indispensable Man (New York: Simon and Schuster, 2012), 255, 368.

5. Amanda Foreman, A World on Fire: Britain's Crucial Role in the American Civil War (New York: Random House, 2010), 169–170.

6. Harriet Chapell Owsley, "Henry Shelton Sanford and Federal Surveillance Abroad, 1861–1865," Mississippi Valley Historical Review 48 (1961): 212–221.

which large numbers of arms and great quantities of saltpeter were acquired and shipped to the United States for use by Union forces.[7]

As the first year of the war drew to a close, Sanford's diplomatic skills helped preserve particularly tense Anglo-American relations following the capture of Confederate commissioners traveling on the British mail steamer *Trent*. This incident, together with the Union blockade that cut off Southern trade from European ports, created a crisis that required his influence to mediate the situation short of war. In his official capacity Sanford argued successfully that the maintenance of good relations between Britain and the United States was in the best interests of Belgium and other European states and that the Belgian court should act as an intermediary for peace. As a result, King Leopold I, a close confidant of the recently widowed Queen Victoria, used his influence to intercede with the British monarch to avoid a conflict.[8]

∎ ∎ ∎

American slavery arose as an important issue to Europeans during the Civil War, and England in particular became increasingly concerned because emancipation was not one of the Union's war initial aims. Having ended slavery in its own colonies in 1834, British opinion had grown ambivalent about the Northern cause, especially in light of the *Trent* incident and the economic impact of the Union blockade. Henry Sanford was astutely aware of the importance of emancipation as a factor of European support for the struggling Union cause and emphasized its importance in correspondence with his superiors in the State Department. His efforts alone were unlikely to have prompted Lincoln to issue the Emancipation Proclamation in the fall of 1862; however, the information he presented provided evidence that addressing this issue was an important factor in preventing foreign recognition of the Confederacy. Support of emancipation helped sustain

---

7. Fry, Henry S. Sanford, 59.
8. Ibid., 56–57.

a policy of European neutrality until Union military successes and the Republican Party electoral victory in the 1864 elections convinced them that support of the Southern cause was hopeless.[9]

Despite his successes, Henry Sanford's efforts in Europe during the crucial war years also made enemies among his fellow diplomats. His energetic surveillance system, innovative purchasing operations, and widespread propaganda activities undoubtedly made a substantial contribution to the North's victory; however, his strong personality and zealousness alienated diplomatic colleagues who questioned his methods and felt that his special assignments frequently intruded on their territory. One in particular drew much negative attention. It derived from a desire by President Lincoln and Secretary of State Seward to recruit Giuseppe Garibaldi as a Union army commander following military reverses early in the war. Seward called upon his friend Sanford for the delicate and uncertain task of approaching the Italian hero. Although conducted in confidence, the negotiations were closely followed and publicized by the press. The situation was further complicated by the ongoing conflict for Italian unification and misunderstandings over the nature of Garibaldi's command, and he ultimately turned down the offer. The mission's collapse had recriminations for Sanford and a number of observers blamed him for its failure. Sanford's attempt to have Congress elevate his diplomatic position brought further enmity, and in 1869 he lost his post in Belgium.[10]

■　■　■

9. Christopher Ewan, "The Emancipation Proclamation and British Public Opinion," Historian 67 (2005): 7–8, 15–17; Kinley J. Brauer, "British Mediation and the American Civil War: A Reconsideration," Journal of Southern History 38 (1972): 62–65; Kinley J. Brauer, "The Slavery Problem in the Diplomacy of the American Civil War," Pacific Historical Review 46 (1977): 448–449; Sadie Daniel St. Clair, "Slavery as a Diplomatic Factor in Anglo-American Relations during the Civil War," Journal of Negro History 30 (1945): 274–275; David Herbert Donald, Charles Sumner, part 2, Charles Sumner and the Rights of Man (New York: DaCapo Press, 1996), 26.
10. Fry, Henry S. Sanford, 64–66, 84–86.

Henry Sanford's diplomatic career had implications for his personal life as well. His engagement with Janey Howe, the recipient of his western letters of 1846, cooled during his European assignments, and he broke off the relationship the three years later. Ever the gallant with the ladies, he lived extravagantly and remained an eligible bachelor without attachments until falling in love with Gertrude Ellen DuPuy, descendant of a prominent Pennsylvania family who was living with relatives in Europe, and a woman twenty years his junior. They married in September 1864 and occupied a luxurious residence in Brussels, maintaining an opulent lifestyle during his tenure in Belgium. Eventually the mother of seven children, Gertrude DuPuy Sanford begrudgingly assisted her husband in his work, which she acknowledged always seemed to be of the utmost importance to the committed Henry. Despite his efforts to maintain their way of life, Henry struggled to overcome the business failures that left the family in reduced circumstances. As his fortunes declined in the 1870s and 1880s, the Sanfords' relationship suffered and added to the disillusionment that characterized the later years of his life.[11]

■   ■   ■

While still in Belgium, Henry Sanford expanded his investments to include several agricultural projects in the postwar American South. The first two involved the acquisition of existing plantations with the intent of restoring production through the infusion of new capital and profiting from the result. In 1868 he leased lands on Barnwell Island, South Carolina, from William Henry Trescott, with whom he had earlier worked on the Aves Island dispute. Trescott's fortunes had suffered during the recent war, and Sanford offered to assist him by managing the plantation in exchange for a share of the cotton crop raised. Problems with labor, local opposition, and crop failures resulted in losses so severe that Sanford abandoned the

---

11. Richard J. Amundson, "The American Life of Henry Shelton Sanford" (PhD dissertation, Florida State University, 1963), 20, 24–29; Fry, Henry S. Sanford, 76–77.

project the following year and turned his attention to sugar growing in Louisiana.[12] Rising sugar prices during the late 1860s encouraged him to join his brother-in-law Samuel B. Rogers in a sugar-making scheme to produce cane sugar for Rogers's Philadelphia refinery. Together they purchased and expanded the Oakley plantation in Iberville Parish. In the face of railroad competition for local black labor, the Sanford-Rogers partnership turned to other sources, employing immigrants as well as convict labor. Again labor problems plagued the enterprise, and a series of bad harvests, deteriorating machinery, and the destruction to crops and levees by the catastrophic Mississippi River floods in 1874 and 1882 doomed the enterprise, which Sanford sold at a loss in 1889.[13]

■　■　■

Sanford's final investment in postwar southern agriculture was perhaps his most ambitious. Responding to travelers' accounts and promotional literature that touted the state of Florida and the potential profitability of citrus growing, Sanford purchased two orange groves near St. Augustine in 1869 and, a year later, 12,547 acres on the south shore of Lake Monroe in Orange County, to develop as a citrus-growing and settlement colony. He invested heavily in the venture, planting orange groves, building a wharf, a sawmill, a store, a slaughterhouse, and two hotels and in 1872 founded the town of Sanford. Largely an absentee owner, Sanford left the management of his business to subordinates whose ineptness and untrustworthiness compounded the problems of attracting reliable labor to an undeveloped area that was just emerging from a frontier. With his fortune now invested in Florida lands, Sanford spent the last decade of his life attempting to make a success of the project. Despite his incorporation of the enterprise as the Florida Land and Colonization Company in 1880, its fortunes continued

---

12. Richard J. Amundson, "Trescott, Sanford, and Sea Island Cotton," *South Carolina Historical Magazine* 68 (1967): 31–36.
13. Richard J. Amundson, "Oakley Plantation: A Post–Civil War Venture in Louisiana Sugar," Louisiana History 9 (1968): 21–42.

to decline as a result of high shipping costs, foreign competition, and poor crops stemming from the groves' unsatisfactory locations, plant diseases, and especially the destructive freezes of 1886 and 1894–1895.[14]

■   ■   ■

Henry Sanford's ties to Leopold II and his support of the king's African ventures during the 1870s and 1880s opened perhaps the most controversial phase of his diplomatic career. Eager to acquire a colony, the Belgian king looked to the Congo, a vast territory in the interior of Africa yet unclaimed by any European power. As director of the International African Association organized to explore the region and open it to commerce, he sought to employ the services of famed explorer Henry Morton Stanley, who had recently returned from the Congo. Anxious to continue in public service after losing his official position at the Belgian court, Sanford gladly accepted a board membership in Leopold's association and the king's offer in 1878 to employ his diplomatic talents to recruit Stanley as his agent. In Leopold's service, Stanley's efforts opened the Congo River to trade and established a monopoly on commerce through dubious treaties with the societies of the Congo Basin. Portraying the success of the International African Association as an altruistic venture representing indigenous African states, Leopold sought international support for the company's regional sovereignty as the Congo Free State. In the capacity of Leopold's agent, Sanford promoted his interests overseas and successfully lobbied for its recognition by the United States in 1884.[15]

■   ■   ■

Henry Sanford remained a central figure in Leopold's efforts to establish control of the Congo. In hopes of gaining an administrative position in

---

14. Fry, Henry S. Sanford, chaps. 5 and 6, 95–104, 106–111, 117–118.
15. Adam Hochschild, King Leopold's Ghost: A Story of Greed, Terror, and Heroism in Colonia Africa (Boston: Houghton Mifflin, 1998), 58–59, 71–79.

the Congo Free State, Sanford represented the king's interests while serving as plenipotentiary of the United States at a conference called by European states to resolve conflicting African territorial claims and other issues relating to the continent's colonization.[16] Although his goal remained unfulfilled, he nevertheless was granted permission to form a trading company on the Upper Congo River and its tributaries. Like his earlier ventures, his Sanford Exploring Expedition, organized in 1886, suffered from mismanagement and insufficient funding, and he found little support from Leopold. Sanford's efforts to solicit additional capital from American investors also fell on deaf ears, and insolvency followed. In December 1888 a Belgian-based association absorbed the company, leaving him with little more than his shares to sustain his family in the last years of his life.[17]

．　　■　　■

When Henry Shelton Sanford died in the spring of 1891, he left behind a life of contradictions. Born into a wealthy family whose business prospects offered opportunity and security, he opted for a diplomatic career that promised neither. Despite the influence and sage advice of his father and uncle, Henry never acquired their capitalist acumen and habitually made bad financial investments. Early on he also chose to ignore debilitating illness and risk his health for the sake of adventure. He did not suffer fools easily, and his self-assurance and occasional arrogance worked to negate his skills as a negotiator, generating needless chaos and creating enemies. Perhaps his greatest curse was the naïveté reflected in his business failures as well as his political judgement. Often oblivious to problematic conditions and unwilling to become involved personally in his enterprises, he proved to be a poor judge of character who ignored

---

16. "General Act of the Conference of Berlin Concerning the Congo," *American Journal of International Law* 3, no. 1, Supplement of Official Documents (1909): 7–8.
17. Fry, Henry S. Sanford, 160–163.

or condoned mismanagement and waste that hastened the decline of his businesses and his fortune. Sanford's experience in King Leopold's Congo venture left him poorer, bitter, and disillusioned. Nevertheless, the success of his diplomatic efforts in Latin America promoted antebellum American interests as a hemispheric power, and his successes in Europe during the Civil War made him one of the Union's most important foreign agents. Despite the dubious impact of his efforts in support of Leopold's nefarious Congo Free State, Sanford's diplomatic activities overall promoted the growth of international American commerce. And finally, although his Florida experiment largely failed as a business venture, it contributed substantially to the development of the citrus industry as well as the state's growth.[18]

In many ways Henry Sanford's later life reflected his early adventures in the West. Willing to take great risks for goals of dubious value and ignoring danger and the consequences of his actions, he forged ahead, ever convinced of eventual success. Only in the last years of his life, when the results of this energetic but uncertain strategy brought financial and personal setbacks that threatened his livelihood, his domestic tranquility, and his health, did its impact bring about a final decline. Sanford's life, with its mixed successes and failures, left a legacy that mirrored both the optimism and insecurity of Gilded Age America and perhaps is best seen as a microcosm of the larger, challenging cultural milieu in which he lived.

---

18. Ibid., 173–175.

BIBLIOGRAPHY

Manuscript Collections

Henry Shelton Sanford Papers, Sanford Museum, Sanford, Florida

Nehemiah C. Sanford, Journal, Western Trip, May–July 1839, Box 2, Folder 7

Henry S. Sanford, Journal, Connecticut to Michigan, July–September 1844, Box 3, Folder 1

Henry S. Sanford, Journal, Buffalo Hunt, July–September 1846, Box 3, Folder 5

Henry S. Sanford, Journal, Two Weeks' Tour of Great Britain, April 1845, Box 3, Folder 3

Western Lands: Accounts, Booth, W. L., 1843–1863, Box 62, Folder 7

Western Lands: Accounts, Berrien, Cass, St. Joseph [Counties], 1836–1887, Box 62, Folder 8

Western Lands: Accounts, Dibble, S. D., 1859–1864, Box 62, Folder 9

Western Lands: Accounts, Miscellaneous, 1840–1873, Box 62, Folder 10

Western Lands: Accounts, Williams, M. L., 1860–1870, Box 62, Folder 11

Memoranda: Lists of Michigan Lands, 1840–1866, Box 64, Folder 13

Correspondence: Booth, W. L., 1843–1863, Box 63, Folder 2

Correspondence: Dibble, S. D., 1859–1866, Box 63, Folder 5

Correspondence: Jones, J. P., 1858–1864, Box 63, Folder 7

Correspondence: Sherman, E. B., 1837–1845, Box 63, Folder 14

Correspondence, Nancy Bateman Sanford and Nehemiah Curtis Sanford, 1823–1840, Box 69, Folder 10

Correspondence, Edward N. Shelton, 1830–1844, Box 73, Folder 1

Correspondence, Janey Howe, July–September 1846, Box 93, Folder 15

Michigan Historical Collections, University of Michigan, Ann Arbor

Bela Hubbard Papers

Minnesota Office of the State Archaeologist, Fort Snelling History Center, St. Paul, MN

Archaeological Site Files

Missouri Historical Society, St. Louis

Taylor, David G. "Journal of Steamer *Clermont* from St. Louis to the Mouth of the Yellowstone River of the Missouri, July 7–28, 1846." Steamboats and River History Collection, 1802–1986, Box 1, Folder 9.

Van Pelt and Opie Library, Michigan Technological University, Houghton, MI

Charter Oak Mining Company, Articles of Association. Charter Oak Mining Company Collection, MS-680.

Articles and Books

Abel, Annie Heloise. *Chardon's Journal at Fort Clark, 1834–1839*. Pierre: South Dakota Department of History, 1932.

Albion, Robert Greenhalgh. *The Rise of New York Port (1815–1860)*. New York: Charles Scribner's Sons, 1970.

Amundson, Richard J. "The American Life of Henry Shelton Sanford." PhD dissertation, Florida State University, 1963.

———. "Oakley Plantation: A Post–Civil War Venture in Louisiana Sugar." *Louisiana History* 9 (1968): 21–42.

———. "Trescott, Sanford, and Sea Island Cotton." *South Carolina Historical Magazine* 68 (1967): 31–36.

Andreas, A. T. *History of Chicago, from the Earliest Period to the Present Time.* Chicago: A. T. Andreas, 1884.

Audubon, Maria R. *Audubon and His Journals.* 2 vols. New York: Charles Scribner's Sons, 1897.

Bain, David Haward. *Empire Express: Building the First Transcontinental Railroad.* New York: Viking, 1999.

Baptist, Edward E. *Creating an Old South: Middle Florida's Plantation Frontier before the Civil War.* Chapel Hill: University of North Carolina Press, 2002.

Barillas, William. "Michigan's Pioneers and the Destruction of the Hardwood Forest." *Michigan Historical Review* 15 (1989): 1–22.

Barnett, LeRoy. "Internal Improvement Lands: A Down-to-Earth Solution for Developing Michigan Transportation." *Michigan Surveyor* 25, no. 5 (1990): 10–12.

Barnow, Victor. "Chippewa Social Animism." *American Anthropologist*, n.s., 13 (1961): 1006–1013.

Bartlett, Richard A. *The New Country: A Social History of the American Frontier, 1776–1890.* New York: Oxford University Press, 1974.

Beardsley, Levi. *Reminiscences.* New York: Charles Vinten, 1852.

Berghofer, Robert F. *The White Man's Indian: Images of the American Indian from Columbus to the Present.* New York: Vintage Books, 1979.

Berlin, Ira. *Many Thousands Gone: The First Two Centuries of Slavery in North America.* Cambridge, MA: Belknap Press of Harvard University Press, 1998.

Berry, Brian J. L. *Geography of Market Centers and Retail Distribution.* Englewood Cliffs, NJ: Prentice-Hall, 1967.

Bidwell, Percy Wells, and John I. Falconer. *History of Agriculture in the Northern United States, 1620–1860.* New York: Peter Smith, 1941.

Birch, Brian. "British Evaluations of the Forest Openings and Prairie Edges of the North Central States, 1800–1850." In *The Frontier, Comparative Studies,* vol. 2, edited by William W. Savage and Stephen I. Thompson, 167–192. Norman: University of Oklahoma Press, 1979.

Bishop, Levi. "Recollections." *Michigan Pioneer and Historical Collections* 1 (1877): 125–126.

Blegen, Theodore C. "Armistice and War on the Minnesota Frontier." *Minnesota History* 24 (1943): 11–25.

Blois, John T. *1838 Gazetteer of the State of Michigan*. Knightstown, IN: Bookmark, 1979.

Bodenhorn, Howard. *State Banking in Early America: A New Economic History*. New York: Oxford University Press, 2003.

Bogue, Allen G. "Land Credit for Northern Farmers, 1789–1940." *Agricultural History* 50 (1976): 68–100.

Boughter, Judith A. *Betraying the Omaha Nation, 1790–1916*. Lincoln: University of Nebraska Press, 1998.

Brauer, Kinley J. "British Mediation and the American Civil War: A Reconsideration." *Journal of Southern History* 38 (1972): 49–64.

———. "The Slavery Problem in the Diplomacy of the American Civil War." *Pacific Historical Review* 46 (1977): 439–469.

Brewster, William. "The Present State of the Wild Pigeon (*Ectopistes migratorius*) as a Bird of the United States, with Some Notes on Its Habits." *The Auk: A Quarterly Journal of Ornithology* 6 (1889): 285–291.

Brisbin, I. Lehr. "The Passenger Pigeon: A Study in the Ecology of Extinction." *Modern Game Breeding* 4, no. 12 (1968): 13–20.

Brooks, Noah. "The Boy Settlers." *St. Nicholas* 18 (1891): 509–517.

Brown, E. Lakin. "Autobiographical Notes." Edited by A. Ada Brown. *Michigan Pioneer and Historical Collections* 30 (1905): 424–494.

Buckman, David Lear. *Tales and Reminiscences of the Stirring Times That Followed the Introduction of Steam Navigation*. New York: Grafton Press, 1907.

Burton, Clarence M. *History of Detroit, Financial and Commercial*. Detroit: By the author, 1917.

Burton, William Evans. *Appleton's Cyclopedia of American Biography*. New York: D. Appleton, 1900.

Busch, Janet. *People and Places: A Human History of the Apostle Islands; Historic Study of the Apostle Islands National Seashore*. Omaha, NE: Midwest Regional Office, National Park Service, United States Department of the Interior, 2008.

Butler, Albert F. "Rediscovering Michigan's Prairies." *Michigan History* 31 (1947–1948): 267–286; 32 (1948): 15–36; 33 (1948): 117–130, 220–231.

Campbell, Daniel R. "Village and the World: The Shaping of Culture in Marshall, Michigan." PhD dissertation, Michigan State University, 1986.

Carter, George E. "Lord Selkirk and the Red River Colony." *Montana: The Magazine of Western History* 18 (1968): 60–69.

Casagrande, Joseph B., Stephen I. Thompson, and Philip D. Young. "Colonization as a Research Frontier: The Ecuadorian Case." In *Process and Pattern in Culture: Essays in Honor of Julian H. Steward*, edited by Robert A. Manners, 281–325. Chicago: Aldine, 1964.

Catlin, George. *Letters and Notes on the Manners, Customs, and Conditions of the North American Indians*. 2 vols. New York: Dover Publications, 1973.

Chamberlain, E. *Indiana Gazetteer, or Topographical Dictionary of the State of Indiana*. Indianapolis: E. Chamberlain, 1849.

Chambers, Thomas A. "Seduction and Sensibility: The Refined Society of Ballston, New York, 1800." *New York History* 78 (July 1997): 245–272.

Chase, Lew Allen. "Hiram Moore and the Invention of the Harvester." *Michigan History* 14 (1929): 501–505.

——— . *Rural Michigan*. New York: Macmillan, 1922.

Clark, Caven P. *An Archaeological Survey of the Lower District of St. Croix National Scenic Riverway*. Lincoln, NE: US Department of the Interior, National Park Service, Midwest Archaeological Center, Technical Report 126, 2010.

Clark, George P., ed. *Into the Old Northwest: Journeys with Charles H. Titus, 1841–1846*. East Lansing: Michigan State University Press, 1994.

Clark, John G. *The Grain Trade in the Old Northwest*. Urbana: University of Illinois Press, 1966.

Clark, Thomas D. *A History of Kentucky*. Ashland, KY: Jesse Stuart Foundation, 1992.

Cochrane, Willard W. *The Development of American Agriculture: A Historical Analysis*. Minneapolis: University of Minnesota Press, 1979.

Cole, Arthur H. "Cyclical and Sectional Variations in the Sale of Public Lands, 1816–1860." In *The Public Lands: Studies in the History of the Public Domain*, edited by Vernon Carstensen, 229–251. Madison: University of Wisconsin Press, 1963.

Cole, Maurice F., comp. *Voices from the Wilderness*. Ann Arbor: University of Michigan Press, 1961.

Colton, C. *Tour of the American Lakes, and among the Indians of the North-West Territory, in 1830*. 2 vols. London: Frederick Wesley and A. H. Davis, 1833.

Coolidge, Orville William. *A Twentieth Century History of Berrien County, Michigan*. Chicago: Lewis Publishing Co., 1906.

Cothren, William. *History of Ancient Woodbury, Connecticut from the First Indian Deed in 1659 to 1854*. Waterbury, CT: T. Bronson Bros., 1854.

Cronon, William. *Changes in the Land: Indians, Colonists, and the Ecology of New England*. New York: Hill and Wang, 1983.

———. *Nature's Metropolis: Chicago and the Great West*. New York: Norton, 1991.

Danhof, Clarence H. *Change in Agriculture: The Northern United States, 1820–1870*. Cambridge, MA: Harvard University Press, 1969.

Densmore, Frances. *Chippewa Customs*. Bulletin 86. Washington, DC: Smithsonian Institution, Bureau of American Ethnology, 1929.

Devoy, John. *A History of the City of Rochester from the Earliest Times*. Rochester, NY: Post Express Printing Co., 1895.

Diedrich, Mark. *The Chiefs Hole-in-the-Day of the Mississippi Chippewa*. Minneapolis: Coyote Books, 1986.

Disturnell, John. *A Trip through the Lakes of North America*. New York: J. Disturnell, 1857.

Donald, David Herbert. *Charles Sumner*. Part 2, *Charles Sumner and the Rights of Man*. New York: DaCapo Press, 1996.

Downing, A. J. *Rural Essays*. Edited with a Memoir of the Author by George William Curtis and a Letter to His Friends by Frederika Bremer. New York: George P. Putnam and Co., 1853.

Dunbar, Willis F. *Lewis Cass.* Grand Rapids, MI: William B. Eerdmans, 1970.

Dunn, James Taylor. *The St. Croix: Midwest Border River.* New York: Holt, Rinehart and Winston, 1965.

Durant, Samuel W. *History of Kalamazoo County, Michigan.* Philadelphia: Everts & Abbott, 1880.

———. *History of Oakland County, Michigan.* Philadelphia: L. H. Everts, 1877.

Dwight, Benjamin W. *The History of the Descendants of John Dwight of Dedham, Mass.* New York: John W. Trow, 1874.

Eckert, Kathryn Bishop. *Buildings of Michigan.* New York: Oxford University Press, 1993.

Edwards, Abraham. "Sketch of Pioneer Life." *Michigan Pioneer and Historical Collections* 3 (1881): 148–151.

Edwards, Richard. *Statistical Gazetteer of the State of Virginia.* Richmond, VA: By the author, 1855.

Ellis, Franklin. *History of Berrien and Van Buren Counties, Michigan.* Philadelphia: D. W. Ensign, 1880.

Ewan, Christopher. "The Emancipation Proclamation and British Public Opinion." *Historian* 67 (2005): 1–19.

Faber, Don. *The Toledo War: The First Michigan-Ohio Rivalry.* Ann Arbor: University of Michigan Press, 2008.

Fanning's Illustrated Gazetteer of the United States. New York: Ensign, Bridgman, & Fanning, 1855.

Farmer, Silas. *The Emigrant's Guide; or Pocket Gazetteer of the Surveyed Part of Michigan.* Albany, NY: Packard, 1830.

———. *History of Detroit and Wayne County and Early Michigan.* Detroit: Gale Research, 1969.

"Far-Sighted Builder-Promoter Creates Vast Financial Empire." *Rathbun-Rathbone-Rathburn Family Historian* 2, no. 1 (1982): 4–8.

Fisher, David, and Frank Little, eds. *Compendium of History and Biography of Kalamazoo County, Mich.* Chicago: A. W. Bowen, 1906.

Fisher, R. S. *Gazetteer of the State of Maryland.* New York: J. H. Colton, 1851.

———. *Gazetteer of the State of Maryland.* New York: J. H. Colton, 1852.

Folsom, W. H. C. *Fifty Years in the Northwest.* [St. Paul, MN]: Pioneer Press Co., 1888.

Foreman, Amanda. *A World on Fire: Britain's Crucial Role in the American Civil War.* New York: Random House, 2010.

Fry, Joseph A. *Henry S. Sanford: Diplomacy and Business in Nineteenth Century America.* Reno: University of Nevada Press, 1982.

Fuller, George N. *Economic and Social Beginnings of Michigan: A Study of the Settlement of the Lower Peninsula during the Territorial Period, 1805–1837.* Lansing, MI: Wynkoop Hallenbeck Crawford, 1916.

——— . *Historic Michigan: Land of the Great Lakes.* Vol. 3. Dayton, OH: National Historical Association, 1924.

——— . *Michigan: A Centennial History of the State and Its People.* Vol. 1. Chicago: Lewis Publishing Co., 1939.

Gaskin, L. J. P. "Centenary of the Opening of George Catlin's North American Indian Museum and Gallery in the Egyptian Hall, Piccadilly, with a Memoir of Catlin." *Man* 40 (1940): 17–21.

Gates, Paul W. *The Farmer's Age: Agriculture 1815–1860.* Vol. 3 of *The Economic History of the United States.* New York: Holt, Rinehart & Winston, 1960.

——— . "The Role of the Speculator in Western Land Development." In *The Public Lands: Studies in the History of the Public Domain,* edited by Vernon Carstensen, 349–367. Madison: University of Wisconsin Press, 1963.

Geiger, Joe, Jr. "The Tragic Fate of Guyandotte." *West Virginia History* 54 (1995): 28–41.

"General Act of the Conference of Berlin Concerning the Congo." *American Journal of International Law* 3, no. 1, *Supplement of Official Documents* (1909): 7–25.

Gibbs, Mary V. "Glimpses of Early Michigan Life in and around Kalamazoo." *Magazine of American History* 24 (1890): 457–464.

Glover, L. H. *A Twentieth Century History of Cass County, Michigan.* Chicago: Lewis Publishing Co., 1906.

Good, Mary Elizabeth. *Guebert Site: An 18th Century, Historic Kaskaskia Indian Village in Randolph County, Illinois.* Memoir 2. Wood River, IL: Central

States Archaeological Societies, 1972.

Goodrich, Enos. "Pioneer Sketch of Moses Goodrich and His Trip across Michigan in February 1836 with His Brother Levi." *Michigan Pioneer and Historical Collections* 7 (1886): 480–490.

Goodspeed, Weston A., and Daniel D. Healy. *History of Cook County, Illinois.* Vol. 1. Chicago: Goodspeed Historical Association, 1909.

———. *History of Dubuque County, Iowa.* Chicago: Goodspeed Historical Association, [1911].

Gordon, Douglas H., and George S. May, eds. "The Michigan Land Rush, Michigan Journal, 1836, John M. Gordon." *Michigan History* 43 (1959): 1–42, 129–149, 257–293, 433–478.

Gordon, Thomas F. *A Gazetteer of the State of New York.* Philadelphia: T. Belknap, 1832.

———. *A Gazetteer of the State of Pennsylvania.* Philadelphia: T. Belknap, 1832.

Greenberg, Amy S. *A Wicked War: Polk, Clay, Lincoln, and the 1846 U. S. Invasion of Mexico* New York: Alfred A Knopf, 2012.

Groom, Winston. *Kearny's March: The Epic Creation of the American West, 1846–1847.* New York: Alfred A. Knopf, 2011.

Grove, David. "The Function and Future of Market Centres." In *Man, Settlement, and Urbanism,* edited by Peter J. Ucko, Ruth Tringham, and G. W. Dimbleby, 559–565. London: Gerald Duckworth, 1972.

H. Lee Huntington & Co. and James Sutherland. *State of Michigan Gazetteer and Business Directory for 1856–57.* Detroit: By the authors, 1856.

Halsey, John R. "Copper from the Drift." *Michigan Archaeologist* 56 (2010): 1–42.

Hamilton, Charles S. "Memoirs of the Mexican War." *Wisconsin Magazine of History* 14 (1930): 63–92.

Harlow, Alvin F. *The Road of the Century: The Story of the New York Central.* New York: Creative Age Press, 1947.

Hart, John Frazier. *The Look of the Land.* Englewood Cliffs, NY: Prentice-Hall, 1975.

Hartley, William G. "Council Bluffs/Kanesville, Iowa: A Hub for Mormon Settlements, Operations, and Emigration, 1846–1852." *John Whitmer*

Historical Association Journal 26 (2006): 17–47.

Harwood, Herbert. *Impossible Challenge II: Baltimore to Washington and Harpers Ferry from 1828 to 1994*. Baltimore: Barnard Roberts, 1994.

Hawes, George W. *Illinois State Gazetteer and Business Directory for 1858 and 1859*. Chicago: George W. Hawes, 1859.

———. *Indiana State Gazetteer and Business Directory for 1858 and 1859*. Chicago: George W. Hawes, 1859.

———. *Michigan State Gazetteer and Business Directory for 1860*. Detroit: F. Raymond & Co., 1859.

Henry, Gary. "Galena, Illinois during the Lead Mine Era." MA thesis, Eastern Illinois University, 1976.

Hibbard, Benjamin. *A History of Public Land Policies*. Madison: University of Wisconsin Press, 1965.

History of Jackson County, Michigan. Chicago: Interstate Publishing Co., 1881.

History of Jo Daviess County, Illinois. Chicago: H. F. Kett & Co., 1878.

History of Northern Wisconsin, Containing an Account of Its Settlement. . . . Chicago: Western Historical Co., 1881.

History of St. Joseph County, Michigan. Philadelphia: L. H. Everts, 1877.

Hochschild, Adam. *King Leopold's Ghost: A Story of Greed, Terror, and Heroism in Colonia Africa*. Boston: Houghton Mifflin, 1998.

Hoffman, Charles Fenno. *A Winter in the West*. Vol. 1. New York: Harper & Brothers, 1835.

Holbrook, Stewart H. *The Story of American Railroads*. New York: Crown Publishers, 1947.

Horsman, Reginald. "Changing Images of the Public Domain: Historians and the Shaping of Midwest Frontiers." In *This Land Is Ours: The Acquisition and Disposition of the Public Domain*, 60–86. Indianapolis: Indiana Historical Society, 1978.

Hoyt, William C. "Early Recollections." *Michigan Pioneer and Historical Collections* 5 (1884): 61–63.

Hubbard, Bela. *Memorials of a Half Century*. New York: G. P. Putnam's Sons, 1887.

Hungerford, Edward. *Men and Iron: The History of the New York Central*. New

York: Thomas W. Crowell, 1938.

Hunt, John Warren. *Wisconsin Gazetteer, Containing the Names, Locations, and Advantages of Counties, Cities, Towns Villages, Post Offices, and Settlements . . . in the State of Wisconsin*. Madison: Beriah Brown, 1853.

Hurt, R. Douglas. *American Farm Tools: From Hand-Power to Steam-Power*. Manhattan, KS: Sunflower University Press, 1985.

Ingalls, Walter Renton. *Lead and Zinc in the United States: Comprising an Economic History of the Mining and Smelting of the Metals and the Conditions Which Have Affected the Development of the Industries*. New York: Hill Publishing Co., 1908.

Jackson, Jerome A., and Bette J. S. Jackson. "Once upon a Time in American Ornithology: Extinction; The Passenger Pigeon, Last Hopes, Letting Go." *Wilson Journal of Ornithology* 119 (2007): 767–772.

Jakle, John A. *Images of the Ohio Valley: A Historical Geography of Travel, 1740–1860*. New York: Oxford University Press, 1977.

Jamison, Knox. "The Survey of Public Lands in Michigan." *Michigan History* 42 (1958): 197–214.

Jenkins, Warren. *The Ohio Gazetteer and Traveler's Guide*. Columbus: Isaac N. Whiting, 1839.

Jensen, Oliver. *The American Heritage History of Railroads in America*. New York: McGraw-Hill, 1975.

Jensen, Richard E. "The Pawnee Mission, 1834–1846." *Nebraska History* 75 (1994): 301–310.

Johnson, Crisfield. *History of Branch County, Michigan*. Philadelphia: Everts, 1879.

Kaatz, Martin R. "The Black Swamp: A Study in Historical Geography." *Annals of the Association of American Geographers* 45 (1955): 1–35.

Kalamazoo County Directory with a History of the County. Kalamazoo: J. M. Thomas, 1869.

Kalamazoo Ladies Library Association. *Quarter Centennial Celebration of the Settlement of Kalamazoo, Michigan*. Kalamazoo: Gazette Print, 1855.

Keith, Hannah Emily. "An Historical Sketch of Internal Improvements in Michigan, 1836–1846." *Publications of the Michigan Political Science*

Association 4 (1902): 1–48.

Kirkland, Edward C. *A History of American Economic Life*. New York: F. S. Crofts, 1939.

Kittridge, G. L. "Note on the Song of 'Mary Blaine.'" *Journal of American Folklore* 99 (1926): 200–207.

Kuhm, Herbert. "Wisconsin Indian Fishing." *Wisconsin Archaeologist* 7, no. 2 (1927–1928): 61–114.

Lake, D. J. *Atlas of Berrien County, Michigan*. Philadelphia: C. O. Titus, 1873.

Lanman, Charles A. *A Summer in the Wilderness: Embracing a Canoe Voyage up the Mississippi and around Lake Superior*. New York: D. Appleton, 1847.

Lanman, James H. *Adventures in the Wilds of the United States and British American Provinces*. Vol. 1. Philadelphia: John W. Moore, 1856.

———. *History of Michigan, Civil and Topographical, in a Compendious Form with a View of the Surrounding Lakes*. New York: E. French, 1839.

Lay, Ezra D. "Condensed Early History, or Beginnings of the Several Towns in Washtenaw County." *Michigan Pioneer and Historical Collections* 17 (1890): 450–462.

Lee, Susan Previant, and Peter Passell. *A New Economic View of American History*. New York: Norton, 1979.

Lehmer, Donald G. *Introduction to Middle Missouri Archeology*. Washington, DC: US Department of the Interior, National Park Service, 1971.

Lewis, Kenneth E. *The American Frontier: An Archaeological Study of Settlement Pattern and Process*. Orlando: Academic Press, 1984.

———. *West to Far Michigan: Settling the Lower Peninsula, 1815–1860*. East Lansing: Michigan State University Press, 2002.

Limerick, Jeffrey W. "The Grand Hotels of America." *Perspecta* 15 (1975): 87–108.

Mahar, William J. *Behind the Burnt Cork Mask: Early Blackface Minstrelsy and Antebellum American Popular Culture*. Urbana: University of Illinois Press, 1999.

Mansfield, J. B. *Great Lakes Maritime History*. Vol. 1, *1831–1840*. Chicago: J. H. Beers & Co., 1899.

Martineau, Harriet. "Harriet Martineau's Travels in and around Michigan, 1836."

Michigan History 7 (1923): 49–99.

Marvill, Lewis. "First Trip by Steam on Lake Superior." *Michigan Historical Collections* 4 (1883): 67–69.

Mather, Frederick G. "Water Routes from the Great Northwest." *Harpers* 63 (1881): 415–435.

Matheson, Katy. "Niblo's Garden and Its 'Concert Saloon,' 1828–1846: The Evolution of a Performance Space." MA thesis, New York University, 1991.

Mathews, Alfred. *History of Cass County, Michigan.* Chicago: Waterman, Watkins & Co., 1882.

McCulloch, J. R. *McCulloch's Universal Gazetteer.* New York: Harper & Brothers, 1845.

McMahon, Eileen, and Theodore J. Karamanski. *North Woods River: The St. Croix in Upper Midwest History.* Madison: University of Wisconsin Press, 2009.

Meinig, D. W. *The Shaping of America: A Geographical Perspective on 500 Years of History.* Vol. 2, *Continental America, 1800–1867.* New Haven: Yale University Press, 1993.

Meints, Graydon M. "Michigan Railroad Construction, 1835–1875." Ann Arbor: Transportation Library, University of Michigan, 1981. Typewritten.

——— . *Michigan Railroads and Railroad Companies.* East Lansing: Michigan State University Press, 1992.

Memorial Record of the Northern Peninsula of Michigan. Chicago: Lewis Pub. Co., 1895.

Merry, Robert W. *A Country of Vast Designs: James K. Polk, the Mexican War, and the Conquest of the American Continent.* New York: Simon & Schuster, 2009.

The Mexican War and Its Heroes: Being a Complete History of the Mexican War. Philadelphia: Lippincott, Grambo & Co., 1848.

Miller, George J. "The Establishment of Michigan's Boundaries: A Study in Historical Geography." *American Geographical Society Bulletin* 43 (1911): 339–351.

Murphy, Lucy Eldersveld. *A Gathering of Rivers: Indians, Métis, and Mining in the Western Great Lakes, 1737–1832.* Lincoln: University of Nebraska Press, 2000.

Neill, Edward D. *Occurrences in the Vicinity of St. Paul, Minn. before Its Incorporation as a City*. [St. Paul]: D. Mason & Co., 1890.

Neill, William Duffield. *The History of Minnesota from the Earliest French Explorations to the Present Time*. Philadelphia: J. B. Lippincott & Co., 1858.

New York Central Railroad Company. *The New York Central Railroad, 1831–1915*. New York: James Kempster Printing Co., 1916.

The New York State Tourist. New York: A. T. Goodrich, 1842.

Nolan, Louis Clinton. "The Relations of the United States and Peru with Respect to Claims, 1822–1870." *Hispanic American Historical Review* 17 (1937): 30–66.

North, Douglass C. *The Economic Growth of the United States, 1790–1860*. New York: Norton, 1966.

Nutter, David Charles. "Malaria in Michigan." Master's thesis, Michigan State University, 1988.

Orcott, Samuel, and Ambrose Beardsley. *The History of the Old Town of Derby, Connecticut, 1642–1880*. Bowie, MD: Heritage Books, 1998.

Owsley, Harriet Chapell. "Henry Shelton Sanford and Federal Surveillance Abroad, 1861–1865." *Mississippi Valley Historical Review* 48 (1961): 211–228.

———. *Register: Henry Shelton Sanford Papers*. Nashville: Tennessee State Library and Archives, 1960.

Parker, N. Howe. *Iowa as It Is in 1855: A Gazetteer for Citizens*. Chicago: Keen & Lee, 1855.

Parkins, Almon Ernest. *The Historical Geography of Detroit*. Lansing: Michigan Historical Commission, 1918.

Parks, Robert J. *Democracy's Railroads: Public Enterprise in Jacksonian Michigan*. Port Washington, NY: Kennikat Press, 1972.

Peck, James Mason. *A Gazetteer of Illinois*. Philadelphia: Grigg & Elliot, 1837.

———. *A New Guide for Emigrants to the West*. Boston: Kendall and Lincoln, 1837.

Peters, Bernard C. "Changing Ideas about the Use of Vegetation as an Indicator of Soil Quality: Example of New York and Michigan." *Journal of Geography* 72 (1973): 18–28.

Peterson, William J. "Steamboating in the Upper Mississippi Fur Trade."

Minnesota History 13 (1943): 221–243.

Phillips, Paul Chrisler. *The Fur Trade.* 2 vols. Norman: University of Oklahoma Press, 1961.

Pilcher, Elijah H. *Protestantism in Michigan: Being a Special History of the Methodist Episcopal Church.* Detroit: R. D. S. Taylor, 1878.

Porter, Phil. *The Eagle of Mackinac: The Establishment of United States Civil and Military Authority on Mackinac Island, 1796–1802.* Mackinac Island, MI: Mackinac State Historic Parks, 1991.

Pray, Carl E. "An Historic Michigan Road." *Michigan History* 11 (1927): 325–341.

Prucha, Francis Paul. *The Great Father: The United States Government and American Indians.* Lincoln: University of Nebraska Press, 1984.

———. *A Guide to the Military Posts of the United States, 1789–1895.* Madison: State Historical Society of Wisconsin, 1964.

Quimby, Robert S. *The U.S. Army in the War of 1812: An Operational and Command Study.* East Lansing: Michigan State University Press, 1997.

Rasmussen, Wayne D. "Introduction to U. S. Land Policies, 1783–1840." In *Agriculture in the United States: A Documentary History,* edited by Wayne D. Rasmussen, 273–280. New York: Random House, 1975.

Rerick, Rowland H. *Memoirs of Florida.* Edited by Francis P. Fleming. Vol 1. Atlanta: Southern Historical Association, 1902.

Reynolds, David S. *Waking Giant: America in the Age of Jackson.* New York: HarperCollins, 2008.

Richter, F. E. "The Copper Mining Industry in the United States, 1845–1925." *Quarterly Journal of Economics* 41 (1927): 236–291.

Riggs, Stephen R. *Mary and I: Forty Years with the Sioux.* Boston: Congregational Sunday School and Publishing Society, 1883.

Robbins, Roy M. *Our Landed Heritage: The Public Domain, 1776–1970.* Lincoln: University of Nebraska Press, 1976.

Robinson, Doane. "Joseph LaFramboise, First Settler." *Monthly South Dakotan* 11 (1901): 353–358.

Rogers, Howard S. *History of Cass County, Michigan from 1825 to 1875.* Dowagiac, MI: Captain Samuel Felt Chapter, the Daughters of the American

Revolution, 1942.

Rohrbough, Malcolm J. *The Land Office Business: The Settlement and Administration of American Public Lands, 1789–1837*. New York: Oxford University Press, 1968.

Romig, Walter. *Michigan Place Names*. Detroit: Wayne State University Press, 1986.

Rothman, Joshua D. *Flush Times and Fever Dreams: A Story of Capitalism and Slavery in the Age of Jackson*. Athens: University of Georgia Press, 2012.

Rowland, O. W. *A History of Van Buren County, Michigan*. Chicago: Lewis Pub. Co., 1912.

"The Sac and Fox Treaty of 1842." *Annals of Iowa* 12 (1920): 375–381.

Santer, Richard Arthur. "Historical Geography of Jackson, Michigan: A Study on the Changing Character of an American City, 1829–1969." PhD dissertation, Michigan State University, 1970.

Schenck, Theresa M. *The Ojibwe Journals of Edmund F. Ely, 1832–1849*. Lincoln: University of Nebraska Press, 2012.

Schilling, K. E., and C. F. Wolter. *Water Quality Improvement Plan for Raccoon River, Iowa*. Iowa City: Iowa Department of Natural Resources, Geological Survey, 2008.

Schoetzow, Mae E. *Brief History of Cass County*. Dowagiac, MI: A. Castle, [2000].

Schoolcraft, Henry R. *Narrative Journal of Travels from Detroit Northwest through the Great Chain of American Lakes to the Sources of the Mississippi River in 1820*. Ann Arbor: University Microfilms, 1966.

Schramer, James, and Donald Ross. *American Travel Writers, 1776–1864*. Detroit: Gale Research, 1997.

Scott, James L. *A Journal of a Missionary Tour through Pennsylvania, Ohio, Indiana, Illinois, Iowa, Wiskonsin, and Michigan*. Providence, RI: By the author, 1843.

Sellers, Charles. *The Market Revolution: Jacksonian America, 1815–1846*. New York: Oxford University Press, 1991.

Seymour, George Dudley. "David Hoadley, Architect." *Art and Progress* 3 (1912): 545–546.

Shaw, Ronald E. *Canals for a Nation: The Canal Era in the United States, 1790–1860*. Lexington: University of Kentucky Press, 1990.

Shaughnessy, Jim. *Delaware & Hudson: The History of an Important Railroad Whose Antecedent Was a Canal Network to Transport Coal*. Berkeley, CA: Howell-North Books, 1967.

Sheehan, Bernard W. *Seeds of Extinction: Jeffersonian Philanthropy and the American Indian*. New York: Norton, 1974.

Shirreff, Patrick. *A Tour through North America*. Edinburgh: Oliver and Boyd, 1835.

Shortbridge, Wilson P. "Henry Hastings Sibley and the Minnesota Frontier." *Minnesota History Bulletin* 3 (1919): 115–125.

Smith, Dwight L. "The Land Cession: A Valid Instrument of Title of Transfer of Indian Land." In *This Land Is Ours: The Acquisition and Disposition of the Public Domain*, 87–102. Indianapolis: Indiana Historical Society, 1978.

Smith, G. Hubert. "Fort Pierre II (39ST217): A Historic Trading Post in the Oahe Dam Area, South Dakota." In *Smithsonian Institution, River Basin Survey Papers* 18, 83–158. Washington, DC: Government Printing Office, 1960.

——— . *Like-A-Fishhook Village and Fort Berthold, Garrison Reservoir, North Dakota*. Anthropological Papers 2. Washington, DC: US Department of the Interior, National Park Service, 1972.

Smith, J. Calvin. *The Western Tourist and Emigrant's Guide . . . of the States of Ohio, Michigan, Indiana, Illinois, and Missouri*. New York: J. H. Colton, 1840.

Smith, Joseph. *The Doctrine and Covenants of the Church of Latter Day Saints*. Nauvoo, IL: John Taylor, 1844.

Spencer, Edgar W. *Geology of the Natural Bridge, Sugarloaf Mountain, Buchanan, and Arnold Valley Quadrangles, Virginia*. Charlottesville: Virginia Division of Mineral Resources 1968.

Spieles, Beth A. "Lake Shetek." In *Draining the Great Oasis: An Environmental History of Murray County, Minnesota*, edited by Anthony J. Amato, Janet Timmerman, and Joseph A. Amato, 113–123. Marshall, MN: Crossings Press, 2001.

St. Clair, Sadie Daniel. "Slavery as a Diplomatic Factor in Anglo-American

Relations during the Civil War." *Journal of Negro History* 30 (1945): 260–275.

St. Lawrence Seaway Management Corporation. *The Welland Canal Section of the St. Lawrence Seaway.* Cornwall, Ontario: St. Lawrence Seaway Authority, 2003.

Starr, Calvin H. "Some Beginnings of St. Joseph County." *Michigan Pioneer and Historical Collections* 18 (1891): 513–517.

Starr, Walter. *Seward: Lincoln's Indispensable Man.* New York: Simon and Schuster, 2012.

Steere, Joseph H. "Sketch of John Tanner, Known as the 'White Indian.'" *Michigan Historical Collections* 22 (1899): 246–250.

"Steps to Statehood." *Annals of Iowa* 27 (1946): 217–219.

Stewart, Charles D. "The Pigeon Trap." *Wisconsin Magazine of History* 24 (1940): 20–24.

Stone, Joel. *Floating Palaces of the Great Lakes: A History of Passenger Steamships on the Inland Seas.* Ann Arbor: University of Michigan Press, 2015.

Swan, Lansing B. *Journal of a Trip to Michigan in 1841.* Rochester, NY: George P. Humphrey, 1904.

Sylvester, Nathaniel Bartlett. *History of Saratoga County, New York.* Philadelphia: Everts & Ensign, 1878.

Tanner, Helen Hornbeck. *Atlas of Great Lakes Indian History.* Norman: University of Oklahoma Press, 1987.

Tanner, John. *A Narrative of the Captivity and Adventures of John Tanner, (U. S. Interpreter at the Sault Ste. Marie), during Thirty Years' Residence among the Indians of the Interior of North America.* Minneapolis, MN: Ross & Haines, 1956.

Temin, Peter. *The Jacksonian Economy.* New York: Norton, 1969.

Thomas, James M., comp. *Kalamazoo County Directory, with a History of the County from Its Earliest Settlement.* Kalamazoo, MI: James M. Thomas, 1869.

Thwaites, Reuben G. *Travels in the Interior of North America by Maximilian, Prince of Wied.* Translated by Hanniball Evans Lloyd. 2 vols. Cleveland, OH: Arthur H. Clark Co., 1905.

Todish, Timothy J., and Todd E. Harburn. *A "Most Troublesome Situation": The*

British Military and the Pontiac Uprising of 1763–1764. Fleischmanns, NY: Purple Mountain Press, 2006.

Treuer, Anton. *The Assassination of Hole in the Day*. St. Paul: Minnesota Historical Society Press, 2011.

Turner, T. G. *Gazetteer of the St. Joseph Valley, Michigan and Indiana*. Grand Rapids, MI: Black Letter Press, 1978.

Tyler, Alice Felt. *Freedom's Ferment: Phases of American Social History from the Colonial Period to the Outbreak of the Civil War*. New York: Harper & Row, 1944.

US Census Office. *Population of the United States in 1860*. Washington, DC: Government Printing Office, 1864.

Van Buren, A. D. P. "Some Beginnings in Kalamazoo." *Michigan Pioneer and Historical Collections* 18 (1891): 605–608.

Wade, Richard C. *The Urban Frontier: Pioneer Life in Early Pittsburgh, Cincinnati, Lexington, Louisville, and St. Louis*. Chicago: University of Chicago Press, 1959.

Walker, J. R. "The Sun Dance and Other Ceremonies of the Oglala Division of the Teton Dakota." *American Museum of Natural History, Anthropological Papers* 16 (1917): 51–221.

Waitley, Douglas. *Roads of Destiny: The Trails That Shaped a Nation*. Washington, DC: Robert B. Luce, 1970.

Western Traveler's Pocket Directory and Stranger's Guide. Schenectady, NY: S. S. Riggs, 1834.

Widder, Keith R. *Battle for the Soul: Métis Children Encounter Evangelical Protestants at Mackinaw Mission, 1823–1837*. East Lansing: Michigan State University Press, 1999.

———. "Founding La Pointe Mission, 1825–1833." *Wisconsin Magazine of History* 64 (1981): 181–201.

Williams, J. Fletcher. *A History of the City of St. Paul, and the County of Ramsey, Minnesota*. [St. Paul]: Minnesota Historical Society, 1876.

———. *History of Ramsey County and the City of St. Paul*. Minneapolis: North Star Pub. Co., 1881.

Wilson, Craig. "What Is Gained but Mackinac? The Battle of Mackinac Island." *Mackinac History*, 4, leaflet no. 5. Mackinac Island, MI: Mackinac State Historic Parks, 2014.

Wisconsin and Minnesota State Gazetteer, Shippers' Guide and Business Directory for 1865–66. Indianapolis: Geo. W. Hawes, 1865.

Wittke, Carl. *A History of Canada*. New York: F. S. Crofts, 1941.

Wolf, Hazel C. "Campaigning with the First Minnesota: A Civil War Diary." *Minnesota History* 25 (1944): 11–39, 117–152.

Work Projects Administration. *Michigan: A Guide to the Wolverine State*. New York: Oxford University Press, 1941.

Yarrow, H. C. *Introduction to the Study of Mortuary Customs among the North American Indians*. Washington, DC: Government Printing Office, 1880. www.nanations.com/burialcustoms/scaffold_burial.htm.

Yater, George H. *Two Hundred Years at the Falls of the Ohio: A History of Louisville and Jefferson County*. Louisville, KY: Filson Club, 1987.

Yates, Norris W. *William T. Porter and the Spirit of the Times: A Study of the Big Bear School of Humor*. Baton Rouge: University of Louisiana Press, 1957.

Newspapers

Albany (NY) Argus, 1840

Alexandria (VA) Gazette, 1839

Augusta (GA) Chronicle, 1846

The Bee (New Orleans), 1831

Buffalo (NY) Commercial Advertiser, 1839–1844

Buffalo (NY) Daily Courier, 1844, 1854

Charleston (SC) Courier, 1845

Cleveland (OH) Daily Herald & Gazette, 1837–1839

Cleveland (OH) Weekly Herald, 1847

Commercial Advertiser (New York), 1844, 1846, 1847

Connecticut Courier (Hartford), 1856

Daily Picayune (New Orleans), 1841, 1843, 1846, 1847

Daily National Intelligencer (Washington, DC), 1844, 1845, 1846

Daily National Pilot (Buffalo, NY), 1845

Daily Sanduskian (Sandusky, OH), 1849

Daily Union (Washington, DC), 1845

Detroit Daily Advertiser, 1843, 1844

Detroit Free Press, 1862

Evening Post (New York), 1843, 1846, 1847

Erie (PA) Observer, 1838

Ithaca (NY) Journal, 2005

MSN News, 2015

Marine Review (Cleveland, OH), 1891

Massachusetts Spy (Worcester), 1845

National Daily Pilot (NY), 1845

New York Daily Tribune, 1845, 1847, 1855

New York Herald, 1845

New York Times, 1891

Niles (MI) Gazette and Advertiser, 1835–1836

Opinion Cabinet (NY), 1849

Oswego (NY) Palladium, 1839

Richmond (VA) Whig, 1846, 1847

Rondout Freeman (Kingston, NY), 1846

Spectator (New York), 1846

St. Albans (VT) Daily Messenger, 1898

Syracuse (NY) Post-Standard, 2005

Western Herald (Sandwich, ON), 1839

INDEX